Moreau

Moreau

PORTRAIT
OF A
FOUNDER

THE STORY OF FR. BASIL MOREAU
AND THE CONGREGATION
OF HOLY CROSS

FR. THOMAS BARROSSE, CSC

FOREWORD BY BR. PAUL BEDNARCZYK, CSC
PREFACE TO THE NEW EDITION BY BR. JOEL GIALLANZA, CSC
AFTERWORD BY SR. ANN LACOUR, MSC

Christian Classics ⸽ *Notre Dame, Indiana*

Imprimi potest: Howard J. Kenna, CSC,
                    Provincial Superior

Nihil obstat: Louis J. Putz, CSC,
                    University of Notre Dame

Imprimatur: Leo A. Pursley, DD,
                    Bishop of Ft. Wayne–South Bend

Originally published as *Moreau: Portrait of a Founder* by Fides Publishers, Inc. Notre Dame, Indiana, 1969.

Foreword © 2024 by Br. Paul Bednarczyk, CSC

Preface to the New Edition © 2024 by Br. Joel Giallanza, CSC

Afterword © 2024 by Sr. Ann Lacour, MSC

Founded in 1865, Ave Maria Press is a ministry of the United States Province of Holy Cross.

www.avemariapress.com/christian-classics

Paperback: ISBN-13 978-0-87061-324-1

E-book: ISBN-13 978-0-87061-325-8

Cover image of texture © E+/ Getty Images Plus. Fr. Basil Moreau's signature courtesy of the United States Province of Holy Cross. Illustration of Fr. Basil Moreau by Cecilia Lawrence. Photograph of Notre Dame de Sainte Croix, Le Mans, France, courtesy of Br. Joel Giallanza, CSC.

Cover design by Samantha Watson.

Interior text design by Esther Moody.

Printed and bound in the United States of America.

Library of Congress Catalog Card Number 75-92021

CONTENTS

FOREWORD

It was during my early formation years that I first met Fr. Thomas Barrosse, CSC, the ninth superior general of the Congregation of Holy Cross. His reputation for being an intellectual, aesthetic, and holy religious preceded him, and therefore, contributed to the anxiety I felt with my classmates in anticipation of our meeting with him. He was to speak to us on our founder, Fr. Basil Moreau, which was to be followed by a period of questions and answers.

Wearing worn, black trousers and a navy-blue shirt sweater, his kindly eyes and warm handshake soon put us at ease. It was my first time meeting a superior general, and I was quickly taken by his simple, humble presence. As he began his talk, I remember being struck about how he spoke so passionately of the founder and with such familiarity. He quoted Moreau, told stories about him, and spoke about his spirituality and his desires for the congregation. I remember asking myself, what was the allure of this nineteenth-century French priest that captivated this man so ardently? I wanted to know more, and began my own pursuit of studying more deeply Fr. Moreau's writings, life, and spirituality. Little did I know then that almost fifty years later, I would be one of Fr. Moreau's and Fr. Barrosse's successors, myself.

As you read this book, you will discover that Fr. Basil Moreau was a visionary. In the hierarchical Church of post-revolutionary France, he desired to unite his three societies of Holy Cross priests, brothers, and sisters into one Congregation modeled after the Holy Family. His progressive proposal was too extreme for the Holy See, and they decided that the women should function as their own congregation independently of the men. At a time when schools were based on the classical system of education, Fr. Moreau saw the value of a more wholistic education integrating the fine arts and emerging sciences within a rigorous academic program while providing time for spiritual, social, and physical activities as well. Although the needs in post-revolutionary France were great, Fr. Moreau was far from provincial in his thinking. He thought globally and risked sending missionaries to Algiers, Bengal, Poland, and North America. Because of his desire for Holy Cross to expand beyond his native France, Holy Cross priests and brothers now live and minister in nineteen countries worldwide.

Fr. Moreau's vision made him a man ahead of his time, but his unshakable faith in God made him an extraordinarily holy man of his time. Yes, he was a well-respected seminary professor with an uncanny gift of preaching, but it was his holiness rooted in a humble acceptance of all things as the will of Divine Providence that made him stand out among his fellow priests and confreres in Holy Cross. Whether it was in his ambitious dreams for his newly founded institute or in his sufferings as a result of his failures, he found God in all things. As he wrote to Mother Mary of the Seven Dolors, "I have searched for nothing but the Spirit of God, and the rest is always secondary to me."[1]

Fr. Moreau's search for God often led him to the Cross of Christ, where he found his only hope. As you will read, Fr. Moreau endured many trials in his life. He suffered from a strained relationship with his bishop, he grieved the tragic loss of several of his religious who died on mission, he faced financial bankruptcy, and he endured the slander and calumny of his confreres, which eventually led to the ultimate disgrace of his resignation as Superior General and separation from the congregation he founded and so deeply loved.

Despite all of this, Fr. Moreau willing surrendered to God's will, harboring no bitterness or resentment against anyone, persevering in his faith and vows, and remaining devoted to the congregation until his last breath. As he preached to the Holy Cross religious at Saint-Laurent in Montreal, "Life is in the Cross and no place else. But we must not only take up the Cross, we must carry it with courage. . . . Let us follow the path that Jesus has walked for us and we will arrive at a happy eternity."[2]

Fr. Moreau is also a man for our time as well. In our divided and fragmented world, Fr. Moreau's message of the primacy of the "union of hearts" has relevant overtones to our current, global situation. He believed that such union will prove to be the "powerful lever with which we could move, direct, and sanctify the whole world."[3] Moreau's philosophy of "educating the hearts and minds" of students has endured almost two hundred years and continues today to be a hallmark of Holy Cross education in our schools on five continents. Fr. Moreau's commitment to place the common good before his own presents a refreshing alternative to some modern-day leaders driven by power, prestige, and privilege. Finally, Moreau's quiet acceptance of life's sorrows as grace-filled opportunities to model our Lord's journey to Calvary offers inspiration to the suffering, giving us comfort and hope that in the Cross of Christ, "all is swallowed up in victory."[4]

I extend my thanks to Ave Maria Press and to Br. Joel Giallanza, CSC, editor, for updating this foundational biography of our beloved Founder of the Congregation of Holy Cross. As Fr. Thomas Barrosse once introduced me to the extraordinary life of our founder, I am delighted that in this book he is being introduced again to a new generation of Holy Cross religious, colleagues, collaborators, and all who seek to be inspired by Fr. Moreau's hope in the Cross of Christ, his trust in Divine Providence, and his zeal for the mission. It is my hope that Fr. Barrosse's mastery and familiarity with the life and holiness of Fr. Moreau will touch your heart in the same way as it touched mine many years ago.

Blessed Basil Moreau, pray for us. *Ave Crux, Spes Unica!*

Br. Paul Bednarczyk, CSC

Superior General

September 15, 2024

Feast of Our Lady of Sorrows

PREFACE TO THE NEW EDITION

"This book is neither a biography of Fr. Moreau nor a history of the origins of Holy Cross." In the preface to the original edition of this book, Fr. Thomas Barrosse, CSC, presents this approach to exploring the life, ministry, and personality of Basil Moreau, founder of the family of Holy Cross. He creates a portrait, illustrating the many colors and tones shaping the founder's life, ministry, and personality. Within this portrait, Fr. Barrosse includes more than sufficient and well-researched biographical and historical material to create an accurate and engaging picture. Though this book was written almost 100 years after Basil Moreau's death, Holy Cross was in the early stages of studying Moreau.

The canvas for this portrait is the aftermath of the French Revolution, a tumultuous decade (1789–1799) that disrupted every segment of society. Moreau was born during the last year of the Revolution and so did not experience all its horrors; nevertheless, that aftermath continued for most of his life. He firmly believed that he was called by God to respond to that disruption; his response involves cross and resurrection, faith and hope, possibility and promise.

SIMPLE COUNTRY PEOPLE

Fr. Barrosse emphasizes that Moreau was born of "simple country people." God called him beyond his tiny village to become a serious student and scholar, an effective administrator and engaging conversationalist, a gifted preacher, a person who could mingle with all strata of society. He was known by many Church ministers, from priests to prelates to the pope, but he did not lose touch with his simple country background. He could correspond with government officials, entertain a variety of guests, and then help the novices prepare vegetables for dinner while telling stories of revolutionary heroes. He could oversee the development of a premier primary and secondary school, organize the sending of missionaries, and still volunteer in rowing a boat to rescue flood victims.

This simplicity is a constitutive aspect of Moreau's personality. Fr. Barrosse uses this as a major brushstroke in this portrait: "Basil Moreau, a simple man, so simple as to be incapable of devious ways and incapable even of understanding or tolerating them." This simplicity gave Fr. Moreau a bluntness that some found disarming. While never intending to insult or unsettle, it made no sense to him that an obvious fact or truth could be pretended away. Such a simple and straightforward approach to people would lead to the cross.

CONSCIENTIOUS

Another major brushstroke that Fr. Barrosse uses for this portrait is Moreau's conscientiousness, which reflected a passion for what he was doing and a determination to do it well because he believed this was God's will. Fr. Barrosse presents Moreau as a man whose passion spans his whole life, from his desire to pursue priesthood, to his concern and love for Holy Cross even in the darkest days of administration, to his generosity for ministry until death.

These qualities compelled Moreau to take up everything he did with a thoroughness and an attention to detail that left others amazed. Fr. Barrosse relates Moreau's tireless efforts to succeed at his studies, to prepare himself for seminary teaching, to organize all the elements of Holy Cross, and to guide and nurture a growing international religious congregation. Genuine commitment underlies everything. Moreau cared deeply about what he did and about the people for whom he did it. Fr. Barrosse wrote, "Basil Moreau was a warmly affectionate man full of love for Christ, full of love for those who shared his labors."

VISION OF APOSTOLIC POSSIBILITIES

Moreau was from a small village but developed a large vision. Fr. Barrosse writes that Moreau's "vision of the apostolic possibilities of the community was as broad as his appreciation of the needs of the Church." This vision was grounded in the very real needs of the people and the practical responses to those needs. It was a graced vision that would lead Moreau to found the Auxiliary Priests, to accept the administration of the Brothers of Saint Joseph, to establish the Holy Cross Sisters, and to engage colleagues. These groups developed into the Family of Holy Cross, which would take on pastoral, educational, catechetical, and retreat ministries, expanding far beyond the borders of France to become an international force for transformation.

Fr. Moreau was convinced that the religious vows, prayer, and community were the stable foundations upon which the mission would unfold. He did not hesitate to insist upon integrity and fidelity, nor did he shy away from recruiting strong people to be part of this community. Many who came shared his vision, others wondered about it, still others opposed it; nevertheless, he remained convinced that grace would bring the vision to reality.

SORROW AND JOY WITH PEACE

Fr. Barrosse uses broad strokes to portray the reality of the cross in Basil Moreau's life. The final decade and a half of his life were enveloped by intrigue, misrepresentation, lies, and abandonment. The origin of that betrayal can be traced to those who had been confidants and close associates, and Fr. Barrosse notes the personal and painful toll this took upon Fr. Moreau. Some stories are hard to read, so filled are they with deception and duplicity from those whom Moreau should have been able to trust.

This portrait makes clear that neither the number nor weight of the crosses laid upon Moreau robbed him of the joy in doing God's will or the peace that remained firmly rooted in his heart. Fr. Moreau's capacity to forgive those who created the heaviest crosses for him never diminished. These crosses invigorated Moreau, transforming him into the image of God, whom he loved and followed. Fr. Barrosse characterizes Fr. Moreau as a "sign of contradiction and a man of sorrows, who considered his choice of our Lady of Holy Cross as patroness of his work an inspiration, who thanked God for having found him worthy to suffer something on the occasion of works undertaken for God's glory."

A MAN OF HIS TIME AND COUNTRY

Fr. Barrosse's use of stories and texts is among the noteworthy characteristics of this book. That material has not had a wide circulation among Holy Cross religious and their colleagues. The stories and texts bring Moreau to life, revealing his gifts and griefs, blessings and burdens, feats and flaws, holiness and humanity. Even though Fr. Moreau is "a man of his time and his country," this portrait is not frozen in history. Fr. Barrosse paints a living portrait, continuing to be refined by Moreau scholarship and by those who live Moreau's legacy.

Fr. Barrosse opens this book by indicating that he wants "to show what kind of man Basil Moreau was." He closes the book by citing a text from Saint Paul's letter to the Romans (8:28) which was among Moreau's favorites: "For those who love God, all things work together for good." Moreau was a man for whom all things did work for good, a man who was an "enthusiastic and tireless worker" for God, for others, for his country and, ultimately, for the world.

Br. Joel Giallanza, CSC
Editor of the new edition
September 15, 2024
Feast of Our Lady of Sorrows

PREFACE TO THE FIRST EDITION

This book is neither a biography of Fr. Moreau nor a history of the origins of Holy Cross. It is an attempt to show what kind of man Basil Moreau was: his personality, his strengths, his weaknesses, his attitudes, and his ideals, and how all these influenced his work.

Since a man shows what he is by what he says and does, these pages constantly draw on his writings and the records others have left of him. Unless the footnotes indicate other sources, statements of fact are based on the biographies of the founder of Holy Cross published by his nephew Fr. Charles Moreau and by Canon Etienne Catta and Mr. Tony Catta. Documents cited, unless a published source is indicated, are found in the general archives of Holy Cross. In general, I have followed existing English translations usually done by Fr. Edward Heston of original French texts. At times, however, I have preferred to alter the version or to do a new rendering. Throughout I have followed the usage of these translations, retaining "Lord" or "Lordship" for the French episcopal titles. I have departed from earlier usage in regularly translating "Sainte-Croix" as "Holy Cross" and "Notre-Dame de Sainte-Croix" as "Our Lady of Holy Cross" in order to reproduce in English the ambiguity found in the documents quoted: at times the former expression refers to the Sainte-Croix suburb and, later, quarter of Le Mans where the congregation was founded, at times to the mother house which was there and which, with the school attached to it, is also called Notre-Dame de Sainte-Croix, and at times to the congregation itself. I have also translated most of the Latin expressions, largely biblical quotations, found in the original texts.

The presentation of a man whose life was so active and full as Father Moreau's must inevitably omit countless interesting details. An event so filled with future promise as his replacing a sick pastor on the very day of his first Mass cannot be omitted by a biographer of the founder of a society of auxiliary priests; but since the incident reveals nothing of Fr. Moreau's personality, there is no reason to recount it in this volume. Or again, every man has attitudes of lesser importance that color his personality and work relatively little or not at all. For example, Fr. Moreau's deep-seated patriotism and his conviction of the important role France had to play as a Christian nation seem not to have marked his work in any perceptible way. So too with the popular devotions of the time which found their way into his life. Devotion to the Precious Blood and to the Holy Face and even the way of the cross and the observance of the months of Mary and Joseph had their place for him, but left little mark on the Congregation of Holy Cross beyond the tradition of devotion to Mary and Joseph. His own life would probably have been no different if his spirituality had not expressed itself in these ways. His occasional interest in the unusual—in particular, in miracles and visions—had no influence on the course of his life, let alone on his work. The presence of these and similar elements illustrate how much he was a man of his time and his country, but discussing them lies beyond the scope of the present book. We shall have ample material and shall succeed better in appreciating Basil Moreau if we limit ourselves to more central elements of his personality and work.

Thomas Barrosse, CSC
January 20, 1969
Ninety-Sixth Anniversary of Fr. Moreau's Death

CHRONOLOGY

July 14, 1789 After years of financial struggle and volatile class relations, the French Revolution begins with the storming of the Bastille prison.

February 13, 1790 The National Assembly prohibits monastic vows and abolishes all religious orders, except those dedicated to teaching and charity.

November 27, 1790 Priests throughout France are required to sign an oath of loyalty to the new French nation.

February 11, 1799 Basil Anthony Mary Moreau is born in the French village Laigné-en-Belin.

July 15, 1801 Concordant between Rome and the Emperor Napoleon, restoring Roman Catholicism in France.

1814 Basil Moreau begins high school and then matriculates to St. Vincent's, the diocesan seminary at Chateau-Gontier.

July 15, 1820 Fr. Jacques Dujarié founds the Brothers of St. Joseph.

XXII | MOREAU: PORTRAIT OF A FOUNDER

August 5, 1841 Seven Holy Cross religious depart Le Mans to begin a mission in the United States: Fr. Edward Sorin; Brs. Vincent, Joachim, Lawrence, Mary, Gatien, and Anselm.

April 1852 The Sacred Congregation for the Propagation of the Faith begins reviewing the affairs of Holy Cross.

May 13, 1857 Pope Pius IX approves the constitutions of Holy Cross but separates the Marianites to develop as an independent congregation.

1860–1866 Period of financial and institutional struggle for Holy Cross, especially for Fr. Moreau.

August 1863 General chapter authorizes the creation of both a French and North American Province for the congregation. French Province established.

May 1865 North American Province established at Notre Dame, Indiana.

June 10, 1866 Pope Pius IX accepts Fr. Moreau's resignation as superior general of Holy Cross.

February 19, 1867 Constitutions and Rule of the Marianites first approved by the Bishop of Le Mans.

July 1869 Marianites in the United States become an independent religious congregation known as the Sisters of the Holy Cross.

January 20, 1873 Fr. Basil Moreau dies at age seventy-three.

January 1883 Marianites in Canada become an independent religious congregation known as the Sisters of Holy Cross and of the Seven Dolors.

1955 The Cause of Fr. Moreau formally opens.

July 21, 1955 Fr. Moreau declared "Servant of God," the first of four stages toward canonization.

May 1961 The Promoter of the Faith for the Cause of Fr. Moreau submits to the Vatican Congregation of Rites the required supporting documents testifying to Fr. Moreau's heroic virtues, which are necessary for declaring him "Venerable."

October 1962 Pope John XXIII convenes the Second Vatican Council, postponing the Cause toward Fr. Moreau's canonization.

April 12, 2003 Fr. Moreau is declared "Venerable" by Pope John Paul II.

April 2006 Pope Benedict XVI promulgates an authorized miracle attributed to the intercession of Fr. Moreau, thus ensuring his beatification.

CHAPTER 1
BACKGROUND

I. THE REVOLUTION

The French Revolution (1789–1799) formed the background to the life of Basil Moreau who was born as it ended and grew up in its aftermath. A quick glance at what it did to the Church and her institutions is indispensable for an understanding of the needs to which his life was a response.

From the very year of the proclamation of the Republic (1789), the new government began to confiscate Church property and outlaw religious communities. Within two years it had imposed on priests the oath of the civil constitution of the clergy. Many took the schismatic oath; many refused. Of those who took it, some did so with mental reservations, and others later retracted. Those who refused to take it, the "nonconstitutional" clergy, were exposed to imprisonment, deportation, or execution, while the members of the constitutional clergy were considered intruders by the people.

The constitutional bishop of Le Mans, installed in 1791, was opposed by his entire cathedral chapter and most of the clergy and people of the department of La Sarthe.[1] Though he remained there until 1802, it was the vicar general who really ran the diocese in secret, even sending men to Paris to have them ordained to the priesthood by bishops there who formed part of a complex secret organization dating back to the beginning of 1792. Not one of the eight hundred parishes of the Le Mans diocese was left without spiritual assistance from the nonconstitutional clergy during the Revolution, though these priests often had to disguise themselves as peddlers, shepherds, farmers, and the like to be able to minister secretly to the people.

Throughout the Revolution, the Republic never controlled more than half the department of La Sarthe. Furthermore, even the local officials and the courts set up by the new government often proved halfhearted about applying the sanctions of law to nonconstitutional priests. At times—for example, in 1794—the laws against Catholics assembling were relaxed. But there were martyrs in the vicinity from the early years of the Revolution until as late as September 1799.

The confusion all this could produce is illustrated by an incident which occurred at the very beginning of 1800.

> The mayor [of Grand-Lucé near Ruillé-sur-Loir, where the church was in schismatic hands] had tried to appease the Catholics by having an altar transferred from the church to a barn. It was there that Fr. Jacques de la Haye [the priest in charge at Ruillé-sur-Loir, where he had Fr. Jacques Dujarié as an assistant] or one of the priests attached to his mission came to celebrate Mass. The justice of the peace . . ., a former assistant pastor at Grand-Lucé, a priest who had taken the oath and then married, could not tolerate this infraction of the laws . . ., which stung all the more under the disgrace of his apostasy. He had Fr. de la Haye arrested by the National Guard just as he finished celebrating Holy Mass. There was a scuffle. The guards dragged the priest away by the hair. The mayor hurried to the scene, followed by the Catholics who succeeded in freeing Fr. de la Haye. He took refuge in the mayor's home, but the justice of the peace had issued a warrant for his arrest which was still hanging over him at the moment of the Concordat.[2]

After Napoleon came into power and negotiated a concordat with the pope (1802), Catholic worship could be resumed with impunity. However, in many places the Church remained humble, poor, and despoiled. Religious communities remained without legal recognition (except the Christian Brothers from 1808)—a situation which was to raise doubts about the force of the vows of such communities in the minds of bishops and even in the minds of these religious themselves.[3] Napoleon attempted to invalidate the superiority of papal power by his unilateral addition to the concordat of the Organic Articles, an official reassertion of the "liberties of the Gallican Church."[4] In fact, however, this step encouraged the development of ultramontanism, which vigorously stressed papal supremacy, and there arose a tension between the ultramontanists and the Gallicans among the clergy—a tension not fully resolved until the definition of papal infallibility in 1870.

The new bishop of Le Mans chosen by the government and accepted by the pope, Michel-Joseph de Pidoll from Trèves, was installed in 1802. He found himself faced with the needs and problems created by the Revolution—needs and problems that it would take decades to solve.

Perhaps the fundamental need was the re-Christianization of the people. Missions had been organized for this purpose at Le Mans in the brief lull of 1796. They were organized on a larger scale especially after the concordat and above all after Napoleon fell from power and the Restoration monarchy replaced the Empire in 1814. They encountered opposition, as the young Fr. Moreau's description of the Paris missions of the early 1820s shows:

> The mission, which is to make the rounds of all the parishes of Paris, is succeeding as well as could be expected. This initial success is not passing unnoticed in the law faculty. Fr. Duponceau, who came to see me, told me that the students

passed notes around during classes inviting one another to go to hiss the missionaries. Recently one anticlerical was bold enough to shout at Fr. de Rauzan: "You're a liar!" but the trouble did not last long. When firecrackers were set off in the same audience, the preacher remarked: "All this trouble is coming from individuals who cannot make any noise in the world with their talents; so they try to attract attention with their firecrackers!" On another occasion they threw around the room a drug that could have asphyxiated the entire audience, but fortunately there were some druggists present and in a short time they produced a still stronger odor to counteract the first, which was already beginning to make people dizzy. These are the things that we learn from those of the missionaries who come to see us occasionally.[5]

Another need, hardly less great, was the restoration of Church institutions, especially the schools.

For some idea of the neglect experienced by the generation born since the outbreak of the Revolution, it is sufficient to recall what Chaptal wrote in his Report on Public Instruction in 1801: "Public education is practically nonexistent everywhere. The generation now reaching the age of twenty is irrevocably sacrificed to ignorance. Primary schools exist nowhere and as a result the bulk of the nation is without instruction."

We know the causes which had brought on this lack of schools. Teaching had been "one of the first victims of the social upheaval of 1789." Before that date, there had been in all the dioceses a large network of schools, which for all practical purposes were exclusively in the hands of the Church.

The lack of schools was not the only element which could have endangered the future of the generation born during the Revolution. The few wandering teachers to whom the children were entrusted were often incompetent or unworthy. "I know," wrote the grand master of the university in 1809 in a circular letter which opened an investigation on teaching personnel, "that there are in their ranks some whom crass ignorance should bar from teaching, or whom evil habits make unworthy of this profession."[6]

The government of the Restoration, like that of the Empire, allowed congregations to organize and to function without any legal authorization. There still remained, however, the question of legal recognition, without which they were incapable of holding property or of receiving donations. Such recognition could be obtained only through direct action by the government. . . . [The unauthorized congregations were] obliged to have recourse to third parties or to those "charitable associations" which were set up by an ordinance of February 29, 1816, for the establishment of primary schools, and which could receive legal recognition by simple royal decrees. This stratagem, however, did not touch the problem of the acceptance of gifts and legacies. Only the [state] University had the legal right to receive donations intended for such associations. These few facts bring into relief some of the practical difficulties encountered under existing legislation by the founders of religious congregations devoted to teaching. It was, nevertheless, under just such a regime that many religious congregations were founded and went through stages of rapid development.[7]

Other Church institutions besides the schools had been destroyed by the Revolution—for example, hospitals. The state was unable to replace them adequately. In these areas too, the need was great.

The anticlerical and anti-Catholic forces unleashed by the Revolution did not subside with the concordat. Many government officials continually harassed attempts to re-establish organized religion and Church institutions. In particular, the absolute monopoly of the state university over secondary education made Catholic efforts to solve the school problem most difficult. In addition to the lycées and university colleges, only diocesan minor seminaries and certain schools granted the privileges of royal colleges—"full teaching rights"—could engage in secondary education and this only from 1821 on. Newspapers frequently stirred up active opposition to Catholic efforts by editorializing or reporting in such a way as to arouse the suspicious or the bigoted.

Within the Church, the Gallican struggle moved toward its denouement. Government officials expected seminary professors to teach the Organic Articles. Fr. Bouvier, professor and later rector at Saint Vincent's Seminary in Le Mans, had signed a commitment to do so in 1818. In such circumstances Rome could hardly issue a formal condemnation of Gallicanism. But the ultramontanist forces were growing stronger and more outspoken. The books of Fr. Félicité de Lamennais helped. His Essai sur l'indifférence stirred great discussion as early as 1817. His De la religion considérée dans ses rapports avec l'ordre politique et civile even got him into trouble with the police in 1826. The struggle sometimes caused sharp divisions in a diocese. This is what happened at Le Mans.

II. FAMILY, FRIENDS, ACQUAINTANCES

Basil Moreau's parents were simple country people. His father, Louis Moreau, was a wine merchant who probably could not write. His mother, Louise Pioger, came from a family of farmers. They married five years before the outbreak of the Revolution and spent their life at the little village of Laigné-en-Belin, about ten miles from Le Mans.

Basil was born on February 11, 1799, the ninth of fourteen children, eleven of whom survived infancy. The family was not wealthy. The children had little opportunity for an education.

Basil wrote later to his sister Cécile, "washwoman at Laigné": "I address my letter to you because in writing to you I write to my parents, and because you are the only one at home who can answer me, since my other sisters are, as you say, working out all day, or rather are afraid that their brother will make fun of their handwriting."[8] But they were a close-knit family, and their simple and unsophisticated faith had kept them loyal to the Church throughout the trying years of the Revolution. Basil, according to the Laigné records, was baptized by a "Catholic priest" the day after his birth.

The piety of Basil's parents is noted by his nephew and first biographer: "Fear of God, love of the Church, prayer in common, a hard-working life, filial obedience, respect for all authority were for Louis Moreau and his virtuous wife family traditions which they tried to hand on to their children as the best part of the family inheritance. In fact, they had no other means of satisfying their many obligations, after their trust in God, than a little property which Louise Pioger cultivated while her husband sold wine in the neighborhood of Le Mans."[9]

Their son wrote a brief account of their deaths. Of his mother he wrote:

> My poor mother is no longer of this world. She died as she had lived, with sentiments of lively faith and perfect resignation to the will of God. I can say that her last moments were singularly edifying and have left us with precious memories. She had long borne many crosses, following Jesus Christ and imitating the patience of our good master more and more. Her devotion to the Blessed Virgin was great, and I have no doubt that Mary stood before her judge as her protectress. The joyful expression on her face during the twenty-four hours that her body was exposed to the numerous persons who came to pray for the repose of her soul indicated to everyone the peace of her conscience. Some, on seeing the smile on her

lips and the peace on her face, could not refrain from kissing her. Without any agony, she was conscious to the end, and as she died, her eyes fixed themselves on me for a last time. She entered admirably into the dispositions of Jesus Christ at his death, repeating three times interiorly the "Into your hands" as I recited it. Her piety showed itself especially when I had her venerate a particle of the true cross which we had the good fortune to possess in those moments so decisive for her eternity. Fortified with the bread of the strong some days before I arrived, she received extreme unction the day before she died with a presence of mind as great as if she had been in full health. . . . I did not know what it was to lose a mother who sacrificed herself for her children, but I know today.[10]

Of his father's last days, he published an anonymous account in 1846 as "notes found among the papers of a priest concerning the death of his father." Louis Moreau died in 1830, having patiently suffered blindness for more than five years. His son wrote:

"My children," this good father said to us, "I pray the good God to bless you, and I bless you myself with all my heart in the name of the Father and of the Son and of the Holy Spirit." Then we asked him to forgive us, and he answered us: "Everything is erased from my heart." Later in the day he begged my brothers to go to confession and made them promise they would. The same day he asked us to recite the Litany of the Dying and answered each invocation: "Pray for me."

[The next day] Mademoiselle de [Boismont], who had come to see him, asked how he was. "*I* must go to see God," he said. And in the evening: "My God! why did I have to begin to love you so late?" Then, "May your gospel be announced everywhere on earth, may all my children sing your praise, and may your missionaries be accepted everywhere. That is what I wish, as you know, Lord; that is what I want. . . ."

[The following day] he urged us to remain united and to love God. "Oh, if you serve God well when you are young, how happy you will be when you die! . . ." "Do you believe that the good God will give me his paradise?" he said to me. And when I told him I hoped so: "What a gift he is going to give me!"

[The day after, he said] to me and my brothers: "Goodbye, my children; here at last is the moment I am longing for, because it is going to put an end to my sufferings and unite me with God." Then as I offered him a little syrup, he refused; when I gave it to him and asked him to drink it out of obedience, he then took it and said: "He took gall, and you give me syrup. . . ."

On Sunday, at ten o'clock he lost consciousness while the Salve was being sung at high Mass for a lessening of his sufferings; then he became delirious, and coming to his senses toward evening, he said: "God does not want me; death passed over my bed twice and left me. Lord, have mercy on me! My God, take my soul!" In the middle of the night: "God has forgotten me." Later: "Let's go! Courage! Let's be firm, and this time let's try not to miss."

On Monday morning: "Now at last the time has come. I am going to rest tonight." He took his crucifix in his hands, kissed it from time to time, answered "Amen" to my exhortations. At about 11:30, as I was reciting the Litany of the Dying and the following prayers, at the moment when I was saying, "Give your soul into the hands of God; may the angels come," etc., his chest filled up, his arms stiffened, and he expired.[11]

In his boyhood, Basil knew priests and laymen who had been heroes during the days of the Revolution, and he heard stories of persecution and fidelity to the Church from their lips. Fr. Julian Le Provost, the pastor at Laigné, ministered in Le Mans at the risk of his life during the 1790s. With the help of Mademoiselle Dufay de Boismont, who had hidden priests during the

Revolution, Fr. Le Provost operated the simple boys' and girls' schools where the Moreau children received the little education they got. Basil wrote of them later to his sister when he learned of their ill health: "I am anxious to get news of the rectory. You are certainly right to tell me how much you regret so great a loss! I share your alarm and your affliction! He is my father. She is my mother. I am their son in Jesus Christ. They raised us and taught us when we were children! How many lessons, how much helpful advice and encouragement they gave us all in their charity! . . . Our entire family . . . will have to mourn the misfortune about to befall us . . . I will never forget them, and I hope to see them, if not during my next vacation, at least in eternity."[12]

Fr. Huard, pastor of the church of Notre Dame de la Couture in Le Mans, who had suffered imprisonment for refusing the constitutional oath, was a frequent visitor of the pastor of Laigné. He, Fr. Le Provost, and Mademoiselle de Boismont seem to have helped finance Basil's education, and it was with Fr. Huard that Basil spent his vacations while he was in the seminary.[13] Fr. Horeau, principal of the little college at Château-Gontier, where Basil received his first really formal schooling (it had only 198 students when he arrived in 1814), had also been imprisoned during the Revolution.[14] The superior of the seminary of Saint Sulpice, where Basil spent a year of study in Paris immediately after his ordination, had helped negotiate the concordat of 1802.[15]

Association with people like these could only provide encouragement for a young priest wishing to rise to the challenge of his time. Additional encouragement came from the enthusiasm of beginnings, for it must have seemed that everything was beginning all over again. The college of Château-Gontier had been reopened only eleven years before the young Basil Moreau got there. The Le Mans seminary had been installed in the old Saint Vincent's Abbey in the very year he entered: 1816. The seminary of Saint Sulpice, shut down by Napoleon in 1810, had been reopened in 1814, seven years before he came. The Le Mans authorities opened the seminary of Tessé as a house of philosophy after Basil finished his own philosophical studies, and so in 1823 he went to teach in a house where he had not studied.[16] A priest of Le Mans, Fr. Jacques Dujarié, had organized a community of teaching sisters which was still developing; and yet in 1820, one year before Basile's ordination, he organized a community of teaching brothers.

CHAPTER 2

PREPARATION
(1799–1823)

I. EARLY LIFE

Very little is known about Basil Moreau's early life beyond the information which his first biographer provides:

Among all his pupils, the pastor of Laigné took special notice of Basil Moreau because of his open and affectionate character, his liveliness, his quick and active mind, his good judgment, and his surprising memory. But what attracted the priest most of all about this child was his solid piety, his purity of life, and his precocious maturity. These things seemed to him good indications of a holy vocation. According to some of Basil's early companions who are still alive, he was the one who organized the boys' games and assigned everyone his role, taking care to exclude those whose behavior at the rectory or elsewhere had given grounds for suspicion. He was also the one who taught the more able of his companions to serve Mass and to take part in various other church ceremonies. For this purpose he used a table in his room as an altar at which he himself took the celebrant's part, not omitting the sermon, which his good mother and his sisters tried to listen to with irreproachable gravity.[1]

His sisters, however, did not always maintain the desired seriousness if we are to believe Br. Marie-Antoine, who notes that on occasion when they giggled, Basil turned to his mother and said: "Mother! Make them keep still! I don't want them to laugh."[2]

> Fr. Le Provost, after having brought his pupil as far along as his modest program of elementary education permitted, did not hesitate to inform Basil's parents of the hopes he founded on the boy's good dispositions. . . . Basil's father asked for time to reflect on Fr. Le Provost's proposals. He was afraid that his son, who was just twelve years old, would end up by losing, through his books, the habit and taste for household chores, in which he had to share outside the time of his classes. [Finally the father permitted his son] to begin the study of Latin with three young boys of the village. . . . However, only later did Louis Moreau excuse his son from pasturing the cows, which was his responsibility among the family chores. The boy worked this task in with his studies, which meant so much to him, by carrying a stool out to the pasture, upon which he did his assignments.[3]

These few lines give the impression of serious and devout youth, with some ability to assert himself, to lead others, to be determined. His seriousness and piety made Fr. Le Provost feel he had a vocation to the priesthood. His ability to assert himself and to get others to follow stands out in his organization of his companions' games and his exclusion of those whose conduct made them suspect. His determination appears as rather uncommon from his readiness to study even while pasturing the family cows.

His studies enabled him to enter the fourth class at the college of Château-Gontier, about sixty miles from Laigné, in 1814 at the age of fifteen. The college then served also as a preparatory seminary, and this is why Basil went there. His studies were certainly paid for, at least in part, by the pastor of Laigné and

Mademoiselle de Boismont. Of the latter, Basil wrote of her after her death in April 1833 in *La Gazette du Maine*: "She contributed with generosity to defer the expenses of the education of many young priests." He spoke from experience.

The boy impressed the principal of the school, Fr. Horeau, just as he impressed the pastor of Laigné if we can believe his biographer:

> Basil justified the high hopes of the principal by his exemplary behavior, constant work, and outstanding success in his studies. The esteem which Fr. Horeau had shown him from the beginning appeared more and more justified as the mind and the heart of the pupil revealed themselves. Years later, when Basil was still only a subdeacon, the venerable principal of Château-Gontier told the bishop of Le Mans of the excellent memory which the student had left at the college and asked His Lordship to assign him as his assistant, with the hope, he wrote, of being able to find in him after some years, the successor that his advanced age and infirmities suggested he prepare for himself.[4]

Basil knew of Fr. Horeau's intention. It is possible that the principal appointed Basil as one of the prefects and even entrusted him with one of the lower classes during his time at the school.[5] In any case, the request made by Fr. Horeau of the bishop shows that he noted some leadership ability in this student from Laigné.

The assistant superior, Fr. Louis-Jean Fillion, a priest ordained just the year before Basil's arrival at Château-Gontier and entrusted with the spiritual direction of the students, also formed a favorable impression of the boy. A close friendship grew up between them, and for most of the next forty years Fr. Fillion was Basil's confessor or spiritual director or both.

Letters to two of his older sisters and a little speech read to his parents in the presence of his brothers and sisters and in their name one feast of Saint Louis (August 25) date from his years at Château-Gontier. They show his deep feeling and, in particular, his strong attachment to his family. They show the seriousness and even the touch of solemnity that marked much of his later writing and preaching.

The first letter is addressed to his sister Cécile shortly after her feast day—probably only a month after he had left home.

> My dear sister,
>
> Your feast day, far from being a day of joy for me, was only a day of sorrow. The farther away from you I am, the more I feel affection and love for you and for all my brothers and sisters. I could not offer my prayers to God for your happiness without thinking of the sad separation which I have just made. You were before my eyes the whole time, and this thought troubled my mind and my soul. I experienced feelings which I had never had before. At times I thought of people who let themselves be fascinated by the apparent glitter of the false pleasures of this world; at times I thought I heard Saint Cecilia chant the praises of the Lord and play melodies on her harp. O great saint, I said to myself, let me take part one day in your heavenly pleasures—that joy so pure and continual—and my whole family too. Don't let the prayers that I offer you for a sister so exposed to all sorts of dangers be vain. Let them be heard, and let all of us be united after death in the heavenly Jerusalem, that homeland which can only be reached by roads that are so slippery. I have to admit that I thought that day of going off to the desert and spending the rest of my days there. I hope that this thought will often come back to my mind because it encourages me to virtue. Perhaps you will laugh at all this, but I tell you that I was beside myself. May the saint whose name you have obtain for you a place in heaven.[6]

The second letter is dated November 20, 1816. Like the preceding, it was mailed from Château-Gontier.

> My dear sister Victoire,
>
> I was deeply touched by your show of affection for me, and I can tell you that if you shed tears when you left me, I was not very far from crying myself and that I have not gotten over it yet. What troubles me is that I see a very hard year ahead for my godmother.
>
> After the affection which you showed you have for me, I am sure that you will not refuse what I am going to ask of you and of my sister Cécile too. Of all the things that you can do for me, what would give me the greatest pleasure is that you make things easy for our good mother because she has real need of that. What a consolation it would be for me if, once I reach my goal, I can spend the rest of my days with her, with father, and with you, if you are willing to follow a brother who loves you very much.[7]

The following little talk was probably given on August 25, 1816, during the last vacation period which Basil had with the family before moving from Château-Gontier to Saint Vincent's Seminary. It was the feast day of Louis and Louise Moreau as well as of one of their sons.

> My dear father and mother,
>
> If I speak today, it is not out of an obligation of civility which this occasion imposes upon me, nor is it to pay you the sort of respects that are ordinarily only refined lies or base flattery. Guided by a purer motive and heeding only the voice of the gratitude that inspires me as well as my brothers and sisters, I want to speak to you the language of truth.
>
> How many interesting things strike my imagination at this happy moment! How many precious memories present

themselves to my mind! With what transports of joy I celebrate this day, which is for you, as it is for all of us, a solemn
feast day! If I go back in spirit to my cradle, I discover pressing
motives of gratitude. If I reflect on the beautiful days of inno-
cence which I spent among you, if I consider the beginnings
and the progress of each of my brothers and sisters, I see you
involved in the care of a difficult business to obtain for us the
necessities of life and to raise us in the proper way. Here I see
a hard-working father traveling from city to city and across
the countryside, there a mother concerned about every day
of her children's lives and always worried about what would
become of them.

Yes, how much care, how many worries, how much effort
and labor our education cost you, how much fatigue you bore
to assure a comfortable life for us. Up to the present you have
spent your days in the bustle of affairs, and you can say with
lively sentiments of gratitude at the sight of your children
here assembled: "Here, my God, are those whom you have
given me for the consolation of my old age. Here is the flock
which you entrusted to me. I give thanks to you that you have
kept them safe and sound for me while so many other families have been destroyed by the loss of children who have
perished on fields of battle."

And now, dear parents, rejoice in the happiness of having
raised your children so successfully. Rejoice in the consoling
sight of all of us capable of conducting ourselves prudently
in the affairs of the world. Rejoice in the pleasure of perhaps
seeing one of your children called to fulfill one day the fear-
ful responsibilities of the priesthood, and perhaps to give his
life for the faith.

Live on, then; be happy. May peace and concord give joy to
the rest of your days. May religion have an ever greater attraction for you so that after having received the powerful helps

which it has to offer its children, you may be received among the number of the blessed.

There, parents dear to our hearts, are the hopes which the hearts of your children form for you. There, Louis, powerful protector of France, is the favor that we beg of you to obtain from the Father of mercies.

Great saint, from the height of your heavenly abode, cast a compassionate glance on a father whom we cherish, on a mother who is dear to us, and on a brother whom the Church has entrusted to your care in naming you as his patron. Take under your powerful protection all those among us who have the honor of bearing your name. Be their intercessor with God, their guide during the rest of their lives, their defender at the moment of death, and their protector at that terrible moment when time is no more and eternity begins. Grant, finally, that as all of us are assembled here, so also one day we may all be reunited with you in happiness.[8]

The portrait these lines give us is that of a solidly devout young man with determination and seriousness to the point of solemnity, with strong attachments to family and friends, and with the ability to bring others to follow him.

II. STUDIES FOR PRIESTHOOD

a. Saint Vincent's

In 1816 at the age of seventeen, Basil entered Saint Vincent's Seminary at Le Mans to begin his philosophical and theological studies. He received tonsure on September 18, 1816, and minor orders three years later. There he found Fr. Bouvier, a theologian of some stature who was later to publish volumes that would have widespread influence in the French Church. He chose him as his confessor. There he carefully learned a thoroughly Gallican theology in Latin syllogistic argumentation from professors who had signed a commitment to teach the Organic Articles the year before his arrival. There he also learned to counter the rigidity of Jansenism with the moral theology of Saint Alphonsus Liguori. On May 27, 1820, he was ordained subdeacon by Bishop Claude de la Myre, the recently installed successor of Bishop de Pidoll, and on April 7, 1821, he received the diaconate. Priestly ordination came for him and forty-one companions at the end of his theological studies on August 12, 1821. He was then 22 years and 6 months of age.[9] He celebrated his first Mass at Laigné in the presence of family and friends, assisted by Fr. Le Provost and with the sermon preached by Fr. Huard.

Practically nothing is extant from his years at Saint Vincent's—no letters, no notebooks. We have only a later record in his own hand of the private vows he took before the subdiaconate—an act which shows his idealism and his attraction for a life of simplicity, poverty, and austerity:

> Vows which I made before the subdiaconate
>
> 1. Vow of perpetual chastity.
> 2. Vow of obedience, that is, not to seek out any position and to accept everything.
> 3. Vow of poverty, that is, not to amass riches, to wear only common and ordinary material and never silk.
> 4. Vow to fast on Friday and to drink nothing but water at supper as long as I live in a seminary—in order not to place myself in an embarrassing situation during vacations. The first reason for this mortification is to do penance for my sins, the second to obtain an ever greater love of Jesus Christ.[10]

The same sort of idealism showed itself in his dream of the foreign missions at ordination time—a dream which he did not press beyond manifesting it to his bishop.

b. Saint Sulpice

The bishop decided he should prepare to teach in the Le Mans seminary and sent him to spend two years with the Sulpicians—a year of study in Paris at the Seminary of Saint Sulpice and a year at Issy on the outskirts at the Sulpician "Solitude"—a novitiate of sorts meant to provide special spiritual training for future seminary faculty members. Fr. Bouvier, now vicar general and rector of Saint Vincent's Seminary, certainly had an important voice in this decision: Fr. Moreau's letters to others from Paris are full of references to what the superior of the Le Mans seminary desired and to their correspondence, which is no longer extant.[11]

From his two years in Paris an abundance of material has come down to us: his notes on several of the courses he took at Saint Sulpice (in which he unlearned the Gallicanism he had learned at Saint Vincent's), his little notebook of resolutions from Issy, and a number of letters to his sisters, to Fr. Fillion (who by then had left Château-Gontier to become superior of the new philosophy seminary of Tessé), and to Fr. Huard.

The letters show him warmly attached to the family and friends that he had left in Le Mans, impressed by Paris and eager to profit from his stay there as much as he could, but especially impressed by the piety and devotion of the Sulpicians who were his instructors.

Of his attachment to his family, he wrote to one of his sisters some time after arriving at Saint Sulpice:

> I am happy when I receive a letter, but I jump with joy when I have two to read, because I am sure you know, my dear sister, that the farther a man is away from his homeland, the more he wants to hear people talk about it, and I understand today the whole truth of what Saint Augustine said: that when a man is separated from his friends, he experiences

a more lively feeling of friendship for them than when he is in their presence. I am beginning with the intention of filling these three big pages; I don't know if the time will permit me to satisfy my desire, but because you want me to let you pay for this letter, I am going to try to satisfy you completely and to write at least ten sous' worth. While you were playing at chestnuts, your brother Basil was at prayer with the community, and there he was speaking to the good God about his family, who occupy his mind too often, and about the good people of Le Mans, the thought of whom is becoming more and more dear to him. Which of us two do you think has the better part? I don't know if you were happier than I.[12]

In the same vein he wrote to Fr. Fillion on November 25, 1821:

God be blessed and praised be Jesus Christ: I am at home at Saint Sulpice. Who would not be happy with such holy people in whom affability and charity make you find only so many brothers and friends! However, I will confess to you that I am constantly aware of what Saint Augustine said: that a man experiences a livelier feeling of friendship and affection for his friends when he is separated from them than when he is in their presence, and I need the support of the hope that one day I will fall into your hands or into those of good Monsieur Bouvier, to whom I beg you to offer my respects and the assurance of my lively gratitude. More than once every day I find myself in spirit in the midst of your numerous [seminary] family; at times, I am even there for your dinner, your spiritual reading, and I take a walk on your terrace. . . . Whatever you think of this joking, you can see from it how distracted my mind is and how I make my meditation. . . . You must pardon this scribbling of mine; I write to you with the confidence of a son in his father.[13]

Of his sightseeing in the capital during the vacation at the end of his year at Saint Sulpice, he wrote to his sister: "I have seen the mint. I made a hundred-sou piece myself. I'll have to tell you how it's done. I have been to see a glass works, a porcelain factory, etc. I have climbed the towers of Notre Dame, etc. That is how I am spending my vacation. It is going to end within two weeks, and then I must think only of God. I wanted to see Paris before the October retreat, because I will not come back any more. . . ."[14]

He noted with enthusiasm the efforts made to revive Christian life in Paris:

> The mission, which is to make the rounds of all the parishes in Paris, is succeeding as well as could be expected. You'll find some details on this matter in the last letter I wrote to Mademoiselle de Boismont. I'll add here only that this initial success is not passing unnoticed at the law faculty. Fr. Duponceau, who came to see me told me that the students passed notes around during classes inviting one another to go to hiss the missionaries. . . . This is the sort of thing we hear from the priests who are giving the mission and come to visit us from time to time. One of them told us that people were beginning to go to confession and that there wasn't a single missionary who did not have at least a marriage to straighten out. Archbishop Quélen is distinguishing himself by his really apostolic zeal. He has reserved a confessional for himself in every parish where, he says, he is waiting especially for the poor, whom he wants to help not only in their spiritual needs but even in their temporal needs as far as lies in his power. Fr. Mesnildot, a missionary, assured us that they are getting him to do whatever they want for the good of their work and that he was even going to morning prayer at five o'clock now in one church, now in another. The sight of this prelate must necessarily make a great impression on the common people.[15]

He was deeply impressed by the piety of his Sulpician masters and their devotion to their priestly vocation:

> On the feast of the Presentation of the Blessed Virgin, we had a ceremony so touching that I must tell you a little about it. I am sure that you'll be edified by it. On that day the Sulpicians renew their clerical promises. We had as celebrant Fr. de Quélen, [archbishop of Paris and] former student of the house of Saint Sulpice; the most distinguished of his assistants were the archbishops of Rheims and of Arles, Fr. de Frayssinous, former director of the seminary and now first chaplain of the king, etc., etc. Immediately before the renewal of the promises, the archbishop gave an exhortation, really short, but full of zeal and unction. Then we saw good Fr. Duclaux [the superior] advance toward the altar to renew his consecration to the Lord. It was a most impressive sight. You really have to have seen it to image it, and I cannot take the time to describe it in detail. I will only tell you that it was impossible not to be moved. And that evening he told us that he had been almost carried away, that he had then offered or presented all of us to Mary; he spoke to us, in a word, with so much openness of heart that we were moved to tears. I also had the happiness of renewing my promises in my turn, and I assure you that a morning passed in that way is worth twenty years of worldly pleasures and enjoyments. I skip many of the interesting circumstances to tell you that these distinguished people ate with us in the refectory where we had a dinner which was very well served and permission to speak during the whole meal. I cannot think of a holier day.[16]

He was in Paris to prepare himself for the task of a seminary faculty member. He seems to have anticipated his work with seminarians by providing at least one of them with financial support.[17]

He was at Saint Sulpice to prepare for teaching. The many carefully and closely written notebooks which he kept and which are still partially extant attest to his seriousness about his classes. His unwillingness to risk losing them by sending them through the mail indicates the value he set on the courses. The obvious interest with which he furnishes Fr. Fillion an abundance of detailed information and arguments, especially on Lamennais' ideas and the reactions of others to them, shows a vital interest in the philosophical and theological issues of the time.[18]

Regarding his future task as a seminary faculty member, he was much more concerned about the seminarians' formation in the spiritual life than about their formation in academics. He wrote Fr. Fillion concerning discussion of a rather explosive philosophical question: "Permit me to offer the observation that it seems best to me not to let your seminarians discuss this question too much because feelings run high and charity is hurt in more than one way. For myself, I have taken the resolution never to speak of systems during recreation or at least not to argue about them; class is quite enough especially since it is useless, above all on this subject, because the greatest lights do not see clearly."[19] The influence of Fr. Mollevaut, the director of the Solitude at Issy, may be suspected here.

In any case, he was struck by the importance of his future task. He wrote to Canon Fillion from Paris:

> If I fall into your hands [at the philosophy seminary of Tessé], I will sing a Te Deum, although I will also tremble, because I am terrified by the very thought of hearing seminarians' confessions and making a decision about their vocation; but if I am sent to preach the gospel in some country place, I will bless God and my bishop. I burn with this desire, and I wish I were already there. Do I have to tell you that at times I experience such a desire that I feel a fire all over inside me? When I get into bed, which I look upon as my tomb, I would like to

wake up in the morning in the midst of some poor peasants. How I would instruct them! How I would lead them to God! Is this a desire to be noticed, self-love or pride, or is it a devout inclination, holy inspirations? God knows. What I know is that this desire is devouring me while I am studying Beth's and Radeh's; while I am arguing to an atqui or an ergo, the soul of my brother is perishing. For the rest, God will arrange everything, and at the first sign I will leave the solitude of Issy, although with regrets.[20]

Some time after he arrived at Issy, he wrote:

Pray . . . that this year of blessings, which I look upon as a year of graces gratis datae *(freely given)*, will not be without fruit for my salvation and that of so many brothers in Jesus Christ who will perhaps be confided to my care only too soon. To form priests! What a ministry! I do not consider any other task as great as this one, which is yours and that of your entire staff. May I at last learn how to govern without commanding, how to obey without reflection on the order given, how to edify by my modesty, how to show everyone the kindness and the charity which we have here for one another, and especially never to forget my own nothingness and my sins—this will be my daily occupation, the object of my study every day.[21]

Three months later he wrote: "His Lordship [the bishop of Le Mans] told me that the seminary is going very well. Blessed be God, and praised be Jesus Christ. It will go still better when you inspire your young men to a very great devotion to the Blessed Virgin." Then he continued: "I tremble in all seriousness when I think that if I am lukewarm, all my pentitents will be lukewarm, etc. Please—I am counting very much on your fervent prayers, etc.: for the rest, I do not think I could be any happier than here at the Solitude."[22]

Frequently in his correspondence with Fr. Fillion he showed a real concern over the rumors he had heard of the unbecoming behavior of some of the Le Mans clergy, or over the piety and discipline which seemed to him marks of any seminary that was to train worthy priests and which seemed to be deficient at the Le Mans seminaries. In fact, he went so far as to urge him—with apologies for his boldness—to encourage a better observance of silence at the seminary of Tessé.[23]

c. Issy

When he moved to Issy in the summer of 1822 for a year at the Sulpician Solitude, he looked forward to the opening retreat and the months he would spend there as a time of conversion. He wrote to Fr. Fillion on July 8, 1822, at the end of his year in Paris and eleven months after his priestly ordination:

> I am going to shut myself up at the Solitude, full of fear, even beside myself at the thought of the three hundred sacrifices [of the Mass] which I offered this year. I will begin retreat on the twenty-first. . . . O Lord, what an account I would already have to render if I had been ministering! What is going to happen later? If I do not become a saint, what a damned soul I will make! Frankly, I tremble, my hair stands on end, when I realize that I am taking the place of a seminarian here who would have become a great saint, because if you do not become one here, you will never be one. So pray for this miserable sinner who every day abuses so many graces, and do not be offended if, once I become a solitary, I break off a correspondence which, edifying and interesting as it may be, would only distract me, for my misery is so deep that every bit of news whether from Le Mans or from my family distracts me and makes me lose the fruit of many meditations. . . . The sacrifice will not be without merit on my side because it will cost me very much. Be so good as to offer my respects and esteem to Fr. Bouvier, and tell him that he should not

be surprised if I write to him less often than in the past. The result will be a little good both for the individual concerned and for the souls who are waiting for him. What would you think of me if I left here just as I had come?[24]

To Fr. Huard he wrote about a month later of his two superiors, Fr. Duclaux the preceding year at Saint Sulpice and Fr. Mollevaut that year at Issy: "If the former had, in my opinion, the kindness of Saint Francis de Sales, the latter has the charity of Saint Vincent de Paul. Both are worth canonizing; and I do not know more interior men. Miserable as I am, I am not correcting myself in such a great school, and I have hardly taken a single step forward in the interior life."[25]

At the Solitude he formed a fast friendship with the director, Fr. Mollevaut, who became his personal spiritual director and remained so until the decline of the Sulpician's mental powers a few years before his death in 1854.

Of Fr. Mollevaut, Basil's first biographer writes:

Once he became superior of the Solitude, Fr. Mollevaut consecrated his life to training ecclesiastics. His great means of teaching and persuading was example. Every morning he was up by four o'clock. He went at 4:15 to bring a light and a Christian greeting to the solitaries who lived in the same building as himself. Then he made his mental prayer and celebrated Mass, which were preceded every day by the taking of the discipline. He had no one to take care of his room; he himself swept it, made his fire, went to get water from the fountain, cut down, split up, and carried his wood, bought his clothes, which were of the most common material, and mended them. Fr. Mollevaut had an extraordinary desire for the hidden life, but it was difficult for him to indulge it since everyone sought him out.[26]

Basil himself wrote to one of his sisters from Issy: "We love one another here as brothers, and we make up a little family of fourteen members whose father is a saint, but a hard saint. He is hard on his own body, but he spoils us. However, he is training us in the spiritual life, and I am in the best possible school. You know how much I need these lessons. Pride, jealousy, self-love, and anger made me commit so many faults when I was among you that I tremble over this at times. I didn't realize how necessary meekness is!"[27]

His notebook of retreat resolutions from Issy give us a look into the young priest's life that his letters do not permit. He prepared for the opening retreat by a very detailed planning of all the free time of the eight-day period and by specific resolutions that show his desire to give himself completely to making a good retreat.[28]

The outcome of the retreat was several pages of resolutions on mortification of the senses, mortification of the vices, external mortification, and prayer and devotional exercises. They deserve being quoted, at least in part, since they show a young man vigorously determined to control his natural propensities and to spend himself on others and yet, for all his vigor and determination, very much aware of his need for guidance. Among other things he resolved:

> Pride, a) I will not say anything good or bad about myself or about things that relate to me; b) I will be obedient and subject to everybody and everything, especially my superiors, my confessor, and the director of my conscience; c) I will never argue with anyone, but if there is reason for disagreement, once I have modestly put forward my reasons, either I will agree with the other person's judgment or I will say nothing; d) with devotedness I will take up those tasks in which I can exercise greater humility, and all the more so, the more my pride and vanity draw back from them; e) finally, I will frequently consider, especially when I desire to be known and taken note of, 1) Christ spending thirty years in solitude and

in a life of silence, 2) my sins, my defects, my tendency to evil, and my slowness to good.

Anger, a) I will go so far to avoid taking revenge that I will not even defend myself when I can; b) with the greatest meekness I will bear the defects and mannerisms of others, especially those that bother me; c) I will strive never to be burdensome or troublesome to anyone in word or action but rather to be kind. . . .

Selfishness, a) I will spend myself completely on others; b) I will not think or say anything of my neighbor that is not favorable, especially of those who bother me; c) I will do for my companions with all the more generosity and joy those things that are more displeasing to me. Finally, I will follow after all the enemies of my salvation, and I will not turn back until they have given up. Therefore I will take care to have and to choose several monitors to point out my defects.

As long as I live in a seminary I will observe the abstinence which I vowed for the Friday of each week and the use of nothing but water at the evening meal on Friday. . . .

In winter, unless a doctor, my director, or necessity demands it, I will never put up heat. . . .

Finally, as soon as my director permits it, I will take the discipline on Friday or wear a hair shirt on that day, but I resolve to do nothing in this matter without his permission.

To reveal my interior every week to my director, on Sunday.

To celebrate Mass . . . on Sunday for the souls which will be entrusted to me later on and for all ecclesiastics.

To recite . . . lauds for the souls who will be entrusted to me.[29]

In his retreat resolutions reading of Scripture and reading of the *Imitation of Christ* figure prominently—practices which he learned from the Sulpicians.[30] The rule of life he drew up for himself at Issy kept them in a prominent place. He decided to memorize passages from the *Imitation*: he resolved to begin each day by reading a chapter of the Old Testament as soon as he had risen and to read the *Imitation* and memorize certain passages during breakfast and in moving from one activity to another.[31] His rule of life also made ample provision for frequent lengthy visits to the Blessed Sacrament and for devotion to Mary. While at Issy, he planned to go on pilgrimage to Chartres before taking up his work at the seminary in order to consecrate his ministry to Mary.[32] He doubtless received warm encouragement from Fr. Mollevaut in all the details of his rule which influenced the rest of his life.

Especially enlightening are his reflections on December 1, 1822:

> Today I am making my monthly retreat, and during meditation, which I made on the faults committed since the [last] retreat and on the graces received, I recognized in myself five obstacles to my spiritual advancement.
>
> The first and the greatest of all is my unfaithfulness to my particular rule [of life].
>
> The second is precipitation in my actions and especially in my words.
>
> The third is lack of mortification of my senses and especially of my imagination and my will.
>
> The fourth is a lack of union with God in the different activities of the day, especially during study.
>
> The fifth is a certain horror of whatever wounds self-love, a secret passion for esteem and a good reputation, a blind habit of not receiving as coming from God little circumstances that contradict my natural inclinations and my will.[33]

Four weeks later, on December 29, he wrote:

> Today I am making my monthly retreat. I recognize that I have corrected 1) my haste in conversation, in the recitation of the Vent Sánete, and in the sign of the cross; 2) my spirit

of contentiousness at recreation; 3) I prepare my meditation better . . . ; 4) I have been more faithful to my particular rule . . . ; 5) since I have made practically no progress in contempt for myself and for the esteem of others, I continue the resolution taken during the last monthly retreat on this matter.

Recognizing that I have gotten nothing but disadvantage from letting others know what I do not like, I have taken the resolution not to speak of such things anymore except to my director, and I have bound myself under pain of venial sin not to speak to anyone except my director of what happens at the parish [where I help]; I have kept this little vow well for the last four days.[34]

A month later, on January 26, 1823, he concluded: "Humility, meekness, and charity being the virtues of which I have the greatest need, and the first involving the other two with itself, I take the resolution to apply myself exclusively to the practice of this virtue, to make it the subject of my examinations of conscience during the month, and to continue until I have begun to desire contempt."[35]

Some time later he wrote:

To hold on to doors as I open and close them.
Not to mimic others.
Not to go to the kitchen.
While thinking of my vow and under pain of venial sin, I will not speak deliberately, whether for good or for ill, either in particular or in general, of persons whose confessions I have heard.[36]

These numerous quotations show Fr. Moreau shortly before his twenty-fifth birthday as a strong, even ardent, personality who was very much determined to control himself, a student most conscientious and industrious about preparing for his future work, a man of strong affections desirous of spending all that he had on others but at the same time clearly—almost overly—aware of his need for guidance. His insistence on his need to obey almost sounds like an abdication of initiative and responsibility. His whole life was a proof that this was not the way he understood these statements. His affection for family and friends and his desire of giving himself to or for others, he expressed with a simplicity and straightforwardness that were almost ingenuous. The rest of his life would prove that his love was discerning and knew how to be firm, how to mistrust on occasion, and how to rebuke. Finally, in his life the spiritual held the primacy. His sense of his need for God was sharp, and his insistence on the primacy of piety and prayer so vigorous as to sound at times a bit anti-intellectual. His work in the years that followed his days in Paris and at Issy proved amply that he was in no sense anti-intellectual. It may be that his expressions were influenced by his spiritual director, who seems to have been somewhat anti-intellectual as a result of the vanity that marked his life as an intellectual before his conversion.

We should not consider young Fr. Moreau overserious. His resolution not to mimic others suggests that he had a lighter side. He could write to his sister shortly before the end of his stay at Issy: "Do not think that I am somber and sad. I am most certainly not. You will find me quite lighthearted, although a bit thin for I have wasted away somewhat. But I am getting along well, and I hope to do even better when I get to Laigné."[37] Stories he told some years later picture him caught by a fit of laughter with the other priests in the Solitude refectory as the reader mentioned the name of certain saints in the martyrology and even at times during community prayers.

There is little to indicate that his leadership qualities developed during these years. The only evidence we have are later letters of Fr. Mollevaut which refer to his "example," which all remembered, and his initiative in establishing observances for the month of May at the Solitude.[38]

He owed a great debt to the Sulpicians. They had formed him for the work to which he would devote the next thirteen years of his life—although, when he left Issy, he probably thought it would be the rest of his life. The work for which they had formed him was their own. He had developed close friendships with many of them. It is not surprising that shortly before the end of his stay at Issy he should write to Fr. Fillion: "Tell me if there would be opposition to my becoming a Sulpician."[39] But as with his attraction for the foreign missions two years earlier, he seems to have pressed this one no further.

CHAPTER 3

BEGINNINGS
(1823–1835)

The first thirteen years of Basil Moreau's ministry were important years because of the services he rendered the diocese of Le Mans. They were important too because they permitted his talents to develop and mature. They were important perhaps most of all because they determined the course of the remainder of his life.

During these years we find in Fr. Moreau a seminary professor who labored very conscientiously at the task he had been given to do, but also one for whom the seminary was much too small a world.

I. SEMINARY DUTIES: PROFESSOR, ADMINISTRATOR, SPIRITUAL DIRECTOR

These years were busy years. He was assigned first to teach at Fr. Fillion's philosophy seminary of Tessé. For anyone as conscientious and thorough as he was, the preparation of the courses he taught demanded much time and effort. He was at this task only two years when in 1825, he was transferred to Saint Vincent's Seminary, where Fr. Bouvier was superior, to teach dogmatic theology. There he had a whole new set of classes to prepare. A bit of tension between the Gallicanism of the superior and the ultramontanism of the dogmatic theology professor, with whom most of the other faculty members sided, made his task harder, and finally led to Fr. Bouvier's having the new bishop of Le Mans, Philip Carron, transfer him in 1830 from the chair of dogma to that of Holy Scripture. Once more he had a completely new set of classes to prepare. Four years later when Fr. Bouvier became bishop of Le Mans, Fr. Moreau became vice-rector of the seminary and assumed administrative duties. These duties included much that the rector, Fr. Heurtebize, would have done had he not been so hard of hearing. Nor were teaching and administration enough: a large number of the seminarians chose him as spiritual director, and many of them continued to come for his help after they had concluded their seminary studies.

Moreau's conscientious approach to his teaching responsibilities is evident. Fr. Mollevaut's correspondence with him alludes frequently to the advice he asked of the Sulpicians who had been his instructors in Paris. His notes for a course on the Church (which date from a later period when he published them for his novices) show him to be a man for whom it did not suffice simply to hand on the ideas he had received from others. His still extant annotations on the psalms, on the life of Christ, and on the Pauline epistles show that he labored hard and researched much in preparing his classes while at the same time following the advice Fr. Mollevaut gave him on March 26, 1830:

> The teaching of Sacred Scripture is a very holy task and demands a good bit of holiness, humility, and prayer. Vanity can encourage research inspired by curiosity, as well as involved discussions, superfluous, useless, and dangerous explanations. As a result, anyone may be as dissipated and vain in this study as in that of Homer or Virgil, and often the students carry away less taste and respect for the word of God and less appreciation of its usefulness than if they had not had it explained to them. There, my dear friend, are the dangers. You will avoid them by calling on the Holy Spirit, who inspired the sacred writers and who alone knows their

meaning and can make it known and make people profit from it. Then you must often meditate the sapere ad sobrietatem *(wisdom that leads to seriousness)*. . . . Remember that the majority of your students will minister in country places among good peasants, and decide in the light of that what will be most profitable for them.[1]

Fr. Moreau's effort apparently succeeded in making him a good professor because a year later, on May 15, 1831, Fr. Mollevaut could write: "You have had the consolation of being able to interest your students in so important a class, in which the word of God is studied and they learn to love the wonders of our faith— nothing is better calculated to form a good priest."[2]

Fr. Moreau's extensive library reveals scholarly and pastoral interests; it includes, for example, many works of the Church Fathers, Mansi's 34-volume collection on the Church councils, the works of Alphonsus Liguori, and several works against Jansenism.

The seriousness with which he fulfilled his administrative duties might be illustrated by his efforts to improve the curriculum at Saint Vincent's. For example, some months after he became vice-rector, he introduced a course in physics which was taught by the outstanding scientist of La Sarthe, who was a good friend of his.

His concern about the spiritual formation of the seminarians recurred repeatedly in his letters to Fr. Mollevaut. It extended to seminary discipline as well as to his own work of spiritual direction.

He wrote of his worry over a spirit of dissipation at Saint Vincent's while he was still at Tessé. Fr. Mollevaut replied on March 17, 1825:

I share your concern about the neglect of silence at the major seminary. Encourage your young people to be faithful to it, despite the bad example, as to a basic point on which piety and good studies rest: use all the influence you have to get them to avoid falling into the dissipation which can in two weeks cause the loss of several years' efforts at practicing virtue. You can hardly form them too much to the habit of recollection, self-denial, humility, prayer, and obedience; without that their progress will be doubtful, and their fervor will disappear.[3]

After his assignment to the major seminary, he asked advice as to how to behave in regard to practices with which he did not agree.[4] In his very first year at Saint Vincent's, F. Mollevaut had to urge him not to be so insistent on what he felt was for the good of the seminarians or so outspoken with the superior:

As for what seems to you to be for the good of the seminary, do not insist on it too much; leave it to those who are responsible for it. . . . Whenever you experience temptations of disgust with your present ministry leave them to be examined six months later. As for the uneasiness, we experience it at times without knowing why. But, my dear friend, what ever gave you the idea to tell your good superior that you did not like the way things were? Don't you see that if we had meditated on that statement in the presence of our Lord, it would not have come out of our mouths? Didn't it rather cause pain to someone who had the right to expect something completely different from us? And all that, in the last analysis, is just wanting others to see things the way we do, to consider us infallible. If I were you, I would give a good bit of reflection to these precipitous moves, and to practice divine abnegation, I would take the resolution not to speak out all the offensive things that suggest themselves to my mind and to blame the superior. Let us spend our effort on that, and it will be worth much more than going to the foreign missions.

There is nothing like explaining one's opinion with moderation while fearing interiorly that if we do not know how to guide and control ourselves we should not pretend to guide others. Saint Vincent de Paul was delighted when somebody made known or adopted an opinion different from his own.[5]

The recently arrived faculty member apologized, and Fr. Mollevaut wrote two weeks later:

I thank our good master for what he inspired you [to do] in regard to your superior [Fr. Bouvier] and your director [Fr. Fillion—Fr. Moreau's confessor, to whom Fr. Mollevaut usually refers in this way]. Let us remember that these retractions are not enough to acquire the spirit of abnegation and that a man can humiliate himself before everyone and all the while remain attached to his ideas and the good opinion he has of himself, along with contempt for others. [True abnegation] is the object of a very special grace which makes saints, produces peace, evenness of temper, hatred of contentiousness and a great interior meekness in regard to everyone. How great a thing it is to work at acquiring kindness! To do so, let us put into practice the maxim you know: to suffer everybody and to make no one suffer; that is the best and the most perfect of all mortifications.[6]

Three years later, however, Fr. Mollevaut was still urging Fr. Moreau to preserve interior peace despite something at the seminary which troubled him:

The more you devote yourself to preserving peace, the more you will find treasures and lights. There is no other way to belong to God and to acquire virtue. What you have seen in your seminary has been a real affliction for your good heart, and you were inclined to attribute the good that happened to your unwillingness to bend. But experience will convince you that peace, patience, meekness, prayer are the real sources of all good, and that only a great charity, condescendence, and inexhaustible kindness will form the hearts of seminarians, that everything lies in gaining their trust and their affection, and that you achieve this by the continual exercise of humility, love of crosses, and perfect trust in divine Providence. There you have the three sources of peace.[7]

It is difficult to determine how much Fr. Moreau was personally responsible for the change, but in 1831 Fr. Mollevaut indicated that a change had occurred at Saint Vincent's:

What you tell me about your seminary fills me with joy. You need not be afraid of speaking to me of it too much. This is the only kind of news that I enjoy more each time I receive it. Once fervor has been introduced into these holy houses, young people can be led as far as one wishes and can be inspired to love and practice all the priestly virtues; and, as Saint Vincent de Paul said, there is nothing greater, more divine, or heavenly that can be done in the Church of God.[8]

However, with a change of administration which brought him increased responsibility for the seminary in 1834, Fr. Moreau's preoccupations returned. His director wrote on October 31 of that year:

As for the seminary, devote yourself entirely to it, but with an absolute and blind dependence on the superior. Be always convinced that nothing good will be done except in union and peace, that peace is worth more than all the good one might imagine he can do, that this is where you will find the abnegation without which nothing can be done. Remember always that you are the second and the instrument. You will have enough to do in directing your young men as you should. Keep in mind that in your position you must give an example of the most punctual regularity and of all the ecclesiastical virtues, and that this can be done only by habitual union with our Lord and by humility.[9]

Fr. Moreau's concern with the spiritual formation of the seminarians appears perhaps most of all in the advice he asked of Fr. Mollevaut regarding his work as spiritual director. From the first months of his work as a seminary faculty member, we find him receiving advice on the calm, simplicity, gentleness, joy, and firmness which should characterize the spiritual director and on the consolation, encouragement, and support the director should give. On November 22, 1823, Fr. Mollevaut wrote to him at Tessé: "You will find young people full of docility and goodwill, getting along admirably. Adore the Holy Spirit in their hearts. He alone can penetrate there and do what he pleases. For the rest, accustom them to direction, and in direction console them, encourage them, and always show yourself serene, happy, and kind."[10] We can read in Fr. Mollevaut's letters the advice Fr. Moreau asked about encouraging seminarians to frequent communion, about helping those who lacked docility or did not observe silence, about advising those whose ordination had to be delayed, whose fitness for the priesthood was doubtful because of difficulties during vacation or during seminary studies, who hesitated over the commitment to celibacy, and about sending a seminarian to another director.[11] We can read the encouragement his Sulpician director gave him in his continued concern for those whom he had directed after they had left the seminary and in the continued contact he maintained with them after they began their own priestly ministry.[12]

Two bits of advice offered by Fr. Mollevaut show both how effective a spiritual director Fr. Moreau must have been (since so many seminarians chose him as director) and how conscientious he was about fulfilling this responsibility (since he had to be cautioned not to bring too much pressure to bear on those who came to him and had to be reminded that he was doing his best).

On November 23, 1826, Fr. Mollevaut wrote:

> You tell me that you are overburdened with penitents. I would believe it if it were not the will of the good God, who, in giving us work, gives us also the necessary time, lights, and graces, not to mention the infinite honor he does us and the merits attached to all that is done in his name and for him. What overburdens us is usually our preoccupation, worry, and reflection on ourselves to see if we are capable of doing what cannot be done except by him who holds all hearts in his hands. For direction, let matters develop gently one after another, be concerned about the needs of your penitents, but do not force. Some will come more often, others less—provided that we are always ready and that by our kindness we instill in them a real desire for this openness.[13]

On February 20, 1828, he wrote: "You are doing everything you can, but you will always find that there is still much lacking: all will not profit as they should, but the prayer, the example, and the instruction they have received will not be lost, and especially the zeal and the kindness that we have shown them."[14]

The tension that existed between the superior and Fr. Moreau during the latter's years as professor of dogmatic theology, complicated by the rumor that theology professors would have to sign a commitment to teach the Organic Articles, probably explains Fr. Moreau's being unsettled about his own situation.[15] To these years belong almost all the occasions when he questioned his place in the seminary, and frequently this questioning was explicitly linked with his disagreements with Fr. Bouvier. In 1825 he began to teach at Saint Vincent's. In 1826 he dreamed of the foreign missions and of preaching missions.[16] In 1827, 1828, and 1829, he thought of becoming a Sulpician. The only other instance of questioning was in 1835 when once again the superior, this time Fr. Heurtebize, was involved, but by that time Fr. Moreau's religious vocation was probably already becoming clear.[17] In any case, Fr. Bouvier was responsible for Fr. Moreau's transfer from dogma to Sacred Scripture (he admitted it in letters to Sulpicians in Paris), and Fr. Moreau knew it. This did not make for a better relationship between the two, although it did resolve the tension which came from Fr. Moreau's conscientiousness about his responsibilities in the dogmatic theology classroom.

II. OUTSIDE ACTIVITIES: PREACHING, BROTHERS OF SAINT JOSEPH, OTHER PROJECTS

These years as a seminary faculty member were busy not only because of Fr. Moreau's responsibilities inside the seminary, but also because of the increasing demands made upon him from outside—preaching, contacts with Fr. Dujarié's community of brothers, various tasks with which the bishop entrusted him, and projects of his own.

Requests for preaching several sermon series outside the seminary began hardly a year after his return from Paris. They continued over the following years. As he did for his classes, so for his preaching, he asked advice of his Paris professors through Fr. Mollevaut, and he conscientiously labored at composing the lengthy discourses which his sermons were. Fr. Mollevaut urged him to allay his preoccupations: "Fr. Hamon [his professor of preaching in Paris] . . . feels that you should be able to preach the passion in the parish that invited you; but try to calm the desires you experience, and prefer to approach the occasion with a good bit of humility, counting only on the grace and the mercy of our good savior: that is the way to succeed. If you are unable to write the sermon out, have a plan which is simple and solid, historical and practical, not complicated"[18]

The success of his early preaching can be seen in the vivid memories with which it left his hearers, in his notes or sermon drafts still extant, and in the reactions that some of his preaching aroused. A priest who had been with him at Issy vividly recalled fifty years later his description of the crucifixion.

In 1835 he preached the eulogy of his close friend and bene-factor Fr. Huard at the service celebrated a week after the latter's death. It so moved those present that they asked him to print it. He yielded only after repeated urgings and after a newspaper's threat to publish notes people had taken while the preacher was speaking! Some printed copies still exist: a 38-page discourse consisting of an introduction, a treatment of the life and virtues of the deceased, and an emotional conclusion. The booklet does not bear the name of the author but has this note on the cover: "Profits from the sale of this brochure will go to the establish-ment of the Good Shepherd monastery."

A glance at the Sermons,[19] a publication of the remnants of a much larger collection of manuscripts which was gradually de-pleted over the years at least in part by loans to other priests, can help us to appreciate his style of preaching and the personality of the preacher. One of his sermons on confession[20] begins with the words of Jesus in the Gospel of Saint John 8:46, "Who among you will convict me of sin?" The preacher begins: "No one but the savior of the world could speak in this way." He goes on to devel-op the thought of human sinfulness and from there passes to the value of confession. He indicates the three points he wishes to consider in his reflections on the sacrament: it is given by Christ as an easy and infallible remedy for our weakness, is intended by the humiliation it causes us to make up for our sins, and is able to provide some control over our evil inclinations in the very shame that accompanies the admission of our weaknesses. "A few reflections on these truths will be enough to free you from a fear that may perhaps have proved fatal to you and to bring you to submit yourself, not out of necessity but out of love, to a law which is meant only for your own good." He then develops each of these points. In developing the second (the humiliation involved as reparation), he raises the objection, "But it costs too much." And he repeats it—only to refute it—seven times over.

In a few introductory remarks on the exercises of a parish mission preached by him and one or more companions,[21] he explains quite simply that the exercises will consist in preaching, catechism, and confession. The preaching will be done especially with an eye to the poor "for whom we have great esteem and affection." The preachers promise that they will keep to the schedule that has been published so that those who come will not be late for their work. They also promise that the instructions will be within the reach of everyone.

His "allocution" at the marriage of his niece Victorine to Joseph Bouleau on April 27, 1847, is the only one of his sermons printed during his lifetime besides the eulogy of Fr. Huard, and it was certainly printed by the family, not by the preacher. Hardly filling eight small pages, it is a short and simple presentation of the holiness of marriage, of its sacramentality, and of the rite itself. The preacher draws his reflections on the holiness of marriage mainly from the Old Testament, those on its sacramentality from the New, providing a commentary on the passage in chapter 5 of the epistle to the Ephesians which treats of the union between Christ and the Church, and those on the marriage rite from the ceremony itself. He concludes with a prayer that God may bless the union which he is witnessing.

His first biographer makes it clear that Fr. Moreau took pains to work out in detail the sermons and conferences he gave and yet that he could preach well even when he had to improvise. He writes:

> Basil never willingly relied on improvisation. . . . He had to do so when he gave the funeral eulogy of good Fr. Pierre Henri Marchand, who died with a reputation for sanctity on January 6, 1833, at Aubigné, where he had been curate for over fifty years without interruption even during the Reign

of Terror. People took advantage of Basil's passing through Aubigné on the day of burial to ask him to render this excellent priest, whose merits he well knew, the public homage which the entire parish was expecting. Unable to make them accept as excuse either his lack of preparation or his need to depart immediately, he recollected himself for a few moments in the rectory garden, taking along the proper office for deceased priests according to the diocesan liturgy of the period. Then he mounted the pulpit and satisfied the devout desire of the clergy and the faithful, who were deeply moved.

Long remembered was the fine and fruitful retreat which he was wholly unexpectedly called upon to give at the seminary when the preacher for whom they were waiting informed them at the last moment of his absolute inability to come.[22]

Br. Marie-Antoine went so far as to say: "There was energy and fire in his preaching, and he never did so well as when he was called on to preach unexpectedly and without preparation."[23]

Fr. Moreau's contacts with Fr. Dujarié's community of brothers began the very year he returned to Le Mans from Issy. This was only three years after their foundation. He served at first only as a confessor assigned by the bishop to help at the annual retreat. Later he became spiritual director of some of the brothers. Gradually, at the invitation of the bishop, the founder, and the brothers themselves, he assumed a more important role.

The community had been founded by Fr. Dujarié in 1820 at the request of the Le Mans clergy and with extensive advice from Fr. Bouvier. The clergy had wanted a community like the recently founded Brothers of Christian Instruction of Ploërmel. So in his parish of Ruillé-sur-Loir at some distance from Le Mans, Fr. Dujarié opened a novitiate for four young men,[24] giving the nascent institute the brief and simple rules of the Ploërmel brothers[25] and providing for an annual vow of obedience for those who wished to make it. He gave the candidates a habit, which many of those who came later never wore, and organized a simple program of spiritual exercises for them. They went out either alone or in groups of two or three to operate the elementary schools of villages or parishes. In 1823 a royal ordinance gave them legal recognition as a "charitable association" to serve the elementary schools of La Sarthe and the neighboring departments.[26] This was the year in which Fr. Moreau began to serve as one of their retreat confessors.

In the years 1820–1828 the community grew to 105 brothers with 48 establishments. The next year they had 50 establishments, the highest number reached before Fr. Moreau became their superior. Given their fairly loose organization and the nature of their work, it is not surprising that there were many departures among them each year and that each year they abandoned a number of establishments. In 1828 the membership was less than 50% of those who had entered since 1820: 105 out of 250, and the establishments they were then operating, mostly small parish schools, were 48 of a total of 70 which they had opened since 1820. It is surprising, however, that in 1824 out of a total membership of 33 only 2 brothers made the annual vow of obedience and as late as 1830 out of a total of 95 only 8.

Between 1828 and 1832, the community experienced a frightening decline. The causes were probably the lack of a sufficiently strict religious regime, the absence of religious commitments, and insufficient formation. The Revolution of 1830, which dethroned one branch of the Bourbons in favor of another, was enough to precipitate the departure of many whose bond with the community was rather tenuous. The cholera epidemic of 1832 may have helped too. In any case, departures began annually to outnumber entries, and in 1833 the community had fallen to 66 members with 27 establishments. In 1835, when Fr. Moreau became their superior, they still had only 69 members with only 27 establishments.

In 1831 Fr. Moreau urged Fr. Dujarié and the dozen most devoted among the brothers to sign a pact of union meant to safeguard the community against dissolution.[27] In fact, he even drew up the ten provisions of the text. In 1832, he and the retreat preacher addressed letters to Bishop Carron, asking him in the name of the founder and all the retreat confessors to permit the perpetual vows of religion to some of the brothers, and Fr. Moreau sent an 11-point proposal for an "association" among the brothers whose members would make a vow of stability and serve as a means to keep the institute from disintegrating further.[28] From his letters, it appears that Fr. Moreau was evidently charged by the bishop with more than the responsibility of hearing confessions. When Fr. Bouvier became bishop of Le Mans, he and the brothers urgently requested Fr. Moreau to help them.[29]

The bishop also turned other projects over to him, like the diocesan fund drive of 1831, necessary to save the Catholic schools of Le Mans, which had lost government support after the revolution of the preceding year. Again, there was Fr. Moreau's campaign of 1832 to found a house of retirement for the diocesan clergy— one which he may have suggested to the bishop. He went about carrying it out in his usual methodical way: he asked advice of many of the priests and seminarians of Le Mans, drew up a detailed plan and an explanatory letter to be sent out to the clergy, and began collecting funds.[30] The efforts, however, failed to win sufficiently widespread approval, and the chancery turned the money collected into a retirement fund instead. Fr. Moreau was also prevailed upon by certain ladies of the city to ask Bishop Carron to open a monastery of the Good Shepherd at Le Mans. The result was that he became its founder, ecclesiastical superior and, temporarily, its confessor. He found himself charged with getting the community installed and shortly thereafter finding more ample quarters for it and, of course, with providing for its spiritual guidance and financial support. To furnish the financial support, he founded the Association of the Good Shepherd in 1834, to whose associates he made annual retreats available from 1835 on and for whom he authored a brochure of 103 pages in 1835, which became a 426-page manual in 1836.[31] His work with the Good Shepherd demanded much time and effort; it also occasioned the first big conflict of his life. We shall return to this matter below.

In addition to all the demands made on him inside the seminary and outside, Fr. Moreau nurtured a project of his own. He had been teaching only five years when he became convinced of the need for Christian teachers capable of raising the level of education in secondary schools and seminaries. Four years later he had broadened his idea to a society of priest teachers and preachers and had begun to make plans with the bishop's approval. Fr. Bouvier, still superior of the seminary, appreciated the need for preachers but did not agree with the plan for priest teachers. In 1833, practically on the eve of Bishop Carron's death, Fr. Moreau sent three priests to Paris at his own expense to pursue their studies at the Sorbonne.

III. THE INTERIOR LIFE: WORK AND PRAYER, HUMILITY AND OBEDIENCE, APPROACHABILITY AND RELIABILITY

The incredible activity of these years may create the impression that Fr. Moreau was simply an activist. Fr. Mollevaut's letters contain revealing passages that correct this error.

It is true that Fr. Mollevaut had to remind him frequently not to overwork himself. As early as October 10, 1823, he wrote: "I particularly urge you to watch your health. You need prudence, exercise and relaxation, and moderation in your work."[32] Over the following years he urged him not to do too much, not to take on any task outside the seminary except under obedience, not to skip times of recreation, to spend vacations traveling and taking relaxation, not to preach during vacation unless it would require little effort, and to do what others suggested for the sake of his health.[33] He had to warn him too against his tendency to push himself and others too vigorously to effect what he was convinced should be done.[34] He urged him to be patient with what did not go as he felt it should, to avoid undue enthusiasm, haste, to be patient with himself, and not to become discouraged.[35]

> On October 6, 1829, he wrote:
>
> You ask me how to correct unevenness of temper and character. You need time for that. You need to know how to put up with outbursts of temper without being troubled by them or being discouraged. Then constantly ask the good Lord for the virtue of patience and never cease to study it in the life and the passion of Christ. Next, found yourself firmly in self-denial because the reason why we have these outbursts is that we hold on too tightly to our outlook and ideas, don't want to give them up, but resist everything that contradicts us. Finally, the ultimate source is humility, and it is the first thing to acquire. When you work all day long at self-contempt, at distrust of all your judgments, at rating yourself below others in your thoughts, in your heart, and in your talents, and at avoiding stubbornness in certain opinions always inspired by an excessive pride and a great contempt for others, then, my dear friend, you begin to become meek, patient, considerate, and you concern yourself with only one task: that of coming to know your misery and living in obedience and humility of spirit. But to get there you must know how to put up with yourself for a long time and to see in yourself only an abyss of miseries and to have a limitless confidence in the God of mercies.[36]

However, Fr. Mollevaut did not disapprove of Fr. Moreau's activities. On June 28, 1827, he wrote: "I am not displeased that from time to time you are extremely busy and do not even have the time to take a breath. That will give you some idea of the apostolic life and the effects of zeal as we see it in Saint Vincent de Paul, who carried on until eighty years of age, involved in a multitude of tasks which never stopped growing."[37]

Nor were the younger priest's efforts at self-control without effect. On May 15, 1833, Fr. Mollevaut could write: "You, my dear friend, experience calm and peace. A thousand thanks to our Lord. You will keep yourself in this happy state through the practice of bearing with your neighbor. How happy a man is when he has understood the excellence of this virtue and looks upon it as the most admirable in Christianity. Gently bearing with our neighbor, his character, his temper, his defects is the most certain mark of a soul that is striving for real perfection and that wants to acquire solid virtues."[38]

When Fr. Moreau moved into new activities, he generally did it hesitatingly and almost unwillingly. He was preoccupied about undertaking his duty as teacher of philosophy. On October 10, 1823, Fr. Mollevaut wrote:

Beginning to teach is always a little difficult because of the preoccupation, the impatience, the aridity you experience, but little by little you manage to trample down a certain desire to make a good appearance and to enjoy esteem. You have a thousand occasions to practice patience, meekness, charity, and self-denial. Then you understand by experience that "piety is useful for all things" and that when we are worried only about serving God well, he helps us marvelously and in everything and cuts our fatigue and labor in half. So if you are faithful to your exercises of piety despite the distaste, dryness, the desire to study, and the fear that you will not have enough time, you will be well rewarded by the peace which you will enjoy and the progress which you will make. To that end, you need to have a good bit of patience with yourself, that is to say, not to become indignant at the sight of your miseries but rather to have recourse to God with holy confidence, to resolve every day to do better, without ever getting discouraged.[39]

Just two months later, on December 30, 1823, he wrote: "Do not be surprised, my good friend, over the interior disturbance and disorder at the very beginning and in a new situation. Ask the good God sincerely for meekness and patience with yourself so that you may then be able to exercise it toward others."[40]

Fr. Moreau experienced the same preoccupation and a real hesitation at the prospect of moving to dogmatic theology. On May 23, 1825, Fr. Mollevaut wrote: "We should rejoice especially in not seeing anything in ourselves to keep us in this new assignment. . . ; reproach yourself for having let your heart doubt even for an instant, you of little faith. Come now, my good friend, this is the time to put into practice our good resolutions to belong completely to God. . . . My heart is ready. And so it will be that the good God will bless you in your new occupation."[41]

The young seminary professor was preoccupied about undertaking an extensive preaching ministry. On March 11, 1826, his Sulpician director wrote:

Anybody else would be preoccupied as you are, and a few sermons to give are just the sort of thing to wear us out mentally until a little experience has shown us that we do not have the sea to drink and that there is nothing more reasonable and fitting than to announce the Word of God, of which we are the ministers. Tell yourself quite simply: "It is not I who sought this out; they asked me, and therefore it is the will of the good God." Then you have only to forget yourself and sincerely pray our Lord to bless the man to whom he has done the honor of making him his representative. Our imagination will present a thousand things to us, one more ridiculous than the other; all that we can do is to recognize that we are all poor human beings, have patience, and be well assured that this trouble will disappear after the thing is done and that we will be quite ashamed for having worn ourselves out by such imaginings.

Keep clearly in mind, my dear friend, what Saint Francis de Sales said: we must not be troubled over having been troubled nor be angered over having been angered.[42]

The move from dogmatic theology to the teaching of Scripture found Fr. Moreau just as hesitant.[43]

Fr. Moreau was very much desirous of a life which would not draw attention to himself. Just after his arrival at Tessé, Fr. Mollevaut wrote of his love for a hidden life: "I was delighted to learn that you have assumed your duties and that the good God has placed you in a seminary in accord with your desires. There you will have the advantage of being able to continue the life of the Solitude which had such an attraction for you, and rightly—a hidden, regular, and obedient life being the most excellent thing in the world."[44] Two months later he indicated the reason for this love: ". . . peace, meekness, considerateness, bearing with others, zeal. You love the hidden life because you think that you will find all of this there, but you will find it only in God. Let us seek a life hidden in God, and we will find solitude even in the midst of duties and external works."[45]

The young seminary professor often wanted to return to the Solitude to spend some time there.[46] He went several times to Trappist monasteries for a retreat.[47] He had a vivid sense of his need for periods of prayer and reflection in order to improve. On September 1, 1831, he wrote to one of his sisters on his way to Issy, where he was going to make a retreat: "Tomorrow morning I will reach Saint Sulpice [in Paris], and then I will go to the country to begin my retreat there. I have a very great need of it, and I earnestly recommend its success to your prayers and to those of everybody who is kind enough to remember me."[48]

Fr. Moreau was most unwilling to promote himself. He never put his name on the title page of a single one of his publications, and in 1825 when Bishop Carron wanted to make him an honorary canon, Fr. Mollevaut had to insist that he accept: "You have no reason to refuse the position of honorary canon, but you should consider before God the holiness and the obligations of such a position, which will be just another means for humility. It would be too subtle and refined a pride to be able to say: 'I refused and despised what others seek after.' It is much better to say: 'I accepted in order to become a holier and more perfect model.'"[49]

Perhaps the clearest example of his readiness to abandon a position once he realized it was wrong is his apology for having taken sides in the Lamennais controversy. After the condemnation of Felicité de Lamennais, Fr. Moreau looked for no roundabout measures but adopted the most direct means at his disposal. One free day at the end of the school year, when all the community had gathered for spiritual reading before the usual afternoon walk, Fr. Moreau came forward and expressed his regret at having taken sides in the controversy. "The eyewitnesses who have reported this incident to us," records Fr. Charles Moreau, "still retained forty years later a most edifying recollection of the scene, without forgetting Basil's faithful and grateful recognition of the valiant services rendered by the ultramontane apologist."[50]

The seminary professor manifested as much preoccupation about obstacles to a generous prayer life as about difficulties in doing his work well. Fr. Mollevaut urged him not to worry about having to forego spiritual reading occasionally or about delaying his thanksgiving after Mass when there was good reason to do so and to avoid mortifications that might attract the attention of others.[51]

> On December 8, 1824, the Sulpician wrote:
> As for meals, do what they tell you, take what they offer you, striving always to purify your intention and to humble

yourself over such strong temptations which sometimes last a whole lifetime. This comes from your temperament. You are certainly right, my dear friend: we must all have a great esteem for the mortification of our Lord. But we need to have more discretion in this matter than in any other and must, above all, keep ourselves in the way of obedience. Never forget that we mortify the body only to achieve interior mortification, recollection, the practice of humility, and self-denial. You can do in this regard whatever your director [Fr. Fillion] counsels you, but be ready to give it all up at the first word.[52]

The frankness and openness with which Fr. Moreau's spiritual director could write to him suffice to show the sincerity of the younger priest's desire for a holy life. The Sulpician wrote of his own "rather savage frankness which you have the goodness to put up with."[53] The value which Fr. Mollevaut set on Fr. Moreau's friendship and the respect he had for the Le Mans seminary professor are enough to show that in his judgment his younger colleague had a deep interior life. On May 9, 1827, he wrote: "The zeal for the salvation of souls and the perfection of priests that you manifested to me gave me such delight last year that the thought of you is always a real joy to me."[54] On June 6, 1835, he finished a letter: "You see how few inhibitions I have with you, but your friendship has put up with me for so long, and you know that I tell you whatever occurs to my poor mind."[55] A few months earlier, on January 11, 1835, the Sulpician had written: "I know the sincerity and the constancy of your affection, and I value it very much. The most consoling thing in our ministry is to be in contact with those who seek only the glory of our good master, and it is a great advantage for me to count on their prayers so that I can have greater confidence in divine mercy."[56]

If Bishop Carron entrusted to Fr. Moreau the many tasks he undertook in these years, Fr. Bouvier was responsible at least in part because of the recommendation he gave his younger colleague.

When Fr. Bouvier became bishop of Le Mans, he continued to count on Fr. Moreau as his predecessor had done. Both Bishop Carron and his successor were well aware of the seminary professor's organizational and administrative abilities. They were also aware of his loyalty. Bishop Carron could write to Mother Saint Euphrasia regarding the foundation which the Good Shepherd monastery at Angers was to make at Le Mans: "Have no worries about dear Fr. Moreau. He is a child of obedience. He will do whatever I order him to do, and I have already told him that I will not allow him to escape the burden which, out of modesty, he seemed unwilling to assume."[57]

The large number of seminarians, the Brothers of Saint Joseph, the priests, and the laity who asked him for spiritual direction certainly did so because they found in him a man of God but just as certainly because they found him available and felt that he would understand them and be able to help them get closer to God.

Members of both clergy and laity were impressed by his generous labors without any thought of self-advancement. In addition to the readiness with which people answered his request for smaller alms, several were ready to give sizable amounts or even properties. In 1831, Mr. and Mrs. Varenne, who had frequently given him financial aid, offered him their house and property near Le Mans, which they insisted he not give away or sell so that he would not end up in a poor house in his old age. In the following year, Fr. Jobbé de Lisle gave him a piece of property in the Le Mans suburb of Holy Cross. He owed Fr. Moreau a great debt of gratitude since the seminary professor had patiently helped him to overcome scruples with which he had been afflicted for more than fifteen years and which made it impossible for him to recite the breviary or to celebrate Mass. Every day Fr. Moreau went across town to recite the breviary with the troubled priest until the older man could do it alone, and had assisted him at the altar until be gained enough courage to celebrate Mass without help. In 1836 Mr. Barré, a rabid anticlerical, offered to rent him his property at a low rate to supply him with the large house which he then needed. Shortly thereafter (in 1837, although it did not become known until his death in 1847) the well-to-do Canon Dubignon, the eldest member of Saint Vincent's faculty, designated Fr. Moreau as his sole heir.

The canon thought highly of the young priest and in 1826 had taken him along on a lengthy voyage through Savoy which included a retreat of several days at the Grande Chartreuse.[58] Many others, priests and laypeople, invited him to spend his vacation with them. In a letter of July 20, 1832, he told his sisters of the various invitations he had received for that summer: Mr. Varenne, Miss Du Rauchet, and different priests of the diocese.[59]

Even people with little respect for the priesthood or the Church found it easy to treat him in a friendly way as a letter written during a trip undertaken in the year following the Revolution of 1830 makes clear. On September 1, 1831, he wrote from the seminary at Chartres to one of his sisters:

> My arrival here was just as pleasant as I could have hoped. Nothing disagreeable has happened since my departure from Le Mans. I got into the carriage with a good lady and a rabid republican accompanied by his wife, who was at least as nasty as her husband, and tried to behave in such a way as to calm them a little. After two hours of conversation, when I was no longer afraid to be known as a clergyman, I took my breviary out of my pocket, said it all, and concluded with a large sign of the cross without anyone's saying anything disagreeable to me. They even seemed discontented that I had not worn my cassock, and they were already offering to escort me in the capital if I had the least worry. That is how I passed the night, except that I had to correct a few gross remarks against the Jesuits and the Carlists.[60]

All of this leaves us with the impression of a hard-working priest with organizational and administrative ability and the capacity to elicit the cooperation of others, rigorous in his pursuit of what he was convinced was for the good of those for whom he was responsible, and unconcerned about his own advantage. He had to struggle to control his own enthusiasm, impulsiveness, and rigor. But far from having an overbearing or forbidding personality, he was open to advice, docile, determined to live in obedience, and ready to retract when wrong. He preferred anonymity and a life of prayer. He was open, friendly, and unpretentious. Others were ready not only to cooperate with him but to open their hearts and their purses to him.

IV. SUFFERING AND CONFLICT: GOOD SHEPHERD GENERALATE

The years 1823–1835 were years of suffering and conflict. They were the years of the great separations. Both his parents and the three great benefactors of his childhood and seminary days, Fr. Le Provost, Fr. Huard, and Mademoiselle de Boismont, died. They were the years of the first really serious conflict of his life. Suffering and conflict often lay bare depths of the personality that are not otherwise seen. The death of his parents and benefactors showed both the strength of his affection for them and the naturalness with which he turned to thoughts of his own eternity at such moments. When he received disquieting news about the health of Fr. Le Provost and Mademoiselle de Boismont, he wrote to one of his sisters from Issy on April 23, 1823: "A few more years, and they will disappear from our midst, and we will follow them down into the tomb. My dear sister, how little life is! How foolish we would be to attach ourselves to a world that vanishes and slips away from us so quickly!"[61] On February 3, 1825, just after his mother's death, he wrote to Fr. Fillion: "It seems to me that I no longer have any desire to go on living except to console the survivors and to become a more and more interior man, since I see that I have not yet begun."[62] The serious conflict of 1834 revealed aspects of his character that we have not yet seen.

The events can be outlined as follows. In October 1832, Fr. Moreau approached Bishop Carron on behalf of two Le Mans ladies who had tried ineffectively to have a refuge of Our Lady of Charity, a "Good Shepherd monastery," founded in the city. In April 1833, sisters from the monastery of Angers opened the Le Mans foundation in a house paid for with alms provided by the two ladies and Fr. Moreau's friends. Despite the seminary professor's unwillingness, the bishop named him ecclesiastical superior and confessor. The Le Mans sisters were delighted with him. One of them wrote: "This worthy priest unites all his good qualities under a humble and modest exterior. To his virtue he joins great knowledge. He is rightfully regarded as one of the lights of the clergy; he has a great facility for preaching, doing this in such a way as to touch all hearts, and he has a special predilection for religious houses."[63] Mother Saint Euphrasia Pelletier, superior of the Angers house, wrote on April 13, 1833: "We cannot thank the Lord enough. And Fr. Moreau! The more I see of the wonders that he does, the more I believe him to be a saint chosen from on high to be our founder and father. We must trust him completely. Tell him how much I desire to see him and thank him." And on April 22, 1833: "What a generous gift, what a father is Monsieur Moreau."[64]

The Angers monastery, with the help of the bishop of Angers, had already approached Rome on behalf of the establishment of a generalate to link the various refuges of Saint John Eudes' Order of Our Lady of Charity under a single central administration. Suspicions of these intentions caused angry reactions from the archbishop and the refuge of Tours, from which the Angers house had been founded. Rome replied that the establishment of a generalate would require the consent of all the houses.

In May 1833, Fr. Moreau signed an agreement with the Angers house that the Le Mans postulants would go to Angers for their religious formation, returning to Le Mans at the request of the ecclesiastical superior. That same month Fr. Moreau had the Le Mans community send a gilded heart to the Angers house as "a visible symbol of the close union" of the two.[65]

After a conflict over authority between the young superior and her older assistant, the latter returned to Angers and accused Fr. Moreau of having told her one thing and written something else to Mother Saint Euphrasia—in short, of duplicity.[66] This was in July. It was at this time that Fr. Moreau was told of the plans for a generalate. He wrote to Mother Saint Euphrasia how delighted he was with them and offered suggestions for realizing them.[67] He even drew up "statutes for a [secret] association [to work] for the establishment of a generalate in the Good Shepherd Monastery of Angers" in thirteen articles.[68] It was placed under the special protection of the hearts of Jesus and Mary (art. 10). The services of the little "association" of priests he was in the process of founding were offered (art. 5) and he himself was named "superior" (art. 13). Apparently he understood what he had been told about the generalate as a request for help. His proposals could hardly have been understood except as an offer to assume the leadership in the efforts being made on behalf of the generalate—an offer that could easily be interpreted as ambition, especially in the case of a man once accused of duplicity. We may even ask if this was not the interpretation of Fr. Perché, Mother Saint Euphrasia's secret advisor who actually held the position Fr. Moreau seems to have thought he was being invited to assume.[69]

At this point Bishop Carron died. Fr. Moreau, unaware of the coldness with which his proposals had been received at Angers, suggested caution until a new bishop had been named. In February 1834, the Le Mans sisters showed Fr. Moreau their new Constitution 52 on the generalate, which had not yet been approved by Rome but which, apparently, they wished to observe. He then recognized that the Angers monastery was bypassing him. He also judged the new constitution canonically indefensible. In April the sisters showed Constitution 52 to their new bishop—Bishop Bouvier. Thereupon Fr. Moreau wrote a letter to Mother Saint Euphrasia which must be quoted in full. It is dated from the seminary of Le Mans, April 15, 1834.

> Very Reverend Mother:
>
> It is to you, and to you alone, that I address myself today, under the seal of the most absolute secrecy, until such time as I allow you to break it, and with sentiments of most lively interest and deep sorrow. I would have written more than a month ago, had I not feared to cause you useless suffering and to afford certain excitable minds the involuntary occasion of suspecting the sincerity of my sentiments in your regard. For the rest, God, who I hope will guide my pen, is witness to the sincerity of my intentions, and had I not vowed to you so much esteem and affection, I would never dare to allow to flow from my pen what it is about to write. But I feel I would be betraying you if I kept silence any longer. Hence, I shall open my entire soul to you despite the recommendation His Lordship [Bishop Bouvier] makes in his letter to me, which I am enclosing for you.
>
> First of all, I must tell you before him who searches the heart that from the very first day the question of your generalate was raised, I never experienced a desire, or even a single thought, which was not in harmony with the sentiments which I made known to you. In so doing, I did nothing but carry out the intentions of your dear daughters in Le Mans, who have never ceased to speak to me and to act with this in view. I shall add that, in entering thus into their views and

into your own, I followed the movement of my own heart and that this heart had always beat for you and for your work. Any one of your religious who would raise the slightest doubt on this score, would be unfair to me and would be formulating an unjust judgment on my entire conduct. I would even call it an act of ingratitude.

I now come to the principal reason for this letter, which I want to discuss confidentially with you as if I were in your parlor and at the point of death. I cannot tell you how deeply I was both pained and surprised two months ago on reading the constitution which you addressed to your dear daughters whose foundation was entrusted to me. I was surprised because, after what had been agreed upon on the occasion of may last trip to Angers, I certainly did not expect that there would be such a sudden change of means for obtaining the establishment of your generalate, especially without giving me even the slightest indication of what had been done. I see now why Marie de Saint-Philippe at the time of her visit to Le Mans wanted to see Bishop Bouvier in private, without admitting me to this mysterious interview. At the time I suspected nothing, and to the best of my knowledge I feel that I have never given anyone reason to distrust me in regard to any of your interests.

I said also that I was pained at reading this constitution because I feared for you what His Lordship mentions at the close of his letter. Had nothing happened to arouse my concern on this score, I would have hoped in time, by making Bishop Bouvier understand that the new constitution was not universally accepted, to leave things as they were at the time of His Lordship's consecration. But he has just been consulted on this affair by Archbishop Berges of Toulouse. Thus, you have been betrayed, and this constitution has fallen into hands which should not have it.

What will His Lordship say? Most likely the same thing he told me on that occasion prior to his consecration, namely, that this document strikes him as being an infringement on the rights of the Holy See. Notwithstanding the rule of Benedict XIV forbidding any additions or changes in your constitutions, you have changed and added several articles which are in opposition to the very same constitutions. This is the reasoning of His Lordship, and I did not fail to make it known to your reverend chaplain [of Angers] on the occasion of his last visit. I did this with an earnestness which certainly must have made him understand all my interest in you and my fear of seeing a storm break loose around you which would be much more unfortunate than the one of which I have already been the unhappy witness.

Oh, reverend mother, how your position pains me, and how badly you have been advised! But do not think that I ever want to abandon you, or that my sentiments in your regard are in any way changed. No; God knows that were I not so devoted to you, I would never have opened my heart to you. Bishop Bouvier will certainly not cause you any trouble and will try to smooth everything over, but you see the embarrassing situation in which you have put me at the very moment when everything was going along so nicely. His Lordship was very much in favor of the generalate, but now he is discouraged by this untimely document, and says that, were he to approve it, he would be acting against his conscience and against all the principles of sound theology. He is sure that the Holy See will certainly be much displeased; that you are risking putting yourself in a bad light in the eyes of the other communities of your order; and that by putting this constitution into effect, you would cease to belong to the institute which has been approved by the Holy See and would no longer be regarded as a regular order but only as a simple congregation.

These are the remarks of the bishop. Keep them for yourself, and count always on my interest. Rest assured that the storm will never come from the bishop of Le Mans, for, notwithstanding his observations based on the soundest theology, he still wants your generalate, but by another means. You will understand, reverend mother, the embarrassment that is mine; I am, so to speak, caught between two fires. On the one hand there is His Lordship, whose viewpoint I have just outlined for you and who urges me to remain silent; on the other hand, there are my dear daughters who are pressing for an approval or at least a sign of consent from His Lordship.

In this state of affairs, I have had to address myself to you with the greatest possible reserve, have an understanding with your charity, arrange everything for the greater glory of God, and thus satisfy my obligations in conscience. The most important point is for the two of us to be in perfect agreement, to avoid whatever might harm the work of the Lord, and to seek out the most prudent means of preventing any possible difficulties from becoming public knowledge.

For the rest, as I have said, I have promised and I now repeat that never will the union of the two houses and the dependence of ours on you be troubled by myself. But I shall not be in any way responsible for obstacles that may be raised as long as I am kept in the dark and the moment I see that I am doing more harm than good to the work of God, I shall advise you and present my resignation to the proper authorities.[70]

In May Sister Marie de Saint-Basile, one of the Le Mans novices, wrote to Fr. Moreau from Angers that she wished to make a vow for the generalate. He replied encouraging her, provided that she was willing to return to Le Mans in accord with the Le Mans-Angers agreement of the preceding May. He also wrote a lengthy letter from the Le Mans seminary on May 30, 1834, to the Le Mans sisters.

My very dear sisters,

I have just reached my room and find here the very sincere expression of your desire to share the suffering with which I am burdened at this moment, a suffering which I was far from expecting and the most painful of all that I have experienced since the origin of the foundation which was entrusted to you. If I had been less attached to your venerable mother in Angers and less devoted to your true interests, I would feel this unhappy turn of events less and would not be at all influenced by the unjust prejudices conceived against me and the indelicate procedures which have followed upon them. But God is my witness that I have promised my esteem and my affection to your two establishments and that I do not separate in my heart the mother and the daughter, not making any distinction of place or of persons.

You know that since the day when I had the good fortune to come to know your venerable superior, all my desires, all my thoughts, all my words and actions had no other end than the prosperity of the two houses and the successful outcome of the undertaking which has become the object of my sorrow after having been the object of my hopes. You know how I have worked to keep you in union with the community which you left in order to come to Le Mans and to keep you in the spirit of most complete dependence toward her who has been charged to direct it. If I sent a heart to Angers, if I preached there for a reception of the habit, if I drew up a rule for the orphans, if I have written several times to your novices, if I have taken so great a part in the crosses of your reverend mother, if I have committed myself to cooperate as far as will lie in my power with the establishment of the generalate for which you long so much, if I negotiated with your general council on the path to take to achieve it—I declare before him who sees my most secret thoughts—I did it only to make the work of God solid without any hidden motives, without any mental reservations. You also know now that it was with the same intention that I had intended to go offer my services to your reverend mother for this year's retreat so as to spare them the expense of a preacher and so as the better to establish minds and hearts in peace and harmony. Finally, there is nothing, not even our new bell, which does not witness how straightforward and frank my intentions were: for its first name [given when it was blessed] is the very name of that person whom I looked upon as the one that would one day be your general.

Who would ever have expected it? While I was spending myself thus on assuring your happiness and seconding all your designs, providing at Rome itself a protection for the implementation of your pious plans, the demon, jealous of the good that was being prepared, sowed distrust against me in the minds of those who should never have done me such injustice and thus prepared little by little the sad situation which forces me today to explain myself to you and yours.

My dear sisters, how much it costs my heart to let you hear words of reproach—you who do not merit them and who are going to see them come from my pen only so that I may justify myself for you and you may communicate them then to Angers, to which I no longer wish to write. While I was thinking of advancing and making solid the work of Providence, a storm was forming threateningly about my head. First of all, I was doubtless not considered enthusiastic enough for the direction of the generalate, and what I regarded as prudence was considered cowardice and treason. Without my knowledge they had you make a vow to a new constitution whose very existence I did not even suspect and which I know now only because you showed it to me in your parlor; for they did not deign to send me a copy or even to say a single word about it to me in all the letters they wrote me from Angers. Then Marie de Saint-Philippe, when she passed through Le Mans, wanted to have a meeting with His Lordship to which I was not judged worthy to be admitted, although I myself brought her to Bishop Bouvier's very door and although it took place in our seminary. Soon it became evident that at Angers there was no longer anything but indifference and distrust for me.

Despite that, I did not even let it appear in your presence that I felt the injustice of such prejudices, and although I did not approve the new path taken to achieve the establishment of the generalate, I carefully kept from saying anything to your community. I even let you remain in peace as regards your new vow, and I limited myself to speaking with Fr. Mainguy [the chaplain of the monastery of Angers] in the interest of your mother in Angers, since I felt that His Lordship would not approve this way of proceeding, although he agreed with the end proposed, and then since I knew that Fr. Berges of Toulouse had written to him to complain about it and since I feared especially that His Lordship of Paris would discover this unfortunate step, which is contrary to the sacred canons. I even wrote only yesterday to Marie de Saint-Basile that she could make the vow in question provided that she committed herself to working for the generalate only in accord with principles in conformity with the authority of the Holy See and in the spirit of your institute. I felt I had to do so out of prudence, and I was waiting for the visit of the bishop of Angers to see how the wisdom of our two prelates would solve these difficulties.

But now from prejudices against me they pass to deeds that I cannot explain: they accuse me of having had the thought of having the generalate established at Le Mans, they want to have our novices make their profession at Angers despite the written agreement between us, they are disturbed about their dowry, and they ascribe to me a dishonest reply through

Mademoiselle Bellot. Here I would betray my ministry and my conscience if I did not break the silence. I call upon my calumniators, then, to tell me on what they base themselves to sow such trouble and division and to ascribe to me what I never intended.

I declare to you, my dear sisters, that I will not permit the violation of a single point of the agreement made between us at the time of the foundation. I add that until today I was disposed to give help to our subjects and, as soon as we could have done so from our funds, to the house of Angers for its foundations, but I renounce these intentions before God until the establishment of a generalate. The novices and the dowries will return to Le Mans as has been agreed, and I refuse to permit that there be the least pressure brought to bear in this matter at Angers until the day when the generalate will be canonically established and approved by the Holy See. From that moment I will again be one of the people most devoted to that work, but I no longer want to have anything to do with it now. I am free of all commitment in that regard, although I protest that I will never say or do anything against whatever is undertaken today for its success. In the same way I will insist on all the other points of our agreement, and no one will ever be able to reproach me for having violated any of them. But I demand too that the Angers council tell me whether or not it is going to observe the agreement made. . . .

If anyone asks me why I do not want to bind myself to the new constitution, I will answer: (1) Because His Lordship has not yet approved it. (2) Because it is contrary to the bull of Benedict XIV, who absolutely forbids anyone at all to do anything in this regard . . . no matter what his authority—this new constitution contains several articles opposed to your statutes, as, for example, the one which concerns the election of the superior and the length of her superiorship,

(3) Because you are abandoning the way indicated by the Holy See, and which we had agreed upon, in order to take another which will lead you nowhere, for though you should have twenty foundations and as many bishops for you, that would give you no right to establish a generalate or to direct in any way another institute which you have made the vow to follow in everything. . . . (4) Because the vow which you are making to this new constitution is contrary to the four others since you have made the vow to follow in everything your constitutions such as they were approved by the Holy See and this [constitution] disagrees with them on many points as I shall demonstrate to anyone who wishes.

Nevertheless, I shall always desire the generalate, without having anything to do with it. I will even permit the making of the vow of which you have spoken to me with the restrictions which I mentioned to Marie de Saint-Basile and, from the moment the pope will have spoken, I will be one of its most devoted supporters. But I repeat, I will never follow you in the way on which you have set out. This is not how Saint Teresa acted. If my explanations do not satisfy you, you have only to tell me, and I will reply to anyone who wishes.[71]

Fr. Moreau then drew up a document setting in parallel columns the new Constitution 52 and contradictory passages from both the papally approved constitutions of the Order of Our Lady of Charity and the year-old Le Mans-Angers agreement.[72] In further letters he demanded that the agreement be kept and that the Le Mans novices return to Le Mans for their profession.[73] In fact, he ordered a novice to declare her mind on the matter in virtue of holy obedience.[74] The Angers reactions were evasive or cold. Bishop Bouvier went to Angers. He wrote from there on June 19:

Already yesterday, my dear Fr. Moreau, the bishop of Angers . . . and I discussed our affair at length. I found him very reasonable, no longer insistent at all on the idea of a genera-late. We spoke of it again this morning, and we have reached perfect agreement on everything.

We then went to the Good Shepherd, and, as we had agreed, the two of us spoke to the superior alone. She seemed quite disturbed by your letters as also by my determination to have our house of Le Mans complete and without any other de-pendence on the Angers house except the bonds of charity and filiation. Thereupon I told her that the bishop of Angers and myself were in agreement on the matter, and when my colleague indicated his approval, she answered that that was not what had been agreed upon but that she could do noth-ing but obey. Only, the Angers house would claim the sums advanced to the Le Mans house; whereupon I said that we could not refuse this if they asked.

I asked to see in private each one of the girls whose names I had, and they granted this immediately.

You can imagine my surprise at finding that not one of them is now willing to agree to return to Le Mans and some, among others Mademoiselle Joubert and Mademoiselle Pétro, not even for their profession. They were shocked that you should have ordered them [to declare their intentions] under pain of disobedience when they had not made any vow: they insist they are free to go wherever they wish; they have consulted the most distinguished ecclesiastics in Angers, who have giv-en them this answer. In fact, I cannot deny this since they can either give up the religious life or choose an order and therefore a house other than the one of which they had first thought. Mademoiselle Pétro showed me a letter that you had written to her in answer to one of hers, telling me that you had completely changed, that she did not want to see you except to beg you to change your ideas on the Angers house and not to separate the Le Mans house from it. Your answer, as you see, did not fit in with her ideas. In general, what you have said to these girls has produced an effect just the opposite of what you intended.

Imagine, my friend, my disappointment and my embarrassment!!!

I went back to the community room where I found His Lordship, the superior, the assistant, and the chaplain. I asked that the assistant and the chaplain leave.

I then told the superior, in the presence of the bishop, after having admitted that they all wanted at least to finish their novitiate here, that I was no less determined to insist on a house conformable to the approved constitutions and rules, and I asked her if she was willing formally to support our house on this condition, sending me to that end of the subjects I would need as long as it would be necessary. She assured me in a most positive way, and the bishop willingly agreed.

There, my friend, is the story of my visit to the Good Shepherd. When I get back, we will talk about it all, and we shall see what position it will be best to take. While you are waiting, do not write to the mother superior or to your daughters, you would gain nothing by it at this moment.

This is a trial which we will have to bear and a good reason for having a novitiate in our house, as I was already convinced.[75]

This move caused Mother Saint Euphrasia to exclaim: "Fr. Moreau. Ah, what an enemy! May God forgive him!"[76]

Tension mounted between the two houses. The Le Mans house sided with Bishop Bouvier and Fr. Moreau. The latter prepared a long memorandum for the bishop of Le Mans. He also sent a memorandum to Rome with letters from thirteen bishops "in support of the ancient order of Father Eudes."[77] The Le Mans house was formally separated from Angers. But some months later Rome established the Congregation of Our Lady of Charity of the Good Shepherd of Angers as an institute distinct from the Order of Our Lady of Charity founded by Saint John Eudes.

These texts show some aspects of Fr. Moreau's character that we already know: he was straightforward and ready to insist with vigor—even to the point of antagonizing others—on matters of principle. They also show how easily he grew indignant in the face of what looked to him like duplicity and perhaps above all in the face of an accusation of duplicity against himself, demanding concrete evidence for affirmations made. Finally, they show what a formidable opponent he could be. His biographers write:

> These events are important in order to make us see how the character of Fr. Moreau stands out at the very outset of his fruitful career. Once he has clearly and honestly seen the goal to be reached, Fr. Moreau does not yield; no obstacle, no consideration can stand in the way. He retains his kindliness and his charity, in the expression of which he goes almost to exaggeration. Nonetheless, he holds fast to his position and, with tenacious obstinacy, because such is his duty, he tirelessly affirms its correctness. By so doing, he brings suffering upon himself and makes others suffer, but it is then that, for his own soul enriched by sorrow and for his works, he harvests the fruits of the cross in the way in which the works of God grow.[78]

Fr. Mollevaut wrote to Fr. Moreau on October 31:

> I admire how the good God is making you pass through crosses and tribulations. That is a certain proof that he wants you completely for himself and that you are acting only for his honor. You must be thoroughly convinced, then, that he is the one who is directing your Good Shepherd work and who is disposing the events which seem to be so contradictory, and that the more you leave things to him, the better they

will go, especially if you are completely detached and ready to see everything collapse and be dispersed. . . . It is when we have such confidence and abandonment that we see things develop.[79]

On January 19, 1835, Bishop Bouvier sent the bishop of Angers this judgment on Fr. Moreau's part in the conflict over the generalate: "I share perfectly in Your Lordship's opinion that Fr. Moreau should have acted with greater kindness, mellowness, and prudence."[80] He placed this observation in the broader context of his views on Fr. Moreau's strengths and weaknesses: "For a long time, I have known how to handle him. It is impossible for me to correct him or even to make him understand that he is in the wrong. He judges everything according to his own intentions, which are excellent, and for fear of causing harm by trying to accomplish a greater good, I close my eyes to many things."[81] It is important to read these lines against the background of the tension which existed between Fr. Moreau and his superior at Saint Vincent's in the years 1825–1830 when the younger priest taught dogmatic theology.

CHAPTER 4
HOLY CROSS
(1835–1841)

On August 31, 1835, Fr. Moreau assumed superiorship of the brothers with whom he had been working closely for some years. In that same month he had organized a little group of "auxiliary priests." This move realized a project that he had pondered for several years. Neither group was a religious community, although the possibility that some of the brothers might profess vows had been discussed three years earlier. Those who joined were attracted to its ministry. Fr. Moreau's ability to organize apostolic ventures effectively was certainly a factor that encouraged many of them. But from the very beginning, he was determined not to leave them simply as communities of work: he wanted to make them into a religious community. In fact, he had proposed vows for at least some of the brothers in 1832. That they were moving toward becoming a full-fledged religious community grew clear to his collaborators only little by little. We shall examine first the development of the ministries of priests and brothers and then see how these apostolic associations developed into a religious community.

I. APOSTOLIC COMMUNITY

The brothers' novitiate was moved from Ruillé-sur-Loir to the de Lisle property in the commune of Holy Cross on the outskirts of Le Mans in the fall of 1835—an area where in pre-Revolution days a chapel of Notre-Dame de Bel-Air had stood. Fr. Moreau immediately began to discuss, to get advice, and to reorganize. Accompanied by Br. Leonard, he spent some time with the founder of the Brothers of Christian Instruction at Ploërmel. In a circular letter he insisted that all the brothers keep orderly and detailed accounts. The brothers began to open more village and parish schools. Fr. Moreau himself carried on negotiations with the mayors or the pastors who wanted schools, and he often visited them.

The new superior decided to transfer to Holy Cross the elementary boarding school which the brothers operated at Ruillé and which then had only five or six students. The prefect of the department of La Sarthe refused to grant authorization. A series of letters from Bishop Bouvier and Fr. Moreau and a trip of the latter to Paris got both that authorization and an exemption from military service for the brothers before the 1836–1837 school year began.

Since the buildings on the de Lisle property were not yet ready, the school was opened in the house just across the street, which Mr. Barré, an antiroyalist and anticlerical, had offered to rent to Fr. Moreau. When in 1837 the local school board tried to block the move from the Barré house to the then ready buildings across the street on the obviously fabricated grounds that the new building was not yet safe for the children's health, Fr. Moreau obtained a certificate from three physicians and a petition from the prospective students' parents and moved. When ordered out of the house, he said he would yield only to force and threatened an appeal to Paris.

In the fall of 1838 he felt the time had come to expand the institution at Holy Cross into a secondary boarding school as already in 1836 he had announced would be done. He bypassed the opposition of civil authorities by obtaining authorization from Paris through the services of a politician whom he had brought back to the sacraments the preceding Lent after thirty years away. But he met unexpected opposition from Bishop Bouvier, who told him, "I do not like your plan, and I have promised to oppose it. Unless you give up this idea, I shall never again set foot inside Holy Cross." Fr. Moreau answered: "In that case, Your Lordship, you are asking for my resignation." Though for several days attempts were made to dissuade him, he did nothing to modify his plans. It is difficult to appreciate the bishop's real intentions. Was it a show of disapproval the bishop had to make in order to avoid becoming alienated from those who opposed Fr. Moreau? To whom had he given his promise of opposition? Fr. Moreau seems really to have intended to resign since Fr. Mollevaut had to dissuade him.[1] In any case, the bishop certainly knew that Fr. Moreau to develop fully the boarding school at Holy Cross as part of the fight against the state monopoly on education. Bouvier did not give a formal order to desist and certainly remained on cordial terms with the superior at Holy Cross, writing letters on his behalf and continuing to visit the school.

In 1839, despite the generally negative attitude of civil authorities to such moves, the school at Holy Cross became an "institution" with the right to teach the humanities. The next step was to work for "full teaching rights," that is, the right to teach rhetoric and philosophy too, and Fr. Moreau directed his efforts toward that goal.

In order to supply a substitute for the unsatisfactory religion text then in use, he published in 1838 a *New Reader*, which was so successful that it saw eight editions in less than thirty years, growing with successive revisions to 439 pages. L'Ami de la Religion wrote of it on June 4, 1839:

> A work entitled *New Reader* has just been published at Le Mans. The modest and capable author has preferred to remain anonymous, but because of the choice and the elevation of his thoughts, the precision and clarity of his style, and

especially the tone of gentle and persuasive piety to be found throughout, no one in the vicinity has been able to mistake his identity. Everyone has recognized a pen employed with uncommon success at making religion known and loved. The book is a complete course of dogmatic and moral instruction put within the reach of all minds, capitalizing as it does on historical events. It would be difficult to present within such limited dimensions any more edifying examples, interesting anecdotes, and helpful maxims. Although the book is meant especially for the young, it will be fruitful reading for all ages.[2]

To offer material and spiritual support to the extensive works carried on from Holy Cross, the superior founded the Association of Saint Joseph in 1837 with Bishop Bouvier's approval. The members were offered a simple program of spiritual life, and they were organized to provide effective financial support. Indulgences were granted them by Rome the very next year.

In 1839 Fr. Moreau authored the first edition of an almanac, the *Etrennes Spirituelles* ("Spiritual Christmas Package"), offered annually from 1840 to 1851 to the associates of the Good Shepherd and of Saint Joseph.[3] It provided them with ample spiritual fare and abundant details on the work of Holy Cross. The Association of Saint Joseph was so well organized and publicized and proved so attractive to those who came into contact with it that by 1843 it numbered 3,000 members.[4]

The two priests and the two seminarians who were Fr. Moreau's first "auxiliary priests" were joined by Fr. Hupier, who was the brothers' chaplain at Ruillé when they moved to Holy Cross. In 1835, the priests went to live at Saint Vincent's, where they met daily in Fr. Moreau's room for common prayer and discussion of Scripture and moral theology. They began their ministry in February 1836. Usually working two together, they preached eleven missions and one forty hours' devotion in the next few months, erecting the way of the cross in the various parishes where they labored. Their superior took part in all this activity while continuing to fulfill all his responsibilities not only toward the brothers at Holy Cross but also at the seminary and as ecclesiastical superior of the Good Shepherd monastery. However, it became evident that the missionaries needed a house of their own, where they would be able to receive those who might wish to make a retreat. Besides, the diocesan administration wanted them to have a house where they could admit priests who had retired because of poor health or for other reasons.

Fr. Moreau was offered quarters for the priests at the Tessé seminary, but this would not have been an improvement; he would have had to carry on his activities over an even broader area. The offer may have been a veiled hint that he and the priests should move from Saint Vincent's. In any case, in the fall of 1836, he was replaced both as assistant superior and as professor of Scripture. It was done rather indelicately. He learned of it after others did. Somewhat piqued, he transferred the priests to Holy Cross. But Bishop Bouvier instructed that the seminary continue to provide him with an annual subsidy to help further the work of the auxiliary priests.

The superior of Holy Cross—or of Our Lady of Holy Cross, as the property was now known—continued to participate in the work of the priests either preaching missions or retreats or at least opening or closing the exercises in which he could not take further part. Nor was this merely a matter of giving the same simple sermon in several different places. It meant working out a detailed plan for missions and giving lengthy and solid instructions.

The number of the priests grew slowly and was hardly enough to answer the requests they received for preaching. Nevertheless, Fr. Moreau introduced them into the work of teaching at Holy Cross. The novice brothers needed instruction. Besides, without them it would have been impossible to open the secondary school there in 1838 since none of the brothers had the required degree. Thus, with Bishop Bouvier's knowledge, Fr. Moreau found himself with priest teachers after all—despite the bishop's earlier unwillingness.

The superior had tried to get sisters to care for the laundry and the infirmary at Our Lady of Holy Cross but had been unable to find a community with religious to spare. Hence, he had to have the help of a number of lay women. In the 1838–1839 school year, he organized the little group of women working there into a community and began even to think of how they too might be auxiliaries, serving, for example, as housekeepers in rectories.

By this time (1839) the community of Holy Cross numbered 114 brothers, 12 priests, and 3 sisters. Their work was prospering and well-known. In fact, the first requests had come for foreign foundations, some of them from the French government and some from bishops directed to Holy Cross by Fr. Mollevaut. By the following year Fr. Moreau thought he could answer some of these requests.

With Bishop Bouvier's approval the superior of Holy Cross answered the request of the bishop of Algiers for brothers by sending four brothers and two priests. Among the brothers was Br. André, one of Fr. Dujarié's first candidates and one of the most generous, faithful, and capable of all those that had joined the community since 1820. Another group of three brothers and one priest left for Algeria before the year was out. The year after, he answered the request of the bishop of Vincennes, Indiana, for brothers by sending six brothers and Father Edward Sorin, perhaps the most capable of all the priests he had.

By 1841 the apostolic possibilities of the Holy Cross community were beyond all doubt. The vigor of their superior, his organizational and administrative ability, and his talent for drawing followers and eliciting cooperation were largely responsible for the development which had taken place during the first six years despite opposition. His vision of the apostolic possibilities of the community was as broad as his appreciation of the needs of the Church, although his basic inspiration had been his perception of the need for an auxiliary clergy and for educators in that part of France. A list of the various types of work which the community undertook or at least seriously considered during his superiorship will help illustrate this breadth of vision. (All but the italicized entries in the following list were already at least contemplated before the end of 1841.)

1. Pastoral ministry (priests): preaching of parish missions, retreats, lenten series, first communions, and the like; assisting and substituting for the diocesan clergy; chaplaincies (hospitals, religious communities, etc.) and parishes; mission posts in various dioceses; foreign missions (that is, responsibility for entire vicariates or prefectures).
2. Strictly educational work: primary and secondary schools; universities; agriculture and trade schools; adult education; special education (hearing and speech impaired); minor and major seminaries; a biblical institute.
3. Broadly educational work: foundling homes; orphanages; homes for juvenile delinquents; care of prisoners.
4. Other: rectory housekeepers (sisters); parish sacristans (brothers); house of retirement for the clergy; hospitals (the sisters were to operate the hospital, the priests act as chaplains, and the brothers ensure maintenance).

Father Sorin got Roman encouragement to open a house for priests under prohibitions after his superior general had told him that it lay beyond the scope of the congregation as determined in the 1857 constitutions. What the superior would have said if the work had been suggested before 1857, it is not possible to determine. But from 1857 on, he looked upon the works specified in the papally approved constitutions as the responsibilities assigned by Rome to the congregation and did not feel free to go beyond them. We shall examine this point below.

The incredible and very efficient activity of the first six years did not mean for Fr. Moreau any lessening of attention to fundamental Christian values: faith, prayer, the cross, kindness. To begin with, the works were undertaken in almost stark poverty. In 1835, for example, the Good Shepherd religious had to furnish the brothers at Holy Cross with food. Frugality was maintained even after the need for assistance ended.

Opposition was not lacking, and Fr. Moreau recognized it as the cross sent by God. On December 27, 1837, he wrote: "If we seek only God's glory and are ready to make every sacrifice for the love of so good a master, then the more trials we have to face, the better everything will succeed."[5] The statement sounds almost like an echo of Fr. Mollevaut's remarks in the letter which he sent to Fr. Moreau near the end of the Good Shepherd controversy. When successes came, it was God's doing too, the superior told the brothers in the circulars he sent to them.

A spirit of Christian love and cooperation marked the work and all Fr. Moreau's collaborators and even the students at Our Lady of Holy Cross, thanks largely to his inspiration. He urged the need of union upon the brothers in his very first circular on November 8, 1835: "To succeed in the important undertaking entrusted to us, we must be, first of all, so closely united in charity as to form but one mind and one soul; for, as you well know, 'In union there is strength' and 'A kingdom divided against itself shall not stand.' It is with a view to cementing this union more firmly and to establishing the greatest possible uniformity in the government of your congregation that I address this circular letter to each and every one of you."[6] Two years later he could write: "Here [at Holy Cross] charity reigns and unites the one hundred and more souls whom Providence has brought together. Let us earnestly ask our good master to make this happy state of affairs last, for it is my greatest consolation and the glory of your institute."[7] How much the Association of Saint Joseph shared in the joys, sorrows, and work of Holy Cross can be judged from the letters and other information published in the *Etrennes Spirituelles*.

The union among priests and brothers was encouraged by Fr. Moreau's personal relationship with them. In his very first circular letter he wrote to the brothers: "I want you to write me whenever you have family troubles, dissatisfaction or discouragement in your work, or when you are faced with opposition from outsiders or even from your fellow religious."[8] Six years later he wrote:

> I . . . have been edified by the docility with which you received my counsels at the last retreat. The humility, obedience, and charity which animated your recent chapters, the frankness you displayed in spiritual direction, and the evident progress of your Association [of Saint Joseph] which, at the request of our good bishop, the pope has already deigned to enrich with numerous indulgences, as well as the persevering zeal of the lady members of the Association's council, has been a consolation. I have been touched by the really admirable conduct of the good fellow priests whom heaven has associated with me in my works and who are so adept at lightening the burden of my heavy charge by sharing it with me, no less than by the good will with which they have received and are following their constitutions. They have manifested a most edifying spirit of union.[9]

II. RELIGIOUS COMMUNITY

A religious spirit was not enough for Fr. Moreau; he wanted a religious community. It will be remembered that he had made vows of chastity, obedience, and poverty before his ordination to the subdiaconate in 1820. In 1832 he had advocated that some Brothers of Saint Joseph be permitted to profess perpetual religious vows. On June 6, 1835, Fr. Mollevaut wrote: "You would like to have a rule and vows."[10] This was in connection with Fr. Moreau's projected foundation of a house of diocesan missionaries. At the close of the brothers' retreat in 1836, which he himself preached to them at Saint Vincent's Seminary, Br. André was the first to pronounce the perpetual religious vows.

That same summer Fr. Moreau and the auxiliary priests drew up a primitive rule for themselves during a retreat at the Trappist monastery of Mortagne. In 1838 he drew up a draft of constitutions for the brothers, based in part at least on the rules which Bishop Bouvier gave Father Dujarié's Sisters of Providence in 1835.[11] Dependence on the sisters' rules appears, for example, in the brothers' celebrating as their special feasts the same three days that the sisters' 1835 rules prescribed: Christmas, the feast of the Assumption, and the feast of Saint Joseph. Provision was made for a fourth vow like the sisters' fourth vow (the instruction of children—for obvious reasons the brothers omitted "and the care of the poor sick"). But they also could make a vow of stability such as Fr. Moreau had suggested in 1832.[12]

On the morning of August 15, 1840, the superior of Holy Cross made his own religious profession, and four of the auxiliary priests did the same that evening. That same year he organized the priests' novitiate on a property he named "The Solitude" near Holy Cross and began a draft of constitutions for them. In 1841 he moved the brothers' novitiate away from Holy Cross to the nearby Charbonnière, the property which Monsieur and Madame Varenne had given him, and he began to send the sisters to the Good Shepherd monastery for their novitiate. Only Bishop Bouvier's unwillingness to have the sisters become religious prevented their taking vows.

In the first six years at Holy Cross, priests and brothers were provided with a religious rule of life, novitiates were organized, and the vows of religion were introduced. These same steps would have been taken for the sisters, but Bishop Bouvier was unwilling. All this was not accomplished without opposition. In

1836, when they realized what direction their reform was taking, twenty-two brothers left, although in the same year twenty-nine candidates entered. The priests were not all interested in becoming religious either. Father Moreau did not insist. Those who wished to remain without vows could do so. The last priest without vows did not leave until 1847, and the brothers who wished to move beyond being a novice could profess the annual vows of obedience and stability until papal approval in 1857.

In this same period the government of the communities of Holy Cross was organized. In 1837 Father Moreau drew up a "Fundamental Act" regulating the financial interests of the communities of priests and of brothers as members of the "Association of Holy Cross." It was signed on March 1, 1837, by fifty-four brothers and eight priests.[13] In 1840 priests, brothers, and sisters had their own elected "particular superiors"; the society of priests and that of brothers each had its own "general council"—a sort of general chapter (the sisters were not numerous enough to have one); the entire Association had a "grand council," or general chapter; and Father Moreau had his particular council to help him in the overall government of the Association. Then a "civil society" was organized for the administration of the Le Mans properties, "the large property at Holy Cross, also called Our Lady of Holy Cross, and the two novitiates," so that Father Moreau's death would not lead to complications for the Association, which did not have the legal right to hold the property. Finally, construction of a "conventual church" was begun, a church which would serve as the symbol and center of the life and work of Holy Cross.[14]

III. THE FOUNDER AND HIS COLLABORATORS: COMMUNITY SPIRIT

From these few facts it appears that in the first six years of the existence of the work of Holy Cross, Father Moreau's inspiration and effort were the chief causes responsible for the extraordinary development of its ministries and of its way of life. It should not be thought that he simply imposed his ideas on his collaborators, however. The fact that those who refused profession were welcome to remain as members of the Association of Holy Cross should suffice to prove this. If any further proof is needed, it can be found in his early organization of chapters and of a large council for himself. He did not want to govern alone either the brothers or the priests, although Fr. Dujarié had, for the most part, governed his communities that way. He did not want simply to be appointed by the bishop but elected by the religious and then only for a limited term. He wrote on January 1, 1840:

> The superior general shall first be elected for three years only and . . . at the end of this period he will cease to hold office. Another election will then be held, and he may be retained in office for three years more. At the end of this term, he automatically goes out of office, but may then be re-elected for life. These provisions will enable you either to remove a superior who would be unsuited for his office, or to retain one who would have proved satisfactory during his two three-year terms.[15]

Fr. Moreau's relationship to the members can be illustrated by several letters requested of the priest novices by Bishop Bouvier in 1841. Fr. Moreau had just been placed in a difficult situation by Bishop Bouvier and had not reacted as the bishop wished. He had been asked to persuade Mademoiselle Philbert, a postulant at the Good Shepherd monastery, to leave since her family was unwilling that she should stay. He spoke with her but refused to bring any pressure to bear. She decided to remain. He told the bishop he could not oblige her to leave but reminded him that he could take the responsibility upon himself and dismiss her. When one of the vicars general tried to get him to change his mind, he insisted that he could not oppose a vocation without sin, though he regretted being in opposition with diocesan authorities. Soon after this episode, one of the auxiliary priests who had chosen not to make vows complained to the bishop that only those who made profession could "preserve their own personal rights" at Holy Cross. Thereupon Bishop Bouvier asked the priest novices to send him a confidential appreciation of their accused superior!

In his letter to the bishop, Father Vérité raised a question: "He has chosen for himself three monitors. . . . Would it not have been possible to advise him through these monitors of the points on which [the complainants] found fault?" He offered his judgment of his superior all the same:

> On numerous occasions when [Father Moreau] was overwhelmed with difficult problems of the greatest importance, I have always admired his self-control, notwithstanding his naturally quick temper. I do not mean that our father does not have his moments of weakness; we all have them.
>
> It is said that he is seeking only to dominate, but, in a novitiate, is it not necessary that there should be subjection to a rule? Are not the novices there to sanctify themselves before undertaking to sanctify others?[16]

Father Champeau wrote:

> I can assure Your Lordship that between the superior and all his priests there reigns the most kindly and most agreeable spirit of abandonment. . . Nevertheless, when I say all his priests, I am speaking in general terms, and I do not mean to indicate that they are all equally well disposed toward him. In a community it is impossible for all characters to be alike and, consequently, for all tastes to be the same. Some will be easygoing and will describe as harshness any act smacking of

energy, while others will be hard to manage and will regard as weakness any act marked with wise kindliness. . . .

Those who have painted Father Moreau for you in the light of one who is seeking to exercise on us a harmful influence have deceived you. In whatever does not fall within the realm of obedience, Fr. Moreau exercises over us no other influence than that of his virtues and his counsels. I have never had occasion to notice in him anything like those imperious commands which would be rather the orders of a master than the kindly suggestions of a friend. In a word, I do not feel that it is possible to have any greater degree of liberty: liberty of conscience, in this sense—that all the priests have faculties for confessions and that all are free to go to confession to any fellow priest of their choice; liberty of direction, consisting in this, that there is perfect freedom to choose one's director, although there is the obligation imposed by rule to render periodic accounts of one's dispositions to the superior. This, however, strikes me as being only just and gives rise to no embarrassment. . . .

In the general administration of the house, in his outside contacts, and perhaps even in his dealing with Your Lordship, he may have shown himself firm and unyielding on more than one occasion. Has he always been in the right? That is not my business. I feel, however, that without this energetic trait of character he would never have accomplished all he has done. But this I say and this I affirm, that with his priests, in community life, he acts like a father. I have on many occasions admired the calmness and the moderation with which a man of this temperament, overwhelmed with work, bothered on all sides, and carrying on only by force of sheer energy, has put up with contradictions which were well calculated to give rise to irritation. Hence, I do not hesitate to declare, Your Lordship, that you have been deceived and led into error regarding this man who is so evidently directed by God.[17]

Three months later, on June 8, one of the malcontents—one who had taken vows—wrote the bishop as follows:

> For several days now I have felt the urge to write to Your Lordship, and the kindliness with which you are pleased to give heed to your children presses me not to delay my letter any longer. I have been very imprudent, Your Lordship, and very frequently I have not weighed sufficiently the meaning of my words since the moment of my profession. If in my difficulties, troubles, and temptations I had been satisfied with opening my soul to Fr. Moreau alone, in whom I assuredly have great confidence, I assure you, my lord, that I would have succeeded in maintaining peace of mind. I know from my own experience that every time I have had enough simplicity to make my troubles known to my superior, I have always felt the better for it, and I am happy to say that I have never made known to him a single reasonable desire which he did not satisfy immediately and which he even often anticipated. Hence, I have been very unjust in his regard, for since the time I entered the seminary and since the time I went to Holy Cross, he has always showed for me fatherly affection, and if I have the happiness to strengthen myself in my vocation, to accomplish some good, and to save my soul, it is to his careful attention that I shall owe all this.[18]

Shortly before this episode Fr. Mollevaut had written the following advice. The letters cited above can help the reader decide whether Father Moreau followed it:

> You know perfectly well what you need in your position: peace, composure, imperturbable calm, prudence and discretion, meekness and union with our good master. Ask and you will receive. But if you need an inexhaustible patience and the ability to bear with others, you must begin by bearing

with yourself. Exterior instruments [of penance] are not what you need at present; such things demand reflection and do not always lead to the goal intended.[19]

You should be delighted that your solitaries have simplicity and like to laugh—it is a good sign. Community spirit demands that everything be done with joy, especially difficult things. The best way to govern is that of Saint Francis de Sales: everything by love, nothing by force. That is how to win hearts and confidence. In that way you will compensate for all the sacrifices which they will have to make to bind themselves to a fixed rule and constantly break with their own wills. It is, above all, your kindness and your meekness which attach people to you, and you should never be afraid of going to excess in this direction.[20]

In 1841 we find the same hard-working priest of earlier years. But by then, his organizational and his administrative abilities had been concentrated on a single, though multiple, work—the one which would be the great work of his life: Holy Cross. He was just as desirous of anonymity, guidance, and advice, just as determined to live in obedience, but just as unyielding in matters of principle. His influence over others had brought him many followers and collaborators. His own generosity and kindness had instilled in them a spirit of union and cooperation. Perhaps he was too kind and should have been less ready to share his worries with his collaborators or to keep among them those who refused to move in the direction in which the work of Holy Cross turned when the vows of religion were introduced.

The vision he had for the great work of his life, the Association of Holy Cross, had become clear. In 1841 he presented it to the brothers in a circular letter that may well be called the Magna Carta of Holy Cross.[21] Father Moreau printed it in the 1843 *Etrennes Spirituelles* as the best way to make the work of Holy Cross known to the Association of Saint Joseph.

It began: "On the eve of attaining the end I had a view in transferring your novitiate from Ruillé to Holy Cross . . ., I feel the need of laying before you in writing the plan of government which I have definitely adopted. I also wish to sketch for you a summary of your duties. . . ."

It presented Holy Cross, first of all, as the work of many:

> Far from me be the thought of attributing to myself the merit of the truly providential works which have just arisen under my direction. After God, who alone is the author of all good, it is to the devotedness of my fellow priests and to your own spirit of cooperation that we owe the astounding work of Holy Cross as it exists today. I have been but a simple tool which the Lord will soon break that he may substitute for it others more worthy. In his plan they are to develop or at least to solidify what I have begun. In the midst of the most painful trials, I have never lost hope in Providence or in your fidelity to the sublime vocation which God has given you. I have counted on the apostolic spirit of the virtuous priests who have willingly shared my labors, on the cooperation of all the members of your institute, and on the charity of the faithful. The five years which have just passed are sufficient evidence that my trust was not in vain.

The founder explained what remained to be done for the full development of Holy Cross—improvement of the formation programs and the methods of ministry as well as a generous religious attitude on the part of all which would create a spirit of union and community:

> This important work which has been entrusted to us is not yet completed. It still calls for many sacrifices and much labor. I am well aware of all that still remains to be done to form our subjects to the religious life, to afford them an intellectual formation in keeping with the needs of the times,

and to establish uniformity in their conduct and their teaching methods.

I firmly trust, however, that the same God who has begun this work under such favorable auspices will carry it through to its completion. This he will do, provided that you strive constantly after the perfect life. This perfect life is characterized by obedience, discipline, punctuality, community spirit, zeal for the interior life, edification, and devotion to work. The perfection of this life stands out particularly in that purity of intention, which seeks not self, but God alone; aims only at heaven and not at anything earthly; strives for nothing but the happiness of possessing Jesus and belonging to him and to his blessed mother; and directs all interests, goods, and rights to the sole honor of the divine master and the salvation of souls. Obedience will so completely animate the whole tenor of such a life that no one will engage in any activity except at the will of the superior. This kind of life will be marked by devotion to regularity and punctuality, by a constant and universal fidelity to the rules and constitutions of the Society, in a spirit of love rather than of fear, and in a spirit of faith rather than for human motives.

This life will promote community spirit by humility, meekness, and charitable forbearance with others. It will follow scrupulously the maxim of the pious author of the *Imitation*: "We must mutually support, console, aid, instruct, and admonish one another." Such a life will give edification by its modesty, its sacrifices of personal viewpoints, its self-forgetfulness, its religious gravity, and its careful avoidance of all criticism, unkind jesting, and even the slightest trace of frivolity. It will be a life of devotion to the work of teaching or of any other employment, to punctuality to the common exercises, and to the shunning of idleness. Lastly, it will be an interior life, elevated to God by the habitual practice of acts of faith, hope, and charity, after the example of Jesus Christ, who is to be the particular model of our conduct. Unless we wish to ruin the work of Holy Cross, it is absolutely essential for us to live with our Lord a life hidden in God.

The basic need was the need of a spirit of union:

Assuredly, all these different works, with which your society is connected in varying degrees, contain many elements of disintegration. Considering them only from the standpoint of human reason, it is difficult to explain how they could begin, organize, develop, and harmonize up to the present. This is particularly true in view of our slender pecuniary resources, the unfavorable political situation, and differences of personal temperament, not to mention the ill will of several who tried in vain to ruin what was being undertaken in a manner which seemed to them so patently imprudent.

Notwithstanding differences of temperament and talent, the inequality of means, and the differences of vocation and ministry, the one aim of zeal for the glory of God and the salvation of souls inspires almost all the members and gives rise to a oneness of effort which tends more and more to a union of hearts which constitutes the bond and strength of Holy Cross.

What is true of a palace whose foundations have been laid and which is rising gradually to completion is verified likewise in a great work of charity. It is not one person alone who builds; nor is it one stone or one single beam of wood that forms it. Each worker contributes something from a personal trade; each workman contributes something from his own trade; each stone is cut to fit into its one appointed place; and each piece of wood is arranged and placed so as to enhance the general effect of the entire building. Union, then, is a powerful lever with which we could move, direct, and sanctify the whole world, if the spirit of evil, which has been allowed to exercise its power over this earth, does not set it-self up against the wondrous effects of this moral force.

In fact, why are the political parties which are disturbing society today powerful enough to bring about revolutions and upheavals? Is it not because they know the secret of unit-ing and working for one same end? Would it not, then, be disgraceful for you and for me not to do for the cause of good, for God and eternity, what the children of the world do every day for the cause of evil, for the world, and for the short day of this life? We who are disciples of a God who died for the salvation of souls who are perishing, we do not realize all the good we could do for others through union with Jesus Christ in the spirit of our rules and constitutions!

The religious should pursue union because it is the teaching of Christ and for many other reasons too:

It is this touching mystery of religious union which our sav-ior unveiled for us in the Gospel when he explained the in-corporation of all the faithful with his divine Person in the body of which he is the head and we are the members. Since we form with him but one body and draw life from the same Spirit, he urges us to remain united in him, like the vine and the branches, borne by the same root, nourished by the same sap, and forming together but one plant.

Read this beautiful simile in the fifteenth chapter of Saint John. There you will find all the motives which could induce you to tighten the cords which keep the works of Holy Cross closely united to one another.

First of all, there is the motive of family pride, for it is our duty to avoid the disgrace of sterility and to win for ourselves the glory of sturdy growth. Just as the branch cannot bear fruit of itself unless it be united to the vine, so neither can we unless we are united in Jesus Christ, the vine of which we are the branches.

We have, too, the motive of holy fear. If we cut ourselves off from this mystic vine, or if we deserve this penalty and thus become divided among ourselves, we thereby expose ourselves to the risk of ruining God's work and bringing down on ourselves the punishments of eternal justice.

There is, moreover, the consideration of our own personal interests and those of the community. From this union there will flow down upon us, as from a rich spring, every grace and blessing.

Finally, there is a motive of gratitude toward the Author and Finisher of our vocation. The fruits of our justice and sanctity will glorify God just as the fruits on a tree are at the same time the glory of the tree itself and of the gardener.

Beholding the fruits of our mutual union, the world will glorify God; and jealous at such great spiritual and temporal prosperity, the devil will endeavor to destroy it at its very root and to disrupt these works by sowing dissension in the minds and hearts of the members. The devil knows full well that all its efforts will come to nothing so long as we remain steadfast in holy union.

The founder offered models of this union:

Here we have a striking representation of the hierarchy of the heavenly spirits, wherein all the different choirs of angels are arranged in three orders which are mutually subordinated one to another.

Our Association is also a visible imitation of the Holy Family wherein Jesus, Mary, and Joseph, notwithstanding their differences in dignity, were one at heart by their unity of thought and uniformity of conduct. . . .

Just as in the adorable Trinity, of which the house of Our Lady of Holy Cross is still another image, there is no difference of interests and no opposition of aims or wills, so among the priests, brothers, and sisters there should be such conformity of sentiments, interests, and wills as to make all of us one in somewhat the same manner as the Father, Son, and Holy Spirit are one. This was the touching prayer of our Lord for his disciples and their successors: "That they may be one among themselves, Father, as you and I are one."

This it is which prompts me to say to you, my dear sons in Jesus Christ, as the apostle said to the Philippians: "If an exhortation made in the name of Jesus Christ can impress you, if the love I have for you can touch your hearts, if there is among us a union of minds, if you have for me some affection, if you feel for me in my sorrows, fill up my joy by thinking alike, having the same charity, with one soul and one mind. Do nothing out of contentiousness or vain glory; but in humility, let each one regard the others as superiors, each one looking not to self-interests but to those of others."

He concluded:

Hence—leaving aside for the moment the sisters—unless you want to see everything crumble and fall into ruin, the rules and constitutions must establish between you [the Brothers of Saint Joseph] and the priests of Holy Cross, between the particular superiors [of each society] and the superior general, the same interdependence which exists between the branches of a tree and its trunk, between the rays of the sun and its fire, between brooks and their source. This trunk, this sun, this source, though merely an instrument, signifies the common origin of the existence and preservation of these three works. Since it is of itself without vitality, light, or water, it must be closely united to God through Jesus Christ, and to Jesus Christ through Mary and Joseph, in order to receive the sap of the spiritual life, light, and the saving waters of grace.

To cement better this union and this imitation of the Holy Family, I have consecrated and do hereby consecrate anew, as far as lies in my power, the auxiliary priests to the Sacred Heart of Jesus, the shepherd of souls; the brothers to the heart of Saint Joseph, their patron; and the sisters to the heart of Mary pierced with the sword of sorrow.

CHAPTER 5

GROWTH
(1842–1850)

By 1841 Father Moreau's vision for Holy Cross was substantiality realized. The years 1842–1851 were years of development and consolidation—development and spread of the Association's works, clarification and consolidation of the Association's goals.

I. MINISTRY

They opened with a setback to the foreign work of Holy Cross: because the civil and church authorities made their situation impossible, the religious had to leave Algeria in 1842. But the setback was only momentary. The next year Father Moreau obtained from the Paris government official recognition of the brothers as teachers for the French possessions of North Africa,[1] and they returned there in 1844. In 1847 a colony from Holy Cross settled in Quebec. In 1848 a foundation was made in New Orleans, and a priest and a brother accompanied to Guadeloupe the Holy Cross priest who was named apostolic administrator there. In 1850 Father Moreau made a foundation in Rome.

The multiplication of foreign foundations continued until 1864. Holy Cross sent out colonies to open new foreign missions approximately every two years from 1840 until 1864, except for the period from 1857 until 1860 when a moratorium was called in order to consolidate existing foundations. In addition, colonies of clerics, brothers, and sisters numbering from three or four to twelve or more left Holy Cross almost every year from 1840 to 1860 to strengthen foundations already made, sometimes several groups leaving the same year. The foundations made from Holy Cross constituted only one-third of those which were given serious consideration. By the end of Father Moreau's time as superior general, of all major regions in the world only the South American continent and the South Pacific lacked Holy Cross communities, and this only because the founder had had to decline invitations to open houses in Australia and Argentina. Of the foreign foundations discontinued before Father Moreau's resignation, not one failed because of misplanning by the general administration. Interference from government officials or supposedly diplomatic moves on the part of religious in the foundations (for example, Father Drouelle in Italy) or local maladministration caused all of them.

In France the work of the auxiliary priests continued. In their first ten years their number had grown from five to twenty-six. Although many of the Holy Cross clergy were outside France or were novices or seminarians, the auxiliary priests had preached eighty-three missions or retreats in France by 1845—a fairly large number if we recall that they usually preached two, three, or four together.[2] Though their number increased by only three, they preached eighteen missions or retreats the next year and nineteen the year after.[3] They found it hard to accept all of the invitations offered them, and enthusiastic letters from the pastors of parishes where they had worked swelled the correspondence files at Holy Cross. Regularly the priests left behind them a number of converts, some of them very influential persons brought back to the Church after decades away and determined to make up for their neglect. Some of these gave generous and important help to Father Moreau in his work. At times the auxiliary priests left organizations behind them. For example, during a mission preached early in 1844, Fr. Moreau was prevailed upon by those who heard his convincing preaching to organize their efforts against blasphemy and cursing. So, in his usually thorough way, he drew up statutes for an Association of the Holy Name of God, in which members pledged to avoid the vices of blasphemy and cursing and to do what they could to impede them in others or at least to whisper an invocation in reparation when they heard God's name blasphemed or used to curse. A medal was cast. Members were registered and organized into small groups. Fr. Moreau obtained Roman recognition of the Association. By the end of the year it numbered more than 3,000 members.[4]

The brothers' work as elementary educators continued to develop. From the 26 elementary schools operated by about 50 brothers in 1835, they had about 100 teachers in almost 60 schools in 1845. They were doing the same work they had done in Father Dujarié's day, for the most part living one or two in rectories or village schools and offering adult education or special education in addition to their teaching of children.[5] With an eye to obtaining a more extensive government recognition of the brothers than the 1823 authorization as a charitable organization for elementary instruction in La Sarthe and neighboring departments, in 1842 Fr. Moreau circulated a letter to the French bishops enlisting their support. By the end of the next year, fifty-seven bishops had replied, most of them very encouraging and some even enthusiastic in their support.[6] But he could get government recognition only for their work in the French possessions of North Africa. Nevertheless, requests continued to come from all over France, and in 1846 he had to announce that no further foundations of schools would be made until 1850.[7]

The Association of Holy Cross had no establishments which it owned in France beyond the three Le Mans properties: Our Lady of Holy Cross and the two novitiates, where candidates studied both the religious life and the subjects they hoped to teach.[8] For the rest of the founder's life, the Association worked for the most part operating institutions owned by ecclesiastical or civil authorities and remained with relatively few institutions or even properties of its own. Not only the priests but the brothers too were really auxiliaries. The same situation existed in the foreign foundations.

The Institution of Our Lady of Holy Cross continued its development. Though it is difficult to measure the caliber of the preaching or the elementary instruction given by the members of the Association except by the enthusiastic response of those whom they served, the caliber of the work at the secondary school at Holy Cross gives a good indication of the thoroughness with which Fr. Moreau and his collaborators went about doing things.

In 1843 a student society, the Academy of Holy Cross, was organized to encourage scholarship. It numbered among its honorary members many church, civil, and academic leaders not only of the area but of the country. Usually one or more of them came to its sessions.[9]

In 1844 a conference of Saint Vincent de Paul was established among the students so their apostolic development could keep pace with their academic development.[10] However, the students had never been strangers to the apostolic labors of the Association of Holy Cross. In 1840 the students of the North African minor seminary of Saint Augustine in Mustapha, directed by the priests and brothers, had addressed a letter to the students of Our Lady of Holy Cross.[11] Priests and brothers who had spent years in a foreign foundation told the students about their work when they returned to Holy Cross or, like Father Sorin from the United States and like Fr. Voisin from Bengal, sent them letters.[12] From Fr. Moreau's remarks in his circular letter of January 1, 1851, about the students at the minor seminary at Orléans, conducted from 1850 by priests and brothers of Holy Cross, it would seem that they enjoyed the same relationship to the Association as the students at Holy Cross did.[13] These facts can serve not only to show that the students of Our Lady of Holy Cross shared the apostolic outlook of the priests and brothers but also that a sense of common purpose, even a family spirit, bound religious and students together.

Fr. Moreau was not satisfied with getting advice from other educators. The parents of the students had something to offer too. Early in 1850 he felt he could organize a "family council" to help in developing "the Institution, to aid its director to profit from the reflections of the public on this establishment," to consider "all the disciplinary regulations and the curriculum . . . and all the questions relative to the physical and moral well-being of the students."[14]

The same spirit which bound the students of Our Lady of Holy Cross to the work of Holy Cross marked the Association of Saint Joseph (as also those of the Good Shepherd and the sisters of the Good Shepherd monastery). In the *Etrennes Spirituelles*, which the associates received, they read, for example, in 1844: "In this little book we set down all our plans for developing the work of Holy Cross."[15] They learned of the works of Holy Cross by reading there most of the documents referred to in the last several paragraphs. They read of requests for foundations, of the approval given by various bishops to the brothers' rules, of the development of the sisters' society, of the edifying death of one of the students at Holy Cross.[16] They also learned the truth when calumnies spread against Holy Cross or its founder: he simply published in the *Etrennes Spirituelles* all the correspondence and other documents concerning events in which his conduct or that of a religious had been slandered.[17] The associates were also provided with a variety of items that might prove of interest to them, such as details on the Potawatomi language, advice to a young person just beginning to take up work in the world, and details[18]

II. CONFLICTS AND SUFFERING

At almost every step along the way of this development, the work of Holy Cross, and of the founder in particular, met opposition. On January 5, 1844, he wrote to the entire Association in a circular letter:

> Were I to judge of the trials which may be reserved for us during the new year by those I have been through during the year just passed, I would prepare myself for all kinds of contradictions. I have had countless obstacles to surmount and numerous false rumors to denounce. Not to mention certain difficulties which seemed on the point of stopping the construction of our conventual church, malicious reports have been spread abroad regarding my conduct and the future of our institute. Some, for example, were bold enough to assert that I was robbing families to build up the work of God. . . . Others claimed that we could not take our boarding students beyond the fifth class. . . . It was falsely reported that I was planning to set up a printing press of my own and to open a dry goods store. The purpose of these rumors was, undoubtedly, to put me in a bad light before the merchants of the city. . . . It was asserted, lastly, that we were giving up the apostolic ministry in the diocese and that we were incapable of continuing it, although we have continued to preach retreats, which God has been pleased to bless in the past.[19]

On January 4, 1845, he listed among the trials of the preceding year: scandalous behavior within the Association, including the violation "of the most essential points of the rule without regard for the vows of obedience and of poverty," the departure of many novices, the death of Br. André and two of the other older brothers, sicknesses, a shipwreck which almost claimed a colony intended for Indiana, the fact that "an ill-willed newspaper printed a letter dictated by inexperience," numerous complaints which caused the closing of a store that had been opened in the interests of Our Lady of Holy Cross and forced the abandonment of certain building projects already started which were then resumed almost immediately, "incredible delays" in the sending of needed articles of clothing to the brothers in the various schools, and "the unavoidable anxiety occasioned by the large number and the youth of the students entrusted to the zeal of those in charge of our splendid institution, and by the poor health of the reverend mother prioress of the Good Shepherd."[20]

The beginning of really serious conflicts in the work of Holy Cross dates from 1844. In that and the following year the authorities at Vallon and Sablé attempted to take undue advantage of the brothers in their schools in these localities. The tension finally rose to such a point that Fr. Moreau was publicly portrayed as a man concerned only with money and at odds with everyone. Since the slanders aimed at bringing the brothers' society into disrepute, Fr. Moreau published all the facts in the *Etrennes Spirituelles* of 1845, and also published a lengthy memorandum to Mr. Salvandy, the minister of public instruction. This only antagonized the opposition, which retaliated by publishing a libelous pamphlet of its own. Fr. Mautouchet, steward at Saint Vincent's Seminary, involved himself in the machinations of the Vallon authorities and even corrected the proofs of their pamphlet. Once he had made the truth known, Fr. Moreau no longer feared losing face before his benefactors and took the matter no farther, leaving the pamphlet unanswered. But Bishop Bouvier, more conciliatory in his approach to government officials, was especially angered because Fr. Moreau had introduced his name into the dispute. The incident paved the way for more serious differences later on between Fr. Moreau and his bishop.

That same year (1845) the anticlerical mayor of Mansigné refused a certificate of good morals to the brother teaching at the local school; without it he could not teach elsewhere, and, of course, rumor would suggest reasons why he had been refused. This led to another struggle, the details of which appeared in the 1847 *Etrennes Spirituelles*.[21]

In 1848 the February Revolution, which overthrew the Restoration Monarchy and established the Second Republic, raised fears that the horrors of the 1790s would recur. In his circular letter of January 5, 1849, Fr. Moreau commented on the repercussions on Holy Cross:

> Some of our number . . . took fright. . . . Four priests left us to engage in the priestly ministry elsewhere, and three brothers who had their diplomas also withdrew. Two others who had at first edified us by their spirit of religious devotedness abandoned their post of duty. . . . Their departure occasioned me particular sorrow because their offer to go to Canada or Africa had given me grounds for counting on their perseverance. . . . Frightened by the threats of fire and pillage when the republic was proclaimed, several postulants ran away from Holy Cross. Some novices too requested permission to return home for a time. As a result of these threats and for lack of our usual sources of income, I was obliged to take most of the young brothers who were at the Solitude of the Savior and send them to the other houses. Consequently, the novitiate of the mother house has been temporarily closed.
>
> Had I heeded the orders of certain men who in these days of anarchy have assumed leadership of the revolutionary movement in the interests of public order, I would have sent away from Our Lady of Holy Cross the students of our institution and also the priests, brothers, and pious women who are devoting themselves so unreservedly to the service of this house. I would have withdrawn from the house myself. To remain at the post of duty assigned by Providence, I had to resist the most pressing pleas of my fellow priests, friends,

and even strangers, who kept warning me constantly of designs on my life. . . .

As a measure of prudence, nevertheless, I was forced to dismiss our boarders temporarily. From this, several persons received the impression that I was abandoning the work of their education, and even insinuated that the Institution of Our Lady of Holy Cross was definitely closed. In this connection it was noised abroad that I had gone to America and had thus deserted a house which was doomed to ruin. The truth of the matter is that I did not even for a moment leave my post of duty or my usual occupations. Soon after, the boarders returned, notwithstanding the fact that a few troublemakers had warned me not to reopen the boarding school under penalty of seeing our buildings set on fire.

Our students, unfortunately, brought back with them from their associations a spirit of independence which it was difficult to curb. This spirit was only a natural outcome of the feverish desire for liberty which is today consuming the people of Europe. Their excitement and their desire to return home were so great that one of the students, doubtless at the instigation of the enemy of all good works, conceived the idea of setting fire to the house. He felt quite sure that if his plan worked, we would be obliged to send him home. In fact, he actually stole some sulphur matches and during the night threw them on the mattress of an empty bed. The fire was already spreading when, fortunately, one of the students, then the brother prefects noticed it and put it out at once. . . .

The spirit of insubordination . . . had one consoling aspect. Our students were never entirely deaf to motives of faith; they never defied any of their teachers; and my presence always reestablished order. Thus it was that, even at the height of their unrest, it was enough for me to appear on the scene to quiet them and make them resume their duties. Besides, to atone for their faults, they not only imposed a general penance upon themselves at the following meal, but gave an alms to the poor, went to the chapel in silence, made the way of the cross, and went to confession. All this proves that in spite of the difficulties of the times, Christian education was exercising an influence on the minds and hearts of these dear children.

As always, calumny has tried to blacken our reputation. The most absurd and contradictory rumors have been circulated about our establishment and especially about myself. Because we had thought it prudent to show ourselves to the public just as we were rather than remain off by ourselves, I had our [student] musicians appear on three or four more solemn occasions in order to make them face the workmen whose threats were a source of fear. I also had them sing patriotic songs during the recreations to forestall feelings of fears aroused by conversations in which there was always some element of false rumor and of more or less alarming reports from the outside. As a consequence, I was accused of aims unworthy of my position and character. On the one hand, among the families of the old aristocracy, I was passed off for a wild democrat and almost a red; on the other, a representative of the people, a devoted friend, warned me that I had been denounced to the government as a reactionary and a royalist who was teaching the students of Holy Cross antirepublican ideas. . . . They attributed to me ideas, correspondence, and acts altogether unworthy of a priest and even of a man of honor.[22]

A lengthy document entitled "Mutiny at the Institution of Holy Cross," found in the general archives, recounts what happened on April 10, 1848:

During recreation the students liked to sing the patriotic songs of the day. They sang the Marseillaise . . . in chorus.

They repeated the refrain "to die for the fatherland" with feverish energy. At first they sang in groups; then they wanted to sing while marching like soldiers. . . .

To understand why this singing was tolerated, it is good to note here that the reverend father rector continued to be the object of recriminations and accusations from the different parties; the complaints went even as far as the minister. While the royalists accused him of being republican, because they heard the students singing these songs, the republicans accused him of being a royalist. . . . They spied on his actions and his words. They interpreted his silence. They did not forget the first attempts made by the revolutionary authorities in regard to Holy Cross. The rector was not unaware of the dangers in the toleration he was showing. . . .

However, such a state of affairs had to come to an end. It was announced that the military marches and the songs had to stop. This prohibition aroused reaction. . . . After the rector spoke to the students in the refectory—a talk to which they listened in cold silence—the older boys were sent off to study. They left the refectory in good order, but it was a threatening calm. For the past month, their study hall, at their own request, had been prefected by a boy chosen by all of his fellow students, and it must be said that until then they had been rather faithful to the responsibility they had taken on their honor. But that evening their minds were forming another plan. Because they could not sing their patriotic hymns inside the house, they said, nothing would keep them from going to sing . . . in the streets of the city to prove . . . that the youth of France were animated by sentiments of true republicanism. . . .

When they got to the study hall, the students all went to their respective places, but it was not Horace or Homer that interested them at that moment. . . . Mr. [Leroi], the student prefect at that study period, was invited to come down from his place. But he answered that since they had put him there, he would betray the confidence which the father rector had placed in him in accord with their own choice if he deserted his post, but that he had no authority to keep them from doing as they pleased. They acted on this last observation. They left the prefect in his place. But they took down all the oil lamps, pushed the tables and chairs against the doors, and after having barricaded themselves in they began to sing the hymn of all insurrections, the Marseillaise, to the accompaniment of the noise they made with the tops of their desks and boxes.

The rector quickly learned of the uproar. He tried to get in, but the door was solidly closed. He called the brother locksmiths, who lifted the door off its hinges. During that time the uproar inside got louder and louder. Doubtless the boys expected to see the prefect of discipline come in, for whom such a bold act might have had unpleasant consequences. The brothers present did not want to permit the rector to go into this tumultuous study period alone. But he pushed them off despite their protests and went in to an explosion of furious shouts. When they recognized the superior of the house himself, they became completely quiet. Everyone sat down in his place. They waited, but without giving any sign of fear or regret. The only thing that showed itself was their habitual respect for him. The father rector silently went to the prefect's place, then looked for a moment on the disorder all about him. "Who took down that oil lamp?" "I did," answered a student. "That other?" "I did." "Who moved that table?" "I did."

To each question a different student answered, admitting his guilt, and then without much objection consented to put right what he had done. But finally one of them got up and

refused to obey. This was a dangerous example. He was ordered out. He left. "All of you take your books and go back to
work," the rector said. As they hesitated, he turned directly to
one of the most ardent agitators and said: "Go to work or get
out." "I'll go," the boy said insolently, "'but I won't go alone."
He got right up and invited the boy next to him to follow him.
Fortunately, the latter, who has since gone to the major seminary of Le Mans, the only one who in the midst of all the
tumult, had the courage to keep out of it and continue with
his work . . . did not move. His neighbor let him alone. But
he left, walking proudly before the superior. Another who,
at that hour of confusion and mistakes, forgot that till then
he had been a very good example in the house, also got up
and went out in the same way, but starting up the inevitable
Marseillaise in a loud voice. A humiliating correction hurried him out and kept the other students in their places. [The
boy himself, André Manceau, in his own account of the event
wrote: "The superior hurried him along . . . by giving him a
kick in the pants."]

Until then not a word had been spoken by anyone except
the brief dialogue reported earlier. Everybody was waiting for
the rector to say something. Perhaps an all-too-well merited
reproach imprudently addressed to them then would have
broken down the last dike holding back a new explosion because the students inside could hear the noise and the loud
singing of those who had gone outside. These songs stopped
only when the boys who had been thrown out were separated
from one another by teachers who each took one to his room
and tried to reason in a friendly way with him.

At the same time the rector brought those inside little by
little to calm down. He did not blame the students, but the
spirit of evil, the source of all evil inspirations, who wants
to destroy everything that troubles his reign on earth and

whose blind instruments men are deceived into becoming. He showed what the consequences of their imprudence would be for them, for their families, for the house where they had been educated. He appealed to the religious sentiments of the students and added: "I am not going to punish you. You have faith. It will tell you what you have to do." Then he announced that since it was especially God who had been offended, they were going to go immediately to the chapel to ask his pardon by the prayer Parce Domine (Spare me, Lord).

In the chapel Fr. Moreau added a few more words, which impressed the boys profoundly, on the insults done to our Lord, so to speak, even in the very place where he dwelt, and he ended by saying that he was going to pass the night in prayer before the Blessed Sacrament so that God would bless their sleep and make their rising next morning calm. . . .

That evening those who had compromised themselves the most asked to spend the night at the foot of the altar. Two of them in particular begged for permission to do this with tears, but their request was not granted. The next day all of them gave up something at their meals, refrained from recreation all day long, and in the evening all went to confession.

The boy mentioned above, André Manceau, in the account he wrote two years later, was evidently still smarting at the memory of what had happened. He presented a somewhat different version of the end of the "uprising." He wrote that the superior said he was willing to forgive the boys who were responsible on condition "that everyone sign a promise, which he would dictate, never to undertake to countermand the orders of the superior but would obey blindly everything that he should order, and that the older boys in the study hall should go without recreation and dessert for the following eight days, etc."!

An illustration of the opposition that Holy Cross had to withstand from anticlerical newspapers and of the vigor with which the founder withstood it is found in a letter addressed to a newspaper which was willing to allow the founder to answer the slander of another journal.[23] The offending paper, the *Courrier*, had "refused to publish it on the grounds that it was too insolent." Fr. Moreau commented: "Frankly, I did not think the *Courrier* was so scrupulous in matters of this kind." He continued:

> But pray tell me, which expression is so shocking? A careful rereading of the letter, which I felt obliged to write [to the *Courrier*] and which you have faithfully reprinted, reveals only one word which strikes me as being somewhat hard for the *Courrier* to stomach. I called the statements of this newspaper lies. Surely, for an editor who is privileged to wield a pen and to use it in the service of others, the charge of falsehood is a serious one. If I did not prove my charge, I in turn would fear being classed as a calumniator. The question, then, is to see if my charge is founded in fact.
>
> I hereby declare unhesitatingly that my charge is well founded and I defy anyone to prove the contrary. Here, then, is one fact, since the *Courrier* asks us for facts:
>
> "I, the undersigned, public watchman of the Commune of Holy Cross, hereby declare that the Institution of Fr. Moreau had nothing to do with the unfortunate incident which took place last Sunday, April 2nd, in rue Notre-Dame. I have also heard it said very positively that the editor of the *Courrier* knew the facts of the case before he published in his paper the article which attacked the said Institution.
>
> Given at Holy Cross April 5, 1849.
Leveau, public watchman"
>
> Now if it be true, as I could prove if need be, that the *Courrier* knew the truth, and the whole truth, in this deplorable affair;

if, as I heard it said to the public watchman, the editor of the *Courrier* was requested not to drag the Establishment of Holy Cross into this affair, since it was in no way implicated, how else can we describe the language of a man who dares to publish as true what he knows is false?

For the rest, Mr. Editor, the *Courrier* is wasting its time in trying to embitter the working classes against us. Anyone who has seen or who sees the house of Our Lady of Holy Cross at close range knows well that those who live there are not in the habit of carrying clubs and mauling the Republicans who go singing past its walls.

Perhaps this letter, simple as it is, will provoke further attacks from the *Courrier*. The prospect does not frighten me; I even pardon them in advance. Once the editor, by the requested insertion, retracts the lie which gave rise to a police investigation and aroused the hatred of the workers against me, he can count on my unbroken silence, no matter what he may invent in the future.

Fr. Moreau continued with this information for the religious: "Under orders from the bailiff, the *Courrier* reproduced the above letter."

All these struggles ended with Our Lady of Holy Cross receiving the long-sought full teaching rights over a year before the law diminishing the state monopoly on secondary education was proposed.

Trials of another kind followed these. In 1847 typhoid fever struck the communities in Indiana at Notre Dame and in Canada at Montreal, taking a heavy toll in the former. In 1849 cholera struck most of France, North Africa, and New Orleans. A large fire destroyed part of the buildings at Notre Dame. In the same year Catholics learned that Pius IX had had to flee Rome. Father Moreau's response to these calamities was the institution of perpetual adoration of the Blessed Sacrament in the Association of Holy Cross. But we shall return to this point later.

III. RELIGIOUS LIFE: VOWS, UNION AND COMMUNITY, GOVERNMENT AND AUTHORITY, GOSPEL AND RULES

As in the first six years of its existence, the Association of Holy Cross developed not only in its work but also in its internal organization and the delineation of its ideal.

The sisters became religious. Bishop Bouvier had opposed having another community of religious women founded in his diocese. Fr. Moreau agreed that the sisters would remain simply "pious women" meant only for housework at Our Lady of Holy Cross. However, his intention from the first had been to make them religious and to have them engage in other works besides the housework they did at Holy Cross. If the bishop of Le Mans would not make them religious, other bishops would. He wrote Fr. Sorin in 1841 asking him to have them established as a diocesan community by one or more American bishops, and Fr. Sorin did. They received recognition in the archdioceses of Montreal and New Orleans.

Fr. Moreau professed those sisters who went to the American and Canadian foundations and provided them with a set of provisional constitutions. He sent Sister Mary of the Seven Dolors, their superior, to Canada so that she could be a professed religious. He made no secret of these moves, unable to see how Bishop Bouvier could raise any reasonable objection to what his fellow bishops did in their dioceses as long as the founder respected his desires regarding his own diocese. In 1843 the *Etrennes Spirituelles* explained that the sisters were intended for educational work and in 1845 that they had received approval as a diocesan establishment in Detroit.[24] Fr. Moreau began that year to address his circular letters to "his dear sons and daughters in Jesus Christ." There can be no doubt that the bishop took a less simple view of the matter than the founder did.

The priests were all religious, or novices who intended to make vows, by the end of 1847. That year saw the departure of the last of the auxiliary priests who had remained at Holy Cross with the intention of never making religious profession. The bishop was involved. He invited this man and two others who had left Holy Cross in similar circumstances to form a band of diocesan missionaries to do precisely the work that the auxiliary priests had been founded to do and were doing so effectively. In fact, without even notifying Father Moreau, he dispensed two professed priests from their vows so that they could join the new group. On November 20, 1847, the founder wrote to Father Sorin about the departure of the last one who had intended to remain without vows: "Fr. Gauthier has just left us, without any discontent, to join Fr. Cottereau in preaching missions." Then he added, alluding to Moses' reaction to the prophesying of two men who had refused to associate themselves with the group of elders with him (Numbers 11:29): "Would that all Israel might prophesy! We have two new candidates to replace him." A letter from Fr. Vérité to Fr. Sorin six years earlier, October 19, 1841, shows that this attitude was the same as the attitude which the founder had expressed at the departure of Fr. Cottereau, who had been one of his earliest collaborators. Until mid-August of that year, he had been on the verge of making vows. He and Fr. Moreau spent an hour discussing the matter, and during their conference, explained Fr. Vérité, "both of them shed copious tears." The outcome of the discussion was the departure of Fr. Cottereau.[25]

The number of professions among the brothers continued to mount. By 1842, 34 had made vows, and in 1851 the professed numbered 80. However, the novices were still much more numerous (136 in 1851). It was only with papal approval in the mid-1850s that all those who joined the society were expected to profess the three religious vows perpetually. Until that date it was still possible to make only annual vows of poverty and obedience.[26] But that Fr. Moreau intended from the start that the Association become a full-fledged religious community appears in his recommending Saint Alphonsus Liguori's treatment of the religious vocation in the letter with which he introduced the prospective constitutions of 1838 and his printing of the saint's "Reflections on the Vocation to the Religious State" in the 1846 directory.[27]

The details of the organization of the Association of Holy Cross—an organization which Fr. Moreau considered definitive—were worked out in these years. Each house of some importance had a "minor chapter" charged with responsibility for the spiritual and the temporal and presided over by the superior.[28] Each society, priests, brothers, and sisters, had its own "particular superior" aided by a council, with the highest authority vested in an annual "major chapter." The entire Association was governed by a rector (or superior general) with a council and an annual general chapter constituted of most of the members of the major chapters.[29] The organization of the sisters' major chapter seems to have taken place in 1847,[30] but because they were not recognized by the bishop of Le Mans, their rights in the general chapter, which was held regularly at Holy Cross, were represented simply by their particular superior. Common constitutions formed the legislation of the entire Association, and almost identical rules the legislation of each society. This arrangement assured both the autonomy and the collaboration of the societies. It was later disturbed, as we shall see below, by the demands made by the Vatican in view of papal approval.

This organization took for granted that the societies would collaborate in their major apostolic endeavors. When bishops requested only brothers, for example, in Indiana and Quebec, Father Moreau insisted on sending priests and sisters too. When church authorities requested only a priest or priests, he insisted on sending brothers, for example, to Guadeloupe, or both brothers and sisters to Bengal. Often only an external force prevented the two or all three societies from being present, as, for example, when the French government prevented the priests from returning to Algeria with the brothers in 1844.

It should be noted that Father Moreau also wanted the religious to live and work together as far as possible, although he recognized that the needs of the Church frequently made it necessary for religious to live outside local religious communities. He maintained the elementary schools run by single brothers living in rectories. The auxiliary priests frequently went alone to preaching assignments or, outside France, were alone in ministry. However, the founder insisted that the religious should go into such situations only after they had had fairly extensive experience in community life, that they should retain close contact with superiors and fellow religious, and they should return to community often.

He wrote to Fr. Sorin, for example, on May 25, 1843, of the religious he was sending him: "I will limit myself to recommending . . . that you try to keep your entire group living together in community for as long as possible and that you be very sure of the spirit of each one before you send them out." He wrote to the "priests, brothers, and sisters in America" on August 30 of that year: "Your future depends entirely on your fidelity to your rules and constitutions, especially on the length of your residence in common with the rest of the community before leaving for different occupations outside."[31]

The founder insisted that contact be maintained with superiors by spiritual direction, which for religious in the smaller and more distant communities meant letters. From what Father Moreau says of their openness and from some of the letters extant, it is clear that a very large number of religious maintained this contact. On January 5, 1846, he wrote: "I am always pleased to have a thorough account of your dispositions and to be able, at least once a year, to read your souls in the letters of direction which reveal them to me. . . . May God bless all those who thus confide to me the secrets of their conscience and console me by their progress in the virtues of the holy state they have embraced!"[32] On January 3, 1847, he wrote:

> Without such contact with you, how can I direct the three societies whose government is now in my hands? It is obvious that the efficacy of the advice and orders of a superior will be in proportion to his acquaintance with the usual dispositions of those for whom they are intended. Consequently, the scattered members of the community and the head who directs them are in need of heart-to-heart correspondence in order to bring all minds together as to a center toward which all rays converge. . . .
>
> Let us then, dear sons and daughters in Jesus Christ, continue to remain thus united in our Lord, and let us often come together in spirit in spite of the distance which separates us. By these relationships of mutual friendship and dependence, we shall help one another correspond with the designs of Providence in our regard and make a holy use of the rapidly succeeding years which can merit for us in eternity years that will be all the happier for having brought us more trials in our fidelity to our vocation.[33]

He considered the assembling of the religious for the annual retreat at Holy Cross an opportunity to strengthen the bonds of community.[34]

His concern over a spirit of union and community, expressed already in his very first letter to the brothers[35] and emphatically reaffirmed in his important circular of September 1, 1841,[36] recurred repeatedly in his later letters.

On January 10, 1843, he wrote:

> May not a single one among us be unfaithful to the grace of
> his vocation. To that end, let us remain united to one another
> by the bonds of charity, confidence, devotedness, and obe-
> dience to our rules and constitutions. Our work here is the
> work of each and every one, and we are all, individually and
> collectively, responsible for it in the eyes of God and human-
> ity.[37] For the rest, God is witness of the ardor of my love for
> you all in the heart of Jesus Christ. My heart expands for you,
> and more than ever before, I feel that you will not be selfish.
> May your hearts also expand for me, and may you continue,
> dear fathers and brothers, to console me by exemplary fidel-
> ity to all your duties.[38]

On January 5, 1844, he wrote: "Above all, let us work with that
strength, unity, and clear understanding which comes from mutual cooperation and the possession of all things in common. We
must never lose sight of the fact that strength of numbers joined
with unity of aim and action is the greatest of all strengths and is
limited only by the bounds of the possible."[39]

On January 3, 1847: "Let us then, dear sons and daughters in
Jesus Christ, continue to remain thus united in our Lord, and let
us often come together in spirit in spite of the distance which
separates us. By these relationships of mutual friendship and dependence we shall help one another correspond with the designs
of Providence in our regard and make a holy use of the rapidly
succeeding years."[40]

The concern for union rather than any desire to propagate a
particular devotion led him in 1844 to proclaim the feasts of the
Sacred Heart of Jesus, Our Lady of the Seven Dolors (celebrated at
that time on the third Sunday of September), and Saint Joseph the
special feasts of the Association and their vigils as fast days.[41] The
three feasts became in the directories of 1845 and 1846 the feast

of the Sacred Heart of Jesus, the feast of the Sorrowing Heart or of the Seven Dolors of the Blessed Virgin Mary, and the feast of Most Pure Heart of Saint Joseph or the feast of Saint Joseph.[42] To them was added the observance of the anniversary of the dedication of the church of the mother house, which was also celebrated as the anniversary of the foundation of that house. Invocations were prescribed each afternoon to the pure and faithful heart of Saint Joseph, the holy and Immaculate Heart of Mary, and the Sacred Heart of Jesus.[43]

Father Moreau also began to sign his circular letters, "Yours in the Hearts of Jesus, Mary, and Joseph." This conclusion, however, occurs in only three circulars.[44] But he does use it in some other letters of this period and in prescriptions.[45]

The names Salvatorists, Josephites, and Marianites for the members of the three societies also appear in the 1847 constitutions. Though they recur thereafter in official documents, they never seem to have succeeded in completely replacing the earlier "(auxiliary) priests of Holy Cross," "Brothers of Saint Joseph," and "Sisters of Holy Cross" in ordinary usage—except in the case of the sisters when their society was separated from the priests and brothers.

Some time in the 1840s the entire Association began to use a seal depicting the three hearts surmounting an anchor, which itself, in accord with traditional Christian iconography, stood for the holy cross as our "only hope." Each society also had its own seal depicting the heart of its patron.

Although Fr. Moreau was devoted to Mary from his childhood, indications of a noteworthy devotion to Saint Joseph start only from the time he assumed the superiorship of the brothers.[46] His designs for the work of Holy Cross—that is, his preoccupation with union and community—seem to have turned his attention to the hearts of Jesus, Mary, and Joseph. But this attention to the hearts does not seem to have induced any devotion to the three

hearts as such. The founder and the religious directed their devotion to Jesus, Mary, and Joseph, referring to their hearts only
in so far as the mutual union of these three persons served as a
model for the union which the members of Holy Cross wished
to achieve.[47] Nor is it accurate to speak of any particular devotion to the Holy Family as such (working quietly at Nazareth,
for example).

The afternoon invocations of the directory and the observance
of the three feasts are the only manifestations of devotion to the
three hearts; the invocation of the heart of Joseph eventually
became simply an invocation of Saint Joseph, and the feasts of
the hearts of Mary and Joseph were eventually presented in the
directory simply as the feasts of the Seven Dolors and of Saint
Joseph.[48] The only indication of a devotion to the Holy Family as
such seems to have been the founder's plan to dedicate the conventual church under this title,[49] which he abandoned in order
to dedicate it to Our Lady of Holy Cross (Notre-Dame de Sainte-
Croix), giving it the title of the mother house. In fact, the observance of the anniversary of the dedication of this church and of
the founding of the mother house—Our Lady of Holy Cross or of
the Seven Dolors—was the principal feast of the Association. After the separation of the sisters, the feast of the mother church
and house remained the principal feast of the congregation because it was the feast of the center of the entire community.[50] In
that way the church along with the mother house better served
the original purpose Fr. Moreau intended them to have: their
"general plan and symbolism," he wrote on February 4, 1842,
"will embody all the ideals which have guided the foundation of
Our Lady of Holy Cross"—that is, the entire Association.[51]

The government of the Association was by no means highly
centralized or dictatorial as some of Fr. Moreau's opponents later
depicted it. In organizing it, he certainly did not imitate the great
number of religious foundations of his day. He seems to have

been influenced rather by his personal desire not to order and command—a desire which we shall see more clearly manifested later. In the prospective constitutions for the brothers in 1838, he had invested their "general council," that is, general chapter, as "representing the entire congregation" with the right to elect all major officers, to admit novices to profession, to dismiss members, and to examine the acts of the superior general's council.[52] The constitutions of the Association of Holy Cross from the mid-1840s gave these rights to the general chapter of the Association or the major chapter of each society, as well as the right to approve members for the diaconate and priesthood, to permit minor chapters to build, buy, or sell, to make or discontinue foreign foundations, and to elect and depose superiors, novice masters, examiners, visitors, directors of studies and professors, prefects of discipline, stewards and assistants,[53] and in 1847 the general chapter agreed that it could limit the powers of the rector as it saw fit and that the major chapter of one of the societies could limit the powers of its particular superior in the same way![54]

This does not mean that Fr. Moreau refused to take responsibility for decisions that were his to make. He was certainly not hesitant about giving commands in virtue of the vows of obedience or poverty, as his circular letters show. Also, despite the fact that the rules and constitutions of 1847 were worked out largely in committee over the preceding three years,[55] they clearly contain his ideas and the minutes of both general chapter and council meetings show that he took an active part in discussions. The general chapter of 1850 even permitted him to modify the constitutions as he saw fit (with advice) until Rome gave its definitive approval.

Fr. Moreau wanted a sizable council for himself: his council, organized in 1841, consisted of ten assistants![56] He also wanted to remain in office only if the chapter chose to elect him. Once governmental organization had been set up, an election was held for superior; he was chosen for a three-year term in 1843, after which he left office. This was the practice he had written into the directory. Despite his unwillingness, upon which we shall reflect below, he was elected for a second three-year term in 1846, at the end of which he again left office. Finally, he was elected for life in 1849—an election which, as we shall see, caused him deep suffering. At first he had written into the brothers' constitutions that the superior general could never be elected for life.[57] He had altered this, as he wrote on January 1, 1840, to enable them to retain a superior who proved satisfactory.[58] That he was hardly thinking of being elected for life himself seems evident from his unwillingness when the time came.

Perhaps the clearest presentation of his concept of his authority can be found in Fr. Mollevaut's letters of August 3, 1840, and of January 5, 1841, which are cited above, or again in his lengthy remarks of July 3, 1843, in which he began by noting that Fr. Moreau understood the role that he was going to describe:[59]

A thousand thanks to our adorable master who has given you one of the most important and decisive graces for your position: that of understanding what a superior is. This is precisely the thing that is most often not known by those who hold your position. Sometimes activity and moving about, a zeal which prudence does not direct—sometimes susceptibility on the part of authority, the desire that everyone yield and obey, the demand that everyone and everything be perfect, and the inability to bear with human defects and miseries—sometimes, finally, a certain delight in one's works, satisfaction with applause, and unwillingness to receive the observations of others and contradictions: there you have what gives all superiors reason for regret. Then, as in the case of civil authorities, they get very involved in temporal and external administration. That is to say, they do not lay the foundation, which is reducible to this one thing. A superior must be perfect and give the example of all the virtues: prudence above all, that rarest and least known of the virtues, continual and profound humility, imperturbable kindness, ardent prayer, constant union with God, unbroken peace. You have a perfect model for this and the most dependable rules for achieving it in the life of Saint Vincent de Paul, which you ought to read repeatedly, and especially in the advice which he gives to the superiors of his congregation. But when you read it, examine your conscience. . . .

Above all, take great care of the health of your collaborators . . . and try to know all their needs. Be a mother in this regard. . . . Keep your eyes always on the essentials: control your temperament and your temper, bear with everyone, know others very well so as not to ask anything beyond the possibilities of anyone and so as to make yourself loved by all. Finally, never forget to bear with yourself in viewing all the miseries that you recognize in yourself and to count only on the grace and the mercies of the Lord.

If a major defect can be found in the organization of the 1840s, it lies in the lack of provision for extensive development at a great distance from Holy Cross. For example, the distances involved and the hardships of travel made it difficult for members of the societies in foreign foundations to participate effectively in annual chapters in France. But since foreign foundations only began to become numerous in this period, Fr. Moreau could hardly have been expected to make detailed provision for them at this stage. The first attempt to organize the foreign foundations into provinces dates from 1851.[60] It was made only when the American and Canadian foundations numbered several houses and works in a relatively limited area. Although by rule the provincials were simply intermediaries between the various local superiors of their territory and the particular superiors of each society,[61] in fact they governed all the houses in their countries as Father Moreau did the houses in France. He intervened only in the cases prescribed (approving expenditures, etc.) or to give advice (mostly about religious life) or help (financial or personnel).

What Fr. Moreau thought of the organization of Holy Cross proposed in the legislation of 1847 appears from the way in which he presented it. His letter of introduction to the 1847 constitutions began:

> Without doubt the gospel of Jesus Christ is quite enough to serve as a rule of life for religious. Besides, it belongs to God alone to preserve the Association of Holy Cross and to bring it to its full development just as it was he who began it. However, since sin has led our nature astray and inflicted a mortal wound upon it and since we have the example of the holy fathers to guide us in our undertaking, we have judged it necessary to write these constitutions in order to guide more securely all the members of the family of which we have become the head in the way of the service of God, according to the plan of the same Association, desiring in this way to cooperate with the divine providence which preserves and guides it.

The religious life is an attempt to take the gospel at face value. The 1847 constitutions served mainly to organize the life and work of the Association in such a way as to make this possible for those who were called to Holy Cross.

As noted above, Fr. Dujarié had given the brothers no rule. The brief statutes of the Brothers of Christian Instruction of Ploërmel had been taken over with no other change than the substitution of "Brothers of Saint Joseph" for "Brothers of Christian Instruction" wherever the latter title occurred. These statutes contained (1) conditions for foundations, (2) rules of conduct toward superiors, toward the other brothers, toward the parents of students and the students themselves, and a few particular rules: frequency of confession, prayers, keeping accounts, correspondence, etc., and (3) the daily schedule.[62]

In 1838 Fr. Moreau used this and the rules Bishop Bouvier had given the Sisters of Providence to compose a much more detailed set of constitutions. In addition to the supposition that the brothers are to become a religious community (absent from the earlier statutes), these constitutions have two characteristics which will mark all later legislation to come from Fr. Moreau's pen: the involvement of large numbers in government and the presence of passages explaining the reason for various practices—for example, spiritual direction and frequent communion.

In drawing up provisional constitutions for the priests, Fr. Moreau was urged by Fr. Mollevaut to build on the constitutions of the missionaries of France which are "practically the constitutions of the Jesuits"—a bit of advice that the founder seems to have followed.[63] The Sulpician also urged him repeatedly to take Saint Vincent de Paul as his model and to study his writings.[64]

The rules and constitutions of the 1840s show a still more extensive involvement of large numbers in government, lengthier presentation of reasons for various practices, a clear conception of the ideal of union and collaboration, a broad vision of apostolic availability for the needs of the Church throughout the world, and a decided ultramontanist leaning. They also exhibit a tendency to go into details.

As an illustration of the presentation of reasons or inspiration for various practices, we can take an article on almsgiving: "The rector and the superiors, whether particular or local, will not content themselves with giving certain indispensable ordinary alms, but full of compassion for the poor, in whom they will see Jesus Christ, they will try in every circumstance to come to the aid of the needy, while remaining, however, within the limits that prudence traces and taking into account the pecuniary resources at their disposal."[63]

That the ideal of union and collaboration was clear from the very beginning of this period is obvious from the circular letter of September 1, 1841, cited at length at the end of the preceding chapter. The apostolic availability of the priests, brothers, and sisters of Holy Cross is also obvious from what was said about the great variety of apostolates undertaken by 1841 and a readiness to send priests, brothers, and sisters, if any were available, to any diocese that needed help.

The ultramontanist leaning of the legislation of Holy Cross appears, for example, in the adoption of the Roman rite throughout the entire Association and eventually even of the diocesan calendar of Rome.[66] As early as the 1838 draft of constitutions, the work of Holy Cross was presented as a service to the various dioceses with dependence not only on the individual bishops but also on the pope as "the center of Catholic unity."[67]

The tendency to detail appears in the fact that particular rules are provided for most of the assignments the religious could have (examiners, sacristans, archivists, doorkeepers, etc.). The rules and constitutions and his correspondence were not the only means the founder used to assure the religious growth of the members of the Association of Holy Cross. In 1848 he published a 394-page volume of *Meditations* for the use of the Brothers of Saint Joseph of Le Mans according to the method of Saint Ignatius. This was only a first draft. In 1855 a new edition would appear—or rather three distinct editions for Salvatorists, Josephites, and Marianites—entitled *The Exercises of Saint Ignatius and Meditations for Sundays and the Principal Feasts of the Year*, almost twice as long as the first edition (749 pages). In 1859 a third and still longer edition appeared (786 pages). The volume was meant for all the religious, although the novices received special attention and their four weeks of spiritual exercises scattered through the novitiate year (eight-day retreats at the start of the novitiate year, before the feast of Saint Joseph, the feast of the Sacred Heart, and the feast of the Assumption). It supplied extensive information on mental prayer and the Ignatian exercises. The first edition suggested extensive readings from the *Imitation of Christ* to supplement the scripture texts. It also offered the "means which Saint Liguori indicates to novices to preserve their vocation."

IV. ROME

The event which would crown the organization of the work of Holy Cross was, of course, to be papal approval. The pope was the "center of Catholic unity," and since by 1845 the Association was already serving numerous dioceses on three continents, the members naturally thought of approval at a higher than diocesan level. The reorganization of rules and constitutions in the 1840s motivated by the need of unified legislation for the entire Association was undertaken with an eye to Roman approval. As early as 1843 Father Moreau had contacted the apostolic nuncio in Paris and had received an encouraging reply: "I have been intensely interested in the account of your works, and I heartily join your worthy bishop [in his favorable 1840 report to Rome] as well as His Eminence Cardinal Polidori [who acknowledged the report] in congratulating you on your zeal and charity, which have already deserved so well of the Church."[68] But Bishop Bouvier did not now want Roman approval and succeeded in blocking it.

Not until 1850 did the repeated attempts to get approval look as though they might succeed. In that year an old friend of the founder, Bishop Luquet, who had invited him in earlier years to India, urged him to make a foundation in Rome.[69] Father Moreau went. His own description of his impressions of Rome are the best indication of what Rome—and therefore Roman approval—meant to him. He shared them with the entire Association as well as with the Association's students in circular letters and

with many individuals in personal letters. On January 1, 1851, he
wrote to priests, brothers, sisters, and students:

> It would be useless to try to share with you the deep and
> lively joy which has been mine since my arrival here in this
> fatherland of all Catholics. To enable you to understand my
> feelings, I should have to tell you all my thoughts and sen-
> timents, not only at the shrine to Notre Dame de la Garde at
> Marseilles where, on November 8, I had the honor of saying
> Mass to beg the protection of the Star of the Sea for our jour-
> ney the next day, but also at the sight of all the marvels of art
> and especially of all the religious monuments which Rome
> possesses within her walls. I would have to describe to you
> over three hundred basilicas, churches, and oratories, en-
> riched with relics which every Christian holds dear. There are
> thousands of masterpieces of sculpture and painting which
> I am unable to describe adequately. Here we behold the mas-
> sive structure of the Colosseum built by the Jews dispersed
> under Titus, where so many martyrs died gloriously.
>
> Furthermore, I should have to tell you of the venerable cat-
> acombs, that immense network of intricate underground
> passages which were sanctified by the bones of the martyrs,
> by the baptisteries, pontifical chairs, altars used by the two
> great apostles and their successors during the centuries of
> persecution. Above all, I should have to make you see and
> hear what I myself saw and heard in the indescribable audi-
> ences with which I was honored by our holy, venerable, and
> beloved Pius IX. I cannot tell you of all these things in detail
> because of the many difficulties connected with this alto-
> gether novel foundation. I must be continually making visits
> or receiving callers, and there is enough letter writing to take
> all my free time if I had any.
>
> There is one place, however, which I must describe for you
> with special care. It is the Aventine, where I am now living

and where divine Providence has called me to inaugurate a work which, though it holds out such bright hopes for the future, has been threatened with failure.

He then went on to describe the church of Santa Prisca and the work he had inaugurated in the adjoining buildings. After touching on several other points, he concluded:

On this occasion, my dear sons and daughters in Jesus Christ, I feel impelled to open my heart to you. Never, since its origin, has Holy Cross found itself in such solemn and decisive circumstances. The supreme head of the Church, the immortal Pius IX, has deigned to study our Association in detail. He has asked to see the plan of the mother house, and it was my privilege to lay it on his table and to put into the venerable hands which had already thrice blessed us and all the members of our Association with a really overwhelming kindness. He has encouraged us in our weakness by granting us spiritual favors, which I shall be happy to communicate to you in due time, and by words which will ring in my ears until death, so deep was the impression which this strong but fatherly voice made upon me. At the very moment that my heart, more than my pen, writes these lines, this venerable pontiff, who has received from Jesus Christ himself the task of feeding all his flock, shepherds as well as sheep, is affording us an outstanding proof of his confidence and interest by permitting one of his own estates to be worked by the children from Santa Prisca under our direction. If in this undertaking we live up to the expectations of His Holiness, we are assured of the approbation of our rules and the official protection of the Holy See. We can have no greater motive for making ourselves worthy of our vocation and of the good will with which the worthy successor of Saint Peter honors us today.[70]

A month earlier (November 26) he had sent to Fr. Champeau, superior of the minor seminary at Orléans, which had been recently staffed by Holy Cross at the bishop's request, a description of his first audience with the pope:

> At last I have just been to see the worthy successor of Saint Peter face to face and listen to his words. He is just as I pictured him, and he received me as I imagined he would last night, when I did not know an audience was arranged for me this evening. There were princes and cardinals waiting. All of a sudden Msgr. de Mérode, who had notified me that the pope wanted to see me in the evening, arrived to accompany me with my package of crosses, rosaries, and medals. He took me in hand, and my heart was beating more violently than ever before. I went in, made one genuflection, then a second, and lastly a third, which brought me to the feet of the holy father. He smiled at me and said:
>
> "Get up, dear Fr. Moreau."
>
> At once my fear left me, and I was at ease.
>
> "Most holy father," I answered, "allow a poor French priest to remain on his knees for a moment before so worthy a successor of the prince of the apostles, and to unburden my soul after kissing the feet of Your Holiness."
>
> "But you already did that at Saint Peter's on the feast of the Dedication."
>
> "A Roman at heart," I added, "and attached to the Holy See in my innermost sentiments and by my theological teaching, I have long yearned for the happy moment when I could express to Your Holiness my profound veneration, and my filial and boundless devotion. I am only a poor . . ."
>
> Here the pope interrupted me and said:
>
> "You are not so poor as you say, for you have been showered with temporal blessings and a crown is reserved for you in heaven."

I was moved to the point of tears when His Holiness forced me to speak by asking:

"You have a large foundation at Le Mans?"

"Three societies in one, holy father—one of priests, another of brothers, and a third of sisters."

"Do your sisters take special care of the poor, and are they engaged in very lowly works?"

"Yes, holy father, this is the principal reason for their foundation."

"Do your priests teach and preach?"

"Yes, holy father."

"How many brothers do you have?"

"A little over two hundred, holy father. I brought four of them with me and they are now at Santa Prisca."

"How are things going at Santa Prisca?"

"They are beginning to get organized, but I thought it well to tell the commission that it would be a good thing to add agriculture to our trades."

"'You are right, and I regard that as very important. . . . And you had nothing when you began your congregation?"

"That is right, holy father, but to date I have spent more than two million francs all told, including expenses for the Good Shepherd Monastery at Le Mans. The mother superior gave me a modest offering for Your Holiness, and some other persons and our students gave me these two hundred francs. Will you allow me, holy father, to leave them on your desk?"

"Yes, but I shall give them back to you for Santa Prisca."

"Oh, I would much prefer to be allowed by Your Holiness to say that you kept them."

"Very well, then, I shall keep them."

Then a moment later he said with a big smile: "And now I give them to you for Santa Prisca."

When I insisted that I did not want to take them, he said: "Popes receive only in order to be able to give."

At this moment the pope rang for his chamberlain and told him: "I want to give something to this good Fr. Moreau for his work in Rome." Then the pope handed me five thousand francs in bank notes to be invested in railroad stocks, with both the principal and the dividends being turned over to Santa Prisca.

After expressing all my thanks, I asked for another unusual favor, namely that of a daily privileged altar for the chapel of our conventual cemetery. His Holiness granted me this favor over his own signature. I then showed him the plan of Our Lady of Holy Cross. His Holiness examined the road leading to our privileged cemetery chapel and asked me if there was water enough for the whole property. When he learned that there was a steam pump carrying water everywhere, he said:

"That is fine," and then added: "but all that is communism!"

"Holy father, that is what I told the workers of Le Mans when they wanted to loot us in 1848. When I showed them Our Lady of Holy Cross in detail, they set up guards all around to protect us."

The pope laughed and called Msgr. de Mérode. I had already been there a half-hour, and it seemed to me that I was chatting with a father talking to his son. I had him bless all my objects of piety, and bent down to kiss the feet of the holy father, but he held out his ring instead. I went away all impressed with the holiness of this good pope and hurried off to tell Prince Borghese and Duke Torlonia about my audience. Both of them were delighted.[71]

On December 22 he wrote:

I must say that most unusual and almost mysterious things have been happening to me here. A few days ago one of the vicars general of Paris, Fr. Eglée [who had traveled with him from France], saw my worn-out hat, pounded it down with the handle of his umbrella, and put a new one on my head. Today the pope took away my rabat. I was at dinner with Msgr. de Mérode when this excellent prelate told me laughingly: "The holy father intends to take your rabat away from you and he wants it this evening. Let's be on to the audience!" I followed him across the numerous and richly furnished halls of the palace, leading to the simple apartment serving the successor of the prince of the apostles, the vicar of Jesus Christ. There passed before me a large family, part Catholic and part Protestant, which had just come from kneeling before the holy father, and I saw eyes still red with emotion and moustaches still glistening with tears. My turn came, and I entered. I made the first customary genuflection, and the holy father exclaimed: "Ah, there is Fr. Moreau! Have you brought along your brothers and your orphans?" I hurried through my three genuflections so as not to keep His Holiness waiting. But he advanced, put his two venerable hands on my shoulders, and said with a laugh: "I assured Msgr. de Mérode that I would take your rabat away; so I want to take it off you." As he spoke, my rabat disappeared, and I saw it lying on the holy father's desk, while he continued to enjoy the scene. They told me that the next day I would receive a little collar, like the one worn by Saint Vincent de Paul, and they would be happy to see it worn in the future by myself and my religious, including the brothers. What do you think, my good friends, of an incident like that![72]

The founder explained in Rome how matters stood with the bishop of Le Mans but was nevertheless given solid hope for an early Roman approval.[73] To hurry the approval along, the general chapter of 1851 not only elected Father Drouelle superior of the

Roman foundation but also named him procurator general with the task of working for papal approval for the Association.

V. FATHER SORIN

As noted above, the 1840s saw the beginnings of Fr. Moreau's first really serious conflicts occasioned by the work of Holy Cross. Chief among these were those which he had with Fr. Sorin and Bishop Bouvier.

Fr. Sorin had joined the auxiliary priests in 1839 at the age of 25 about a year after his priestly ordination. The next year he was one of the first four priests to profess religious vows on the same day as Fr. Moreau did. One year later, at the age of 27, he left Le Mans with six brothers to become superior of the Holy Cross foundation in Indiana. Fr. Moreau had chosen him as the most capable man he had. Fr. Sorin had had relatively little formation to the religious life. He left when the organization of the Association of Holy Cross was still incomplete. He gave himself fully to the land of his labors, even becoming an American citizen and developing an outlook that fitted nineteenth-century America perfectly. After difficult beginnings, he saw the work of Holy Cross prosper marvelously under his direction at Notre Dame du Lac. He was much more "self-reliant" than Fr. Moreau.[74]

He went to a diocese where the bishop wanted a mother house like Holy Cross and apparently thought Fr. Sorin would agree.[75] Fr. Moreau asked Fr. Sorin to try to maintain his dependence on Holy Cross, but he left this crucial decision to the young priest's judgment since he could not judge the situation from Le Mans. Fr. Sorin decided on dependence, and Fr. Moreau wrote to the bishop accordingly.[76] He then sent additional personnel to Notre Dame in 1843, 1844, 1846, and 1847.

The superior of the Indiana foundation began early to admit candidates, make expenditures, and build, and even to issue notes on Holy Cross without previously notifying the mother house, much less requesting the required authorizations. Nor did Holy Cross receive complete accounts or budgets.

Fr. Sorin wrote he was sure that Fr. Moreau would approve admitting candidates. The financial irregularities are not surprising when we find that as late as 1852 the general chapter could complain that it could not vote on an annual budget because it did not have sufficient information from any house of the Association except the mother house![77] Fr. Sorin's neighbor to the north, the Canadian foundation, was criticized for "very irregular administration" in the general council minutes of November 14, 1849. The cause of this kind of administration is certainly not to be sought in Fr. Moreau's negligence: he repeatedly warned against improper account-keeping in his circular letters. Perhaps he could have used more vigorous sanctions to enforce his directives.[78] But it would seem that the annual general chapter could have done something about this too!

When Fr. Moreau called him to order, Fr. Sorin replied rather sharply. The higher superior replied by insisting on his confidence in the superior of the Indiana mission but demanding that the latter obtain required authorizations. He repeatedly affirmed this confidence[79] but also repeated his demand. At times the tension was great.[80] Nevertheless, Fr. Moreau made Fr. Sorin particular superior of the sisters in view of their becoming religious in the New World and wrote: ". . . you are absolute master like myself. . . . Arrange everything as you think best, and then tell me about it later."[81]

In 1845 the bishop of Vincennes arrived at Holy Cross, and an agreement regulating the relations between the two parties, which Fr. Moreau had tried to obtain from him for three years, was finally drawn up. The bishop had complaints against Fr. Sorin. The council agreed to "trace directives for the Indiana superior" but insisted "that Fr. Sorin's zeal had until then merited only praise and sympathy." Fr. Sorin objected that he had not been consulted but was shown that the agreement had been based simply on what his letters to the mother house had indicated as his desires.

When several letters of complaint against him reached Holy Cross from the bishop of Vincennes and Fr. Theodore Badin, to whom the property of Notre Dame du Lac had originally belonged, the Indiana superior was summoned to France to meet with the rector's council and to attend the major and general chapters of 1846.[82] In the council minutes of May 20, which make somewhat harsh statements against Fr. Sorin's administration, the councilors insist that this "cannot and must not weaken in any way their private dispositions toward a fellow religious toward whom each and every one declares himself personally full of esteem and fraternal affection." The same minutes blame Fr. Moreau for not making known to the administration at Holy Cross all that he knew about the Indiana superior's doings. At this point a bill for nine hundred francs arrived which had been charged against the mother house without authorization by the Indiana foundation! In the council and the chapters, all matters, including the possibility of separation and Fr. Sorin's acceptance of a college at Louisville without authorization from Holy Cross were discussed.

Though everything seemed to have been regulated by this trip, the administration of the Indiana foundation continued as before.[83] Fr. Saunier was sent as canonical visitor in 1847 after Fr. Moreau learned that the Louisville college had been accepted in his name without his authorization and sizable debts subsequently incurred. Fr. Sorin was displeased and hurt and wrote in self-defense. Fr. Moreau replied: "I shall be content with saying that just as soon as your chapter sends me its recommendations on the means of saving you, I shall attempt the impossible in order to get you out of your difficulties."[84]

When Fr. Sorin wrote again that he was thinking of leaving the community and that Fr. Moreau had written to the bishop against him, the rector replied:

> Believe me when I say that I am still sufficiently devoted to you and interested in the work of which you have been the instrument not to forget myself to the point of writing to the bishop against you, and I like to think that there will soon spring up again between us that spirit of harmony which the devil has destroyed and without which no good can be accomplished either at Notre Dame or anywhere else. Try to convince yourself that I will give you back my confidence just as soon as you are ready to follow in the path of our rules and constitutions, and be sure that, notwithstanding our misunderstanding, I have never ceased to love you and to cherish you before God.[85]

Fr. Moreau wrote again on December 4, calming Fr. Sorin's fears that he had been denounced to the founder:

> I have not received, my dear friend, any letter pretending to accuse you of having prevented Father Saunier from fulfilling his office of visitor at [Notre Dame], and I advise you to be on your guard against these calumnies which, after all, I know how to handle, for you must not think that I will take the word of anybody who comes along. I have already told you I will base myself on what the mother superior [of the sisters] and you write to me and on the acts which come from your chapter. Only, on your side, keep to the rules and to my directives as long as circumstances do not justify a modification in the judgment of the most prudent members of your chapter.

Unfortunately, matters were further complicated when at Louisville Fr. Saunier exceeded his mandate and Fr. Moreau had then to repudiate his actions![86] Without authorization from Holy Cross, Fr. Sorin then offered to accept full responsibility for the college and to staff it from Notre Dame. But his offer was not accepted. The general chapter of 1850 decided it had to censure Fr. Sorin for building without authorization and once again demanded detailed accounts.[87]

In mid-1848 Fr. Drouelle was sent as canonical visitor to America. Since he had nothing but praise for what he found at Notre Dame du Lac, good relations between the Indiana foundation and Holy Cross seem to have been restored. Fr. Moreau wrote to the Indiana superior on October 2:

> You must be convinced that I no longer have anything against you in mind or heart, but that I am devoted to you and am confident that you will be straightforward and simple in all your relations with me. For the rest, you could not please me more than by assuring me that there is now greater union and regularity among you because, in fact, the entire future of your work depends on these two virtues. I understand, of course, how difficult it is, when you are still at the beginnings, to avoid those little miseries caused by the expression of offended self-love and violation of the rules. How difficult it is in the midst of countless setbacks to be always patient and even-tempered. I know it from experience, and I feel it more every day. . . .
>
> As for your defection [that is, his intention to leave Holy Cross], I was never really worried because I never had any doubts about your devotedness despite the fact that I felt that I had to blame certain of your acts of administration which seemed to me to deserve it. Be assured then, my dear friend, that between you and me things are now as they were from the beginning, in life and in death, without any distrust.

Fr. Drouelle, however, had not examined the financial situation at Notre Dame, which continued as before. The visitor continued south in late November and, informing Holy Cross only afterwards, opened a foundation at New Orleans—a foundation which would occasion still further tension between Fr. Sorin and Fr. Moreau. Fr. Sorin looked upon the New Orleans house as belonging to Notre Dame du Lac, and Fr. Moreau wanted it to submit its accounts and petitions for profession to Holy Cross through the Indiana house. But he appointed as superior Fr. Gouesse, a religious from Notre Dame who did not get along very well with Fr. Sorin. The subsequent conflict led to Fr. Sorin's declaring Fr. Gouesse expelled from the Association.

The archbishop of New Orleans wrote to France defending the New Orleans superior. Nevertheless, Fr. Moreau named Fr. Cointet of Notre Dame as superior and recalled Fr. Gouesse to France. It was about this time that news reached the mother house of the four brothers that had been sent from Notre Dame to California to take part in the 1849 gold rush, one of whom had died on the way without the sacraments. By this time, it was early 1851. The general chapter scheduled for that summer would be called on to judge all these affairs.

Despite all its difficulties the New Orleans foundation flourished. The orphanage opened there was caring for two hundred children in 1851 and two years later for four hundred.

VI. BISHOP BOUVIER

As we have already seen, some tension had existed between Bishop Bouvier and Fr. Moreau when the two had been at Saint Vincent's Seminary because of the younger priest's ultramontanism. Whether the two men's differences of view lay behind the critical remarks the bishop made to his fellow bishop at Angers after the Good Shepherd conflict is not clear. Nevertheless, it was Bishop Bouvier who in 1835 wanted Fr. Moreau to found the auxiliary priests and to become superior of the Brothers of Saint Joseph.

The bishop's outlook on the work of Holy Cross was very simple. The brothers had been founded by Fr. Dujarié largely because of his own insistence that this means be taken to supply the lack of elementary teachers in the diocese of Le Mans. The diocese also needed a band of diocesan missionaries, and they could well help assure stability to the brothers' congregation. He had no objections to help that might be offered to neighboring dioceses. He saw no need for anything more.

The bishop never abandoned this position. He permitted Fr. Moreau to ask the clergy of Le Mans to help encourage vocations to the brothers even in days of great tension between Holy Cross and the Le Mans chancery, but he never conceived of the priests or of the sisters as constituting societies in their own right like the brothers.[88] Bishop Bouvier was doubtless not happy to see the priests go into educational work, though it is hard to see how Fr. Moreau could have avoided this once he began to develop the school of Our Lady of Holy Cross. How serious the bishop was in his opposition to the opening of a secondary school at Holy Cross in 1838, it is hard to say. Fr. Moreau had offered his resignation. Not only did the bishop not accept it, but he seems to have nurtured no resentment after the opening of the secondary school.

Bishop Bouvier was angered in 1841 when Father Moreau refused to send away a certain postulant, Mademoiselle Philbert, from the Good Shepherd monastery in accord with the desire of her relatives. It is unlikely that the lengthy letter Father Moreau wrote to the bishop's vicar general on February 15 explaining his position dissolved all hard feelings. It presented the specific facts of the case, discussing some of them in detail. It provided a lengthy citation from Saint Alphonsus Liguori's treatise on the religious vocation in which this doctor of the Church not only justified the procedure followed by Fr. Moreau but cited several other saints in favor of it. Father Moreau summarized the quotation and showed that he had acted in accord with the principles it expressed. He said he was not worried how his actions were interpreted as long as his conscience was right before God. He considered one by one the various objections to his way of acting. He concluded: "And there you have more than I should have written to justify myself. I would have spared you these lengthy explanations if I did not value your friendship highly. I cannot tell you how much it has hurt me and how much it still hurts me to see myself in opposition with you in this situation. At least I would like to believe that you will see in what I have done a certain delicacy of conscience and a great amount of frankness."

Accusations against the founder from one of the auxiliary priests who did not want to become a religious led to the bishop's peremptory request for a criticism of their superior on the part of all the priest novices which was to be sent directly to him. This move certainly hurt Fr. Moreau, although the letters, quite favorable to the founder, must have quieted the bishop's qualms.

The request of another priest for a dispensation from his vows in 1842 occasioned more suspicion against the founder on the bishop's part. The priest was certainly unstable at this point in his life, and he seems to have received encouragement from those who were opposed to seeing Holy Cross become a religious community. Father Moreau wrote to the bishop denouncing the "lies" of the younger man and the "deplorable state" in which he was. He concluded:

> What is, then, the source of all the trouble that this poor priest is experiencing? The entire community of Holy Cross would answer Your Lordship, if you consulted them, that it comes wholly from his companionship with those who, despite our rules and the principles of true piety, have never ceased to sow tears and discord. May God forgive them, as I forgive them myself.
>
> What is the remedy? Your Lordship is the judge, and I will carefully refrain from suggesting any. I have been hurt, I am

hurt, and I will be hurt by many another such trial without complaining, but I am nevertheless convinced of the truth of all that I have had the honor to explain to Your Lordship.[89]

In 1843, Fr. Mautouchet, the steward at Saint Vincent's Seminary, had delayed giving Fr. Moreau the annual subsidy of two thousand francs which Bishop Bouvier had promised the seminary would give the auxiliary priests as long as there were at least five of them. After several fruitless attempts to get the money, Fr. Moreau simply sent certain of his bills to Fr. Mautouchet. It was then that he discovered the steward was contesting his right to the money. He wrote to the bishop on July 9, explaining the whole affair and asking whether he had failed in his part of the agreement. Describing the work of the priests, he said: "We have just finished three continuous months of missions, and although some have tried to assert otherwise, the good God has blessed this ministry everywhere." He concluded: "[I understand] now how it has been rumored around the diocese that people wanted other auxiliary priests founded and that, if it were not for Your Lordship, this would have already been done. If I am an obstacle to good, remove me; take away this ministry from me. I will thank Providence, and I will do it without any resentment."

It was becoming obvious that Holy Cross could not count on the support of Bishop Bouvier. He had still not given full approval to the rules and constitutions submitted to him in the late 1830s. Fr. Moreau turned toward Rome. Of course, he would have done it anyway, ultramontanist that he was. On September 25 he sent a report to the nuncio in Paris. The latter sent a favorable answer, suggested that the report be sent to Rome, and noted that it should include a recommendation from the bishop. The bishop's answer to Fr. Moreau's request for this recommendation was noncommittal.

The next month the bishop asked the founder to defend himself against certain rumors. Fr. Moreau wrote, in part, on October 7, 1843:

> Your Lordship asks me, then, if it is true (1) that I tried to turn women away from other communities in order to make them join our Holy Cross Sisters; (2) that I made them think that they were true religious while, in fact, they are only devout oblates; (3) that I gave them the habit with solemnity as if they were true religious? . . .
>
> First of all, Your Lordship, permit me to say to you, as to my former confessor at the seminary, that I would consider myself unfaithful to God, to the work that has been confided to my care, and to my own conscience if I ever tried to influence a vocation, and I can challenge all those who have shown so much opposition to me to indicate a single person, whether a religious at the Good Shepherd or a brother, priest, or sister at Holy Cross, upon whom I had such an influence whether by letter, in conversation, or even by my silence. On the other hand, I could show Your Lordship that many other priests whom you honor with your confidence have not always acted in this way.
>
> Then, Your Lordship, it is good that you know that before training sisters for our needs, I had asked for sisters elsewhere. . . . This may surprise you, but the letter which I have included with this one will convince you of it, and which I ask you to be so kind as to return to me. . . . You will see from this authentic document, Your Lordship, that I did not train sisters for the needs of our establishments until I had knocked to no avail at the door of the communities of your diocese. . . .
>
> Finally, I am accused of giving the impression to anyone who wants it that I established a community of real religious.

On this point too, I can challenge anyone to cite with truth a single person to whom I have spoken in this way. On the contrary, I have pointed out that they were only devout girls and that you recognized them only as such.

It is true that I have given these girls a habit and that the habit is religious if you will, but it is not the habit of any existing religious order, and I thought I could act in this way since I do not know of any civil law or canonical rule opposed to it. . . .

Please, Your Lordship, believe in the purity of my intentions, put more trust in those men and women who love and venerate you and who are only seeking the glory of God and of your episcopate without ever having compromised themselves in anything that could give concern to your administration. Be our father as we want to be your children. Let me accomplish the work of God in peace. Do not trust certain flatterers who deceive you. Let me quietly form our girls and their vocations. . . .

Forgive me, Your Lordship, these lengthy details and the slips I have made in this letter: the nights and the days are hardly enough now for all my occupations, and I hardly have the time to reply to my accusers. I would be so happy to see once and for all that I can count on Your Lordship as on the best and the most devoted of fathers and that I no longer have to fear that distrust and coolness will have a place in your heart, which I would want to spend my entire life consoling and which I would be hurt to see myself obliged to sadden in order to be faithful to the grace of my vocation, or to see, with the best of intentions, a bishop destined to do so much good oppose himself without realizing it to the accomplishment of God's designs!

This letter simply offended Bishop Bouvier, and three days later the founder had to write again:

In what concerns the sisters, before God, I give up all thought of employing them for anything but the service of our houses, since you do not want them to work for the retreats that I was planning or in rectories. As long as you have forbidden me to think of these two things, my conscience is clear, and I have no qualms about the good that might have been done. I beg Your Lordship to be convinced that I say this without any anger or discontent—as long as I will not have to render an account for it in eternity. . . .

I admit that I was wrong in choosing a habit for our sisters without submitting it to you, but since I had acted in the same way for the brothers' habit and there was no objection to this, I quite simply thought that it would be the same thing here. I was wrong. I apologize and promise you that if you permit them to go on wearing it, in the future I will bless this habit without solemnity and in private, not even under the eyes of our priests, brothers, or students, and will do it with the formula found in the ritual, and the sisters will clothe themselves in it in their rooms. . . .

Permit me to add, Your Lordship, that in speaking of flatterers who are opposed to me, I said nothing that I cannot prove; but since, against my intention and my expectations, these expressions offended you, I humbly ask pardon for them.

The bishop was still not satisfied, and on October 12 Fr. Moreau wrote again: "The reply with which Your Lordship honored me demands a final response on my part, and I have therefore the honor to address it to you with all the respect due to a bishop to whom I owe all that I am in his diocese, but also with all the truthfulness that I owe to my position without diminishing in any way the veneration and the gratitude that I have for you." He then went into further details on the bishop's attitude to the brothers' change in habit some years earlier. While showing the truth of what the founder had said, this letter showed that the bishop was wrong. It could hardly have improved the relationship between the ordinary of Le Mans and the founder of Holy Cross.

In February 1845 Fr. Moreau informed Bishop Bouvier that the cardinal prefect of the Sacred Congregation of Propaganda Fide had through the nuncio requested a memorandum on Holy Cross and had asked the bishop to grant the approval of the rules that had been pending for so long. Bishop Bouvier's answer was evasive.

Shortly after this request, the bishop was angered by Fr. Moreau's acceptance of a former seminarian of the Le Mans diocese as a brother candidate. The latter wrote on March 3 explaining his action: "I fear that Your Lordship always judges me severely, and I would be very happy to receive a little encouragement. . . . Permit me to say to Your Lordship with the confidence of a son in his father that I no longer know whether I am acceptable to you or not. However, I will suffer in silence everything done against me. . . ." He then listed the various moves made to block the work of Holy Cross in Le Mans and concluded: "I am sometimes tempted to say with Saint Paul, 'We are the most miserable of all men: to me to die is gain.' Please pardon this outpouring."

The bishop replied on March 5 explaining his position and concluding: "Do not be so quick to judge me and to condemn me." However, Fr. Moreau was convinced that the various points he had mentioned were not merely points of apparent opposition of the chancery to himself, and so on March 9 he wrote taking up each point that he had made and showing why they gave him grounds for worry. He concluded: "Forgive me, Your Lordship, but since I have suffered in silence from certain events that have hurt me deeply and have spoken of them to no one, even at Holy Cross, I needed to let all of this flow from my pen. I am happy now that you are ready to assure me of your affection. . . ."

In October the founder sent the bishop a copy of the *Etrennes Spirituelles* which exposed the Vallon and Sablé affairs mentioned earlier in this chapter and also sent him a copy of his memorandum to the minister of public instruction.[90] The bishop was angry and answered on October 27: "As soon as I learned of your memorandum and of your *Etrennes*, my dear superior, I could only regret these two publications. I know that some highly positioned persons are very much worried about them. In what concerns me, I am as displeased as I was grieved that you had the imprudence to publish, without saying anything to me, an account which was drawn up in my name and which was the property of my administration."

In December just before Christmas, the founder was notified that the seminary would no longer pay him the annual subsidy promised the work of the priests because of its own financial difficulties. It was easy to see who was behind the move. Fr. Moreau wrote on December 24:

> Although this is a rather sad Christmas gift for me and mine, I still thank Your Lordship, and the seminary administration too, for having motivated this suspension of subsidy by the financial embarrassment of the seminary and not by other motives in which I would have been more personally involved.
>
> It is true, Your Lordship, that in reading this deliberation and communication, I regretted not to find that the least word of thanks or the least expression that would show that I have not been unfaithful to the conditions that were imposed on me. I trust that I have not hereby lost anything for eternity, and that is enough.
>
> I would, nevertheless, be happy, Your Lordship, to know if you or any of the members of the administration authorized Fr. Paris, pastor of Vallon, to tell Fr. Chevallier Belaunay recently that I was in open opposition with my bishop. Nothing

would make me unhappier than such a statement, and if I were ever unfortunate enough to deserve its being made, I would want immediately to get your forgiveness and to get back into your good graces or to give up all ministry. I know all too well that every priest in opposition or at variance with his superior cannot be blessed.

I also beg Your Lordship to be so good as to tell me whether or not I should conclude from this correspondence that you want us to give up the retreats and the missions which we give every year, since this document which I have received leaves me in complete ignorance on this point, and I certainly cannot remain in doubt about it. For the rest, the least sign of your desires in this regard will be enough for me to continue our apostolic ministry gratis for God.

The bishop replied that he did not consider the founder of Holy Cross to be in open opposition with himself and that he wanted the auxiliary priests to continue their ministry, but he also recalled his anger of the previous October over the exposé of the Vallon and Sablé affairs.

During the retreat which he made as the end of his second three-year term as superior general approached, Fr. Moreau wrote to the bishop:[91]

I feel the need, from the retreat which I began last Sunday, to ask pardon for all that might have offended Your Lordship until now in my words, my writings, and my conduct, acknowledging at your feet that I am nothing but a proud wretch in every regard.

I have a favor that I would like to ask of you and for which I would be most grateful. It is to permit me to have Fr. Chappé elected superior general in my place. I could remain his assistant. I could prepare minds and hearts for the move with prudence and in such a way that it would cause no division.

You would thus greatly oblige him who has the honor to be, while he asks your blessing, Your Lordship's respectful and obedient servant.

The bishop noted on the top of this letter:

I sent my reply from Laval on the sixteenth . . . that he had in fact several times displeased me very much by a way of acting which was unjust to me and in my estimation imprudent in more ways than one, but that I readily gave the forgiveness which he took the initiative to ask and promised no longer to recall what there may have been unpleasant for me in the past, that the request relative to Fr. Chappé demands at least that serious attention be given to it, and that we will speak of it later.

Fr. Moreau replied on May, 19, 1846:

I gratefully accept the pardon which Your Lordship has been so good as to offer me without attempting to justify myself in any way in the undertakings in which I should rather have been happy to experience the contradictions, calumnies, and opposition of which I was the object, instead of complaining of them or growing sad like the proud and ignorant person that I have been my whole life through. That is what would have brought down the blessings of God on the works whose success is ever more difficult for me to understand.

As for the reproaches which were addressed to me by the minister of worship [Bishop Bouvier had asked him to explain this], it is certainly possible that I deserve them because I am capable of anything. But I would like to see Your Lordship get information on my ministry at Rennes from the chancery or from the pastor of Saint Germain. I am ready to recognize as true anything they may say against me and to do so humbly before God. For the rest, here is what I recall having said, word for word, when I preached the passion before the imposing audience: "How many nations can you count that have remained faithful to Jesus Christ? Can you name the religion of their governments? Do they recognize a divine power which rules them? On what terms do they find themselves with the heavenly spouse of the God-man—the church? Is there a single one whose conduct is directed by faith, whose constitution is based on the gospel? . . ."

I do not know, Your Lordship, whether I can be blamed for anything else.

To tell the truth, it would have been well to add the rest of what I said: "The priest is not a man of any political party but rather a man of God, and as far as I am concerned, I am not desirous of seeing among my hearers royalists, liberals, or republicans but only brothers in Jesus Christ who have no other standard but the cross, no profession but that of the apostles' creed, and no other motto than that of the savior: Love one another." And this statement seemed to please everybody.

On June 27 Bishop Bouvier refused the invitation to preside at the closing of the school year at Holy Cross—a refusal which Fr. Moreau considered humiliating and ascribed to the impression made on the bishop by the libelous pamphlet distributed in retaliation for his publication of the facts of the Vallon and Sablé affairs in the 1846 *Etrennes Spirituelles* of that year.[92] The bishop answered explaining that he had refused only because Fr. Moreau's publication had involved him personally and he did not want to seem to be giving approval by his presence at Holy Cross. He suggested that the humiliation could be avoided if Fr. Moreau set the ceremonies for a day when the bishop could not be there.

In 1846 Fr. Moreau was still trying to get Roman approval through Propaganda. The nuncio obtained for him the favor of being named "apostolic missionary," which gave him faculties directly from the pope. This was certainly an attempt to gain prestige in the face of the position of the Le Mans chancery. Then the founder asked Bishop Bouvier to write to Rome on behalf of Holy Cross as he had done in 1840. The bishop did write. But it was such a denunciation of Father Moreau that the Sacred Congregation of Bishops and Regulars replied that no approbation would be forthcoming for the work of Holy Cross.

In 1847 the founder once more had to defend himself. He wrote on April 28:

> Although I resolved long ago to give no reply to all the calumnies of which I am repeatedly the object, I feel I must tell Your Lordship how much I have been hurt by your recent complaint: that I should have committed the blunder of boasting that I opposed Your Lordship and that I should have been considered capable of it because a reckless man dressed in a religious habit said it and repeated it at Laval. Permit me to say, Your Lordship, that even if I were so ill-disposed as to act in such a way, I would certainly avoid boasting of it. Besides, ever since I had the good fortune to have you as instructor in the seminary, you have known my conscience and my conduct well enough to appreciate that I do not so far forget what I owe to my bishop as a Christian, as a priest, and as a religious. Finally, if those who are so determined to calumniate my intentions and my actions have the courage to follow through with their unjust procedures in my regard, I ask that Your Lordship be so good as to have them appear with me before you or that you indicate writings or facts that can be found to support such an accusation. If I wished to depart from my resignation and from the patience which religion imposes on me, it would be easy for me to prove that I have been the object of uninterrupted opposition: I would have numerous witnesses, evident facts,

and, what is more, writings, publications, including the well-known memorandum of Fr. Mautouchet, who certainly had to have a robust conscience to print what was described to me as contained in this document, which I have not yet read, of which he had the patience to correct the proofs, and which will remain as an authentic monument to the bad faith, calumny, and opposition of which I would long ago have been the victim if I had a bishop who did not know, like Your Lordship does, my intentions, my background, and the works of which I have become the all too unworthy instrument. . . .

I sincerely hope that Fr. Mautouchet does not force me to unmask him and his memorandum. I forgive him for it wholeheartedly. I am disposed even to be friendly to him and to all those who have long disparaged me before Your Lordship. I beg you to believe that the greatest cross which I shall have had to bear in my life will be not to have won your confidence enough to convince you that in all my undertakings I have in view only the glory of God, the honor of your episcopate, the salvation of souls, and that I have never departed, either I or my collaborators, from the sentiments of respect and devotion which I owed to a prince of the Church to whom I am indebted for the time I spent at the Seminary of Saint Sulpice, for my elevation to the priesthood, and for the honorable position which I had at the seminary without assuredly ever having deserved this.

At the death of Fr. Dubignon, who had lived at Saint Vincent's Seminary since Fr. Moreau had taught there, a new problem arose, and once more Fr. Mautouchet played an active part. The elderly priest made Fr. Moreau his sole legatee. The founder refused to accept that part of the fortune that would have legally gone to the testator's niece, taking only what would have gone to his sister, who herself was most unhappy about his refusing the niece's portion. The seminary officials were understandably unhappy over not receiving anything, though Saint Vincent's had received numerous gifts from Fr. Dubignon over the years. When Fr. Moreau went to get the deceased priest's effects at the seminary, he was informed that he could not have them until he paid the board that Fr. Dubignon had neglected to pay over the last few years. It was easy to recognize the influence of Fr. Mautouchet.

When the bishop agreed with this decision, it was enough to evoke all the past opposition of the diocesan administration to the work of Holy Cross. In addition, the implication that Fr. Dubignon had been either so irresponsible as not to pay his debts or mentally failing toward the end of his life angered the founder. The episode initiated a correspondence in which the bishop told Fr. Moreau to take Fr. Dubignon's effects, insisted the debt was real, and declared himself offended. On July 29, the founder wrote:

> Because my language offends Your Lordship and your council, I come humbly to make my apologies, asking you, however, to be so good as to indicate the expressions that I must retract and the facts or assertions that I might have advanced without foundation, being ready to disavow them all.
>
> Forgive me, Your Lordship, if I add that the memorandum of Fr. Mautouchet also requires satisfactory explanations, for if Your Lordship admits its language and the facts given there, I should be subject to penalties. If this language and these facts are the expression of calumny, as it will be easy for me to demonstrate at the proper time, I leave it to Your Lordship to draw the consequences.
>
> For the rest, I repeat, Your Lordship, I only ask justice, and my conscience is my witness that I am ready to apologize to whomever I should just as I sincerely forgive whoever tries to harm me or our works whether in your mind or elsewhere.

He added in a postscript: "If I dared, I would request Your Lordship to ask Fr. Mautouchet how he could tell Fr. Gamón, who told it to me, that three Holy Cross priests made the student Morancé come down from the dormitory to my office to have him make the vow of poverty!!"

The impression which Fr. Mautouchet and other opponents of Fr. Moreau had of the founder of Holy Cross did not, of course, remain their secret. Their closeness to Bishop Bouvier only increased the tenseness of the bishop's relations with him. The situation was worsened by Fr. Moreau's distribution of the revised constitutions and rules of 1847 to the religious at the annual retreat at Holy Cross.[93] The bishop had indefinitely postponed approval of the rules and constitutions submitted to him earlier. The Association had submitted a "summary" of constitutions to Rome and had apparently received some sort of praise for them. Fr. Moreau's move in rewriting the rules and constitutions in the light of this "summary" resembles Mother Saint Euphrasia's publication of the Good Shepherd Sisters' Constitution 52 before definitive Roman approval of the generalate. There is this difference, however: some sort of praise had been given to the "summary," while Constitution 52, which was at variance with the already approved constitutions, had been distributed and a vow taken to observe it before it had even been submitted to Rome. There is this further difference too: the 1847 constitutions of Holy Cross did not introduce any particular novelty in the Association's administration except as regards the sisters. But, of course, the Association was recognized as a diocesan community in other dioceses besides Le Mans, and in these other dioceses the sisters had canonical existence.

In any case, Bishop Bouvier wrote an angry letter to the nuncio on September 14:

> Fr. Moreau, appointed by me as superior of a congregation of brothers founded by a pious pastor of my diocese and with my cooperation, founder himself of a society of auxiliary

priests, is not, unfortunately, living up to my expectations. Not only has he been failing for some time to cooperate with me, but in an ever increasing degree he is acting altogether independently of me. I have learned from several bishops that he has made overtures to them to secure their approval for the constitutions he presented to them, but which have not been submitted to me. They have been printed and are being distributed secretly to the members of the congregation with a prohibition against making them known to me. Several times already these constitutions have been changed or substantially modified.

I have been told confidentially, but with certainty, that Father Moreau is trying to get his constitutions approved by Rome and that Your Excellency is the intermediary. . . .

Success in any such negotiations would be a scandal. I do not hesitate to say so. I have too much confidence in the exalted wisdom which guides all the business of Rome not to be convinced that nothing will be done without at least asking my advice.

Although the twelve hundred priests belonging to the clergy of my immense diocese afford me the greatest possible consolations, there are nevertheless certain individuals who are extremely hard to handle and who think they can find protection in Rome. . . .

Assuredly, bishops must be ready to render an account of their administration to their hierarchical superior, but they also need support against the often intolerable pretentions of certain turbulent characters.

As for myself, I try to do nothing which I shall be unable to justify when summoned to do so by the proper authorities. But, conscious of the authority entrusted to me, I cannot allow it to be misunderstood nor, even less, to be belittled in the eyes of my clergy.[94]

Fr. Moreau did not know of this letter, but he was certainly aware of the bishop's coldness. The upshot of the regrettable Dubignon affair was Fr. Moreau's apology sent on September 30 from the Trappist abbey of Mortagne. As usual, he was ready to retract, but a sincere self-examination failed to show him what he should retract. He wrote:

> As I finish my retreat, I sincerely regret that people have suc-ceeded in alienating Your Lordship from me. I have examined myself before God, asking an account of my entire conduct, and I cannot discover any act or any word for which my con-science would reproach me in your regard. I believe, on the contrary, that I and my collaborators have for Your Lordship all the respect and devotion that you deserve. If I am under an illusion, I will be grateful to Your Lordship to indicate to me anything I have done or written or said that I should retract. I wish you could read in my heart, know better the sentiments which are really ours, listen less to certain people whom I forgive with all my heart despite the difficulties they have caused me, and I am sure that you would do us justice.

In October the bishop used two former auxiliary priests and the last priest without vows to leave Holy Cross—Fr. Gauthier—to open a house of diocesan missionaries and then, without even informing Fr. Moreau, dispensed two other Holy Cross priests from their vows so that they could join this group. We have al-ready seen Fr. Moreau's reaction to Fr. Gauthier's departure and the establishment of another group of diocesan missionaries as contained in a letter to Father Sorin dated November 20, 1847: "Would that all Israel might prophesy."

Other incidents occurred that autumn to prove to the founder of Holy Cross that opposition to his work was not limited to Fr. Mautouchet. In view of the opposition he had experienced in Le Mans, Fr. Moreau submitted the rules and constitutions of 1847 to Bishop Bouvier on November 23 with the request that he show them to no one until the two of them had discussed them.[95] He concluded this letter with a renewal of apologies already offered:

> I hope that I shall receive from Your Lordship the consolations of which I have so much need and that you will find in me complete docility to suppress, explain, or add all that the good of the works of which I have become the instrument will require. With this conviction, I feel the need to apologize for the vivacity with which I took the liberty to explain myself to Your Lordship the last time: my heart had been so swollen, so sore for so many years. I dare to hope from your father's heart, Your Lordship, kindness and forgiveness just as I also forgive those who have done me so much harm in your thoughts right up to the present moment and so alienated me from you, whom I nevertheless have always loved and venerated.

A letter of December 14 shows Fr. Moreau delighted by the show of good will on the bishop's part. He wrote: "I am always happy to have been able to open my soul to you, and I will be even happier not to do anything in the future except in agreement with Your Lordship and, if possible, with your vicars."

However, only a few months later he felt that the good will had vanished. He wrote on October 4, 1848:

> In the midst of trials almost too strong for my weakness, I thought that I had taken all the necessary steps to come to an understanding with Your Lordship and your vicars general since the end of December, but you have not seen fit to reply to my visits, to my other initiatives, to my letters, or even to come to confirm our boarders. I have regretted this, and I still regret it, but there is no longer anything that I can do. I am ready to resign from everything as soon as I will be asked, to remain if I am told to do so, or to leave the diocese, even patiently to accept the penalty of not preaching and ministering.

> These, Your Lordship, are my habital dispositions. I will avoid coming to trouble you by a visit as long as I am convinced that my presence is disagreeable to you, but I will not for all that be less respectful or devoted to you.

Shortly before the general chapter of 1849, Br. Leonard had attempted to organize an effort to separate the brothers from the priests. All but a very small number of the brothers approved rather of Fr. Moreau's intention to maintain union. Bishop Bouvier agreed with Fr. Moreau. The founder, delighted by the tone of the bishop's letter, wrote on August 18: "I cannot resist my desire to thank you for the good which Your Lordship's letter has just done to my soul: it seems to me that I have once more found in you all the affection and the interest which God inspired you to have for me when I entered the seminary. Then I loved you and venerated you more than I can say. And so I feel today that these interior dispositions, which have never really left me, revive and give me peace. God bless you."

Notwithstanding this apparent reconciliation, it is easy to see how extremely unwilling Fr. Moreau was to be re-elected for life by that general chapter. In addition to the usual burdens of organizing a nascent work, of forming candidates without a tradition to offer guidelines, of perfecting an institution that had hardly opened, and of correcting mistakes, he had frequent clashes with civil and ecclesiastical authorities, often having to answer gross calumnies. He had years of a rather tense relationship with Fr. Sorin. Above all, he could not really count on the support of his bishop. Then over the last few years revolution and epidemics had troubled not only the work of Holy Cross but the entire western world and the Church. He wrote on September 3 to sisters who congratulated him on his August 30 re-election:

> I thank you, my dear daughters, for your good wishes and prayers on the occasion of my re-election. If it was a source

of joy to you, it was a source of deep sorrow for me and still troubles me very much because of the responsibility that weighs upon my conscience. But I obeyed, resolved to drink the chalice to the dregs, and I find a real consolation in the thought that I have already learned to count on your devotedness. I appreciate all the services that you are rendering to our work and beg God to reward you for them.

In 1850 the final break between Holy Cross and the bishop of Le Mans approached. Fr. Moreau was invited to assume direction of a trade school in Rome. Bishop Bouvier could not doubt that this would encourage Roman approval of Holy Cross. The founder wrote later: "Wishing to dissuade me from going to Rome, Bishop Bouvier told me time and time again as he refused to give me a letter of recommendation, that I was wrong in answering the requests made of me, that I would be tricked by the Italians, and that our undertaking would never succeed."[96]

VII. INTERIOR LIFE

a. Labor and Poverty, Cross

Years of struggle and achievement, of development and consolidation, the period from 1842 to 1851 found Fr. Moreau no less concerned with the humbler and less striking things of earlier years, and especially with prayer and self-renunciation.

Concern with foreign foundations, revised rules and constitutions, and Roman approval (with all the correspondence these things involved) did not impede his continuing, an extensive preaching ministry. For example, his lengthy New Year's circular of 1843 was written, or at least begun, away from Holy Cross while he was preaching three consecutive missions.[97] His preaching was as successful as ever. For example, the Journal de la Mayenne saw fit to publish on March 29, 1845, an account of the close of his lenten preaching at Château-Gontier that year:

The feast of Easter, always so solemn, was never more imposing at Château-Gontier. Praise and thanks to Fr. Moreau who preached our Lent! Made fruitful by a firm and dignified word, by a closely reasoned and unassailable logic, by an attractive and persuasive eloquence, by a really apostolic zeal, this forty-day retreat has produced abundant fruit.

Before six o'clock, Saint John's Church was full of Catholic Frenchmen who had come for Mass and communion. In addition to the hundreds of women who filled the side aisles, there were in the nave more than six hundred men giving evidence of most edifying dispositions. . . .

At the high Mass there were the same crowds, the same recollection, and during the rest of the day Saint John's Church gave very consoling proof that the faith is growing stronger instead of disappearing under the breath of disbelief.

Fr. Mollevaut had warned the founder on September 26, 1844: "I have learned of the different retreats that you have given. You have great need of prudence. Go more slowly and do not try to do everything at once. This is a temptation which gets the better of us after some years of work and then makes us incapable of continuing our function."[98]

His struggles did not warp his Christian perspective. He was ready to undertake foundations in stark poverty, as happened in Algeria (a foundation which always remained extremely poor and often found itself in downright misery), Indiana, Canada, and New Orleans.[99] Of the American foundations he wrote: "There poverty reigns supreme: the food, the lodgings, everything breathes a spirit of want like that of the savior during his mortal life. In spite of all this, at Notre Dame du Lac they have succeeded in building a church which is quite beautiful for those parts, and there are also hopes of enlarging the university buildings."[100]

He was quite content that the religious should be poor with the poor: the brothers had been founded precisely to teach the poor,[101] and his own early dream had been to work in a poor country parish. He provided a frugal life for the religious. Br. Marie-Antoine wrote: "As regards food, during my novitiate we had as much soup as we wanted and then a piece of dry bread. Those engaged in heavy work had, in addition, a piece of white cheese. . . . Our father founder was very wise. In the rules we read, 'Such and such directives hold good for the province of France. In other provinces, the provincials will decide what concessions can be made.' [At dinner] we had two dishes."[102] And Father Vérité wrote to Father Sorin on October 10, 1843:

> Our reverend father took the resolution never to put up any buildings which did not reflect poverty in every detail. He made an exception for the boarding schools where, he said, things must be done on a big scale in order to attract children belonging to the upper classes. [They were the only ones to go beyond an elementary education.] Consequently, he wanted everything at the boarding schools to be on as large a scale as possible, but everything pertaining to the priests and brothers, as regards either the buildings or the furnishings, to breathe the spirit of poverty as is the case with the Franciscans. . . . That is why the building at the Solitude of the Savior, as you know, has followed such modest plans and why at the present time we are building only in plywood at the Solitude of Saint Joseph. Our good father repeated all this to us during our retreat, quoting Saint Teresa, who was so vehemently indignant against big buildings.[103]

He showed concern for poverty to such a point that when he made the canonical visit of the mother house in 1846, he decided that certain decorations in the rector's, that is, his own, office should be removed and that he should have exactly the same furniture as everyone else.[104]

He realized, of course, that despite the frugal life of the entire Association, certain works, especially those in foreign lands, could demand an unusually great selflessness and strength on the part of the religious sent to these foundations because of the privations to be endured there. Hence, he sent only volunteers and then only if he judged them qualified. He even provided for those foundations by a foreign mission vow. The text of the priests' 1845 rule on the foreign mission vow reads as follows:

> Those who judge themselves divinely called to preach or teach in foreign countries where the society has houses will make this known to the rector and with his agreement may vow to go to these houses in so far as obedience permits.
>
> Care should be taken that the members not live alone in foreign countries but at least two together.
>
> Only those are to be sent who have given proof of faith and a devout life, who have demonstrated that they have contempt for the world and whatever concerns the present life, who are so mortified that they seem to be most immune to the body's needs and indifferent to food, rest, or labor, and who, finally, are men of perfect chastity because of the countless dangers to be found in everything, on all sides and at all times.
>
> Let them remember that this is the most challenging ministry of all, in which they may be called upon to live far from their confreres, where there is no one who sees how they act and there are all kinds of temptation from all sides. Hence, if anyone should doubt whether he is called by God, it is much better to fail to answer an uncertain vocation than imprudently to place one's salvation in jeopardy.[105]

As background to this text we might read the observations of Fr. Mollevaut in a letter of December 8, 1839: "For these missions across the sea you need solidly proven religious with a most lively faith, strong character, a right spirit, and tried purity, who yield in nothing to imagination and sensitivity, who do not have a nervous or gloomy temperament. The dangers in these countries are terrible and even fatal because it is hard to find help and counsel."[106]

Fr. Moreau had himself begun to develop these thoughts of his Sulpician director in his circular of January 8, 1841.[107] The 1845 rules were only a further development of them.

The founder saw the trials that came upon the work of Holy Cross as graces. On January 4, 1845, he wrote after having listed the trials of the preceding year:

> These are, doubtless, a goodly number of crosses for one year, not to mention those which from time to time were provided by ill will, lying, and slander. Far from complaining of these trials, we must learn to love them, for if we bear them as we should, they are worth their weight in gold. These nails and thorns will be changed later into the many precious stones which will make up the crown of glory reserved for those who have been faithful to the duties of their vocation, and have worn lovingly, even to the end, their savior's crown of thorns. I do not know what new crosses await us during the coming year. Whatever they may be, let us not forget that the heaviest crosses contribute most to the general good of our work and to the welfare of each one of us. We must bear in mind that since our divine model remained nailed to the cross even to his last breath, we too must desire to stay with our cross even to death. We should not bother about what the world may say of us, for if in one sense we do not deserve its blame, in another sense we have merited it only too well by our infidelity to the inspirations of grace. At such moments let us remember that the life of all the saints was a mixture of sweetness and bitterness and that, according to the expression of one of the most lovable of them all, "the heart of the servant of God is like an anvil made to be struck and to live on blows and outrages."[108]

On January 9, 1848, he wrote: "The important point for us is to accept everything with equal conformity to the will of God.

We should cry out with the pious author of the *Imitation*, 'If you wish, O my God, that I be in darkness, so be it; if you wish that I enjoy the light, again so be it; and if you wish that I be afflicted, be equally blessed.'"[109] He tried to maintain calm throughout the Association in the aftermath of the 1848 Revolution, reminding all that they "should be persuaded that to 'those who love God all things work together unto good.'"[110] His recognition of God's hand in persecution and opposition enabled him to forgive calumniators and to remain without any grudge against those with whom he came into conflict. His correspondence with Bishop Bouvier and Fr. Sorin amply demonstrates this latter point.

Fr. Moreau knew interior trials as well as exterior difficulties. On July 8, 1843, Fr. Mollevaut offered him support:

> You have nothing to reproach yourself with regarding confession and direction, although you seem to yourself never to have done anything except to please yourself and to gain esteem. The good God permits such obscurities and profound darkness to keep you humble. Also, this comes from your temperament and from an unpleasant and gloomy disposition. The only remedy is to follow blindly the advice of your confessor. I know many persons who are in such states of desolation in which they seem to have lost all confidence and hope: it seems to them that peace is forever banished from their heart. This is one of the hardest and most salutary trials to detach us from the world, from ourselves, and from all our works.[111]

There were certainly other periods of darkness and desolation which, like this one, he kept hidden from all except his director. We know nothing of any others until his great trial of 1855.

Trials from within and without were not enough. Fr. Mollevaut had to restrain Fr. Moreau's tendency to corporal mortifications.

On July 3, 1843, he wrote: "You tend by temperament to external mortifications. In your position, you would do better not to perform any that can be seen, such as drinking only water. Live like everybody else so as not to embarrass anybody. In second place, you must take care of your health, especially of your chest and your voice, which are absolutely necessary for you, and if the doctor recommends that you take any particular precautions or that you follow a particular diet, you should obey."[112] The founder's first biographer comments:

> He had long before accustomed himself to drinking only water, and he no longer drank anything else. When the labors of his heavy administration obliged him to curtail his preaching ministry, he found the prudence which his kindly director had recommended less necessary, and little by little he accustomed the community to his absence from breakfast on Wednesday, Friday, and Saturday—an absence which later became, till the very end, strictly regular except on solemn Church days.[113]

On July 8, 1843, Fr. Mollevaut wrote: "You may continue to sleep on a straw mattress: the sovereign pontiff Gregory XVI does as much; only be careful of colds in winter and take care of your voice because you need it."[114] The biographer comments: "For the bed of straw which his director permitted, Basil felt that he could substitute some years later without any danger to his health, the use of a simple easy chair in front of which he set a footstool. He used it until the end except for some months between 1852 and 1854, the time that was needed to heal some leg trouble."[115]

According to Sister Mary of the Cherubim, it was said that Father Moreau slept only three hours a night. She added: "He took the discipline every night; he wore a belt and bracelets with iron spikes on his arms, his shirts were spattered with blood. He was very light-hearted."[116] On September 26, 1844, Fr. Mollevaut wrote: "As for [external] mortifications, you should give them up completely when you are too busy and when your health is not normal. You have enough to do without them—patience, bearing with others, being considerate and kind; it is ill-advised to prefer something else less important."[117] He rarely seems to have considered himself too busy or ill.

b. Prayer and Simplicity, Kindness and Severity

In the face of exterior trials Father Moreau found all the more encouragement to pray and a reason to pray all the more. In introducing perpetual adoration of the Blessed Sacrament into the Association in 1849, he wrote:

> At the first news of the resistance encountered by our army at the gates of Rome and of the spread of the plague which is devastating Paris,[118] it occurred to me to lay before you a plan for the perpetual adoration of the Blessed Sacrament, which I have had constantly in mind for some months past. The aim of this adoration would be to obtain further blessings from God for the Holy See and for the numerous victims of cholera who are hurled into eternity without even having time to make their peace with God. This desire of my heart grew more insistent as the needs of stricken society became more pressing and the family of Holy Cross, even in the midst of so many calamities, received more touching proofs of God's protection. Still, I was unwilling to burden you with new spiritual practices unless you yourselves could see their necessity; it is this necessity alone which can justify what I propose to your spirit and religious fervor. At the present time I feel that I can prescribe this adoration, because I am quite sure that the sad events which we are witnessing have disposed you to accept it.[119]

A few months later, he wrote:

> [In laying before you a plan for perpetual adoration of the Blessed Sacrament,] my aim was to draw down divine mer-

cy on the numerous victims of cholera and, in particular, to preserve our Association from the inroads of this irresistible enemy, whose attack is always so deadly. Since that time experience has proved to us that our confidence in the Lord is not in vain. As I was thanking God for this favor with heartfelt gratitude and resolving to suspend our nightly visits to the chapel of the mother house because of the fatigue which a great deal of extra work was causing our coadjutor brothers, an announcement which was as painful as it was unexpected [the death of Br. Hilarion in Africa and the beginning of the cholera epidemic there] not only made us continue this practice but at the same time reproached me for having heeded too readily the suggestions of human prudence.[120]

Fr. Moreau found many other reasons for continuing the perpetual adoration, and the general chapter of 1849 agreed that it be adopted definitively by the Association.[121]

The intense activity of the founder and the struggles which he faced at almost every step should not leave us with the impression of an ambitious activist always ready to push and force others toward the attainment of his own goals and unconcerned about the work of others. On occasion he contributed his own manual labor to the building of the conventual church. He also joined the coadjutor brothers and the novices at preparing vegetables for the cooks. Br. Victorien recalled:[122]

Very Reverend Fr. Moreau was friendly with everybody during recreation. He could be seen more than once seated on a bench among the novices and coadjutor brothers washing vegetables with them. It was on these occasions that Br. Marie-Benoit, in charge of the vegetables, who came from the same locality as Fr. Moreau and was a little older, took delight in recounting the little pranks which Basil had played on his mother and others in his childhood. The good father was amused and enjoyed a laugh. And we novices, how delighted we were at hearing a story of the escapades of young Basil Moreau.

The recollections of Br. Marie-Antoine include these stories:

The very reverend father was both feared and loved. People went to him for everything; they even took advantage of his kindness. That was because he was so approachable. Here are a few facts to prove it. One day two brother bakers fell to discussing bread that had been baked the day before. "It's fresh bread," said the first. "It is not," said the other, "because it was baked yesterday." "I tell you that it's fresh. . . ." "And I say that it is not." Not being able to agree, the two silly people went off to disturb our good father with such a foolish quarrel; they started their little discussion all over in his presence. He listened to them, looked at them, and smiled. Then he said: "Go make the way of the cross, and if after you still don't agree, come back." They never came back.

Another day a young brother went to accuse himself of having eaten some sugar-coated almonds which he had taken from the table of our good father. "So you like candy? It would have been better for you to ask for them," he said, "but since you like them, take the box. Here it is: that will be your penance."

About the same time another brother had tried to get a letter to him in order to straighten out certain difficulties. This letter never reached its destination, and the brother was very unhappy about it. Our good father, when he heard somebody speak about the thing, went to the novitiate and asked for the young novice, who was very grateful for so much considerateness in this.[123]

Br. Cécilien recalled: "When the novices had the good fortune to have him with them during their recreation—something that did not happen very often because of his many occupations—you should have seen what religious devotion they showed him! His conversation was so interesting and charitable!"[124]

The same two brothers recounted stories that throw light on the accusations of a quick temper and authoritarianism that would be made later. Br. Victorien told of an occasion when Fr. Moreau called the novices together in his room. "He asked to see a little picture or list that was in a little frame, and they gave it to him all covered with dust. The very reverend father, very displeased, threw the frame on the ground, where the glass broke, and thus gave everybody a good lesson in politeness, cleanliness, and respect for superiors."

Br. Marie-Antoine noted: "The very reverend father was authoritarian but not in such a way as to offend. One Sunday at the high Mass, with the church full of people, he told a priest who was having difficulty in his sermon, 'Go get your manuscript.' The young preacher obeyed and then gave a magnificent sermon: everybody was in tears. That was surely a reward for the promptness of his obedience."[125]

He also told the following story:

> One day two religious had gone swimming without permission; it happened that one of them drowned. When he heard the news, the very reverend father had the bell rung and assembled all the religious in the community room. There, with sorrow in his heart, he gave a forceful sermon on obedience and declared that this event was a punishment from heaven for the breaking of the rule. He added: "Because this religious has chosen to separate himself from his community and to die far from it, he will not be buried with the community; further, he will be deprived of the presence of his fellow religious at his funeral; only his unfortunate companion will be permitted to assist." The steward recovered the body of this unlucky man which was then

buried on the other shore. We think that if the good father acted with so much severity in such circumstances, it was to give an example to the community and that for the rest of his life a good part of his penances were offered for that poor exile.

A few excerpts from the many letters he wrote to individual religious will show how far from impersonal his relations with them were.

To Br. Joachim at Notre Dame du Lac, who had fallen ill, he wrote on July 27, 1843:

So, my dear Joachim, you are sick, and I am really heartbroken at not being able to take care of you myself. Nevertheless, I find my consolation in the thought that you will know how to profit by your illness, in order to detach yourself in an ever increasing degree from this present life, and that in your fellow religious and your good superior you will find all the assiduous care which can be commanded by heartfelt charity. May our Lord preserve you still longer for the welfare of his work, and be himself one day your reward.

To Br. Vincent, who was in New Orleans and having difficulty getting the recent foundation there off to a good start, he wrote on June 3, 1848: "How are you, my very dear Vincent? How I should like to see you again! I know that the administration of your house must be a burden to you, but you have obeyed, and from that moment on you are sure of doing the will of God and of being able to count on the help of his grace. . . . If the combat here is rough and difficult, the victory which follows will be sweet and the rest eternal."

In an undated letter some time around the year 1849, he wrote: "How I thank you for your good letter, my very dear Vincent! It goes straight to my heart, which loves you and esteems you more than I could say. So leave me with the hope of seeing you once more and embracing you again before I die."

The Marianites received the same sort of assurances. Fr. Moreau wrote to one of the French sisters, Sister Mary of Calvary, on May 25, 1848: "So, my dear daughter in Jesus Christ, you are sick, worn out with work and disappointment. How that worries me! Send me news of yourself and, no matter what may happen to you, in life and in death count on the esteem, confidence, and affection which I have long since vowed for you."

To an American sister, Sister Mary of the Nativity, he wrote on June 27, 1850: "I thank you for your rememberance, my dear daughter, and I beg you to rest assured that I have as much affection and interest for you as if you had been born in France and trained in the novitiate at Holy Cross. Courage! Be a worthy daughter of Our Lady of the Seven Dolors."

A letter of May 25, 1843, to Fr. Sorin shows how carefully Fr. Moreau knew and followed each individual religious. He sent to the Indiana superior recommendations on each of the members of the little colony that was departing for Notre Dame:

> Br. Eloi can be of great, of immense usefulness to you, but he has to be approached through the heart and often given encouragement. . . . He will be a big help to you as a locksmith. Fr. Gouesse will be just the man you need for music, and I think he will do as good a job teaching. But there is a bit of levity in him, and he needs the help of someone who will direct and admonish him. In any case, he should never be ordained without my agreement. Fr. Delacoux Marivault is a very devout priest who can do a good job teaching beginners and can hear confessions according to need; but do not let him go too quickly and direct him. He is good, simple, and devoted. The sister assistant ought to be a little more serious; Mary of Calvary needs a little more openness and simplicity; Mary

of Nazareth, humility; and Mary of Bethlehem, greater obedience; but they are good young women and very devoted.

We find in Fr. Moreau a tension between the desire to answer all the needs of the Church and a desire not to draw attention. For example, in the 1847 *Etrennes Spirituelles* he wrote:

> Up to the present, it had seemed to us that publicity was necessary for the development of our works, which were just beginning; today that motive, which was perhaps illusory, no longer exists. Therefore, we give notice to our associates [of Saint Joseph and the Good Shepherd] that, after having given mature reflection to the matter before God, we feel that we must limit ourselves from now on in these *Etrennes* to an account of our two associations, desiring for the future to practice better the rules of humility which Saint Vincent de Paul traced out for one of his missionaries: "It is very opposed to humility to publish what we are and what we do. If there is any good in us and in our way of life, it comes from God, and it is for him to make it known if he judges it expedient. As for ourselves, who are poor, ignorant, and sinful people, we ought to hide ourselves as being useless for any good and unworthy that anyone should think of us. This is why, monsieur, God has given me the grace to remain firm right up to the present in not consenting to the printing of anything that would make our company [the Congregation of the Mission] known and esteemed, although strong pressure was brought to bear on me."[126]

In 1851 Fr. Moreau discontinued this publication. What the founder wrote to Br. Vincent in America during Fr. Sorin's visit to France in 1846 sums up excellently the greatest preoccupations of the founder as the work of Holy Cross seemed to be growing strong and taking definitive shape under his direction:

It is certainly true, my dear friend, that we are all miserable sinners deserving only of the gallows, after so many graces and so little progress. But fortunately we have to do with a God who knows the clay from which we have been made. So then let us strive to be what we will want to be at death, for our life is slipping by. Let us apply ourselves to practicing the presence of God, patience, recollection, and silence. Without these we will never be more than shadows of religious. Besides, we will succeed in doing good only to the degree that we become saints. Above all, fidelity to the rules, no useless running about and gossiping, no direct and overly friendly relationships with the sisters, poverty, simplicity, mortification. There, my good friend, is what we should be concerned about. I thank God for having sent me your good superior so that I can address him of all your spiritual needs, which are more urgent in my eyes than those of the body. . . .

I wish I had the happiness of seeing you again! At least, let us plan on being reunited in heaven, and to that end let us imitate the saints and be united to our Lord.[127]

c. Impressions of Others, Fr. Mollevaut's Last Advice

Something of the impression that Fr. Moreau made on others can be grasped from the description that Louis Veuillot left of him in 1846:

He has . . . the manner of one of those peasant priests from whom you do not really expect very much, and this impression is hardly offset by his Le Mans accent, in which he makes statements of the greatest simplicity. Thirteen years ago he had already been professor at the major seminary for twelve years and more, for he is getting near fifty. That sort of life, in which you must always repeat the same lesson, did not seem very useful to him; he had other projects. He left the seminary without a sou in his pocket and hardly knowing where he was going to sleep. Today he has spent more than 1,300,000 francs and has property worth two million; he still has not a sou in his pocket, but neither has he a sou of debt.

He founded a society which is called the Association of Our Lady of Holy Cross. It is made up today of 15 professed religious [priests], of 150 brothers who have about 50 establishments in France, and of a considerable number of sisters. He has established near his mother house a monastery of the Good Shepherd which cost him 600,000 francs. He has a considerable mission in America at Notre Dame du Lac, in the State of Indiana, whose superior, Fr. Sorin, is a very distinguished young religious. He has built two beautiful convents and is finishing a Gothic church where there are fourteen chapels.

After you have spoken with him for a little, you see that he has eyes full of delicacy, a mind which is simple, solid, and fertile, a heart eaten up by love. He is a man of noble character and a saint.

God has supported him wonderfully. Here is a little story he told me. In the early days, when he was just beginning to build, he once realized that he had a bill of 1400 francs to pay the next day and no money at his disposal. He went to hear confessions as usual, and at seven o'clock found himself with the thought that, if he did not pay, he would become the laughingstock of the town, where he was already considered a fool, and that his works would be finished. He resigned himself and went off to make a visit required by politeness to a woman who was interested in philosophy. She spoke to him about her interests. Without asking her for anything, he let her know of his embarrassment. She gave him a thousand francs. He took them, astonished at this windfall, and went off saying to himself, "I still need 400 francs." He got home. The first thing that he saw on his desk was the sum in four neat piles of coins carefully arranged and exactly counted out. Who had brought the sum? The brother cook told him that it was a gentleman whom he did not know and who had not given his name. No one ever could find out who the donor was.

The same woman, the one with the thousand francs, without giving up her philosophy, was an instrument of Providence on a second occasion. At the Good Shepherd they were in great embarrassment over certain bills that totaled about 10,000 francs, which they did not know how they were going to pay. The superior had the poor children whom the house had taken in make a novena to Saint Joseph. When the novena was finished, this woman put in an appearance and asked that they give her the house's bills. They did so. She paid them, and she left a good supply of wheat besides. "And this woman was not a Christian?" I asked. "No . . ." "Let us hope that God will convert her." "He has already begun," Fr. Moreau said to me smiling.

I had Fr. Moreau and Fr. Sorin for dinner at my home on May 3 [1846].[128]

In a letter to his wife, Veuillot speaks of Fr. Moreau: "I received from good Fr. Moreau of Le Mans a nice little letter, in which he sends his compliments to you. I am going to preserve it with great care, for he is a good man who is going to be canonized. Our grandchildren will be delighted to find this letter in the papers of their grandfather."[129]

Fr. Mollevaut had at his own request left Issy in 1837 at the age of 64. From the Sulpician seminary in Paris, he had continued to correspond with Fr. Moreau. In 1849 the first symptoms of the breakdown which was to be the supreme trial of his life appeared, and he began to prepare for death, which did not come until 1854.

The last of his letters to Father Moreau which are still extant date from 1846. They are most relevant to what lay ahead for the founder of Holy Cross.

On January 25, 1846, the Sulpician wrote:

> It is no longer a matter of politeness between us; bonds formed by pure charity do not break. I know your sentiments: mine are known to you. Often I speak of you and of your works. There is nothing that interests me more in the holy Church. And if I needed any other motive, it would be the difficulties that you encounter, which are the touchstone of divine providence. It is impossible to want to do anything generous for the glory of our adorable master without meeting with contradictions and oppositions from every side, even from those from whom we would least expect it—we must never count on human means. When you read the history of associations, you see that many of them were on the point of being overturned by attacks from within and from without. Fr. de la Salle and Saint Liguori experienced it to the very ends of their lives.[130]

The founder's first biographer cites this text in part and adds:

> Saint Liguori was no stranger to Fr. Moreau. After having learned to follow him as his preferred master in theology and after having advocated his doctrine at the Le Mans seminary as far as prudence would permit at this period, he had made a close study of this illustrious founder; he used to propose him repeatedly as a model for his priests, having them read assiduously the Memoirs on the Life and the Congregation of the saint by Fr. Tannoia, one of his disciples.[131]

On May 18, 1846, Fr. Mollevaut wrote:

> I was finishing my retreat when you were beginning yours. At my age it is more than time to practice the "Be ready." What you ask for yourself, I daily feel greater need of, and so we will pray for one another. Your little acts of humility are always good, and they give good example. It is only this virtue and poverty that keep communities going. On every side missionaries are being demanded; there is an immense good to do. You have a few vocations, but much less than you need. . . . But here too you must simply wait on divine providence and thoroughly put to the test those that offer themselves. Where are we going to find self-denial, humility, and obedience? Often the candidates are numerous enough, but a single one is enough to cause immense evil in a community. That is why St. Vincent de Paul was so hesitant about receiving candidates, and despite that, he was tricked. It is especially on the missions that you need religious such as you will hardly find. Prayer is the great means; the Lord must build the house and set into it the stones that are needed.[132]

The early biographer explains that in 1848 the elderly director told a seminarian at Saint Sulpice who had brought him a message from Fr. Moreau: "Fr. Moreau does great things; heaven is with him because he is humble."[133]

At their last visit Fr. Moreau told Fr. Mollevaut: "Now, Monsieur Mollevaut, you no longer have anything to do but practice the advice that you have so often taught: Love to be unknown and taken for nothing." The Sulpician answered: "My dear friend, that is not what you should say; [instead,] say: and to be taken for a fool." The biographer comments: "This was the final lesson of all his direction which the founder of Our Lady of Holy Cross would never forget. . . . To practice it without faltering, he had in Canon Jean Fillion, his confessor, a sure and affectionately devoted guide" to replace the aging Sulpician.[134]

CHAPTER 6

CULMINATION
(1851–1860)

The years 1851–1860 marked the culmination of Father Moreau's efforts to build the work of Holy Cross.

I. APOSTOLIC WORKS

In France the founder obtained legal recognition of the Good Shepherd monastery and almost obtained it for the Institution of Our Lady of Holy Cross and the brothers' society, which had still been unable to gain any recognition outside Algeria except as a charitable association for elementary education in La Sarthe and neighboring departments. Both these efforts deserve attention.

Fr. Moreau had never ceased to take seriously his responsibilities as superior of the Good Shepherd monastery. The detailed ordinances of the canonical visits he made every year and his work with the associates of the Good Shepherd are only two illustrations of this.[1] For the associates of the Good Shepherd and of Saint Joseph, he published the *Etrennes Spirituelles* from 1841 until 1851. Each year he provided them with a retreat, usually preached by an outstanding missionary. The founder's first biographer writes: "At each retreat there was a special conference for the men, and every year some of those who made it, and whose social position provided an example to others, edified the population by their return to their religious duties."[2] Through the associates or through contacts of his own, Fr. Moreau collected ample money to keep the monastery functioning smoothly. By 1850, 578 persons had been cared for by the sisters.

Because the monastery had no legal existence, the superior had to hold all its property in his own name. He attempted to gain legal recognition in 1842 without success; in 1850 he thought that renewed efforts might succeed. For two years the prefect of La Sarthe, whose wife was head of the Association of the Good Shepherd, attempted with the support of Bishop Bouvier to get the government of the Second Republic to grant the desired recognition. It never came. Just after the coup d'état of late 1851, Louis Napoleon transferred the right to grant authorization to religious congregations from the legislative to the executive power, and on March 6, 1852, the legal recognition was granted.

The struggle, however, did not end there. The transfer of property from his name to the monastery demanded the payment of a fee of seven thousand francs,[3] which Father Moreau did not have and the monastery could not afford. In May 1854 an imperial decree freed the monastery of this payment.

After obtaining legal recognition for this work, Fr. Moreau thought he might succeed in obtaining it for the brothers, who were now active in France far beyond the department of La Sarthe, and for the mother house, since the bulk of the property held by the civil corporation of Holy Cross was still his. The prefect and the local municipal council unanimously recommended that the recognition be given, and the petition was sent on to Paris. But this time Bishop Bouvier was opposed.[4] The recognition was not granted.

The educational work of Holy Cross continued to develop. As an aid to the religious education which the brothers gave, the founder published a 234-page Collection of Hymns for the Use of the Josephites, many of them composed by himself over the years. To improve the brothers' work of elementary education in general, he published his *Christian Pedagogy for the Use of the Josephites* that same year—a text of 154 pages. To this text he appended the hymns, which were also published separately, lengthening the volume to 351 pages. Presenting it to the religious he wrote:

Let us join to truly religious conduct a love of work and especially of study. This point is of fundamental importance for
our educational establishments. . . . It was precisely in order to learn the educational situation in our community and
to be provided with specific information on their methods
of teaching, their textbooks, etc., that I sent out forms to be
filled in by the superiors of our schools or by the prefects of
studies. . . . These considerations gave me the idea of preparing a treatise on Christian pedagogy for use in all our elementary schools. I was obliged to do this work in haste because of
my imminent journey to Rome, but I intend to revise it after
receiving your suggestions.[5]

His biographers describe this work as follows:

This volume . . . sets forth all the educational ideas dear to
Fr. Moreau, such as his concern over the deepening of both
the soul of the teacher and the students. He makes the point
that no one can become a teacher overnight. To be a teacher,
one must have a vocation. . . . If spirituality, as St. Paul says,
is useful for everything, how . . . necessary it is for the work
of education! . . .

Spirituality must . . . be joined with knowledge. On this
point Father Moreau was most exacting. From his religious
he demanded a higher degree of knowledge than from others, and he also wished to see in them an insatiable desire to
learn more and a genuine understanding of good study habits. From the pedagogical viewpoint, he stressed the necessity of clear ideas, exact definitions, and a language which

would be simple and easy while not failing to be correct. This also called for zeal. . . .

The teacher must be strong and demonstrate prestige through a prudent spirit of reserve. . . . The teacher must be ever watchful. . . ., patient, careful not to show anger which invites ridicule and is a source of scandal. . . .

There is a further chapter in which . . . the author takes up all the different types of children found in school: the spoiled child, the dull child, the proud child, the stubborn child, the insolent child, the jealous child, the spiteful child, and the mischievous child. He also treats of the problems presented by the frail child, pointing out special procedures to be adopted by the teacher in regard to all these categories. Most of the time this technique is presented under its positive and encouraging aspect, which is summed up in the principle that the teacher must get the most from the fine qualities found in these students.

The school building itself is to be spacious, its dimensions according to regulations, the classrooms well lighted, and the school furniture comfortable.[6]

This work was intended to improve the quality of education given by the religious; a thorough review of educational practices had been initiated in 1853. On January 2, 1855, Father Moreau had written to the religious:

To implement my desire that the Josephites prepare the textbooks to be used in their own schools, I hereby put the [teachers'] conferences at Saint-Berthevin, Meslay, and Saint-Pierre d'Entremont in charge of whatever concerns arithmetic; to those of Vendôme, Poncé, and Marannes is assigned the field of grammar; and the conferences of Montjean, Arpajon, and Ernée will see to the elementary texts. The secretary of each conference will briefly summarize his work in the form of a treatise, and at the mother house, the committee composed of Brothers Grégoire, Philippe de Néri, and Philippe, with Father Champeau as chairman, will be entrusted with the definitive revision of the work of these conferences.[7]

In 1856, he also wrote:

Thanks to the able direction of our local prefect of studies the secondary instruction given in our school at Holy Cross is most satisfactory. A sufficiently clear proof of this is the success obtained by four of the students who received their bachelor's degrees in letters or science. As to the results of the teaching in our houses abroad, insufficient information prevents us from formulating any judgment. But there is urgent need, it seems to me, of remedying a weakness which could easily prove disastrous to our teaching. I refer to the training of well-formed professors with advanced degrees who will be prepared not merely for the ordinary instruction required in our schools but for the direction of higher studies as well.[8]

Insisting on the need for textbooks, he wrote: the few scattered works which have been produced do not realize "the plans that I set forth in [earlier] letters. Consequently, I renew even more insistently all my former directives and in order to provide for the formation of more efficient teachers, I hereby suspend all new foundations. At the same time this step will permit us to bring back periodically to the mother house those members who are in need of further studies, and will enable us to train them in those common principles which make for uniform teaching methods." How professional the approach to education was within the Association appears from the extensive literary activity of some of the religious, who produced books which were used widely outside the Association.[9]

It was especially the latter half of the 1850s that witnessed the development of the works of Holy Cross in France. In 1856 Father

Moreau announced that Holy Cross numbered 648 members (72 Salvatorists, 322 Josephites, and 254 Marianites) and was operating 114 houses or works, educating 10,000 students.[10] At that time Father Moreau was investigating the possibility of merging with the much smaller community of the Augustinians of the Assumption founded by Father Emmanuel d'Alzon.[11] This merger never took place because Fr. Moreau was unwilling to accept for Holy Cross the obligation of chanting common prayer because it would disrupt ministry, and Fr. d'Alzon did not appreciate the advantages of an autonomous society of brothers. However, for most of the negotiations the founder of of Holy Cross saw no difficulty in the various necessary adaptations he would have had to make in the work of Holy Cross, including the adoption of the rule of Saint Augustine, which he knew as the rule followed by the Good Shepherd Sisters and which might have influenced his important 1858 rule on community spirit. What drew him was the possibility of a more effective ministry because more religious and more resources would be available. The next year again, a merger was considered with the tiny community of the Missionaries of Our Lady of Hope at Saint-Brieuc in Brittany.[12] In 1858 the fusion took place, and Holy Cross assumed responsibility for their flourishing school at Saint-Brieuc.

Early in 1856 an offer had come from La Souterraine to operate a sizable school equipped so well that it would doubtless be possible to open a novitiate in a short time. The offer was accepted. That same year, after some hesitation, Fr. Moreau had accepted the donation of the Maulévrier property and château in the diocese of Angers. To this magnificent site he transferred both the boarding school and the novitiate which Holy Cross had established nearby.

Also in 1856, after even longer hesitation, Holy Cross assumed direction of a school in Paris operated till then by a former religious of Holy Cross. Fr. Champeau became superior, although he had failed as an administrator in the early 1850s both at the minor seminary at Orléans and at that of Nevers. In 1857, however, the general administration decided that it could no longer retain responsibility for this institution. Fr. Champeau's pleas, made when the founder was in Paris on his way to America, dissuaded Fr. Moreau from closing it; "the good superior general, separated from his council, could refuse nothing, provided his conscience did not place him under strict obligation."[13]

Finally, in 1856, Ms. Dubignon, sister of the priest whose will had caused Fr. Moreau so much trouble in 1847, died, and the founder learned that her will constituted him her sole heir. The will was so explicit and vigorous that Fr. Moreau felt that he had to accept.

In 1858 Holy Cross agreed to administer a house of missionaries at Rheims, and the next year the recently professed Fr. Clovis Bolard was named first superior.

The years 1851–1860 were also years of extensive development outside France.

In November 1851 the founder was asked to send religious to the local church in Dhaka in Eastern Bengal (now Bangladesh). Not before the following November could the first group leave Le Mans. Four years later the Sacred Congregation of Propaganda Fide entrusted full responsibility for this local church to Holy Cross since no one else would accept it. Fr. Moreau explained this acceptance later:

> I have been blamed by some for accepting this mission on the grounds that all the other congregations had refused it and that no good can be done there. To this criticism, I have replied, as in similar circumstances I shall always reply, that my principle with regard to foundations is neither to ask nor to refuse anything when all indications seem to point to a plan of Providence. Could I have any greater certainty of such a plan when, to Msgr. Oliff's repeated requests for

> missionaries, was added the desire of the Holy See, as formally expressed by the reply made to my observations by Msgr. Barnabo, then secretary of the Sacred Congregation of the Propaganda and now its cardinal prefect?[14]

During these years, additional houses were opened in America and in Italy, and a foundation was made in Poland. Serious consideration was given other foundations in European countries and in Argentina, Palestine, India, and Australia.

By 1857 the work of Holy Cross had literally spread across the world, and the spread had been so rapid that the founder had to declare a moratorium on foundations to allow for the strengthening of those which had already been made.[15]

II. CONFLICTS AND SUFFERING

The years 1851–1860 also witnessed the papal approval of Holy Cross—but only after a vigorous struggle with Bishop Bouvier and after certain changes introduced into Fr. Moreau's original plan for the Association at the request of Rome. Before reflecting on the changes introduced and the results of papal approval, we must examine the struggle between Bishop Bouvier and the sufferings caused to Fr. Moreau by the foreign foundations.

a. Bishop Bouvier and Papal Approval

During his visit to Rome at the end of 1850 and the beginning of 1851, Fr. Moreau had written several letters to Bishop Bouvier of the warm welcome accorded him in the Eternal City and the suggestion of various Vatican officials that he get his rules approved. He tactfully suggested that the bishop might help.[16] In his letter of December 6, 1850, he noted that someone in Rome had praised Bishop Bouvier: "'There is a very keen theologian,' he told me in poor French"—a text which is probably the closest approach to flattery in all of Fr. Moreau's writings.[17]

Once it became clear that Rome was favorable to the work of Holy Cross, Fr. Moreau's attitude toward Bishop Bouvier began to change. Although he sincerely desired to maintain good relations and dependence, opposition from the bishop of Le Mans was less likely to trouble his conscience: a higher authority than the bishop's had spoken.

In 1851 Bishop Bouvier held a diocesan synod. Before it convened, many members of the clergy began pressing insistently for total adherence to the Roman rite throughout the diocese and for the abandonment of all remaining liturgical usages proper to the Gallican rite. In the eyes of many, Gallican liturgical usages were symbolic of Gallican theology. The bishop's theology was, of course, Gallican, while that of the founder of Holy Cross was thoroughly ultramontanist. Needless to say, Holy Cross stood completely for the adoption of the Roman rite. To make matters worse, it was at this touchy moment that the orthodoxy of Bishop Bouvier's textbooks came into question and talk of a Roman condemnation began.

The different attitudes which these two men had toward Rome became even more sharply divisive when on May 2 Fr. Moreau had published a circular which suggested early Roman approval for the Association in a hardly veiled way.[18] On December 8, the day after Louis Napoleon's coup d'état, he published another, giving a lengthy description of steps taken to obtain approval, noting that the Sacred Congregation of Propaganda Fide would assume the responsibility, and practically promising the approval within a few weeks.[19]

At the start of 1852, Bishop Bouvier was in Rome to forestall the condemnation of his theology texts. On the way he stopped in Paris and complained to the nuncio over the transfer of the question of the approval of Holy Cross from the Sacred Congregation of Bishops and Regulars to Propaganda.

The bishop's attitude toward the founder became more and more evident from incidents like the following. After returning from Rome, he summoned Fr. Moreau one morning at seven o'clock to reprimand him for wearing the Roman collar and for not having made the annual New Year's courtesy visits to his two vicars general. Fr. Moreau replied that he had made the visits but had not been received! As for the collar, the pope had told him to wear it!

A letter of Fr. Moreau to Fr. Drouelle on April 23 shows how strained the relations between the bishop and the founder remained: Fr. Moreau wrote that the prefect of La Sarthe intended to obtain legal recognition for the entire Association of Holy Cross despite Bishop Bouvier's opposition. The bishop's opposition, however, proved an effective block.

In May Fr. Moreau learned that Pius IX had definitively entrusted the cause of Holy Cross to Propaganda despite the bishop's disapproval. He also learned that one of Bishop Bouvier's vicars general had told the prefect of La Sarthe that the bishop intended to go to Rome to block the approval of the Association. His informant was the prefect himself!

Fr. Moreau often did not know how to react. When he received an invitation to dinner from the bishop, he asked advice and then left it unanswered! He explained himself on May 8: "P.S. I reopen this letter to tell Your Lordship that in complaining about my not replying to the honor you did me to invite me to dinner, you forget that you did not judge it appropriate to return our New Year's visit and that I would have thought myself lacking in propriety if I had presented myself in that case at your table."

By the fall Bishop Bouvier was angry that two bishops had come to Le Mans in his absence and had visited Holy Cross and that a third, whom he had asked not to preside at commencement exercises there, had nevertheless made a visit.

In November Bishop Bouvier was once more in Rome, where he learned that his texts would escape condemnation if he corrected them but also that any criticism he might make of Holy Cross would produce a very bad impression.

Fr. Moreau was tiring of the persistent opposition of the bishop. He even wrote Fr. Drouelle on November 22 that he was considering resignation.[20] Then he learned from his procurator of a lengthy bill of complaints against Holy Cross which the bishop had deposited in Rome. He answered on December 12: "As for a rapprochement, I am ready to do everything His Lordship can rightfully and reasonably demand, but nothing more: I would rather immediately send my resignation to the pope." On December 13 he sent a lengthy rebuttal of the complaints, which had to include even an explanation of the allegedly omitted New Year's visits of the preceding January. To this complaint Fr. Moreau replied that he could prove he had tried to make the visits by the testimony of the servants who had met him at the door! Then on December 15 he wrote to the bishop regarding the unanswered dinner invitation:

> I beg Your Lordship to believe that if I acted in this way, it was only after having gotten advice and with the conviction that my presence would have been displeasing to you, given the fact that Your Lordship had me come at seven o'clock in the morning to his house in order to reproach me for not having visited his vicars general at New Year's and since, after I had proved to you that I had been to visit each of them . . ., you thought it your duty nevertheless not to return our visit. If in all this I have offended against the respect due to my bishop, I beg Your Lordship to overlook it, protesting that I am disposed to do everything that I can to please you as long as it does not harm the work of Holy Cross, and declaring to Your Lordship that far from holding to the position of superior in Holy Cross, I would be happy to become the last of all—and I

hope actually to do so in a few years because I will shortly be able to show Your Lordship a material situation as satisfying as that of the Good Shepherd and a personnel befitting the Association which I would be happy to see develop no longer outside your protection but under your auspices.

On February 2, 1853, Bishop Bouvier wrote to Fr. Moreau: "You have just sent me for my approval statutes with which I had nothing to do. You should understand that I cannot approve them without having examined them, conformably to the rules of canon law, which I cannot violate. . . . If we reach an agreement, I shall be happy to work hand in hand with you. . . . But if we cannot reach an agreement, then I shall be obliged to refrain from cooperation, as you have forced me to do."[21]

Thinking this an offer of reconciliation, the founder answered on the same day:

In the reply with which Your Lordship has just honored me, I find a trace of your former kindness toward me. This encourages me and gives me the confidence to write you once again. . . : I have less fear that I may be a bother to you because this letter does not demand an answer.

Your Lordship reproaches me with having acted independently, and I am forced to admit that this was so, but it was assuredly to my own great regret and the heaviest of all the crosses that I have had to bear in the works for which I have been responsible. God is my witness that my greatest happiness would be to hide myself beneath your bishop's mantle, to act only in obedience to Your Lordship, and to be the consolation of your episcopate by the submission which I vowed to Your Lordship when I was simply your disciple and your penitent. Permit me to say that if it has not always been this way, I cannot explain it except by a providence which has made use even of my defects to develop this work because for those who love God all things work together unto good, even their sins. I hope, then, Your Lordship, that your father's heart will pardon me for having crossed you whether in creating an Institution at Holy Cross, which is becoming more and more prosperous (148 boarders at present), or in going without your agreement to found what we have in Rome today, or especially in developing outside your diocese the society of sisters which you would only approve as servant girls for our houses and which Propaganda has called to Bengal and to Buenos Aires. What gives me hope that Your Lordship will forgive me for developing the sisters is that, in addition to this tacit approval of the Holy See, they had your approval as servant girls. . . .

For the rest, I feel the need of declaring to Your Lordship that I now place myself at the disposal of your will and that of the Holy See, that far from entering into discussions, I will submit to whatever Your Lordship will decide with Propaganda without writing to anybody, and that you will find me ready to prove to you with what respect and devotion I am Your Lordship's very humble and obedient servant.

That same day Fr. Moreau wrote to Rome:

I had the honor to inform Your Excellency that I hastened to offer my respects to our venerable bishop immediately after his arrival, and that His Lordship has finally promised to examine our fundamental statutes as the letter from his secretary attests, which Fr. Drouelle will have the honor to present to Your Excellency with two others which show that if the society of the sisters was founded contrary to the will of Bishop Bouvier, this was certainly not true as regards its substance but only its form and its developments. But permit me to point out to Your Excellency that if I had wanted to limit myself to the good pleasure of our bishop, the Association

of Holy Cross would not exist because His Lordship was opposed to all of its developments outside his diocese, as he
was to my trip to Rome.

For the rest, I want to affirm that I will neglect nothing
to re-establish good harmony between Holy Cross and the
chancery, although my conscience does not reproach me in
anything as regards the past.

Nevertheless, the reconciliation was only specious. That same
month, Br. Leonard offered the bishop his services to help spread
within Holy Cross opposition to Roman approval.[22] The bishop
visited Holy Cross on March 10, but on March 17 he refused to
hasten his examination of the constitutions so that he could give
his opinion on the desirability of approving them—an opinion
for which Rome had long been waiting. On March 19 the bishop's
secretary preached at the mother house, but at the same time he
wrote to Rome that Holy Cross stood on the verge of bankruptcy.

Fr. Moreau learned of all these moves from Fr. Drouelle, who
received his information from Propaganda. On April 7 the founder wrote his procurator: "The truth is that the only motive which
is holding His Lordship back from giving his approval is the humiliation of having to reverse certain acts which were characterized by blindness or passion and which the Lord has permitted
that no flesh may glory before God."

Finally, on April 9 Propaganda demanded that Bishop Bouvier
submit his opinion on the constitutions. In early May the chancery had to admit that the copy furnished some time before had
been lost and had to ask Holy Cross to furnish the bishop with
another. At the end of May Fr. Moreau learned that, instead of
submitting a report on the constitutions, the bishop had sent another bill of complaints to Rome, including a letter from one of
the religious opposed to Roman approval!

At this point, exasperated, Fr. Moreau forbade the religious
to correspond with the bishop except through him! He submit-

ted a lengthy refutation of the bishop's accusations. He also asked Fr. Drouelle to find out who had sent the bishop the letter against Roman approval: "Try to find out who wrote the letter which His Lordship used when he wrote to the cardinal prefect. I suspect Br. Leonard, who has always collaborated with the chancery, even when it was a question of having the brothers make vows."[23]

Outward appearances were kept up, however. At the end of July Bishop Bouvier was at Holy Cross for commencement exercises. But in October Fr. Moreau was submitting another long refutation to Rome and in December explaining how hard it was to keep the rift between the chancery and Holy Cross from becoming a public scandal. In fact, in view of the increasingly impossible situation, he asked Msgr. Barnabo to persuade the pope to accept his resignation.[24]

Early in 1854 the harassed founder wrote to his procurator: "If the Holy See knew Bishop Bouvier a little better, they would not hesitate to issue the brief [of praise], which would silence him completely."[25] He asked Fr. Drouelle to unmask the bishop's dishonesty. In response to his request that he be permitted to resign, he was informed that the pope did not want him to leave his post, but at the same time he learned that Pius IX had no intention of using his "authority against a bishop who had just submitted and who had promised to introduce into his theology all the corrections requested of him."[26] Referring to the influence of the bishop of Le Mans within the French hierarchy, the pope said quite simply: "Crossing him means crossing them all."[27] The denunciations of Fr. Moreau and Holy Cross continued, and on June 20 he was informed by Fr. Champeau, who was then in Rome, that Fr. Drouelle had received a nasty letter from the bishop concerning approval; there was no longer any hope.

The general chapter held in the summer of 1854 addressed a letter to the bishop on August 24 asking for better relations between the chancery and Holy Cross. The same day Father Moreau wrote:

> I feel I must inform Your Lordship that if you do not find my signature among those of the members of the general chapter who had the honor to write to you, it is because I chose not to take part in their initiative although I share the sentiments which dictated it. I hereby offer my resignation as superior of the Good Shepherd, suggesting that I withdraw from your diocese so that my presence may no longer be an obstacle to the interest which is needed by those whose direction was entrusted to me. I shall not be any the less devoted to this work or any less ready to show my respect for Your Lordship on every occasion. Permit me to add that if I do not speak of my resignation as superior general, it is because His Holiness, to whom I had the honor to offer it, did not feel that he should accept it.

On October 7, 1854, he wrote to his procurator general: "The way in which you respond to my confidence and the favor which the worthy vicar of Jesus Christ shows you . . . suffice to make up for the trials through which divine Providence is pleased to make me pass, in letting me remain before the Holy See under the weight of the calumnies by which Bishop Bouvier feels he must show opposition to the manifestations of satisfaction which His Holiness chose to show us from the beginning." Then he added: "I hope that God will give me the grace to repeat right up to the end: Yes, Father, for such was your good will. It is a minor matter for me to be judged by any human tribunal: he who judges me is the Lord. For you, my dear friend, go on as you have begun, and may the Lord keep you in all your ways."

But just a few days later he wrote: "I must confide to you, my friend, that worn out by our bishop's opposition to all that can contribute to the development of our congregation, I have resolved, if the Holy See does not think it should do me justice, to resign or to request the transfer of our mother house to Rome, and I authorize you to act toward this end as the occasion may present itself."[28] On the following day he addressed another long defense to Propaganda.

Bishop Bouvier was on his way to Rome. On October 20 he wrote to Fr. Moreau from Marseilles, where he had fallen ill of dysentery, that the founder of Holy Cross had acted as if he were exempt from the bishop's jurisdiction. When Fr. Drouelle told this to the pope, Pius IX seemed to be amused. He said: "Either the bishop will come, and in that case I will take up the matter with him and settle it once and for all; or else he will be unable to continue his trip, and then you can hope that he will leave for a better world. It is quite permissible to desire heaven for someone."[29]

The bishop reached Rome and was able to assist at the definition of the dogma of the Immaculate Conception on December 8. That same day his secretary notified Fr. Drouelle that, in his absence, he would grant permission for Bishop Dufêtre to ordain a Holy Cross seminarian at Le Mans who had come from the latter bishop's diocese. But Bishop Bouvier himself wrote the next day to Bishop Dufêtre that he was displeased by the move and would find it hard to explain. Bishop Dufêtre forwarded this letter to Fr. Moreau! This letter was Bishop Bouvier's last administrative act. On December 29 he died in Rome.

The reputation which this long struggle with diocesan authorities won for the founder appears in an appreciation of Fr. Moreau by Fr. Ambroise Ledru, a historian of the diocese who wrote late in the nineteenth century. According to Fr. Ledru, Fr. Moreau's life was full of unfortunate financial ventures; he "obtained" from Bishop Bouvier the superiorship of the brothers, then left the seminary after having given evidence of bad faith, and later refused to pay the bishop 25,000 francs owed him.

Admitting that he has drawn heavily on the testimony of Fr. Mautouchet, Fr. Ledru concludes: "Obviously Fr. Moreau needed money. Like his friend Dorn Guéranger, he had recourse to blameworthy means to fill his coffer and provide for the needs of his foundations."[30]

The same negative judgment appears in the remarks of the man who had been Bishop Bouvier's secretary for some time when the latter died:

> The works [of Holy Cross] were excellent. Thanks to the activity of Fr. Moreau, they at first developed very rapidly. The bishop of Le Mans applauded, encouraged, and recommended them wholeheartedly; he allowed several of his priests remarkable for piety and zeal to enter the new society and to devote themselves to the work, and he was filled with delight in advance at the thought of the good that he had every reason to expect for his diocese.
>
> Unfortunately, the founder, led astray by his imagination and carried away by his natural activity, accepted no direction, rushed on madly and without reflection, piled up debts which went on increasing year by year and threatened the ruin of the congregation.[31]

These remarks might be compared with those of Br. Marie-Antoine: "Fr. Moreau was blamed for having opened missions too quickly. But he was not wrong, for, especially abroad, these branches did not dry up; on the contrary, they bore much fruit. Our very reverend father, who had broad vision acted like a man who saw clearly: the good God had designs on those foundations. Besides, Fr. Moreau did not have to demolish a single wall at Holy Cross, so accurately did he calculate when he built."[32]

The final years of struggle with Bishop Bouvier began and ended with blows from a quarter from which Fr. Moreau least expected it: Rome. As condition for Roman approval, he was called upon to alter his original plan for Holy Cross. In 1852 Fr. Drouelle notified him that Pius IX would not approve the sisters as part of the Association: they would have to be approved as an independent community. Feeling that his plan was not understood in Rome, he wrote the procurator: "I have learned, my dear friend, of the new trial which God had in store for me, and I hasten to commission you to declare to Monsignor Barnabo that if it is impossible to obtain approval for our three societies, I humbly beg him to have us approved at least as priests; without this all our works are going to suffer. Would to heaven that I had not received any promise or formed any hope or given any hope to anyone else! But yes, Father, for such was your good pleasure."[33] Since the particular superior of each of the three societies was a priest, the founder thought he could thus obtain a sort of approval in principle and work from there to the approval of the brothers and the sisters. However, he insisted to Msgr. Barnabo at Propaganda: "I have always held myself ready to accept wholeheartedly whatever modifications [the Holy See] might wish to impose on me."[34]

Rome demanded other changes too. We shall examine these below. At the moment only one other Roman move calls for attention here. In 1855, just a few months after Bishop Bouvier's death, Propaganda issued the long-awaited decree of praise (June 18), but it approved "the institute according to its primitive form and limits." Since the only direct contact which the Vatican officials had with the ministry of Holy Cross was the brothers' work in Rome at their agriculture and trade school at Vigna Pia and their school in Trastevere, Fr. Moreau rightly suspected a misconception of the work of Holy Cross as a society of brothers directed by priests, and in fact the earliest stage of the work of Holy Cross was just such a community. It now looked as though even the priests and the brothers were about to be separated by Rome. He did not release the Roman document and finally decided that he would have to go personally to Rome to plead the cause of the Association.[35]

b. Foreign Foundations: Father Sorin and Notre Dame, Deaths in America and Bengal

At the end of 1850 Fr. Gouesse whom Fr. Sorin himself had sent earlier to New Orleans as "visitor" was named superior in the Louisiana house but with some dependence on the Indiana superior. The tension between the two men led the Indiana superior to announce to the archbishop of New Orleans less than a month later that Fr. Gouesse was expelled from the Association of Holy Cross and to the religious that they need no longer obey him. The archbishop sided with the New Orleans superior and declared himself satisfied with his administration. The general council found nothing for which it might condemn Fr. Gouesse. Fr. Moreau maintained the arrangement he had decided upon earlier, and the general council thought of sending a canonical visitor. Fr. Sorin reacted angrily, and on the founder's advice the council dropped the idea of the visit and left the whole matter to the general chapter of that summer. Further, in the interests of harmony between the Indiana and Louisiana houses, Fr. Gouesse was recalled to France and replaced by Fr. Cointet from Notre Dame. During this period, Fr. Sorin was still creating financial bills for the mother house without warning.

The general chapter of 1851, at which Fr. Gouesse assisted and which Fr. Sorin said he could not attend, censured the Indiana superior for several matters, among them his having sent four brothers to participate in the California gold rush and his treatment of Fr. Gouesse in New Orleans.[36] It diminished the dependence of the southern house on Notre Dame by deciding that the financial surplus of the New Orleans house would be sent to France rather than to Indiana. Furthermore, the general council, against Fr. Moreau's recommendation, decided to send Father Gouesse back to New Orleans to work under the archbishop.

On learning of Fr. Gouesse's return to New Orleans, Fr. Sorin went to Le Mans to present his accounts to the general council and to discuss the New Orleans house. It was late 1851, and Fr. Sorin had been named "provincial" of the United States. However, the provinces had just been established, and the competence of the provincials was still not clearly specified.[37] The council reaffirmed the chapter decision regarding the relationship of New Orleans to Notre Dame.

Father Moreau permitted Father Sorin to go to Rome before returning to America in May 1852. As the moment of his return drew near, the founder wrote that Father Gouesse had been invited to leave New Orleans and go to Canada.

The general chapter of August 1852 left Father Moreau free to choose as superior of the new Bengal mission either Father Sorin or Father Voisin, apparently preferring Father Sorin since the option was left so that Father Moreau could first assure himself of the situation in America.[38] After investigation and discussion, the general council pronounced itself in favor of Father Sorin's appointment, and he was notified in September. Father Cointet would return to Notre Dame from New Orleans, and since Father Sorin would no longer be American provincial, Father Gouesse could return to Louisiana as superior. Father Sorin answered by declining to accept a position which would eventually call for episcopal consecration. The sisters' minor chapter submitted vigorous objections. The brothers and priests too were opposed.

On October 29 Father Moreau replied to the sisters:

> I have just received, my dear daughters, the letter written by the secretary of your chapter in reply to my own. It saddens me to see that you have misunderstood the point of my letter to you. In fact, I was not consulting you regarding the decision which is to deprive you of Father Sorin. First of all, you

would show very little appreciation for the services he is rendering you and for the need you have of him if you readily agreed to his departure for any reason other than obedience. Secondly, minor chapters, as a general rule, are not empowered to give advice to a major chapter or to the rector's council or to the rector himself, although they may always address their respectful observations, it being well understood that they will then obey. But I was only asking for your ideas as to the choice of a successor, and this is the only point on which I was expecting you to express yourselves.

I cannot understand what you mean when you write that it would be hard on you to see an exaggerated spirit of obedience induce your father superior to agree to this change. Is it possible for religious obedience to have any other limits than those of the rule? Now, is not the change which has now been decided on in principle within the limits of our rules since there is question of a foundation authorized by these rules, one that is within the limits of our vocation and is proposed by the Holy See itself? Besides, who has assured you that Father Sorin is not destined by God for this new apostolate? Consequently, could you be at peace and would you not have grounds to fear the reproaches of our Lord and those of souls who might be lost through your fault if you were responsible for preventing the execution of the designs of divine mercy? For my part, I should not wish to take upon my conscience a similar responsibility.

You add, my dear daughters, that if your superior agreed so readily to leave you, it would give you grounds to feel that his devotion to you was only a dream. What would you have answered to your parents if, in order to prevent your entry into the religious life, they had used such language with you? When we love our Lord, should we not always be ready to sacrifice all sensible relationships with those around us in order to hurry off wherever God is calling us? Have you recalled what the divine master replied to his disciples, namely, that it was expedient for them that he should deprive them for a while of his visible presence? Do you think that God will abandon you because he deprives you of an instrument of his providence which he wishes to use elsewhere for the salvation of other souls? Would you really love God and would you be showing toward him the confidence inspired by simple faith if you opposed a sacrifice which he is asking of you and which sooner or later he will demand through death? What is more, would you be acting in the spirit of faith if you thought for this reason that everything is lost? "O souls of little faith," he would exclaim to you, "why have you been afraid in the midst of the storm?" Is it not a good thing, on the contrary, for God to show you that none of us is necessary for him? As for myself, I feel that if I were suddenly to disappear from this foundation, he would take it upon himself to prove to all concerned that he had no need of my ministry, no matter what some people might think and say.[39]

That same day he wrote to the priests and brothers:

I appreciate, my dear friends, all the considerations which dictated your reply, and I would be really happy to be able to grant your desires. But it is precisely the praises you sing of your father superior which induced our general chapter to choose him as the most worthy of our religious for this new mission. I share this viewpoint of my council, and I cannot reconsider this serious decision. Nevertheless, I shall wait until the month of May and then God will provide.[40]

On October 31 he wrote to Father Sorin:

I have just received your own letter, my dear friend, along with the replies of your chapters. It surprises and baffles me, especially since your two preceding letters are not of this same tone, except as regards the viewpoint of humility. Nevertheless, this very humility should induce you not to regard yourself as indispensable at [Notre Dame], although I understand like everybody else how necessary your presence may be. Neither would I want you to go beyond the limits of our rules by demanding the intervention of the pope when no such intervention is at all necessary. Above all, it is important for you to remain in the spirit of obedience which, according to Saint Francis de Sales, neither asks anything nor refuses anything. Besides, my dear friend, you know that article 9 of our common constitutions requires the intervention of the sovereign pontiff only for dignities outside our Association. . . . Lastly, if you are waiting only for a formal order from your superior, I command you in the name and in virtue of holy obedience. Nevertheless, take your time, dispose the hearts and minds of those around you, make plans for your departure no later than the month of May, and, if necessary, prepare to hand over to Father Granger a power of attorney for that date. How I should like to be on hand to tell you in person what I have just written and to embrace you![41]

When the archbishop of New Orleans learned of Father Gouesse's reappointment, he asked Father Sorin as provincial to come to New Orleans. The Indiana superior went and there informed the archbishop that he was not leaving Notre Dame and that Father Gouesse should not be admitted as superior. The archbishop and Father Gouesse himself asked that his reassignment to New Orleans be reconsidered. Father Moreau upheld the council decision at least temporarily, and Father Gouesse reached New Orleans while Father Sorin was still there. The latter had to admit Father Gouesse as superior but reorganized the New

Orleans administration and left for Indiana with all the cash on hand! It was already January 1853.

Father Moreau began to receive insulting letters from some of the Notre Dame religious, not excluding the novices. He insisted that the Indiana community respect his orders: "Is it possible that anyone at [Notre Dame] could be so blind as to countermand orders which I transmitted to Father Gouesse and Father Cointet? If so, this would be the gravest possible violation of the vow of obedience and of our constitutions and would constitute formal contempt of legitimate authority and rebellion against the mother house. I demand that, in the absence of Father Sorin, Father Granger should answer me in the very next mail, and I order him in the name of Jesus Christ to cancel these counter orders."[42]

On February 2 he wrote to Father Sorin:

> In the midst of the trouble you have been causing me, my dear friend, and with which I have not yet thought it well to acquaint our community, I have never lost sight for a moment of the ten years of generosity, obedience, sacrifice, and trials of all kinds which you have undergone for the work of God. But I deeply regretted that the archbishop of New Orleans was informed of all these miseries, and I am sorry also that you felt justified in acting in a manner contrary to my assignments and directives without even warning me ahead of time. That is why I beg you today to get along better with me and to be persuaded that, although I am saddened by the complaints which rightly or wrongly are made against you and by the opposition which you are encountering from several bishops, I am not letting myself be influenced by these things. I understand readily that Father Gouesse's return to his former position displeased you. Nevertheless, you were asking me to replace Father Cointet without delay because he was sick, and thinking of your appointment as superior of

the Bengal mission, I did not think that I could make a better choice, while leaving myself free to send another priest should occasion so demand, and even someone to replace Father Gouesse, who seems to have improved during his sojourn at Saint-Laurent.

Be this as it may, I am always thinking of your new appointment, my dear friend, and of Father Cointet as your temporary replacement. I understand how much it may cost you to leave work which it was so difficult to found and where your presence would still be so necessary. But think of Saint Francis Xavier performing his miracles and yet being ready to leave his mission at the very first indication of the will of his superiors. Bear in mind that the obedient man will speak of victory and that by removing you from [Notre Dame] God wants to spare you many new contradictions and through your ministry to make himself known in the midst of those twelve million souls who are seated in the darkness of death.[43]

Only a few days after this letter was mailed (February 12), a document was sent from Notre Dame to Le Mans announcing the secession of the Indiana house from the Association. It concluded:

Understanding literally the promise made on the day of our profession to do everything in our power to prevent separation from the mother house on the part of any house to which we are assigned, we hereby declare, being assembled in chapter, that we can no longer in conscience prevent this separation and that, conformably to our memorandum of the tenth of this present month, we feel obliged to free ourselves for five years, leaving it to Fr. Heurtebize at the expiration of this five-year period to take up with the father rector the steps to be taken for the welfare of religion. In any case, until that time, we will try to live as religious.[44]

The memorandum referred to was a long justification of this move. Fr. Heurtebize, the former rector of the Le Mans seminary who had been chosen at Notre Dame to serve as judge, replied that secession meant a violation of vows and would involve the obligation to vacate property which did not belong to the Indiana superior. In May, however, Father Sorin announced to Father Moreau that the bishop of Vincennes had dispensed the Indiana religious from their vows.

In June Father Chappé left France as canonical visitor. In the meantime Father Moreau drew up a report which would serve as the basis of a canonical trial and prepared to refer the matter to Rome.

On July 31 the founder wrote to Father Drouelle: "I do not yet have the courage to read all the lies from [Notre Dame]. They pain me, especially when I realize that I was threatened with precisely what is happening in Fr. Mautouchet's memorandum. May God forgive them and enlighten them. I have been too credulous and patient."

On August 11 Father Moreau wrote to the archbishop of New Orleans: "The visitor should soon be reaching [Notre Dame]; while I deplore the blindness there, I do not want to do anything hastily."[45] The visitor reached Notre Dame only on September 7. He was received not as a canonical visitor but as a "friend" and informed that very few of the religious at Notre Dame knew of the secession! Since he heard only minor complaints against the mother house in the Indiana community, he accepted that statement. But he also learned that all the Notre Dame property was held in Father Sorin's name.

Even before the visitor's arrival, the archbishop of New Orleans had declared himself unfavorable to the break and uncertain of the validity of the dispensation from vows. During the visit a letter from Father Drouelle arrived making it very clear that Rome would side with France and reject the position of the Indiana community.[46]

While Father Chappé was still trying to decide what to do, on September 20 Father Sorin read him a letter of retraction![47] The visitor, prevented from visiting New Orleans by an epidemic of yellow fever there, immediately returned to Le Mans to present the cause of the reconciled secessionists. The general council, however, ordered Father Sorin himself to come immediately to Le Mans. It had already declared null the act of secession and all the recent professions and business transactions for which it had not given required authorizations. It also deposed Father Sorin as provincial leaving him simply as local superior of Notre Dame. The Canadian provincial became provincial of America. But Father Moreau had persuaded the council to add to these decrees: "Father Sorin will not make this present decree public knowledge except to the degree in which he deems it necessary and prudent, and he shall facilitate the execution of this decision in order to rehabilitate him in the eyes of those who have known of the plan of secession."[18] These decisions were sent on October 29. They included the revocation of Father Sorin's assignment to Bengal: he could hardly have been sent at this juncture.

Before this document was mailed, on October 13 Father Moreau wrote to the reconciled superior:

> Just as your declaration of independence hurt me deeply, my dear friend, your resolution of repentance and sincere and unreserved submission brought me joy and consolation. God is evidently watching over his foundation and those who are devoting themselves to it. He has just drawn you back from an abyss into which you and yours were rushing headlong under the spell of a frightening kind of spiritual blindness. With all the members of my council, I thank him for this signal grace which he has granted you. Keep yourself in these holy dispositions with sincere humility. You ask me, my dear friend, to forget the past and to grant you pardon; this I most readily send you. But at the same time I feel bound

in conscience as father and superior to demand of you immediately the same act of obedience against which, to the great scandal of the Association, you have revolted up to now. Consequently, without yielding to any advice or fear, leave [Notre Dame] immediately and come to see me at once. I shall not hide from you, my friend, that my joy would have been much more complete if your minor chapter, which you are under no obligation to obey, had shown me in its report the same sentiments of confidence and obedience which you manifested in your letter. Your example will be an inspiration to them. Come; my heart is open to receive you in our Lord.[49]

Father Sorin spent November and December at Le Mans. After his departure and the arrival of the account of the break as it was presented in the Notre Dame chronicles, Father Moreau wrote him: "I have just finished reading the last page of your chronicles, my dear friend, and I cannot tell you how edified I was, how touched by this account. . . . I have only one desire now—to be able to suppress this phase from the annals of the Association. But perhaps your example will be useful for our successors and your humble submission profitable to all. Be assured in any case that you have lost nothing but gained very much in my mind and heart."[50]

The following June 15 he addressed a circular letter to the entire Association:

Thanks be to God, grace triumphed at the very moment when the enemies of good were rejoicing at the prospect of a scandalous break with the mother house. My heart still overflows with joy when I recall the spirit of genuine submission and humility with which steps were taken to draw these two houses together once again, the house whose right it is to govern and the house whose duty it is to obey.

It is in virtue of this dependence on the mother house, my dear sons in Jesus Christ, that the members of the Association are to form but one same family, united by the sweet bonds of fraternal charity and the religious vows. In this way Our Lady of Holy Cross will resemble, in its developments, a mighty tree whose stem produces numerous branches as it grows, branches that produce others, all nourished by the same life-giving sap. If this is to be so, however, all the members must cultivate the spirit of mutual love and cooperation, and have at heart the welfare and success of the Association as a whole rather than the private interests of egoism and self-love. Were it otherwise, rivalry and dissension would be inevitable. If it is to take root and grow, our Association must necessarily be based on evangelical abnegation and unselfishness. Only grace can produce these dispositions in our fallen nature, but with them, there will not be a single member of our Association who will not make a personal contribution to its progress, according to strength, intellectual ability and particular aptitudes. One will do intellectual work and another, manual labor; this one will teach, that one will administer; and all the while this activity of the individual will help the community, and the activity of the community will, in turn, help each individual. Joys and sorrows will be mutual. If any fail in health or are incapacitated before their time, the others will support them and provide for their needs. Then it is that we shall taste the happiness of a life of poverty, chastity, and obedience in the midst of priests, brothers, and sisters in Jesus Christ, and we shall sing with David: *Behold how good it is and pleasant for people to dwell together as one.*[51]

In early 1854 Father Moreau sent Father Gastineau as a replacement for Father Gouesse. He reached New Orleans only at the end of March and after a week gave up and left for Canada! The fugitive superior's steward, Father Salmon, was named to replace him temporarily. The archbishop, however, refused to let Father Gouesse leave until another priest arrived. Father Sorin began to get very upset over the presence of Father Gouesse in New Orleans and the situation of the southern foundation in general, a situation which Father Moreau was begging him to remedy. It was only in July that Father Sorin announced that he could help the New Orleans religious by sending a superior in the person of Father Cointet, who had been there earlier. But this former New Orleans superior remained at Notre Dame until a new colony for the southern foundation arrived from Le Mans. In September, before Fr. Cointet could depart for New Orleans, the southern house lost Father Salmon by death. Then epidemics broke out both in New Orleans and at Notre Dame, and Father Cointet died. In October the New Orleans religious, dejected, requested that their community be dissolved and they be recalled.

Father Moreau wrote to Father Sorin on October 13: "How many crosses, my poor friend, how many trials for you and for me! May God have mercy on us. I am far from blaming you for not having yet sent anybody to New Orleans. . . . Stop all corporal mortifications, and take good care of your health. You owe it to your house. . . ."

On October 23 he wrote: "Day and night, my friend, I am with you and your sick, and it seems to me that I hear your dead knocking at my door as they leave you one by one for a better life. This will show you how deeply I share in your sufferings and how ardently I desire to see them end. Let us speak no more of New Orleans, except to save this foundation if that is still possible. . . . Even if the Lord should slay us. . . ."

On December 22 he wrote:

> "For those who love God all things work together for good." I have just read attentively, my dear friend, your letter of direction, and I thank you for your openness even though I regret

to see you troubled by a thought which has no foundation on my part and which is in such little conformity with the way I have acted and with my dispositions. I have carefully examined what I wrote or sent to you since your return to [Notre Dame], and I can find absolutely nothing there which should sadden you.

You reproach me for having kept Father Gouesse at New Orleans. But did not the break, which I would prefer not to be obliged to recall, force me to act in that way? Since the wonderful day on which we embraced, have I not constantly tried to recall the superior from New Orleans to the mother house? Was not this the reason why I sent Fathers Gastineau and Salmon? Since then, have I ever ceased asking you to send a superior in order that my recall of Father Gouesse might be realized?

On January 4, 1855, he had to write another letter trying to calm the troubled Indiana superior.

Finally, Father Moreau asked the archbishop of New Orleans to confide the care of the community to a priest of his choice, and Fr. Raymond, a Sulpician, temporarily replaced Father Gouesse, who left for France. In the light of the Sulpician's favorable report, it was decided in early 1855 that the New Orleans foundation would be maintained, that it would eventually become a province, that Father Guesdon would leave France as the new superior, and that a priest from Notre Dame would be his assistant.[52] The founder announced this in his circular of February 3, 1855, at the same time that he announced the re-establishment of the Indiana Province and Father Sorin's reappointment as provincial.[53] The new superior arrived in New Orleans, won the hearts of all, and then, in another yellow fever epidemic that September, died. Father Moreau received this news just as he learned of the tragic deaths of two religious in Bengal and shortly after he had been informed of the death of Father Voisin[54] who had been named superior of the Bengal mission and had proved to be an excellent missionary. Father Gouesse upon reaching France wanted to return to New Orleans! He finally left the Association.[55]

At this point the founder did not know what to do. Without consulting the archbishop, he placed the future of the house in Father Sorin's hands, probably expecting him to send a superior. Instead, the Indiana provincial sent visitors (five brothers and sisters!), who disturbed the community to such a degree that the archbishop intervened and had them recalled. Father Moreau then placed Father Sorin under obligation to send a priest as superior, left the house under him as provincial, but forbade him to reassign the religious without his approval, announcing that he would make a canonical visit of the American foundations in the near future.[66]

It was late 1855. Between that date and his visit in the summer of 1857, scattered incidents occurred like Father Sorin's peremptory transfer of the New York foundation, made in 1855, to Philadelphia in 1856 without consulting the mother house, unauthorized professions, rumors circulated against the mother house in America, and the recommendation given a religious visiting France not to stop at Holy Cross.[57]

While tension was building to its climax between the Le Mans chancery and Holy Cross on the one hand and between Father Sorin and Father Moreau on the other, sickness struck Father Moreau himself: the eye trouble and leg trouble which had bothered him in 1850 became acute.[58] From 1852 to 1854 the leg trouble caused him to leave the chair in which he slept for a bed, and then in 1855 his eye trouble curtailed his work.[59] At the same time tragedy began to strike the Association in the form of epidemics.

In 1852 cholera struck the New Orleans foundation and carried off two brothers and fifty children. This was the second epidemic for this foundation, which had begun in such stark poverty only three years earlier and had been tried by cholera in its very first year.[60] Other houses were experiencing the same sort of poverty. Father Moreau wrote in the summer of the following year:

> I should like to tell you, my dear sons and daughters in Jesus Christ, that each of our houses abroad is as well off materially as Our Lady of Holy Cross. If I did, I would be deceiving you. Despite the generosity of the venerable pastor of Saint-Laurent and the economy of Father Rézé, notwithstanding all the sacrifices of our brothers and sisters under his wise direction, our houses in Canada remain poor. Though their suffering causes us no anxiety for the future, how I long to relieve it! It pains me too not to be able to hurry personally to the aid of our missionaries in Bengal and to share their labors and hardships. At least they will be consoled to learn of the approaching departure of a new colony.[61]

That same summer (1853) yellow fever broke out in New Orleans and typhoid fever in Montreal. After having announced five deaths in the houses at New Orleans and at Saint-Laurent within a single month,[62] Father Moreau begged the religious "to commend to God the sick who threaten to deplete our ranks still more." He continued: "Five sisters are still confined to their beds at New Orleans, where good Father Gouesse has but one brother in good health; in addition, typhoid fever is wreaking havoc with our community at Saint-Laurent."[63] Two weeks later he wrote of the situation in Europe: "Another epidemic of Asiatic cholera, which is far more terrible than yellow fever, is now threatening to ravage our ranks as it did in 1832," and he offered the suggestions of the Medical Gazette on how to arrest it at its first symptoms.[64] These were the months of Father Sorin's secession; the day after the date on this letter, Father Chappé arrived at Notre Dame to plead the cause of reconciliation.

In 1854, as the summer approached, the founder wrote of the trials of the preceding months:

Each succeeding year will bring us new crosses. No work inspired by faith can be long without them! It is not surprising, then, that many new trials have occurred since my report to you a year ago at this time. To begin with the cruelest, you all know the sufferings endured by our religious employed at the orphanage and trade school at New Orleans. Besides the suffering entailed by the death of the brothers and sisters who fell victims to yellow fever or cholera, the survivors and particularly the father director of these houses have experienced untold hardships. Despite all our efforts to come to their assistance, they found themselves alone in the midst of the children who looked to them for help. I cannot tell you how I myself suffered when I saw the very ones whom I was sending to help console them stopped on their way, one by death and three others by unforeseen events. Some reached their destination only to flee, panic stricken. I trust that the two brothers who are leaving for this dangerous obedience will arrive safe and sound and that they will perform their obediences after the example of the saints. Whatever be the future of these distant missions, I shall never forget the unselfishness of those who refused to leave their post of duty in spite of the dangers which threatened them on all sides. I am thinking particularly of the faithful priest who inspired and encouraged them at the peril of his life.[65]

Later in the summer he announced four deaths in various foundations, indicated there were a number of very sick religious at Notre Dame, and gave this news about those who had left Le Mans for New Orleans and Bengal: "The religious who have just reached New Orleans had a frightful passage lasting sixty-four days from Le Havre to New York; four times they were on the verge of being lost. Then there is our colony in Bengal. They too are suffering greatly especially from the climate and are in great need of more missionaries."[66] Ten days later he was announcing another yellow fever epidemic in New Orleans and the death of the new superior, Father Salmon, and at the same time new deaths at Notre Dame.[67] In the Indiana house dysentery had reached epidemic proportions. He cited Father Sorin's letter:

> My days and nights are hardly long enough to visit and help our sick and to give them the last sacraments. . . . Fifty boarders have arrived, and there is not a single professor able to teach a class. . . . I must handle the Latin and French classes by myself besides doing all the office work. My only assistant is a thirteen-year-old boy. The rest of my time is taken up with visiting and caring for the sick, who have practically no one else to help them. I shall probably be on my feet until ten o'clock tonight. I feel the fever in all my bones. Surely God will have pity on us! He is punishing us to make us better religious. If this letter should be my last, permit me to close it by asking your blessing.

Two weeks later, he had to announce further deaths at Notre Dame, among them that of Father Cointet, newly appointed to replace Father Salmon in New Orleans. He wrote: "Is not all this enough to break the spirit of the superior of Notre Dame du Lac and my own as well? Still, let us adore the designs of divine Providence; and while resigning ourselves to even its most severe judgments, let us take care not to lose heart. Let us increase our fervor; and if we hear the voice which calls us to the foreign missions, let us harken to it, no matter what the cost."[68]

Three weeks later, he announced another death at Notre Dame and commented:

> This has brought the total number of deaths to eighteen, including some postulants and some students. The poor superior there is overwhelmed with deepest affliction, and he cannot provide for even the most indispensable employ-

ments because the survivors are exhausted by lack of sleep, weariness, or sickness. Just when the congregation beyond the ocean seemed on the threshold of prosperity, and the college and academy were filled with students from the best families, the epidemic broke out, and all these bright hopes were shattered in an instant. But God be blessed! He has shown the rigors of his justice in these instances only to reveal more clearly the tenderness of his mercy.[69]

In the fall of the following year, when Father Moreau was in the grips of the great trial which we shall consider in a moment, he learned of the death of several religious including the excellent missionary who had been appointed as superior of the Bengal mission in Father Sorin's place and who had been there less than two years.[70] He wrote:

I should have been more prompt in recommending to your prayers four members of our congregation who died some time ago; . . . but a strange presentiment made me fear that I should soon have a new name to add to those already mentioned. This new name, which I have scarcely the courage to write, so great is the grief it causes me, is that of the superior of our mission in Eastern Bengal, good Father Voisin. He died on August 14, worn out by the climate and exhausted by the work of his ministry. Give these souls, so deserving of our grief, the aid of your suffrages, and pray that I may bear up under the burden of the crosses which weigh me down.[71]

Before the month was out, he had to announce further deaths— one of them that of another excellent missionary in Bengal, another that of the new superior in New Orleans, where the yellow fever had broken out again:

These terrible lessons of Providence and the troubles which are weighing upon me make it both a duty and a need for me to speak with you heart to heart. Why has God deprived these two sorely tried missions [New Orleans and Bengal] of their superiors and members who were so badly needed? Why does God add to these crosses the others of sending away the postulants and closing our novitiates so we will not take on obligations that we could not meet even with heroic economy? Impenetrable are the designs of Providence, and we must bow our heads in resignation even under its most painful blows. But are not our sins perhaps the cause of these misfortunes?[72]

Even between epidemics the religious in New Orleans had a difficult life. Father Moreau's first biographer writes of the foundation of the novitiate under the direction of Father Guesdon; he cites the description of the meals provided by the local chronicles: "A little pot of molasses each week was enough to sweeten the tea and the very light coffee, which was the only thing, along with bread, that we had for breakfast and supper. At dinner there was a little piece of meat or, on the three days that we did without it, of salted fish seasoned with water, since there was no butter. The furniture matched the diet, and our clothes did too. Despite all that, there was never a word of complaint; the Lord was the only witness of what was done."[73]

c. Dark Night

Worn out by his struggle with Bishop Bouvier, not sure whether he was threatened with the separation of the societies by the confusing decree of praise from Rome, burdened down by all the worries from the foundations abroad, Father Moreau in 1855 experienced what has been called his "dark night." He described it himself, and one of the priests wrote that description:[74]

I never see the return of the month of October without being deeply moved because it recalls that frightful trial which God allowed to befall me either in the interests of the congregation or in order to give me a greater insight into the spiritual sufferings of others. For several years I had been without my spiritual director, Fr. Mollevaut, and my regular confessor was absent. It all began when I allowed myself to become terribly worried over the political revolution which I feared was imminent and over the high cost of living, which gave rise to serious concern. I saw, or thought I saw, very clearly the impending doom of the entire congregation, even abroad. A strange light seemed to flood my intellect, which was doubtlessly the work of the devil. I beheld this ruin so clearly that there was no further possibility of doubt. The idea obsessed me. Humanly speaking, I could see no way out of it, and I felt I was even stealing the bread I ate. In vain my devoted friends, Fr. Lottin, Fr. Heurtebize, and others, tried to console me. "How can you allow yourself to become so discouraged," they said, "you who used to have such great confidence in Providence?" I could find no satisfactory answer. I could only say that there are moments when those who undertake the works of God must be broken and humiliated—times when everything must be crushed.

My family sorrowfully offered their consolation. But it was useless. Around me there was nothing but desolation. I suffered much from the thought that I was causing so much suffering for the many friends who refused to abandon me. While in this terrible state, I could only recommend myself and the entire congregation to the prayers of the whole community. That is what saved me.

But what I have just described was only the beginning of the anguish. I had already let all the hired help go, stopped building, and cut out all expenditures. I had instructed the members of the community to get whatever they might need for the moment when the impending catastrophe would oblige them to leave. I had sent away all the postulants, regretting that I had burdened the house with them. I myself discredited my administration by insisting that the brothers who offered me money, and even a person outside the congregation who brought me fifteen hundred francs, should not entrust the money to me since all was finished. Every stone I heard being put into place in the choir of our church brought me unbearable anguish. I did not even have the courage to look at the building, and I said to myself: "Fool that you are, what a scandal you have caused in the Church of God!" I declared that we could not in conscience take the students when they returned to class or take money from their parents, so convinced was I that it would be an injustice. The brother steward was the only one who could get me to sign anything. He simply took the pen and forced me to use it. It is remarkable that throughout this whole period no one asked us for money.

Some of his letters from this period give indications of his fears, especially those to Fathers Sorin and Drouelle. To Father Drouelle he wrote in March: "I am afraid of collapsing under the weight of our debts," and on September 22, "Everyone fears that a revolution is just around the corner." To Father Sorin he wrote on September 27: "I am in a continual state of affliction and extreme distress. May God have pity on us and watch over you in a very special way."[75] In fact, even a letter appealing for alms seems to show signs of his sufferings: "The mother house, which has been left to its own resources from the beginning, that is, for the last twenty years, can no longer meet all these needs singlehanded. The high cost of living, which deprives it even of the profit formerly accruing from its boarding school, obliges it, as a measure of prudence, to refuse candidates for admission, and, as a consequence, suspend new foundations abroad."[76]

Father Moreau's own account continues:

But we never abandoned prayer, and you recall how we went sadly every evening to beg Jesus, father of the poor, for bread for the next day. Then, when the community had retired, I remained in the chapel for long hours. What did I do there? I went from station to station, searching for light, for an inspiration, and I found nothing, absolutely nothing. I came back to the sanctuary, went up to the altar, and knocked on the door of the tabernacle. I waited and received no answer, not the least encouragement. At that moment I understood something of our Lord's abandonment in his agony as he went from his Father to his disciples without finding any consolation. I then understood perfectly the suicide of Judas, and it would have been a real favor if someone had taken away from me two objects which I had procured and which were on my desk—a passport, which I had requested from the Ministry of Foreign Affairs, and five hundred francs to pay my passage. I would have yielded to the temptation, had I not kept my eyes fixed on the crucifix. I kept looking at it for days. At night, alone with myself, I suffered still more from a sleeplessness which was practically continual. Still I found the night short! "O God," I said to myself, "how fast the time passes! Is this the sun that is appearing again? Why cannot this night be eternal?" Finally, convinced more than ever that everything was crumbling around me, I saw myself destined to become a beggar from door to door. I saw myself mocked and stoned, and I said: "My God, I consent, provided that the congregation be saved and that you be glorified." At that moment I was somewhat consoled by the thought that, if everything were really lost, I would not have such feelings. And I added, as though in an impossible dream: "Oh, if I could only see the congregation reunited once more in general retreat!" That was a happiness for which I could no longer hope. During that time the rumor was spread abroad that I was insane. Nothing could be more false. I was just as calm as I am today, and I enjoyed the use of all my faculties.

But I saw no escape; I thought it was all over.

According to Sister Mary of the Cherubim, the founder told Father Chappé: "For three days now the devil has been appearing to me, upsetting me, and saying to me, 'Moreau, you are damned, and all the religious under your direction will be damned too. They must leave. You are the cause of it all. . . . All the religious are against you; you are all lost. Get out of here.'"[77]

Br. Marie-Antoine wrote of the reaction of the religious as they saw the founder making the way of the cross: "It was heart-rending to see our venerated father in tears."[78]

Father Moreau's account concludes:

The trial had been going on for about two months, and the community had never ceased to pray for me, when I received a letter which came from a distance of more than fifty leagues [173 miles] from a person who, at least as I supposed, could not have known of my condition. In this letter I found the phrase: "I see you in the same state as Peter when he was sinking in the water." In the twinkling of an eye, light flooded my soul and all my confidence returned. The trial was over.

The letter came from Countess de Jurien, a friend of Father Drouelle. She was a benefactress of Holy Cross and may have been informed of the founder's trial by the procurator. She wrote:

I have read your letter attentively, for I saw you at grips with a temptation of a kind which confronted Saint Peter who, as he saw himself walking on the water, began to see that he was sinking. Our Lord held out his hand to him and scolded him. "Man of little faith," he said, "why do you doubt?" And I, Father, repeat these same words to you with the authority of the master who spoke them first, and I tell you also: "Why do you doubt?" Renew your courage and peace. Peace, but in abandonment to God. This work is from God and not from you. It is up to him and not to you to keep his ark afloat. Hope and pray but do not doubt that, even though I cannot do anything for you at the present moment, God will come to the assistance of your foundation, which he has willed, begun, aided, and sustained up to now, and which he does not wish to see perish. With all my heart I pray for you.[79]

III. ROMAN APPROVAL

a. Alterations in Government

An examination of the changes introduced into the constitutions between 1852 and 1857 and of Father Moreau's reactions to them will help throw light both on his ideals for Holy Cross and on his relations to Rome. Starting with the "fundamental statutes" approved by the general chapter of 1852 and continuing through to the papally approved text of 1857, we can note many changes, although only a limited number have major importance. Unfortunately, it is difficult to know how many of them were demanded by Pius IX or Propaganda, how many were suggested by Father Drouelle on his own initiative, and what reasons motivated each demand or suggestion. In particular, it would be interesting to know whose idea it was that the superior general should be elected for life without any preliminary limited terms.

It is certain that the work of Holy Cross was only imperfectly understood by the Roman cardinals, as the story of the 1855 decree of praise shows. It also seems clear that the procurator made suggestions at least partially on the basis of his understanding of how approved communities functioned and his knowledge of the policies of the Vatican regarding religious communities.

How accurate this understanding and knowledge were is another matter. The letters he sent to Father Moreau during these years contain many suggestions. On his trips to Le Mans and at general chapters, he certainly offered others. In any case, Father Moreau was accustomed to accept whatever he thought was Rome's will without contradiction.[80] What would have happened had he lived in Rome during this period and been able to judge the situation there for himself will have always to remain conjectural.

The founder did not object to the Association's becoming a "congregation"—the latter term had been used frequently before 1845, and the two words do not have very different meanings. Holy Cross had been called an "Association" not because two or three societies were joined to form it but, just as with all the other "associations" Father Moreau founded or planned, because the individual members came together to pool their efforts and, in the Association of Holy Cross, also their lives. The statement made by Father Moreau that he had abandoned the title "congregation" in favor of "association" out of prudence[81] does not mean that the term "association" dates only from that time. It was frequently used earlier—for example, in the "Fundamental Act" of March 1, 1837.[82]

The founder readily accepted the change of his own title from "rector" to "superior general," explaining that he had avoided the latter title from 1840 on because of the negative reaction of Bishop Bouvier and the Le Mans chancery.[53] After some reflection, he yielded to Father Drouelle's urging that the "particular superior" of each society become simply an assistant to the superior general.[84] Father Drouelle said that this move would more effectively assure the union of the societies.

He was reluctant to see the general chapter be made a triennial, instead of an annual event: three years seemed too long a period during which to entrust the government of the congregation simply to the superior general and his assistants, although there were nine of them (six councilors, a secretary, a steward, and a treasurer), in addition to the procurator in Rome.[85] In fact, active collaboration in the government of the congregation and even the organs of consultation were even more restricted after Father Moreau's resignation in 1866. The general chapter became sexennial.[86] The general assistants were reduced from nine to four in 1868. The provincial chapters eventually also ceased to be annual. The minor chapters, renamed "local chapters" in 1857, gradually became simple chapters of accusation, that is, meetings to review and strengthen the members' fidelity to their rules and responsibilities.

Replacing the major chapters of each society with provincial chapters seems to have been the step for which Father Moreau was least prepared, although it followed with some logic upon the suppression of the "particular superiors."[87] As first established, the provincials had been intermediaries between the local superiors of a foreign foundation and the particular superiors of each society. In fact, however, Father Moreau and the particular superiors interfered rarely with what the provincials did. For all practical purposes the provincial, who was simply the most important local superior in a foreign foundation, watched over the other houses and handled whatever exceeded the competence of the other local superiors except in those cases in which an authorization from Le Mans was required. In short, they governed in their area as the mother house did in France. This was why Father Moreau could write "Approved" on Father Sorin's suggestion that the provinces be related to the general administration as the American states were related to the federal government.[88] In 1857 the provincials—or, rather, the vicars; vicariates replaced the earlier provinces until provinces could be organized according to the 1857 constitutions—officially assumed in their provinces the role the rector had held in the earlier period: that of superior of all the religious, not simply those of a house or of one society, and the provincial chapter became in the province what the general chapter had been earlier throughout the congregation: the means of assuring effective collaboration of the societies. But no organ of government assumed the function of the major chapters, which had assured the autonomy of the societies. The autonomy of the societies was so little appreciated after a decade under this new governmental set-up that the general chapter of 1868 proposed suppressing all mention of two societies in the constitutions, a change which Rome did not approve, and took other decisions which disturbed their parity.[89]

The hardest blow to the founder's plans was, of course, the separation of the sisters. Even after the separation became a reality, he hoped that he might still get Propaganda to accept some arrangement in which the Marianites would be linked governmentally to the Salvatorists and the Josephites. As long as he remained superior general of the priests and brothers and responsible for the sisters as their founder, there seemed to be grounds for his hope. He obediently implemented the separation of government and of temporalities between the sisters and the men's community when the latter received papal approval. But he continued his efforts to get Rome to accept that the sisters should retain dependence on the superior general of the priests and brothers at least as the Daughters of Charity do on the superior general of the Vincentians. The effort, however, proved vain.

Despite all of these alterations in his plans, Father Moreau saw the hand of God in what happened.[90] The approval that finally came, however much it altered his dreams, "came from the highest authority on earth."[91] In fact, it made the congregation no longer his. He no longer felt the same sort of responsibility for it as he felt earlier—that of shaping it as its founder. Once it had its canonical existence from Rome and its constitutions had their authority from papal approval, his duty became simply that of a superior general who must see that the work grow in accord with the constitutions given it.[92] But before turning our attention to this new relationship of the founder to his work, we must examine his reaction to the papal approval and the events that accompanied and immediately followed it.

Bishop Bouvier's successor, installed in Le Mans on November 11, 1855, was Jean-Jacques Nanquette, a convinced ultramontanist but broad-minded enough to be conciliatory to the opposition.[93] He gave hearty encouragement to the two ultramontanists who had had the most trouble with his predecessor: Dom Guéranger, the abbot of Solesmes, and Father Moreau. When the founder of Holy Cross went to Rome the following March, he took with him a letter from his new bishop which earnestly recommended the congregation.[94]

b. Approval of Rome, Consecration of the Conventual Church

The decree of praise for the priests and brothers came in May 1856: "Praise is due this institute consisting of priests and brothers, who are nevertheless to be so united among themselves in friendly union, that, while preserving the nature of each society, neither one may dominate the other but both may cooperate in the best possible manner in the attainment of their respective ends."[95] The sisters would receive approval later.[96]

The constitutions were approved the following year by a decree of Propaganda dated May 13, 1857. Already on April 27 the decision had been taken, and on April 28 Father Drouelle notified Father Moreau. On April 29, the founder addressed the following letter to Cardinal Barnabo, new prefect of Propaganda:

> After having poured out my soul to God in thanksgiving in the midst of the community at Our Lady of Holy Cross gathered before the Blessed Sacrament, and shedding tears of joy for the happy news of the approval of our congregation,

I cannot resist the desire to beg Your Eminence to be so kind as to make known to His Holiness the expression of my lively gratitude and to express my sentiments of homage also to the most eminent fathers of the Sacred Congregation, while accepting at the same time the tribute of my own profound gratitude.

Never shall I forget, Your Eminence, that, after God, it is to you that I owe the signal favor with which the Holy See has just enriched the congregation and deigned to take it under its protection. I shall be happy, whenever possible, to give expression to my gratitude by my blind obedience and devotion to the sacred congregation of which you are the worthy prefect.[97]

On June 17 of that year the conventual church was consecrated. To understand what this event meant to the founder, we need only read his justification of the church in his circular of January 1, 1857. He insisted that it would be to no purpose to bless the church "if we, the living and spiritual temples which these stones represent, were not found pure and holy in the eyes of" God. The consecration of the conventual church would, therefore, demand the dedication of the entire congregation to the Lord. He furnished other reasons for building the Church too:

I should like to reply to those who have asked why I spent so much money on the construction of this church. The reason is that I wish to leave to the family of Holy Cross a temple where at times all its members might meet in common prayer, a sanctuary to inspire the respect and build up the spiritual life of the students in the school attached to the mother house and which, at the same time, would be of service to the people of the neighborhood. My idea was to erect a lasting memorial of our love and gratitude to Jesus Christ, the sole founder of our congregation, . . . to Mary, whose protection over our work has always been so evident, and finally to Saint Joseph, who has so often showed himself its guardian. Besides, from the very beginning I have often thought that, if I could build a dwelling place for God which would be as worthy of God as our limited resources could allow, Providence would never leave us without a home in the different places to which we are called and that, above all, God would admit us into the dwelling of eternal glory.[98]

On his tenacity in building this church, we have the testimony of the newspaper La Chronique de l'Ouest:

One man alone, left to his own resources, a humble priest, the founder of a congregation, . . . wanted to build a church, a real church, and he did. For the space of fourteen years, at the cost of personal sacrifice, tenacity of purpose, and confidence in God, and after having been obliged to stop all work for lack of money and to resume work without knowing if he would be able to continue for even six months, this humble priest went on tenaciously and, whenever it became necessary, took his place among the workers, along with his religious.[99]

He described the consecration in a letter which followed the one just cited by two and a half weeks:

I shall not attempt to describe for you my innermost feelings during these days of glorious and holy memory. Neither pen nor tongue could adequately express for you the thoughts of my mind and the emotions of my heart as I beheld the touching spectacle which has just unfolded before me. To my dying day I shall remember with happiness and gratitude this imposing ceremony, wherein it was my privilege to see a prince of the Church, nine venerable bishops [more than ten others wanted to attend but could not], an illustrious follower of St.

Dominic, the famous son of St. Benedict [Dom Guéranger], and many fellow priests from our own diocese and the neighboring dioceses bring to the Congregation of Holy Cross the blessings of heaven and the public expression of their heartfelt interest. At the same time, His Excellency Duke Torlonia, who came from Rome explicitly for this ceremony, the officials of the department [of La Sarthe] and in particular the prefect, the general, the general receiver, the mayor of our city, and his assistants manifested their good will toward us by attending the religious functions and the luncheon which the community served to its illustrious guests.[100]

The religious were there in great numbers, including the members of the general chapter and the students. The day the church was consecrated was certainly one of the happiest of Father Moreau's life.

The members of the general chapter had been convened for the consecration and then met for nine sessions to trace the lines of the reorganization of the work of Holy Cross in accord with the newly approved constitutions. Since many changes had been introduced, the work of reorganization was imperative. Nine vicariates were set up, four in France (Holy Cross, Paris, Maulévrier, and La Souterraine) and five abroad (Notre Dame du Lac; Saint-Laurent, Canada; New Orleans; Rome; and Dhaka), to replace the earlier provinces and were to be organized as the superior general saw fit until a future chapter could petition Rome for the establishment of provinces in accordance with the constitutions.[101] The responsibility for the bulk of the work of reorganization would fall upon the general chapter of 1860—a chapter which Father Moreau would soon come to look upon as the culmination and completion of his work for Holy Cross.

Before the month was over, the superior general was on his way to America.

IV. FINISHING TOUCHES

After papal approval there were two great tasks which the founder had to perform. He had to help the members of the congregation appreciate the new constitutions and shape their lives in accord with them. He had to prepare for the general chapter of 1860—the great chapter of reorganization.

The former of these tasks he addressed first of all by his canonical visits to the Canadian and Indiana foundations and to the establishments in France.[102] He also explained in his circular letters several aspects of the new situation in which the congregation found itself as a result of papal approval.[103] A particularly interesting point, in view of later accusations and complaints, is his insistence that the religious must no longer regularly communicate directly with him but through the newly named provincials.[104] Another interesting point, in view of later developments, is his repeated insistence on keeping accounts properly. Apparently he never succeeded, despite repeated efforts, in convincing the religious of the importance of proper finances.[105] Finally, he published a revised edition of the rules (1858) to bring them into accord with the 1857 constitutions, a third, enlarged edition of his *Meditations* (1859)[106] and a *Catechism of the Christian Life and of the Religious Life for the Use of the Congregation of Holy Cross* (1859). He also worked on constitutions and rules for the Marianites.

a. *Catechism of the Religious Life* and Rules of 1858

An examination of his *Catechism* and of his new edition of the rules will throw further light on his ideals for Holy Cross and the influence of his own personality upon them. An examination of his canonical visit to America and various reactions to it will highlight Fr. Moreau's personality and his relationship to his work.

The *Catechism* was a little volume of 291 pages based in part on the catechism of St. Robert Bellarmine. It contained a description of the "method of [teaching] catechism in use in the congregation."[107] A "summary of Christian doctrine to be learned by heart" followed, a "catechism of the Christian life for the use of the congregation," and a "catechism of the religious life." They were also a "method of prefecting" and a set of "rules in use at the Institution of Our Lady of Holy Cross."[108] This little volume is valuable not because of its originality but rather because it contained the soundest traditional teaching about the religious life and because the founder wanted it, as a catechism, to form the members' perspective on life in Holy Cross.[109]

He writes, for example:

> What is perfection?
>
> It is habitual charity, but so intense that it immediately disposes us to do ordinarily and easily all that God commands with the spirit and in the way that God wills.
>
> How do the vows, which have the evangelical counsels as their object . . ., lead to religious perfection?
>
> By removing the three great obstacles to our union with Jesus Christ or to divine charity, for the vow of poverty puts off the desire for riches, the vow of chastity the love of sensual pleasures, and the vow of obedience the love of independence or the suggestions of pride and of one's own spirit.
>
> What is the excellence of the religious life?
>
> Its excellence is such that the holy doctors compare religious profession with baptism and martyrdom because in making it we give to God all that we have and all that we are.
>
> How can this gift of ourselves and of what we have be compared to baptism and to martyrdom?
>
> Because in thus giving oneself forever, the religious does for God and for personal sanctification the most generous thing that charity can inspire after the sacrifice of one's life.[110]

The 1858 edition of the rules Father Moreau presented in this way:

It is sufficient to say that this new edition of the rules became necessary not only because the previous one was depleted, but also because the constitutions which the Holy See deigned to approve at the same time that it approved our congregation demanded this revision. Consequently, I set to work immediately upon my return from America and have constantly devoted to this task the greater part of my time.

You would have received these constitutions and rules sooner had I not feared to compromise the success of my efforts by too great haste and had I not wished, before finishing the work, to cull from the experience of the past the lessons which it offered me. Here I think it well to explain all the different modifications and changes which have been introduced into these rules from the time of the first draft in 1838 up to this last revision. I am well aware that oftentimes surprise was expressed on this score and sometimes even complaints. And yet what was more simple and more natural?

If I could have foreseen the development of the Congregation of Holy Cross from the outset, I could then have regulated and coordinated everything in advance. If such were the case, however, the congregation would have been a merely human combination and not the work of divine Providence. The fact of the matter is that it began and developed in a manner so mysterious that I can claim for myself neither credit for its foundation nor merit for its progress. Therein lies the indubitable proof that God alone is the founder of this congregation since, according to St. Augustine, when we cannot find the cause of a good work, we must recognize that the Lord is its beginning and author. In the fight of this truth, I had either to follow the designs of Providence by modifying our rules according as God's plan unfolded before our eyes, or wait, as did St. Vincent de Paul, to give them to you in my declining years. By adopting this latter plan, however, I would have left all the scattered members of the family of Holy Cross without rules or directives. I would have had to give up the idea of establishing uniformity of administration in all the houses of the congregation and to live in constant fear of being surprised by death before putting the finishing touches on this extremely important part of my work. I would also add that my drawing up and promulgating these rules according as the need arose has already prepared you to accept and put into practice whatever changes the future might demand because their principles remain always unchanged.

In sending you these rules, dear fathers and brothers, I regret that I cannot make them more authoritative by vesting them with the sanction of the general chapter. Nevertheless, I am convinced that the general chapter will accept them with gratitude, while at the same time reserving to itself the right to make such changes and additions as the spirit of God will inspire. Besides, to secure the approbation of the general chapter, I would have been obliged to defer the publication of these rules until its next session. This would have entailed too long a delay since the chapter will not be held until 1860. Besides, not to mention my fear of not having then the full use of my sight, which is failing so rapidly, I am convinced that it was necessary to complete this revision, first, because the last edition was depleted and, secondly because on the occasion of my visit to Canada and the United States, repeated requests were made for the rules in English and German for the postulants and novices who speak only these languages. . . .

Yet, notwithstanding all my care in this revision, I am far from presenting it to you as perfect. This work always remains liable to new changes according as experience will prove their usefulness. For this reason I have reserved the right to make at our annual retreats and especially at the general chapter any interpretations which may be deemed advisable, and I shall willingly accept any and all modifications which may be recognized as useful or necessary. But, dear fathers and brothers, I offer you this revision, such as it is, as my last and most important task. I present it to you with the heart of a father and a friend, trusting that you will receive it with your customary docility and that it will be the source of the blessing of God on the congregation in general and on all the individual members.[111]

The rules treated of various aspects of the Christian and religious life, drawing inspiration mainly from the Bible and entering into practical details.

Of faith Father Moreau wrote:

As the holy Council of Trent teaches, faith is the root and foundation of all our justification and therefore of all the virtues. Without the root the tree does not receive sap, does not bear fruit, and the least wind can uproot it; without the foundation the edifice cannot be built, or it will certainly fall. . . .

The religious will try to have a faith which is so simple, solid, and lively that it will not only enlighten their minds but animate their thoughts, their affections, their words, and their actions.

They will often demand of Jesus Christ, the author and finisher of our faith, the spirit of faith, saying to him for one another as his apostles did: Lord, increase our faith.

To put this virtue into practice, they will walk in God's presence and will fear giving offense and incurring God's judgment more than any evil on earth. They will adore God as the absolute master of all things; they will love God as a parent; they will pray with respect, attention, fervor, and confidence. They will undertake all things out of obedience for God's glory and the salvation of souls; they will have pure intentions, ardent zeal, burning charity.[112]

Of humility:

> Since humility is the foundation and source of fraternal charity, [the religious] will make special efforts to acquire it, having recourse to the divine Heart of Jesus Christ, who is its principle and its model and who says to all his disciples: Learn from me because I am humble of heart.
>
> Now humility is born especially of self-knowledge, which produces contempt of self at the sight of one's nothingness and sins. Therefore, they will try to know themselves well, asking this grace of God. Far from esteeming themselves, they will have the lowliest sentiments of themselves, reserving all esteem and all love for God, who is alone worthy of praise. Therefore, they will never seek high positions or praises, but rather to be forgotten, obscurity, and humiliations, out of respect for the incarnate Word, who emptied himself.[113]

Of mortification: "Those who belong to Jesus Christ, says Saint Paul, have crucified their flesh with its vices and concupiscences, and this is, in fact, the only means of putting to death or mortifying the old self."[114]

Of charity:

> Since our Lord recommended nothing to his disciples so much as fraternal charity, [the religious] will try to practice it always and everywhere as the second and the greatest of his commandments after that of love for God.
>
> To acquire, preserve, and strengthen this holy union more and more, they will love one another in God, as God's handiwork; for God, to be pleasing; according to God even as God has loved us. If they have anything against anyone or if they should have offended anyone, they will go immediately to be

reconciled; they will avoid even the least suggestion of particular friendships or hatreds, experience having proved that these two vices are the source of the divisions that ruin communities.

All the members of the congregation will have a great respect, a sincere esteem, and a cordial affection for one another. They will always live together as close friends.

To achieve this aim, they will practice charity as it is described by St. Paul. [Then Fr. Moreau provides a detailed commentary on 1 Corinthians 13:4–7.][115]

Of prayer he wrote: Both mental and vocal prayer are "necessary, as it is easy to see from the Gospel, the teaching of the Fathers of the Church, and the example of the saints, especially of the apostles, who reserved to themselves the task of praying and preaching, leaving the rest to others, because prayer and preaching are the two great means of converting souls."[116]

There are two rules, however, in which Father Moreau himself and his great concerns for Holy Cross stand out most clearly— the rules on zeal and on community spirit.

In the rule on zeal we see depicted the ardent apostle from Laigné himself. He writes from the heart, not indicating any source on which he draws:

> The spirit of faith inspires and animates zeal, which is the sacred fire that the divine master came to cast upon the earth. For how can we believe without fervently desiring that God not be offended? How can we be convinced that humanity must necessarily be happy or unhappy for all eternity without taking the means to assure their happiness and without offering help to save them from hell?
>
> If we have faith and the zeal which faith inspires, we will not be able to think of the outrages done the divine majesty without feeling it to the heart; we will be profoundly moved

at the sight of the unhappiness of those who condemn themselves to hell and of the danger of those who grow careless
on the path of virtue; we will shed bitter tears over them, do
penance for them, and pray for them with fervor; we will be
ready to undertake anything to instruct minds in the eternal truths and to form hearts to virtue, to maintain order and
the rules or repress disorder; we will be disposed to suffer
anything and to go anywhere that obedience may call us to
save the souls that are perishing and to extend the kingdom
of Jesus Christ on earth.

To this end everyone will strive to enkindle and keep alive
within themselves the sacred fire of charity. But zeal must be
regulated by knowledge, by prudence, and by that blessing of
the love of God and neighbor which knows how to direct and
temper its fervor so that the limits traced by the wisdom of
superiors are not exceeded.

The religious will therefore be careful not to imitate those
fiery and headstrong people who see only their own ideas,
wish to follow only their own way, push and overturn everything in their path to achieve their ends, like a stream whose
banks do not hold it in and which destroys the countryside
instead of watering and fertilizing it.[117]

Fr. Moreau gave community spirit the central place in these
rules which he considered his last great contribution to Holy
Cross. The preceding rules (I–XI) addressed the admission and
formation of candidates; some material could be more properly placed elsewhere—for example, confession, communion,
monthly retreat. That these rules are in fact all meant to treat admission and formation is even more explicit in the 1855 edition
of the rules, which served as a basis for the 1858 edition. Then
with rule XII the founder began his treatment of life in Holy
Cross. He did this by describing the spirit that should animate
the members. Here again we see the author himself, for it was

this spirit that he personally communicated to the community at Our Lady of Holy Cross and to the congregation at large.

The text reads as follows:

> Community spirit consists in that intimate union which made of all the first Christians only one heart and soul to such a degree that they put all their goods in common and the pagans, witnesses of this touching spectacle, exclaimed in their admiration: See how they love one another!
>
> It is this spirit that the divine master wants to see in the congregation as in the Church, for he made it the mark by which people will recognize his disciples and he asked God for this when he prayed: That they may be one in us so that the world may believe that you have sent me. Let us, then, endeavor to make evident among all the members of the family of Holy Cross a union that will edify all outsiders.
>
> Since the spirit of unity is the distinguishing mark of the common life, everything in the conduct of the Salvatorists [or Josephites] must tend to make it possible to recognize them everywhere by their charity, their mutual affection, their union of thought, sentiment, word, action, and temporal interests in such a way as to realize the words of the psalmist which are sung on profession day as they exchange the sign of peace: How good it is and how profitable for people to dwell together!
>
> To maintain this fraternal union, everyone will strive to imitate the people of the world who associate for business, put all their efforts, resources, and industry in common, and work and help and support one another in order to succeed in business and amass wealth: religious should be the same, for they are charged with heaven's business.
>
> Or again, they will strive to imitate that tiny people the bees, among whom some stay within the hive, others guard the entrance, while others fly away, labor, gather up a harvest,

and return laden with the spoils, which they then share among themselves; they have laws, a mother, a queen; they watch, rest, and travel together; they gather to drive off the enemy; and, if necessary, they sacrifice their lives in defense of the common roof. Admirable community! Striking example of the union, the indissolubility, which must unite all the Salvatorists and Josephites under the guidance of the same rule, the same father, the same shepherd!

Consequently, they will take special care to avoid all that might trouble this beautiful union, this cordial understanding, like the selfishness that thinks only of self, distrust, sensitivity, singularity, envy, jealousy, rash judgment, detraction, calumny, murmuring, indiscreet conversations, and false reports.[118]

b. Spirit of Holy Cross

To appreciate how much this spirit animated Father Moreau himself and how much he succeeded in instilling it in others, we can examine reactions to his visit to America and reactions to Our Lady of Holy Cross itself. His one quick visit to the American foundations brought him into contact with many religious whom he had not seen in years and many whom he had never met. His and their reactions can show what he expected to find in them and what they noticed in him. "The Visit to Our Lady of Holy Cross . . . by a former student" can show how someone who had received a Holy Cross education was impressed by it or, if the author is really Father Champeau,[119] what the intentions and hopes of the educators were.

i. Visit to America

On July 3, 1857, Father Moreau wrote to the congregation of his forthcoming visit to America:

The word "visit" reminds me of a desire which has been with me constantly, ever since the day when divine Providence guided some members of the family of Holy Cross beyond the seas. This desire is all the dearer to my heart since I am sure you share it too, my dear sons and daughters in Jesus Christ, you whom I have seen leave Our Lady of Holy Cross one by one amid the prayers and sadness accompanying your departure. At this moment I think also of those whom I know only by correspondence. Though you have been begging me for such a long time to come, you are no more eager than myself for the happy moment of our early meeting. If you desire to see me and to speak to me, I too desire more strongly than words can express to see you and listen to you. I regard this as a means of fulfilling one of the holiest and most agreeable duties of my office. I yearn for this visit for your consolation and mine in order to acquit myself of the obligation mandated by our constitutions to solidify your scattered houses in the unity of one same government and spirit by the presence and guidance of your superior general.[120]

From New York he wrote back to Holy Cross:

It is already two weeks since I left you, my dear sons and daughters in Jesus Christ, and in that space of time twelve hundred leagues [4143 miles] of sea have come between us. But for all this, my mind and heart are with you still. In my journey over this immense ocean, which I am anxious to cross a second time to see you again, I often found and will find my thoughts traveling back to you. It seems to me that I can still see you grouped around me in our beautiful sanctuary at Holy Cross. At times I imagine myself receiving once more your last farewells at the top of the sacred steps, from which it was such a sacrifice for me to descend. Again I see myself on my knees before the altar where our Lord heard my parting prayers, or in the crypt before the image of the adorable face, where I am sure you are faithfully keeping a little lamp which is to burn until my return. This is the expression of all our prayerful wishes for Our Lady of Holy Cross.

I was deeply moved when I came out of this crypt and saw you gathered together in the parlor or in the sacristy in order to manifest your affection for me. Beyond all doubt I was quite unworthy of this love, and yet it was a true reflection of my love for you. Hearts which love each other in Jesus Christ can never part without sadness, especially when it is a question of so long a journey. I understood perfectly the anxiety which worried you. At my age it was no small thing to leave so much urgent business, cross the ocean, accustom myself to a new climate and different food, and interrupt for such a long period my daily correspondence.[121]

He described his visit to Canada in a circular letter to the entire congregation:

Landing in New York on August 11, I immediately wired to Montreal, advising the community at Saint-Laurent of my arrival. The next night I arrived at the Sulpician seminary, where I was received with their usual kind hospitality, and the day after I found myself in the midst of our dear Canadians. I was with them for two days before my telegram arrived. "This proves," said Father Rézé, "that the very reverend father general goes faster than the telegraph." No one there was expecting me; the young brother whom Father Veniard sent to announce my arrival to the mother superior at Sainte-Marie received as his thanks the assurance that he was "losing his mind." In the meantime the bells of Saint Joseph's and of the parish church were ringing out. Everyone, fathers, brothers, and sisters, came running to ask the cause of all this excitement; the news went from mouth to mouth, but still they could hardly believe it. Before long there was no further room for doubt. It would be useless for me to try to describe the demonstration of joy which everywhere broke forth. We embraced and congratulated one another on our happiness. Lastly we went to the church to sing a hymn of thanksgiving. All hearts were profoundly touched. As their voices carried up to the throne of God the incense of their homage, we experienced the exquisite happiness of finding ourselves once more, after such a long separation marked by so many severe trials, in the midst of our family in a distant country.[122]

An interesting detail of this visit was his meeting with the novice sister who was later to found the Little Sisters of the Holy Family, now known as Saint Marie-Léonie Paradis. Her request for profession had been refused because of her health. She was urged to appeal to him: "Go see him with confidence; go on, our father founder cannot resist tears."[123] He not only permitted her to make vows, but he himself presided at the ceremony.

He concluded the account of his visit to Canada in his circular letter by addressing the religious there:

For all this, dear sons and daughters in Jesus Christ, I congratulate you and warmly thank you. I am grateful also to the worthy pastor of your parish, who welcomed me with unforgettable courtesy and kindness. The proofs of affection which your charity unceasingly lavished upon me during my too short stay among you will always remain engraved on my heart, and I shall never forget them as long as I live. Continue to live in a spirit of mutual unity, and be always submissive to your superiors, constantly animated with the excellent spirit in which I left you.[124]

A summary of Father Moreau's conferences at Notre Dame du Lac by Father Lévesque recorded the impression made by his visit there:[125]

August 26, Wednesday morning—the very reverend father rector and superior general of the Congregation of Holy Cross . . . arrived unexpectedly at Notre Dame du Lac . . . about nine o'clock in the morning, coming from Canada. . . . The first act of the very reverend father was to celebrate the sacred mysteries with a faith and spirituality which from the very beginning won him all hearts. Practically all the brothers, Salvatorists, and sisters resident at the college were present. . . . After breakfast, which was accompanied by an outpouring of the very paternal heart of His Reverence, who was just meeting all his new hosts, of whom three-fourths were unknown to him until then, he went to the laundry of the good sisters at the school. . . . From there he went to the infirmary, which had only a single patient, good Br. Laurent. . . .

Thursday, Friday, and Saturday, the reverend father rector had two meetings every day with the entire congregation, Salvatorists, Josephites, and Marianites . . . in the big church: besides meditation in the morning at 5:30, at eleven o'clock, when he explained or, better, gave the religious spirit, according to the new constitutions. . . . These explanations, like everything else that he did, had a clarity and a blessing that were really angelic. Several people, in particular, Reverend Father Granger, director of the Salvatorist novices, took notes on them. I really regret not having written them down. And in the evening at five o'clock he read and explained the new constitutions.

Sunday (August 30). The reverend father rector preached at the high Mass, at vespers, and even at the procession of the Blessed Virgin at the brothers' [novitiate]. In the morning he gave a magnificent and rapid analysis of the life of our Lord from the point of view of history and providence, ending with a most happy allusion to the Gospel of the ten lepers [the gospel of the day]. . . .

At vespers, he preached on devotion to the Blessed Virgin, a commentary on the litany which was going to be chanted in the procession that followed—filled with blessing—and on our duties to Mary, whose mercy he implored especially in favor of the house of Notre Dame du Lac, where she is the special patroness. There were many little stories on Mary's protection, some of which were unknown to most of the hearers, whose tears frequently flowed. It was easy to see in him the old missionary who knows quite well the way to the heart. For the rest, his profound spirituality and his inexhaustible goodness of heart gave him at once the key to all hearts. . . .

Friday, September 11, the very reverend father at eleven o'clock read his long directive for the visit—forty-three articles, many of which concern the novitiate of the Salvatorists, in whom he showed a very great interest. What a joy for them to hear from his eloquent lips that incomparable explanation of the religious spirit in which he developed with such clarity and spirituality the three inappropriate desires and their remedies. For my part, I will thank God my whole life through for this great favor at a time so important for me— my eleventh month of novitiate. . . .

Then, after summarizing Father Moreau's remarks on routine and haste in prayer, the author shifted from French to a rather quaint English: "Look about your old foolish and quick temper, grey hair, or better greenhorn, after fifty-one years of life, who let you be robbed by the devil at every moment by this haste? O Jesus, Mary, and Joseph, . . . obtain for me true and continual fervor of heart and soul."

An interesting episode of his travels in America which shows his tireless character was his visit to Philadelphia. He arrived on Thursday evening, heard directions until 1:00 A.M., presided at meditation at 5:30 the next morning, gave several instructions in chapel, organized a council of administration, distributed numerous assignments, and ended by officiating at several receptions of the habit and professions. Another interesting little episode was his farewell to Father Sorin at the Philadelphia railroad station at 1:00 A.M. Father Moreau wrote: "Then we embraced each other with the warmth of two souls who felt themselves united as were the souls of Jonathan and David."[126]

On his way back to France he wrote to those he had visited in Canada and the United States: "Since I cannot record here the many houses and names which are all dear to me, I beg them all to receive this expression of my satisfaction and of my thanks for their touching welcome. Thanks to their docility, the closest union exists among all the members of each house as also among all the houses I have just visited." Then he addressed himself to the rest of the congregation:

> I owe a tribute of gratitude to all those who have accompanied me with their good wishes and prayers during the dangerous and long journey which has brought me so many consolations. Thus, always inspired by the thought which makes me see in the Salvatorists, Josephites, and Marianites of Holy Cross members of one same family united under one same authority, with common sentiments and interests—at least in spiritual things, if not in temporal—I felt the need and regarded it as a duty to share with you all my joys for your edification and your example.[127]

ii. Our Lady of Holy Cross

The pamphlet "A Visit to Our Lady of Holy Cross at Le Mans" by one of the former students of this Institution is signed, "P. Meslay, architect. Paris, April 15, 1858."[128] Whether it was the work of a former student of the school or a former educator, Father Champeau, it shows how the spirit of union, which the founder so emphasized, animated—or was meant to animate—both religious and students at Holy Cross and how its center was Father Moreau himself. The author wrote:

> The first person that I met after I left the chapel was the venerable and beloved Father Moreau, founder and superior general. But how he had changed! His hair had become white and his features profoundly furrowed by work and austerity. I jumped like a child who catches sight of his elderly father after a long absence, and I ran toward him as I greeted him. He recognized me without difficulty, and his fiery eye and kindly smile delighted me. I let myself be taken into his arms; it seemed to me that all the joys of my childhood came back at once and dissipated my preoccupations which had already become so numerous. . . .
>
> To me Father Moreau had been no university official in command of the little regiment of which I was a part; he was a father who had admitted me into his beloved family and who had loved me as a child for many years. This father and his colleagues had devoted all their care to us: they got up early in the morning and prayed long hours for us before beginning their difficult labors; and in the evening, when we went off to bed, they were still awake for us, after having spent themselves on us all day long without hope or desire of other reward for their difficult ministry than our happiness and the rewards of heaven. For them it was not enough to feed minds with a few lessons of science and literature; they saw in young people hearts to be formed and souls to be saved: they aimed higher than earth. . . . The heroism of their charity came from there. How could we not love such people?

After a long description of the grounds and buildings and a summary of the history of the work of Holy Cross, the author continued:

You can see immediately that the needs of the people—of the least favored class—were practically the exclusive aim of Father Moreau's plans; and so the God of love, who became man for the comfort especially of the little and the poor, has so abundantly blessed his undertaking that in just a few years it has developed in an extraordinary way.

The Institution of Our Lady of Holy Cross at Le Mans was the first important establishment of the young congregation. . . . Today it competes [academically] with the [government's] secondary schools and surpasses them by its excellent spirit. . . .

One of the particular marks of a Holy Cross education is the outstanding attachment of the youth to Father Moreau and his work. We attribute it to the family spirit which has always reigned in the house and in the habit which the good superior had of sharing with the pupils in fatherly way practically all his joys and sorrows. We were never strangers to the important affairs of the congregation. When the first groups left to go off to evangelize savage countries, it was for us an event of major importance; no one left without receiving from us expressions of sincere affection and without being accompanied by our hopes and prayers; the stories of their travels and their labors were for us news awaited from people we loved. . . .

I will close this writing, already too long, by informing you how Father Moreau, whose fervent and unconquerable charity had labored so much for the poorer classes, brought the practice of this important virtue into the heart of his students. The Institution formed its own conference of St. Vincent de Paul, which speaks to its students on behalf of the poor, visits the unfortunate in their homes under the guidance of a professor, gives food and clothing to whole families, and, finally, learns generous giving at the same time as it does the other virtues. . . .

All the students that leave Holy Cross are encouraged to form an association in which they pay modest dues, with the aim of offering moral and financial aid to those among them who may be in need in the future.[120]

The years 1856–1858 were, in many ways, the happiest of the founder's life. They had followed upon the excruciating sufferings of several years. They saw the realization of what Father Moreau had labored toward for over twenty years. In 1858 he was convinced that his work for the Good Shepherd was now done and submitted his resignation as ecclesiastical superior. He thought that his work for Holy Cross was practically done too. In the letter which he wrote to Bishop Nanquette, resigning as superior of the monastery, he said: "Since the monastery of the Good Shepherd can now get along without my direction, thanks to the wisdom of the superior and the enlightened zeal of the chaplain, I come to ask you humbly to relieve me of being superior for this foundation so that I will be able to occupy myself henceforth wholly with that of Our Lady of Holy Cross, which I hope also to place in the hands of His Holiness within a few years."[130] He also wrote to Father Drouelle on April 22 of the same year, referring to his work on the rules: "My task is finished." The final touches would be put on the work by the 1860 chapter.

c. Preparation for the General Chapter of 1860

Extensive preparation for the general chapter of 1860 began in the year preceding the sessions with Father Moreau's announcement of the membership of the various chapter committees and suggestions about the procedure they might follow. He then published the agenda in some detail. Finally, he also published a set of suggestions for the consideration of each chapter committee.[131] From the very beginning he pleaded that all the members of the congregation participate in the preparation:

I do not believe that I should wait for the opening of our general chapter to call your attention to this important assembly. Though there are but few of you destined to take part in it, yet all have an interest in its happy outcome, and consequently it is to your interest to pray for this intention. Besides, it has occurred to me that it would help you to know beforehand the matters which are to form the principal subjects of our discussions and to know who are on the committees which I thought it well to appoint, in order that you may address your observations to them. This will provide those attending with a clear knowledge of the needs of the congregation and enable them to give to each problem well-considered attention.

Convinced that I shall not regret having shown complete confidence in you in this grave circumstance, I shall lay before you very frankly the plan I should like to see followed in this chapter and thus give you time to weigh well your various reflections.

I have but one request, dear sons in Jesus Christ. It is that you in all your communications with the general chapter delegates and they in turn in their examination of your suggestions be animated with that supernatural intention which protects all discussions against self-love and bitterness as against all that prejudice which would make one insist on being right in the face of any and all objections.

Since I truly desire to have suggestions on all points of administration, which up to now I have had the painful responsibility to bear almost alone, I shall be pleased and grateful to accept light from every source. Do not be afraid, then, to make your observations, after seeking light from God; send them on to me either directly or through the intermediary of the committees in all freedom and frankness. Bear in mind, however, that after offering your suggestions, you are obliged in conscience regarding chapter decisions to submit unreservedly, without ill-feeling and especially without criticism, to whatever measures it shall deem advisable for the interests of the entire congregation or any of its houses or members. You would owe the chapter this obedience even if you were not free to make known your own opinions.[132]

V. NEW CONFLICTS

These years (1856–1858) were, in fact, a culmination for the founder, but they were also a beginning—the beginning of sufferings even more excruciating than those he had already undergone.

a. Dubignon Legacy

In 1856 Mademoiselle Dubignon's excluded heirs (her niece and the niece's husband, Monsieur and Madame Houdbert) contested her will and threatened a lawsuit. Several members of the Le Mans clergy encouraged them, among them Fr. Mautouchet. Bishop Nanquette left Father Moreau free to act according to his conscience. On December 28, 1856, the founder wrote to him:

Notwithstanding the advice I have received from reliable persons who have made the study of law a lifetime occupation, notwithstanding the advice of ecclesiastics of well-known piety whose uprightness of conscience would certainly be able to correct me if I were on the point of making a mistake, and notwithstanding the fact that all these counselors affirm that justice and equity are on my side in the will in question and assure me that it is my duty to accept the legacy made to me by Mademoiselle Dubignon—notwithstanding all this, I would renounce this legacy, if Your Lordship so desired. But since you do not at all disapprove the vigorous battle I intend to wage in the lawsuit threatening me, I wish to thank Your Lordship for the fatherly words which you so kindly addressed to me this morning and to assure you that out of this lawsuit no harm will come to the reputation of the priest whom Your Lordship designs to protect and who, although he is superior of a congregation dependent on the Holy See, will always be subject to you as the most respectful of diocesan priests.[133]

On May 1, 1857, he explained the entire matter to the congregation in a circular letter, presenting the contested will in full and replying to the charge that he dispossessed families.[134] The Houdbert position was that their deceased aunt had really left her fortune to the Congregation of Holy Cross—that Father Moreau was simply a "third party" who received it for a congregation which could not legally possess. This was one of the first times this approach was taken: it was to prove most useful later on for liquidating the holdings of unauthorized communities. Members of the Le Mans clergy, including Fr. Mautouchet, testified against Father Moreau. The court gave a verdict upholding the will in early 1858.

Father Moreau wrote to the congregation on April 13:

Faithful to my consoling practice of informing you of my principal worries—a habit which has hitherto done me much good—I shall not close without giving you news of the lawsuit filed against me as a result of the Dubignon legacy. Although this is my own personal affair, nevertheless what concerns me interests all of you too closely not to preoccupy your hearts and minds. I put my case in the hands of Lamothe, an extremely capable lawyer at Laval. There were two verdicts rendered by an unbiased and enlightened court of first instance at Laval. The first exonerated me from the odious accusation of having fabricated the will, the second from having ingratiated myself into the good will of the testatrix. The question of a supposed trust fund, which had been advanced as a third and last resort by my adversaries, was also settled in my favor, thanks to the skill of Mr. Bethmont, lawyer and former president of the bar of Paris, who undertook the defense of my cause and pleaded it admirably. As for the tribunal before which this learned lawyer pleaded, it appeared to me that no serious difficulty would arise since the deceased had, in a will written in her own hand, manifested the solemn expression of her last desires, namely, that she bequeathed to me personally all her property and that she did not obligate me in any way to devote it to any specified work of charity. Notwithstanding this decision, handed down after long investigation by magistrates better placed than anyone else to appreciate the real importance and value of the testimony given before the court, it is possible that the case may be appealed to the imperial court at Angers. In view of this, I cannot, until further orders, regard myself as undisputed proprietor of the legacy, and I must be prepared for new annoyances.

In spite of all this, we have every reason to thank God for his conduct toward me in this painful situation. Here I am not thinking so much of the outcome of the suit which has thus far been in my favor, but rather of the fact that the testimony adduced on both sides has not occasioned any scandal for religion nor injured the good name which is so indispensable for your superior general. Should, however, anyone be astonished at seeing me engaged in such a lawsuit, I reply in the words of St. Vincent de Paul, "I grieve deeply to go counter to the counsel of our Lord, who does not wish his followers to plead in courts. If I have done this, it is because I could not in conscience renounce property which I had so legitimately acquired." I could add further that I determined to fight this case only because venerable prelates and a prince of the Church assured me that I could not refuse the legacy of Mademoiselle Dubignon without showing weakness and betraying the pious intentions of the deceased.[135]

The case was appealed.[136]

At this point yellow fever struck the New Orleans foundation again. Within six weeks Father Moreau had to announce the deaths of five religious and the serious sickness of several more, including the new superior, Father Sheil. He ended the last announcement by an appeal for replacements: "If any feel themselves called to devote their lives to the poor orphans of New Orleans where, notwithstanding all these trials, our congregation has such a beautiful future, I would ask them to notify me of their desires in the course of the year."[137]

During the second hearing of the Dubignon case, a publication of pamphlets by both sides took place, as was not uncommon at the time. However, the plaintiffs' pamphlet contained such libelous allegations by Fr. Mautouchet against Father Moreau that the latter asked Bishop Nanquette for an ecclesiastical trial on January 14 and 26, 1859, and even requested that the bishop preside. Finally, to offset the bad effects the pamphlet might have on the court proceedings, Father Moreau published a lengthy reply. The ecclesiastical arbitrators pronounced both priests' publications unjustifiable and offensive but said nothing about the truth or falsehood of the allegations made. Father Moreau was indignant.[138] Worse yet, the court reversed the decision of the lower court and the founder wrote to the congregation to announce recent deaths and to notify them of the court decision, on February 24, 1859:

> If it is true, as we cannot doubt that God chastises those whom he loves and that the road which leads to heaven is one of tribulation, we have good reason to bless Providence. So heavy are the blows which have just fallen upon us that I am almost afraid to trouble your souls by announcing them

to you. I trust, however, that grace will sweeten the bitterness of all these sacrifices and that in the end you will rejoice with me that the divine master has found us worthy to drink of the chalice of his humiliations and sufferings. It is thus that he wishes to purify us, detach us from this present world, and lead us toward a better life. If, then, we have the happiness to see things as he does in his mercy, we shall all have gained much by losing what is so dear to us in two genuinely religious. I, in particular, must learn this lesson, since by reason of losing my lawsuit and because of the libels published against me I must pass for a wretch without conscience or honor. Thanks to your prayers and to those of so many persons who are devoted to the Congregation of Holy Cross, my soul is not at all troubled thereby, and if I am never to make use of [the Dubignon property], I shall thank the Lord of the universe for depriving me of this enjoyment. . . .

I close by thanking those among you, my good friends, who hastened to come to my assistance in defraying the expenses of my lawsuit, and by informing you that my lawyer has advised me to appeal my case to the court of cassation. This is also the opinion of my director, as the good of religion seems to demand it. I have not yet made up my mind on this point.[139]

Father Moreau asked other advice besides his director's. He furnished further details on both his appeal and the libelous attack on March 24, 1859, explaining that whatever the outcome of the appeal, his responsibility to the testatrix and to the cause of religion would have been discharged and his conscience would be at peace.[140]

b. Fathers Champeau and Drouelle

From Father Sorin there seems to have come little more than consolation for the founder. In fact, Father Moreau was even embarrassed by a request from the Indiana provincial in early 1860—the request that the founder leave his hand to Notre Dame du Lac so that it could be enshrined there, raised in everlasting blessing over the Indiana foundation! On March 9, 1860, Father Moreau answered:

> I could not be more touched, my dear friend, by all your manifestations of affection, but surely charity has blinded you in my regard. I would be extremely embarrassed to let others know of the letter that your good heart has just addressed to me, and my conscience tells me that I have no right to the honor that you want to do me. Besides, my soul would suffer too much as a result, for while people would think me in heaven, I would be in purgatory and so much the longer because people would pray less for my eternal repose. People can do as they like with my body, and I will never be bothered by it. To be forgotten is all that I deserve in this regard, and there is only one thing that I ask: to live in God; if I dare to express a thought, it would be to have inscribed on the cross on my grave: Lord, be merciful to this sinner.

Father Champeau in Paris, however, was giving cause for concern. Already in 1856 he had sharply accused Father Moreau of putting him in complicated financial difficulties. As 1860 approached, he was amply proving that his administrative talents were far inferior to his literary ability. The general administration was becoming alarmed at the Paris superior's refusal to submit proper accounts and even to supervise the finances of his steward, Br. Marie-Julien.

Father Drouelle in Rome was proving to be a better diplomat than administrator and showing great readiness to blame his administrative difficulties and the consequent closing of houses in Italy on the mother house! Already in 1857 Father Moreau had asked him not to act so independently of the general administration while assuring him that he had not lost his superior general's trust. The members of the chapter of 1857 witnessed a nasty outburst on the part of the procurator: at the session of June 21 he took the floor without being recognized and launched into recriminations against the mother house. Father Moreau had to appoint a committee to study the finances of the Roman foundations.[141]

His spirit of independence grew especially after the procurator became provincial, or vicar, of Rome (that is, of the Italian houses). Father Moreau was amazed at his insults and threat of recourse to the Holy See. The superior general wrote on December 31, 1858: "Since Father Drouelle replies by ruse, insult, and threat of scandal to what was a pure act of kindness on my part, I feel that I must set down the facts and the forgotten obligations and justify my administrative council." Father Moreau then went on to explain that he had been perfectly within his rights in disposing of the funds and objects that came from the novitiate at Ferentino which had been closed. He took up article by article the pertinent parts of the constitutions. He denied that Father Drouelle and his council had the right to appeal directly to the Sacred Congregation of Propaganda without having referred the matter to the general chapter first.

The relationship did not improve. Father Moreau had to insist that a provincial depends on the general administration,[142] and on September 22, 1859, he wrote:

> I thank you, dear friend, for your frankness in passing on to me the complaints that have been made to you against me, but I am neither troubled nor angered by them. I will simply justify my administration before the general chapter and, if need be, before the Holy See.
>
> I cannot understand the complaint that I have been arbitrary in the movement of personnel, and I would like facts. It is a gross calumny to say that we do not have novitiates and

that the professed are not persevering. Let names be given and facts about this arbitrary movement.

Let me be told how we are not making progress, and I will reply with facts. I maintain on the contrary that we have, since the last chapter, grown in number, in religious spirit, and in natural resources, etc.

What is lacking to the direction of the work for its stability? What rule, what constitution have I violated, etc.?

Those who say that I have treated them like dogs say nothing about how they have pushed my patience to the limit: besides, it is a fact that since the retreat we have all been in peace here. . . .

Please, my friend, give me facts, and if they are well founded, I will thank you. After all, I am ready to submit my resignation to the general chapter.

The state to which the relationship between the two men had disintegrated is clear from what happened at Father Drouelle's visit to Le Mans in 1859. A report was drawn up by the general council to be submitted to the 1860 general chapter.[143] The report also shows that Father Moreau had not reduced the pace of his activities in the least. It can be paraphrased as follows:

Father Moreau returned to Holy Cross from Saint-Brieuc where he had spent two weeks doing business for the congregation and taking part in the inauguration of the chapel of Saint William, which was to be administered by Holy Cross religious. He found that Father Drouelle had arrived four days earlier without having informed him that he was leaving Rome and without having made known the reason for his trip.

After having answered his correspondence, heard confessions, and received visitors, Father Moreau convoked an extraordinary meeting of his council so that Father Drouelle could explain the reason for his coming. Before the end of this session Father Drouelle left to go to dinner at the bishop's house without troubling to find out whether he would find Father Moreau at the house later, probably supposing that he would remain at Holy Cross for some time. But since Father Moreau had delayed his regular visit to Rheims for two months and had rescheduled it for the following days and since the cardinal archbishop was waiting for him, he had to leave at 11:30 for this foundation.

The superior general spent three days there to regulate definitively all the matters that were pending and without remaining for the installation of the archbishop of Rheims, went to Paris where Father Champeau needed a preacher for the first communion retreat. He got to the capital on Wednesday evening, opened the retreat, and continued that while making visits and doing errands in Paris until Sunday at five o'clock in the evening. After having spent an hour at the Council for the Propagation of the Faith on behalf of the Dhaka mission, he returned to Holy Cross at one o'clock in the morning.

After having answered his correspondence, heard his penitents, and prepared the departure of a brother and a sister for Canada, he asked about Father Drouelle and was surprised to find him absent. He held a council meeting during which a committee was named to draw up a report that the council had demanded earlier. Then Father Moreau made preparations for the first communion retreat at Holy Cross and gave examinations to forty-eight children.

When Father Drouelle appeared on Tuesday afternoon, he violently reproached Father Moreau for not having given him the time he needed. Thereupon he left and did not reappear until that evening after supper when he sent Father Moreau, during spiritual reading, a letter from Vigna Pia, in which Father Prudhomme, who had written it, said that Fr. Drouelle's hasty departure from Rome had occasioned the visits of creditors and especially of one to whom a rather sizable sum was due; hence, Father Prudhomme urged him to return without delay to Saint Bridget's.

Father Moreau was amazed to find at the end of the letter the following lines by Father Drouelle, and he read them in council: "I will return to Rome only on one of the two following conditions: either the congregation will provide me with the means to honor my commitments, or it will authorize me by a notarized act to sell the house of Saint Bridget's on the best possible terms with the responsibility of returning to benefactors the gifts that they made for the restoration of this house."

Father Moreau finished as quickly as he could with visits from a vicar general and the secretary of the bishop of Le Mans, who were urging him to accept an invitation to dinner with a visiting prelate. He wanted, if possible, to settle the embarrassing Roman situation at once, since it was to the interest of the congregation that he return to preach the ordination retreat at the seminary at Saint-Brieuc. He charged Br. Grégoire with immediately convoking the council and inviting Father Drouelle to attend. But he learned then that the latter, whom he had not seen at any community function, was sick in bed. Father Moreau charged Br. Grégoire to convoke the council in Father Drouelle's room, promising to get there just as soon as the account of what had happened up to that point had been read to Father Drouelle and his observations had been given. However, after an hour's delay the council could not meet because of the absence of Father Lemarchand, who had to prefect the retiring of the students, and that of Father Charles. Finally, Father Moreau succeeded in assembling the councilors in his room, and after having observed that no religious had the right to create the dilemma in which the closing remarks on the letter of Father Prudhomme had placed him, he took several decisions on the regulation of the entire affair with the agreement of the councilors.

To make the founder's position more difficult, the five vicariates in France had proved themselves nonviable. Father Moreau could do nothing but reduce them to one—that of Holy Cross.[144]

The only provincial, or vicar, to object was Father Champeau, who thus seemed to have failed once again, this time as provincial. But Father Drouelle sided with Father Champeau and criticized the procedure "as the expression of the overpowering habit of governing men as one governs a herd of cattle"![145] The event was most inauspicious, coming so close to the chapter of 1860. To make matters still worse, the recently professed Father Bolard, who had more recently been named superior of the Rheims house, had been elected as a delegate to the general chapter from the Paris vicariate before it was suppressed and then by his scandalous behavior and irregular conduct proved himself incompetent as a superior and had to be removed! His removal came in June 1860, but he refused to leave Rheims or even to turn over the administration of the house to his successor! He then turned up in Le Mans for the provincial chapter immediately preceding the general chapter, determined to lead a revolution against the authority of the superior general.

CHAPTER 7

RESIGNATION (1860–1866)

The general chapter of 1860 can be viewed as the final great turning point in Father Moreau's administration. From that time on, it became progressively clear that he no longer had effective control of the congregation and that he could not count on Rome to regain it. He tried to resign, but the general chapters always refused, and the Vatican also refused until 1866.

I. CHAPTERS OF 1860 AND THEIR AFTERMATH

The chapter of 1860 was a disappointment. Important members were absent. Opposition to the founder began to organize. The chapter failed to accomplish what Father Moreau hoped it would do.

Father Sorin and Bishop-Elect Dufal arrived only after the chapter closed; hence, the superiors of the Indiana and the Dhaka vicariates were not there to represent these important foreign foundations.

Even before the chapter Father Bolard had published and circulated a pamphlet entitled Historical and Canonical Notions on the General Chapters of Religious Congregations, which was nothing less than an attempt to achieve the deposition of the superior general. He dedicated it to Father Moreau![1] Over the founder's objections the provincial chapter seated this priest, who had been removed as superior of the Rheims house and who, before the subsequent general chapter concluded its sessions, was dismissed from the congregation, by the unanimous vote of the priest capitulants, for immorality.[2] Despite his disgrace he had sounded the call for organized opposition, and it was taken up by others. Father Champeau and especially Father Drouelle were most outspoken in their criticism of Father Moreau in the chapter.

An attempt was made to have the suppressed French vicariates re-established, but this move failed to carry. Father Moreau suggested that the chapter request of Rome the establishment of three provinces: France, the United States, and Canada. The chapter voted this move, which meant the eventual suppression of Father Drouelle's province of Italy and further alienated the procurator general.[3] Because of Father Moreau's insistence that his assistants should reside near him, Father Champeau lost his seat in the chapter: the chapter chose to leave him in Paris as local superior and therefore did not re-elect him general assistant. This certainly did not improve his relations with the founder.

The chapter did not accept the 1858 rules, which Father Moreau had considered his last great contribution to Holy Cross. Instead, the capitulants set up a committee under the chairmanship of Father Charles Moreau to prepare a further revision for the chapter of 1863 after consultation of the entire congregation.[4]

Recognizing that he had become a sign of contradiction, Father Moreau begged the chapter not to let him be "any longer an obstacle to peace and union of hearts" in the congregation; he asked the delegates to accept his resignation or to permit him to offer it to the pope. They refused.

The Marianite chapter met at Holy Cross in the same months as the priests' and brothers' chapter. The sisters decided to reopen the house they had earlier in New York. Since they now formed an independent congregation, Father Moreau did not consider this move contrary to his promise to Father Sorin in 1857 that no house of the congregation would be opened there which was not dependent on Indiana. However, the move greatly antagonized the Indiana vicar. It seems also to have alienated the Indiana sisters from the mother general. In fact, Father Sorin demanded that she leave the Indiana sisters in his hands for three years in accord with his bishop's desires, and at the request of the mother general Father Moreau agreed.

Despite Father Moreau's opposition to his plan to open a house of retirement for priests at Notre Dame, Father Sorin obtained encouragement from Rome through Father Drouelle and without the superior general's knowledge. When Father Moreau learned that Rome had approved the foundation and that an appeal for funds had been launched, he could only offer a futile protest.

In October Father Moreau urged Father Champeau to keep closer watch over the financial ventures of his steward, Br. Marie-Julien. In fact, similar carelessness on the part of other superiors led to his writing a circular letter to the entire congregation underscoring the responsibility of superiors for the activities of their stewards.[5] This appeal went unheeded by Father Champeau, who wrote a scathing letter of denunciation to Cardinal Barnabo against Father Moreau's administration. The Paris superior suggested that Rome make an apostolic visitation of the congregation. The procurator general too painted an unattractive picture of Father Moreau's administration for the cardinal and began retaining communications that his superior general sent through him to Propaganda.

Father Moreau's letters to Father Drouelle during this period give evidence of the increasingly negative attitude of Cardinal Barnabo toward Holy Cross and the increasingly strained relations between the superior general and his procurator. A letter of October 24 refers to Father Drouelle's report of Cardinal Barnabo's complaint that the founder's correspondence wore him out. Father Moreau reacted: "I will avoid giving him further grounds for complaint and, above all, for laughing at my simplicity. I thought they had more charity there. Three consultations in three years wear someone out!!!" A letter of December 29 shows the attitude of the procurator to the founder: "I regret, my friend, always to be receiving recriminations from you, which I do not think I have deserved."

But this period was not completely without joy. On November 25, 1860, Bishop Dufal was consecrated in the conventual church as vicar apostolic of the congregation's mission in Eastern Bengal. For Father Moreau this event was a great "favor from God, who [thereby] raised one of our members to the episcopate, enriched the Congregation of Holy Cross with the fullness of the priesthood, and, so to speak, crowned our institute."[6] He felt the need to prepare for the occasion by a retreat.[7] As always, this favor was for the founder an added reason for the "exemplary fidelity" of the religious, and he consequently urged the observance especially of silence and prompt rising with fidelity to meditation.[8] The day of the episcopal consecration was probably Father Moreau's last day of great joy as superior general. With 1861 an almost unbroken succession of trials began.

II. SCANDALS AND SUFFERINGS OF 1861

In December 1860 the general council became alarmed over the ventures of the Paris steward.[9] Then in January 1861 the scandal broke. Frightened, Father Champeau appealed for help to Father Moreau. Legal "protests" were being filed against the Paris school for promissory notes it was unable to pay, opening the way to court action. The Paris superior even contemplated running away.[10]

It gradually became clear that the steward, Br. Marie-Julien, was a gullible victim for swindlers. He had signed numerous promissory notes for all sorts of charitable enterprises, including the works of Frs. Sorin and Drouelle, Peter's pence, and a benefit fund called "The Bank of the Good Samaritan," which was meant to provide help for prominent persons who might "eventually be visited by misfortune."[11] Father Sorin had even named the chief swindler president of a projected "Association for the Development of Catholic Schools in the United States," for which he asked the blessing of Rome![12]

The archbishop of Paris insisted that Holy Cross assume responsibility for the debt to avoid scandal,[13] and Father Moreau could do nothing but agree. After the presentation of the first unpaid promissory notes, there followed several months of excruciating expectation during which the full amount of the debt remained unknown as new promissory notes came successively to light. On March 8, 1861, Father Moreau wrote to Father Sorin: "O God, what a trial for the end of my life!" Only on July 6 could he announce that he had finally learned the full sum.[14]

The unfortunate steward first went into hiding and then left the congregation. The superior general worried where the unfortunate man would find lodging and, even when he decided to dispense him from his vows, declared himself ready—"out of consideration for the brother's good faith"—to have him "return, live, and die in the congregation."[15]

Father Moreau asked permission of Propaganda to borrow money in order to meet the debts. He urged Father Drouelle to acquaint Cardinal Barnabo with the situation "without putting Father Champeau in a bad light for his poor administration."[16] No answer came, and in order to pay promissory notes coming due, the superior general had to risk exposing himself to the accusation of improper administration by acting without the required Roman permission.

Another heavy blow fell with the court decision which deprived the founder of the Dubignon legacy. On June 7, 1861, he wrote to the congregation:

At last the will of God in my appeal against the verdict of the court of Angers is known to me. Although it is not as I should like to see it naturally speaking, still I adore this will, I bless it, and I beg of you not to be saddened by this new trial. By depriving me of a considerable sum of money which I had in no way sought, this new decision makes me more detached from the things of earth and gives all of us a new opportunity to suffer for the love of Jesus Christ. My conscience, however, bears me witness, that I have done my duty to the testatrix. . . .

Doubtless I would have been most happy to offer to the congregation a property whose value exceeds the debt with which the community has been so unjustly burdened. This would have removed from your minds a harassing anxiety regarding the temporal future of the Congregation of Holy Cross. God, however, has been pleased to deprive us of this consolation in order to deepen our confidence in him and to oblige us to abandon ourselves to his providence in this matter as in the affair of our eternal salvation. May this heavy temporal loss, then, obtain for us the grace of greater detachment from the world, a fuller spirit of self-renunciation, and a more absolute trust in the designs of heaven on the congregation. Oh, if God would be so good as to establish us in these holy dispositions, how the loss of [the Dubignon property] would turn to our advantage! Could we not then say as does the proverb: "Losers win"?

Let us dwell on these thoughts, reverend fathers and dear brothers. Let us make these sentiments our own and, far from allowing our confidence in God to be shaken by events which run counter to human views, let us endeavor to practice these words of him who, although he was Lord of the universe, still had nowhere to lay his head:

"Seek above all God's kingdom and justice, and the rest will not be wanting to you. Do not be solicitous for your life, what you shall eat, nor for your body, what you shall put on. . . . If God so clothes the grass of the field which is today and tomorrow is cast into the oven, how much more you, O you of little faith? Do not be solicitous, therefore, for all these things, for your Father who is in heaven knows that you have need of all these things."

This does not mean, reverend fathers and dear brothers, that our Lord here forbids foresight and human initiative. He recommends elsewhere work, order, and economy in the use of temporal things, but he forbids all anxiety because this is a reflection on his paternal providence.[17]

Well before the Paris disaster came to the knowledge of the general administration—just after the 1860 chapters—Father Moreau had noted a spreading lack of religious spirit. He wrote several letters on various aspects of the religious life in the latter months of 1860: chastity and study, rule and chapter of accusation, obedience and perseverance in vocation, mortification and generosity.[18] In the painful months during which the extent of the Marie-Julien debts gradually came to light, he published a lengthy circular on devotion to Saint Joseph.[19] Just as the final promissory notes were presented, he published a long letter on poverty.[20] Far from causing him to lose sight of the primacy of religious values, the trials and anguish of these months only made him more aware of them. Nor, through it all, did he lose his interior peace. On May 5, 1861, in the middle of the long uncertainty about the extent of the Marie-Julien debt, he wrote to Father Chappé, superior at Maulévrier: "I thank God for the calm and the resignation which . . . grace has given me."

The Paris house was not the only source of worry. The French vicariate was still not satisfactorily organized. By mid-April 1861 the vicar, Father Desprez, did not want to accept responsibility for the vicariate debts![21] In the summer of 1861 other setbacks and financial scandals occurred in France: the donation made to Holy Cross at La Souterraine was revoked, and debts amounting to several thousand francs came to light at the schools of Flers, where a court seizure was threatened, and of Brûlon—all this despite the founder's repeated pleas and orders regarding poverty and financial administration.[22]

Nor was the French vicariate the only source of concern. The situation in America became most disquieting with the outbreak of the Civil War. Father Moreau wrote to Father Sorin on July 3 that a letter from the Indiana superior on the problems in America had filled him with anxiety. He added that he would, were he "without faith, fall beneath so many crosses."

Within the Indiana community a serious problem arose when Br. Amédée, who had been assigned by Father Moreau to organize the Notre Dame accounts and who found himself in continual conflict with his superior, fled to Canada in the spring of 1861 with a number of blank promissory notes, announcing to Father Sorin that he had him at his mercy. The Indiana superior appealed to the superior general, who in turn through Father Rézé, the Canadian superior, gradually got all the promissory notes back from the fugitive. Father Moreau wrote several letters before the end of the incident, no less than three on July 20 alone, intended to reassure Father Sorin.

Finally, in August Father Drouelle informed Father Moreau that Rome had decided on an apostolic visitation and had appointed the bishops of Le Mans and Angers to make it.[23] For the founder—given his outlook on the papacy—a visitation by the Roman authorities could only be a blessing. He even complained when it was eventually somewhat delayed. But the procurator also forwarded to his superior general a list of complaints made to Rome against him. One of them, of course, was the charge of authoritarianism. Father Moreau wrote to Cardinal Barnabo in reply: "Notwithstanding the exaggerations contained in these accusations, I recognize the consequences of an unduly violent character, for which I humble myself every day. It should induce the general chapter, as well as the Holy See, to accept my resignation and to put me in the last place in the congregation." He continued: "There remains for me now only to await the apostolic visitation and then humbly to beg Your Eminence to regard me as your respectful, submissive, and grateful son and to continue your kindness in order that my very poor health may not break under the weight of so many trials. For life has become a burden, and for me to die is gain."[24]

There was some consolation for the founder in the full endorsement which the French provincial chapter that August gave to his handling of the financial situation and in the financial help which came from New Orleans, Canada, and even Poland and Bengal.[25]

But despite the encouragement he found in the approval or help that came from various quarters, he was finding himself increasingly alone. In September Canon Fillion died. Father Moreau wrote to the congregation:

> It is with deep emotion that I must advise you of a new trial which it has pleased God to add to all those you already know. . . . This trial [is] the sudden death of a devoted friend of our congregation, the confidential sharer of my joys and my sorrows for more than forty years, my support, my consolation, in a word, my director, since the death of venerable Fr. Mollevaut. What makes this cross all the heavier is that I was unable to hear his parting farewell or receive his last sigh. . . . The cup of the Lord is full. May it please God not to oblige me to add [more] because of new trials: but the dregs have not yet been drunk.
>
> Yet I feel that my heart is ready for everything. Thanks to God who strengthens me, I am also confident that all these heavy blows will serve to consolidate his work if we know

how to live in a spirit of faith, fraternal charity, good order, economy, recollection, modesty, obedience, chastity, and poverty.[26]

Denunciations to Rome continued, and Father Moreau could see little improvement within the congregation. On October 23 he wrote again to the cardinal prefect of Propaganda: "I cannot resist the desire to confide to Your Eminence the pain I feel at seeing the incessant denunciations to the Holy See of which I am the object and the regret I experience that no answer has come to the request which I have already twice made to have my resignation accepted since there is no longer any confidence in my administration and my sins are drawing down divine wrath upon the work of Holy Cross."

The image of the founder which the preceding texts reveal is a man repeatedly thrown into anguish at threats of ruin for the work for which he was responsible. Nevertheless, he maintained real concern for the very people that caused his worries and remained unwilling to humiliate or hurt them. He saw God's providence in all the setbacks and maintained a degree of interior calm through them all. Sensing his increasing isolation and ineffectiveness and seeing his faults as an important element in the congregation's problems, he came to the logical conclusion of offering his resignation once again as he had in the general chapter of 1860. It was not accepted. After all, an apostolic visitation of Holy Cross was pending, and any changes would best be delayed until its conclusion.

III. CANONICAL VISIT OF AMERICA AND APOSTOLIC VISIT OF HOLY CROSS: 1862

Because of the death of Bishop Nanquette, the friend of Holy Cross entrusted with the apostolic visit of the congregation in France, the visit was not made until after the installation of his successor in the summer of 1862. By that time Father Moreau had sent one of his assistants to make a canonical visit of the American houses. The background to this latter visit lies in events which occurred toward the end of 1861.

The Marianites had reopened their New York house in August. During the next three months Father Sorin insisted that it be closed, writing to Le Mans and to Rome and finally announcing that he was considering withdrawing from the congregation. At the same time, Bishop Luers of Fort Wayne, Father Sorin's ordinary, had been demanding, according to the Indiana superior, that the Marianites' mother house be transferred to his diocese. In a letter to the bishop dated November 19, Father Moreau explained at length that the sisters had been canonically established years before outside Le Mans because of Bishop Bouvier's opposition, that he could not now transfer their mother house without the agreement of the bishop of Le Mans, and that the sisters' situation in Indiana was hardly normal since the separation of their material goods from those of the priests and brothers which Rome had ordered had never been carried out at Notre Dame. Nevertheless, he agreed to ask the mother general to take up residence at Saint Mary's!

Father Sorin informed the founder that this letter did not satisfy Bishop Luers and suggested that Rome might have to offer the final solution. At the same time Father Moreau learned that the Indiana superior had begun unauthorized building at Saint Mary's. He wrote to Father Sorin on November 26: "I will refrain from speaking to my council of your building . . ., my friend, because they would ask by what right you were doing it without having submitted plans. . . . Refrain from writing to Rome regarding the sisters, or you will ruin everything. . . . My trials have reached the limit, and I beg you not to add to them, or you will drive me into a kind of agony."

When he learned of the opposition that had become active against the sisters' New York foundation, he wrote to Father Granger:

> I am deeply pained, my dear friend, to see you abandoning once again the way of obedience and so incapable of understanding that, after having averted a scandal for you in the Amédée affair, I am now forced to fear a new and still greater one. Do you not see that the New York foundation cannot ruin yours in any way whatever, that to give the archbishop [of New York] grounds for complaining against Father Sorin in Rome is to lose everything, that to be disturbed over the matter is simply to fall, perhaps with great scandal to fall, perhaps with great scandal. . . . No, a hundred times no, it is not the spirit of God, but the enemy of our work who is blinding you at the very moment when I am undergoing the agony of an extremely cruel trial to which you are contributing by not reimbursing what you owe in justice and what I have so pressing a need of! I conclude. I shall limit myself to weeping and praying since you still refuse to recognize my authority. But beware of the consequences.[27]

In December 1861 the founder decided that the most effective way to solve the American problems would be to send a canonical visitor. He chose one of his assistants, his nephew Father Charles Moreau, because of this priest's ability to speak English. The visitor reached New York on December 31, although the visit was not officially announced to the congregation until the circular letter of March 26, 1862.[28] The visitor spent the first six months of 1862 visiting the congregation's houses in various parts of the New World, leaving Notre Dame until last. Father Sorin, who, after all, was superior of the Indiana vicariate, grew increasingly angry over the impending visit and the visitor's procedure.[29]

Against the background of the scandals in France and perhaps because he feared that the American problems would develop into a scandal, Father Moreau used the letter in which he announced the visit to plead for union as the strength of Holy Cross, the desire of Christ, and the will of the pope for the congregation. He wrote:

> Never more than now have I experienced a keener realization of how necessary it is for me to be united with you and for all our houses to be united among themselves and with the mother house. This need of union has been emphasized by our financial disasters, the increased rage of Satan against the Church of God, and the war in America, which has cut me off from all correspondence with our vicariate of New Orleans. It is these considerations which impel me to stress very particularly at this present time that union without which our efforts to establish the reign of God among souls would result only in the ruin of the congregation and our own confusion.
>
> In fact, faith as well as reason and experience demonstrate conclusively that "in union there is strength." Union gives rise to strength by blending all the parts into the whole like the mortar which holds the stones of a building together and unites them all with the keystone. Disunion, on the contrary, dissipates strength by separating the parts from the whole. Its effect is the same as when, for want of mortar, the stones of an arch pull away from the keystone, which is the center of symmetry, and bring the entire structure crashing down in ruin. Thus the forces of evil are ever hard at work to destroy sacerdotal union by alienating, if possible, priests from their bishops and bishops from the pope; thus does the demon detach columns from their base and from their capital according to the well-known proverb of Machiavelli: Divide and conquer.
>
> If we would be strong against the enemies of our congregation, let us be one just as our Lord Jesus Christ asked this unity for us of his Father. It is only on this condition that God

will give us his own strength. This strength it is which flows from charity, mutual harmony, oneness of mind, and the sweet bonds of communal love. From this charity and harmony there arises a twofold power, without which we shall never accomplish anything for the salvation of souls: power before God, who is the source of our strength, and power before others, whom union brings under its influence as the effect of grace and supernatural help.

Let us, then, tighten our ranks, my dear sons and daughters in Jesus Christ; like the Israelites let us march forward as one. No matter what the cost, let us remain united with our superiors through obedience and united among ourselves by the bonds of that love of which the Sacred Heart of Jesus is the burning center and which, so to speak, should form a chain linking together all the members of Holy Cross. This, moreover, is the recommendation of our divine Lord to his apostles. It was the object of his touching prayer to his heavenly Father for us when he said: "Holy Father, I pray that they may be one in the unity of one spirit, one faith, and one love, and that just as you are in me and I am in you, so also they may be one in us."

This is our sublime ideal. If we model our lives on it, we shall form a glorious brigade marching into battle in the might of union, and this army drawn up in battle array will strike terror into the devil and the world. But if we are not united, we shall be only a motley and disorganized army, unable to resist the enemy.

Consequently, in the name of God's glory, in the name of our most sacred interests and those of our congregation, in the name of the holy father, who has deigned to approve our constitutions—while leaving to me for the present the government of the Marianite sisters—and whose fatherly heart would be sorely tried by the least sign of disunion among us, let us generously make all the sacrifices demanded by union and harmony. Let us avoid all intrigue, which would be for unity like a gnawing worm; all hypocrisy, as though it were a cancer; and flattery, which begets only corruption. We must be on our guard against selfishness which would be our ruin, egoism which gives rise to the whims of self-love, and all rivalry among the various houses. We must avoid the accumulation of temporal interests in individual houses to the detriment of the community, and all unfounded claims to domination, great or small, which may tend to minimize the authority of the superior general. Otherwise the general administration would be hampered in its activity by the destruction of that unity of government which has been established by the Holy See. Each house would have its own local spirit instead of taking its inspiration from Our Lady of Holy Cross.[30]

Before the visitor reached Notre Dame du Lac, the founder had received greetings on June 14 from many religious for the feast of his patron. The manifestation of loyalty and affection renewed his courage. On June 15 he wrote:

On Saint Basil's day, the feast of my glorious patron, I was overwhelmed by an avalanche of letters of congratulation. Most of them were beautifully worded and filled with sentiments of affection expressed in a way that is most flattering to self-love, which is so open to deception. But, thank God, I see in all this only the excess of your charity for me, and I am really affected only by the prayers which you are so kind as to offer for me. . . . The future of our congregation is still in our hands, and, notwithstanding the deep wounds inflicted on her by some of her very own members, her life is not yet drained. Our congregation will come out of this trial more vigorous than ever before if we but follow the guidance of our constitutions and rules and especially if we act in a spirit of faith out of zeal for God's glory, our own sanctification, and the salvation of the souls entrusted to our care.

Thus, my dear sons in Jesus Christ, in spite of the many inroads on my health which have been caused more by my many trials than by the infirmities of old age, I feel new confidence and courage, especially during these days which bring me the testimony of your affection and devotedness. Among the letters occasioned by my feast day, those which come from you have a special attraction for my mind and heart. For this reason I should like to reply to each of you individually, congratulating some, encouraging others, and exhorting those who are negligent in God's service not to expose themselves to the curse uttered against the lukewarm.

Since I cannot do so, however, both for want of leisure and because of my weakening eyesight, I have recourse to the customary circular letter to thank you one and all for your good wishes and prayers on my behalf. Ah, I am so sorely in need of prayer! In it rest all my hope and consolation. Let us pray, then, and pray much. Let us gather before the throne of God, united in the hearts of Jesus, Mary, and Joseph, without ever missing prayer at the hours indicated by the rule from the moment we get up until we retire.[31]

In addition to the joy of the letters he had received, came encouragement from the new bishop of Le Mans—the nephew of the founder's recently deceased confessor. He arrived in Le Mans in early June, and although Fr. Sorin had alerted him to the "crisis" at Holy Cross, he showed only respect and veneration for the founder, paying a friendly visit to Holy Cross shortly after reaching his immense diocese.

Fr. Charles Moreau reached Notre Dame on July 11 or 12, and whatever renewed hope Fr. Moreau may have felt quickly disappeared. Fr. Sorin resigned when the visitor arrived, and in a letter of July 14 he announced his move to Fr. Moreau: "My conscience now obliges me to resign from all administration. If I cannot do this without leaving the Congregation of Holy Cross, Your Reverence is humbly requested to grant me my dispensation from vows or rather permission to pass to a more perfect order."[32]

Fr. Charles refused to accept the resignation. He began the visit of the sisters, who signed and sent to Fr. Moreau a written renewal of their vows and the promise of "inviolable fidelity to the constitutions and rules" of their "venerated founder."[33] Summoned by Fr. Sorin, Bishop Luers arrived and forbade Fr. Charles to do anything important with the sisters without Fr. Sorin's agreement. Fr. Sorin resumed authority over the sisters and ordered their provincial to leave Saint Mary's. She left for France, and Fr. Charles left for Illinois. Shortly thereafter a petition left Notre Dame and Saint Mary's for Rome with Bishop Luers' approval; it requested an apostolic visitor! This brought matters to a standstill.

It was August, and the apostolic visit of Holy Cross was still pending. The annual chapter of the vicariate of France was held. Fr. Galmard, secretary of the chapter, delivered scathing attacks on the ineptitude of the founder and his administration which disturbed the chapter as much as Fr. Bolard's booklet had disturbed the chapter of 1860. The chapter went so far as to censure the 1860 reduction of the French vicariates to one! However, its criticisms were not limited to the founder; it also censured Fr. Drouelle's finances.

Fr. Moreau's requests finally led to the appointment of Bishop Fillion to resume the apostolic visitation of Holy Cross. He completed it in the wake of the stormy provincial chapter, dating his report to Propaganda September 16. The visitor found the mother house solvent despite the staggering debts of other houses which it had assumed and, at the cost of great effort, was paying off. He found the religious formation and religious spirit satisfactory. He wrote of the superior general:

> Very Reverend Fr. Moreau is simultaneously superior general of the entire congregation, provincial of France, local superior of the professed house and the college, master of novices for the brothers and the priests, and professor of theology. . . . Although the reverend father superior assured me that at the beginning of the next school year he would turn over the direction of the college and the novitiates to serious-minded and capable priests, it would not be out of order for Your Eminence to insist on this important point and to obtain from Reverend Fr. Moreau a commitment that, after appointing these priests to these offices, he will not hamper their activity by excessive interference. The religious, who without exception spoke to me with great liberty, point out the fiery, domineering, and oftentimes unduly sharp and changing character of their superior. But all of them add that he is filled with faith and love for the Church, and that even in his excesses his zeal is always animated with the purest of intentions.[34]

To appreciate the observation that Fr. Moreau held so many offices, we must recall several facts. (1) The founder was acting as provincial. Repeated attempts to organize the vicariate of France had all failed. In May Fr. Moreau proposed reorganizing the vicariate, suggesting as vicar Fr. Champeau![35] This priest had been named vicar in June. Perhaps the sickness which kept him from assisting at the general chapter of 1863 had already incapacitated him by August.[30] (2) The founder was local superior. Other major superiors regularly acted as superior of the house where they resided (for example, Fr. Champeau in Paris when he had been provincial), and no objection had ever been raised. (3) The founder was novice master. The history of the two Le Mans novitiates shows that Fr. Moreau assumed this office, after the first few years, only at intervals when the incumbent novice master was needed at another post and a replacement was not readily available. (4) The founder was also a teacher. Many of the other religious at Holy Cross held several offices. The superior general did not keep a secret of his many occupations. In the triennial report which he submitted to Rome at the end of 1860 he had written: "For the last ten years, each Sunday I have given homilies on the gospel, the epistle, and the liturgy to all those who live at the mother house and, in addition, during Advent and Lent dogmatic conferences. Further, each week throughout the entire year there are catechism periods for the brothers and the students. Before having undertaken this teaching, I spent fourteen years as professor either of theology or Sacred Scripture at the seminary of Le Mans."[37]

The appointment of the officers mentioned by Bishop Fillion was implemented before the middle of October. Nevertheless, Fr. Drouelle painted a dark picture of Rome's outlook on Holy Cross, an outlook which he was helping to create.[38] Fr. Moreau wrote Mother Mary of the Seven Dolors on October 18:

> It must be admitted that we were certainly right in taking the title of Our Lady of Holy Cross and of the Seven Dolors in making this foundation. Neither of us was expecting so many tribulations, but Providence has its own plans. Our only course now is to pray and work; the time for rest will come later. But never was it so difficult to govern souls as it is now, and Satan is really unleashed against us. . . . Nevertheless, the pope has just promised to forget our financial and moral weaknesses [according to news from Fr. Drouelle] on condition that we take effective measures to prevent them from happening again.[39]

Fr. Moreau wrote to Fr. Drouelle that he would resign at the approaching general chapter but that if Propaganda intervened to order the continuation of the visit in Indiana and the separation of the material goods between the men's and women's communities there, there were grounds for hope.[40]

On September 23 he wrote to the sisters in America that they were to regard as not binding in conscience anything that Fr. Sorin did contrary to the visitor, that if Bishop Luers opposed their following their rules and constitutions they could immediately leave the diocese, and that if they refused to obey the directives he sent, they should consider themselves as no longer belonging to the society of the Marianites.[41] He had written to the bishop to the same effect on September 1.

In the meantime, the Marianite provincial arrived from Saint Mary's to provide firsthand information on the visit, and a letter reached Mother Mary of the Seven Dolors from one of the American sisters: "The mystery is clear: they want separation; everyone, even Fr. Granger, is against the founder."[42] On October 16 Fr. Moreau wrote to Fr. Sorin:

> Without wishing it, you are filling up the measure of my suffering and are occasioning a great scandal. You should, first of all, have permitted the visitor to carry out his obedience, and then have appealed to the superior general against his decisions if they seemed to you irregular or imprudent or unjust, then against my replies to the general chapter, and finally against that authority to the Holy See. You have felt entitled to do just the contrary. You will have to answer for it.
>
> Furthermore, you have chosen to answer nothing to my order to reimburse me, and you are exposing me today to prosecution. I do not have the courage to add anything more except that I will pray and weep at the foot of my crucifix until the storm passes.

On October 22 the founder sent a directive to Fr. Sorin and all the priests and brothers in Indiana in virtue of their vow of obedience and under penalty of answering to the general council, the general chapter, and the Holy See. He ordered Fr. Sorin to apologize to the visitor and the latter to try to have an understanding with Bishop Luers over his role. He invalidated sisters' professions made without the permission of the mother general. He ordered that the Notre Dame community withdraw its petition for an apostolic visit until Fr. Charles' visit had been completed.

The procurator general finally decided to send a report to Propaganda. Cardinal Barnabo and Pius IX saw it. Fr. Drouelle informed Fr. Granger of their very negative reaction. However, a second report from Fr. Drouelle kept Propaganda from laying the blame on Fr. Sorin; it urged the intervention of Rome to resolve the "conflicts and misunderstandings."[43] In January 1863 Cardinal Barnabo's letter ordering the continuation of the visit reached Notre Dame.

Fr. Moreau, however, had by now recognized clearly that, despite the apostolic visit, he could no longer effectively elicit the collaboration of the priests and brothers and that he could not count on Rome's support. He wrote to Cardinal Barnabo at the end of 1862:

> The ease with which all sorts of calumnies against my administration have been accepted even in Rome and the measures which authority has felt obliged to take as a result of these accusations leave me no further room for doubt that I have completely lost the confidence with which Your Eminence previously honored me, as also His Holiness Pius IX. But thanks be to God, I do not feel I have abused this confidence.
>
> From this I can conclude that I have lived in a state of blindness regarding the duties of my office—for my conscience

does not reproach me in anything—or that my sins are the cause of all this. But I am not thereby justified.

Hence, Your Eminence, while respecting the wisdom of the conduct of the Holy See in my regard, I now have the honor to offer my resignation as superior general just as I resigned as superior of the Good Shepherd house in our city after having founded it and secured for it governmental recognition.

Consequently, I shall be grateful to Your Eminence if you would be so kind as to have my resignation accepted by His Holiness. I would have offered it sooner, were it not for the difficulties of all kinds created for me by our house in Paris.

He concluded: "I hope that, with the help of Your Eminence, the difficulties which have arisen will disappear and that I shall be able next year to submit constitutions for the sisters to the Sacred Congregation and then to live as a simple religious in our congregation or with the Trappists at Mortagne."[44]

To the congregation he could only address a plea to do what neither his pleas nor his orders had thus far succeeded in persuading them to do. On January 1, 1863, he began his New Year's letter to the religious:[45]

The misfortunes which have befallen us during the past year as inevitable consequences of the financial and disciplinary disorder of the preceding twelve months have been too terrible for us not to strive to prevent a recurrence of them during this coming year. Such should be the object of all our efforts. . . .

What a difficult situation was thereby created for the mother house and particularly for the superior general! My life during this period has been nothing short of agony. One must endure torture of this kind to understand really what it costs our poor human nature.

He concluded: "Oh, how I would bless God if, before I die, I could see all our houses walking in the path traced out by our

constitutions and rules on financial management and the observance of regular discipline. I would then go to my grave without
any anxiety for the Congregation of Holy Cross, and I would rejoice in having been called, notwithstanding my unworthiness,
to be an instrument in realizing the designs of God on each one
of you."

IV. FAILURE OF THE CANONICAL VISIT, CHAPTER OF 1863

After learning that the visit would be resumed, Fr. Moreau decided that the best solution to the Indiana problems would be
to request papal approval of the Marianites' constitutions with
establishment by Rome of the mother house at Le Mans and to
convoke the sisters' general chapter in Philadelphia at the end of
March. On February 15 he wrote to Fr. Charles, preparing the way
for these steps: "I have received at last, my dear friend, the news
of your imminent departure for Notre Dame, where I hope everything will be restored to order. . . . Write me how the visit goes;
modify my orders, and approve ordinations and professions.
After that, await further instructions from me before leaving Indiana. . . . I have been receiving letters of submission from everybody at Notre Dame except from the sisters."[46]

On the same day he wrote to Fr. Granger notifying him of his
intentions for the sisters and commenting on the impending
"peace": "I have received your telegrams, my dear friend, and also
the letters from Fr. Sorin. They console me in proportion as I was
previously saddened when the enemy of good stirred up so many
miseries against us."[47]

Three days later, after learning from Bishop Fillion that his request for approval for the sisters' constitutions would be acted
on favorably, he wrote to Mother Mary of the Seven Dolors: "I am
in a hurry to send you this letter, my dear mother, and to advise
you that I am convoking the general chapter in Philadelphia. Hell

has worked so hard against us that some great grace, like that of your approbation, must be in store for us."[48]

Cardinal Barnabo informed the founder that he had not lost the confidence of Pius IX and that his resignation was not called for. Bishop Luers invited the visitor to return to his diocese. Two sisters from Saint Mary's had reached Le Mans to explain their situation to the founder. It was now mid-March. Matters seemed to be on the verge of a solution. But all of this was a mere deceptive appearance.

When Bishop Luers learned of the plans for a general chapter and papal approval, he forbade Fr. Granger to communicate to anyone, without his approval, anything from France which might disturb the peace. This meant that the Indiana sisters never learned of the convocation of the chapter, which Fr. Charles then decided should not be held. The sisters who had gone to Le Mans had gone to obtain the help of an influential Visitandine nun in presenting to Propaganda the request of two American archbishops that the Marianites' constitutions not be approved, and Fr. Moreau discovered the reason for their trip.[49] In Rome, Fr. Drouelle presented Cardinal Barnabo a memorandum on the American visit from Fr. Sorin but not the one from Fr. Charles. In fact, Fr. Drouelle wrote Fr. Sorin that the two of them and Fr. Champeau with the help of the bishop of Le Mans would have to find a solution to the congregation's problems in the approaching general chapter and even discussed the question of a successor for the superior general. Cardinal Barnabo informed Fr. Moreau through Fr. Drouelle that he wanted the sisters' chapter postponed. The procurator explained that the cardinal regarded the convocation as "arbitrary"!

At this point the founder wrote to the procurator general: "Let them do with the sisters as they wish: on this point I will obey beyond what they ask, for I will no longer have anything to do with them. I am ready to do the same for the priests and brothers, and

I will bless God the day when I will no longer have authority over anyone."[50] On May 7 he went so far as to write:

> Since, without even waiting for a word of justification from me, Rome has felt justified in by-passing the general authority in the affair of the Indiana sisters, treating the regular convocation of the general chapter of this society as arbitrary and making the visitor, the founder, the mother general with her council, and all the general capitulants bow to a cabal of a few sisters without any mission who, because of visits they have made and influence they have managed to exercise, have surprised the good faith of one or two bishops, you can tell the cardinal, my friend, now that you have the evidence, that if this scandal is sustained any longer, if Fr. Sorin is permitted to continue the resistance into which he has pushed his sisters out of spite and pride, and Fr. Granger, at his instigation, is permitted to intercept my correspondence, I will withdraw secretly from Holy Cross and leave to everyone before God the responsibility of his acts.

Despite his helplessness in the face of a situation he regarded as patently irregular, the founder still retained an inner calm, which he manifested, for example, in the letter he wrote to the superior of the sisters at Saint-Laurent:

> When we walk in the path of obedience, we are assured of being on good terms with God and, consequently, can count on his assistance. What else is necessary in order to live in peace in the midst of the storm and not to be troubled by the tempest raised by human passions? It is neither you nor I who are to be pitied but rather those souls who forget their sacred promises and go astray on paths unknown to the simplicity of faith. Hence, take courage. . . . In calm and prayer await orders from above and live in fidelity to your rules, being assured of the future of your society.[51]

Bishop Luers informed Fr. Moreau that he had appealed to Rome for an apostolic visitor and warned him not to remove Fr. Sorin unless the mother house was willing to assume the Notre Dame debts. Fr. Moreau replied with a lengthy but precise presentation of facts about the relations between Notre Dame du Lac and Holy Cross and a denial that he had any intention of removing Fr. Sorin. The visitor finally returned to France.

The date of the general chapter was approaching. In July the superior general sent a 25-page report to all the delegates on the state of the congregation during the three years since the 1860 chapter. It began:

> Religious congregations, like political societies and individual persons, encounter in the course of their existence circumstances that decide their destiny. None of us are unaware that since our last session the work of Holy Cross has undergone one of those fatal crises in which its future has been so gravely compromised that it would have perished without the special assistance of Providence because of the bad administration and other faults of some members. If these deplorable events should have nothing to teach us, I would despair of the survival of an enterprise which is, nevertheless, in accord with the designs of heaven because it has been approved by the august representative of God on earth. We cannot, therefore, without incurring a frightening responsibility, avoid the duty that our office imposes upon us today, and woe to the religious whom the situation caused for us by the spirit of evil should find apathetic or indifferent! With confidence, therefore, I submit to you a report which, while it offers you a picture of the material and disciplinary status of our congregation during the last three years, will permit you better to appreciate my administration, our present needs, and the measures which we must take to avoid new misfortunes. I recommend that you make it the subject of

your most serious reflections and that you pass over nothing that demands a reply or mature deliberation.

It concluded:

There is now nothing more for me to do except to ask you to accept my resignation both in order to form my successor to the office of superior general before I disappear from your midst and for the peace of my conscience and the greater good of the congregation. I have already sent this resignation to Rome, but I was asked to have it accepted first by the chapter, and this is what I am now doing, begging you not to refuse it. I will be no less devoted to the work in the post which obedience will assign me, and which I hope will be the lowest possible, in order that I may do reparation in the humility of submission for the faults which I committed in exercising authority over you.[52]

The general chapter opened on August 11 with Bishop Fillion presiding as apostolic visitor at Fr. Moreau's request. In preparatory sessions on August 9 and 10 the officers of the chapter were chosen, and the chapter proceeded to the election of ex officio members whose terms of office had expired. The chapter membership asked the superior general to give his advice on the election of two general officers: an assistant and the procurator general. The minutes read:

His Reverence saw no difficulty in the re-election of Br. Grégoire as assistant. As for the office of procurator, he thought that this position no longer had all the importance which it had enjoyed in the past [before approval of the constitutions], and after having praised Fr. Drouelle for his devotion and his ability as procurator, he would be inclined to give Fr. Drouelle a more important post, and, without any intention of influencing the election, he would be inclined to entrust the position of procurator general to Fr. Tréhu, who is presently at Rome and can remain there without any great difficulty.

The chapter thereupon proceeded to the elections by secret ballot: Br. Grégoire was elected assistant for six years and Fr. Tréhu procurator general also for six years. His Reverence straightway promulgated these two elections and immediately named Fr. Drouelle vicar of France to replace Fr. Champeau, whose state of health does not permit him to take any part in the chapter.

On August 11, after Bishop Fillion had given an address and the non-delegates had withdrawn, the superior general, in accord with chapter procedure, made his accusation before His Lordship and finished it more or less in these terms: "[I accuse myself] of having been, since the beginning of the congregation to this day, an obstacle to the development of this work because of my predominant fault, which is compulsiveness, violence, and a lack of union with God and of a spirit of prayer. Therefore, seeing in Your Lordship the representative of the sovereign pontiff, I beg you to have His Holiness, through Cardinal Barnabo, accept my resignation as superior general, noting that because of my advanced age I have great need of repose, not physical—I am not looking for that—but moral, in order to prepare myself for eternity; and so that my presence will not make the position of my successor difficult, I ask to be sent to another house, the smallest of all, far from Holy Cross."[53]

On August 12 at the very end of the fourth meeting of the chapter a portrait of the founder was discussed:

Mr. Eugene Moreau having completed a portrait of the very reverend father, several members of the general administration wanted to have a certain number of photographs of this work made. But, certain that His Reverence would not authorize an expense of that kind and would even destroy the portrait if he saw it, fearing on the other hand to violate their vow of poverty if they acted on their own, they wrote to His Lordship as apostolic visitor and delegate to obtain the necessary authorization, and His Lordship granted it in the presence of the chapter despite the opposition of His Reverence.

On the next day at the fifth meeting of the chapter immediately after the reading of the minutes, Fr. Moreau asked to speak:

His Reverence then begged His Lordship to reverse his decision of yesterday regarding the portrait and explained that he had always refused permissions of this sort which had been asked by the religious and blamed those who had had portraits made of themselves without asking him, and that he had made an exception only for the bishop of [Dhaka]. His Lordship answered that the religious of whom he was speaking could not be compared to a founder and that the Sulpicians kept the portraits of all their superiors general. The very reverend father insisted, saying that he would not be able to see his portrait without asking himself whether this was the picture of a man who would be saved or damned and that it would be a real torment for him. His Lordship maintained his first decision, adding that his portrait could only be a subject of edification and consolation in all our houses, and for this the chapter expressed its unanimous gratitude.[54]

During the chapter there were several clashes between Fr. Moreau and Fr. Sorin, Fr. Drouelle regularly siding with the latter. Bishop Fillion repeatedly played the peacemaker and suggested compromises. All the financial and other problems of the past three years in France, Indiana, and Rome were discussed, including the reactions of Cardinal Barnabo and the interventions of Bishop Luers. Fr. Sorin wanted Br. Amédée expelled from the congregation. The bishop suggested that obtaining a legal release of Fr. Sorin from the brother's claims would be enough, and the chapter agreed "almost unanimously."[55] Before the end of the same session, some words were exchanged about the difficulties between the visitor and those visited in Indiana. "His Lordship expressed the desire that in these personal matters both sides be satisfied with the kiss of peace."

After lengthy discussions the chapter decided to petition Rome for the canonical establishment of two provinces—France and America. Paris was proposed as the residence for the French provincial at Fr. Drouelle's suggestion.[56] A disagreement arose over the place of residence for the American provincial house: Fr. Rézé, until then provincial of Canada, wanted a neutral territory, that is, not Montreal, Notre Dame, or New Orleans, and Fr. Séguin suggested Philadelphia. The matter was consequently left to the judgment of Bishop Fillion.[57]

When Fr. Moreau presented the complaints of a number of religious from Indiana that their correspondence with the mother house had been interfered with, Fr. Sorin admitted withholding the letter of a sister "because she had no judgment" and said that he could not answer for all manifestations of distrust against him. Fr. Moreau "readily consented to drop the matter."[58]

After Fr. Drouelle's proposal that the chapter recognize the correctness of Fr. Sorin's financial dealings with the mother house, to which Fr. Charles Moreau objected, Bishop Fillion "suggested that the chapter decide to do justice to the devotedness of all, that misunderstandings on both sides be forgotten, and that from now on there be peace and union founded on mutual esteem, trust, and affection. The entire chapter gave a rousing vote of agreement."[59]

The chapter accepted the proposal that the rules be shortened and that their contents be reorganized. It charged the general council with publishing a new edition before the end of the next school year.[60]

At the final session "the very reverend father requested a secret vote on the matter of his resignation in view of a letter from Cardinal Barnabo asking the thought of the chapter on this matter. The result of the ballot opposed his resignation."[61] Only three votes out of twenty-three favored it.[62]

Since the agenda had been completed, His Reverence thanked His Lordship for the favor of his presidency during this session, from which there was reason to hope for the best results. The very reverend father once more assured all the delegates, especially those who were returning to foreign foundations, of the sentiments of sincere paternal affection and complete confidence which he had in their regard. His Lordship said that, despite many difficulties, the situation of the congregation was far from giving grounds for serious worry. . . . His Lordship concluded by recommending to us, above all, the spirit of devotion to the congregation, the spirit of union and charity. He then blessed the chapter members as apostolic delegate.[63]

On August 22 Fr. Moreau reported on the chapter to the congregation, concluding:

> After these observations, there remains for me but to recommend to you, dear fathers and brothers, that you bear in mind what you saw and heard during the annual retreat, especially at the retreat held at the mother house. . . . Let us recall particularly [the preacher's] insistence on poverty, chastity, and obedience, and on the spirit of mutual union. It is this union, the fruit of sanctifying grace, which will strengthen us against the world and the devil, while being at the same time the source of our success and consolations. It is like the mortar which holds and binds together the stones of the building we have undertaken, for without it everything will crumble and fall into ruin. This is why Jesus Christ so earnestly recommended union to his disciples and why in his last moments from the heights of that pulpit of which,

so to speak, one side rested on the cenacle and the other on Calvary, he made of union a formal command, his command of preference. For this reason also, addressing himself to his Father in a most sublime and moving prayer, he earnestly asked that his disciples might be united with one another as are the three divine Persons of the Trinity in such a way as to make them one. Oh, who will grant us this grace?

United to those in authority and to one another by the indissoluble bonds of obedience and charity, we shall triumph over our individual enemies and over those of the work entrusted to our care. Let us, then, stand in closely united ranks and, far from separating and scattering, let us live in such a manner that, as it beholds the members of our family, the world may say of us as the pagans did of the first Christians: "See how they love one another!"

This is the most burning desire of my heart. In order that it may be the better realized, I here declare that I wish to forget everything which could have saddened me on the part of certain religious so I may give them once again all my affection and confidence. In turn I beg of you to forgive anything in my words, actions, or writings which may have caused you the least pain. I promise to cooperate to the best of my ability with all those who share with me the government of the congregation either in France or abroad and to respect scrupulously all the orders, appointments, and elections made by the provincial chapter in France or by the general chapter.[64]

V. AFTERMATH OF THE CHAPTER: CONTINUED OPPOSITION

Fr. Sorin requested permission to take the chapter decrees to Rome. Fr. Moreau refused on the grounds that Fr. Sorin had repeatedly insisted that his presence was needed at Notre Dame.

Fr. Sorin persuaded Bishop Fillion to recommend to Rome a delay of the implementation of the chapter's petition for the establishment of a single American province because of the American Civil War. At this move Fr. Moreau recognized that he could not expect the sorely needed collaboration he had requested and once more offered his resignation to Bishop Fillion, who refused to forward it to Propaganda. The first biographer explains:

> That day his sorrow was so great that after the last exercise of the evening he called his councilors together to confess the temptation he had for a moment to abandon his post and the congregation. He knew, and this was his great sorrow, that the stream of denunciations was reaching the very feet of the sovereign pontiff, who one day in the presence of three Brothers of Saint Joseph, let these words of pity escape from his lips: "Poor congregation! Poor mother house! Poor superior general!"[65]

The bishop wrote Fr. Moreau:

> This would be an inappropriate moment to forward to the cardinal prefect of Propaganda the request you have just addressed to me. In my letter to him yesterday giving him an account of the chapter, I told him how deeply I had been edified, and I spoke of hopes aroused in me by the good spirit of the delegates and the union reigning among them. If the Holy See were inclined to listen to any of the calumnies against which you protest, it would be sufficiently enlightened by the vote of the chapter, which showed so eloquently that it wished to keep at the head of the congregation him who is its founder and father as well as its solid support. In the face of the protestations of the chapter, you had to force your humility to yield. In the light of the chapter's vote, you know how to sacrifice the sentiments which dictated your letter, and also how to take up valiantly the cross which divine

Providence had laid upon you. You will not lay down the cross without an order from God.[66]

On August 29 Fr. Sorin wrote Fr. Moreau a rather cold letter. The question of the Indiana sisters inspired the remark: "Abraham allowed Lot to go his own way. Just as it was for them, the earth is large enough for us, and if these dear souls cannot meet in the peace of God, it is much better to give them the peace of separation."[67]

The efforts against the founder's administration which had preceded the chapter continued after its conclusion. In October the superior general pleaded with the religious for an end to slanders. He wrote:

Inasmuch as Fr. Drouelle has entered upon his duties as provincial of France and its dependencies, I now have a certain amount of leisure which I have never previously enjoyed. I wish, then, to take this opportunity to call to your attention a serious fault of which several members of the congregation are guilty. I refer to detraction and especially to calumnies or false rumors in general. These reports are circulated particularly against the mother house and my administration and against the general chapter itself, some of whose acts have been maligned even to the authorities in Rome. . . .

What makes this evil all the more dangerous, reverend fathers and dear brothers, is the ease with which we allow ourselves to fall into it and the illusions we build up with regard to the terrible responsibility which we thus incur before God. How many there are, in fact, who feel no remorse, and go to holy communion without confession after having spoken ill of one another, of their fellow religious, their superiors, other houses, councils, chapters, and even the entire congregation! In this connection I am acquainted with certain facts which are really deplorable and which, if not remedied, would end by dividing the members of our family, preventing or weakening certain vocations, seriously endangering the prestige of the general administration, creating countless difficulties and thereby frustrating the designs of Providence on the congregation which God has founded. . . .

Everyone, reverend fathers and dear brothers, should give serious thought to this point, keep watch over himself for the future, and bear in mind these words of the wise man: "There are six things which the Lord hates, and the seventh his soul detests: a haughty air, a lying tongue, hands which shed innocent blood, a heart which forms evil designs, feet light and ready to run to evil, the lying witness who testifies to lies, and he who sows dissension among his brethren."[68]

Fr. Drouelle considered his recall from Rome a "demotion."[69] It unleashed verbal attacks against both Fr. Moreau and the new procurator general as well as denunciations to Cardinal Barnabo and even to Pius IX on the part of some of Fr. Drouelle's religious and lay friends, whom he had apparently initiated into the congregation's affairs. The first version of the chapter which the cardinal received was given by the former procurator at his return to Rome for his belongings. This report provoked a complaint from the cardinal that Fr. Moreau had opposed the separation of temporalities between the Marianites and the congregation! Fr. Moreau's reaction was another offer of resignation on October 9: "After the manner in which I am being treated in Rome and at the mother house in the presence of anyone who happens along and without ever having been given an opportunity to explain myself, I have no other choice but to notify Your Eminence not to count on me any longer for the government of the congregation."[70]

Less than two weeks later he wrote to the superior of Saint Bridget's: "I give up any attempt at self-defense, and, even were

I placed under interdict, I want to repeat until the very end: Yes, Father, for such was your good pleasure."[71]

In November Cardinal Barnabo informed Fr. Tréhu, the procurator general, that he wanted the superior general to come to Rome along with Fathers Drouelle and Champeau to discuss the accusations made against him. Fr. Moreau replied by once more offering his resignation and by sending Fr. Séguin, the general secretary, to Rome with all the documents needed to justify his administration. Fr. Séguin wrote from Rome: "The cardinal has been showered with signed letters and especially with anonymous communications. I told him that you had no enemies except among those whose debts you had paid. His Eminence complained at length that, since the approval of the constitutions, he has been left out of the picture. He knows our congregation only by the complaints he has received against it. In these latter years His Eminence has heard from the mother house only every four months."[72]

Fr. Séguin thus began to uncover the intrigues of the former procurator general and saw the numerous letters against the founder which had filled the files of Propaganda.

At this news Fr. Moreau wrote to the general secretary:

> When I learned, my dear friend, the whole mystery of intrigues that you have revealed to me, I cried out spontaneously: Iniquity has lied to itself. But also, how good is the God of Israel to those who are of right heart. What surprised me most is this battle cry raised against me after the very chapter in which a secret ballot on my resignation registered only three votes in favor out of twenty-three as well as the ignorance in which Fr. Drouelle kept His Eminence of our affairs for three years although I was telling him everything, writing him everything, sending him all the documents, and thinking that he was keeping nothing back from

the cardinal prefect, to whom we owe our approbation in Rome.

Another inexplicable mystery for me is how, despite my failings, I am on good terms with my bishop, with all the civil authorities of our city, with the government itself, and with all the cardinals, archbishops, and bishops of France who know me, with the possible exception of the bishop of Angers, in whose regard my conscience does not disquiet me in the least. Surely the temper which I am supposed to have should have caused me to compromise myself in letters I wrote or things I did. . . .

Did I say or do anything violent during our general chapter, where I certainly had the occasion to do so against several people who paid no attention to my advice or even my directives at Paris, at [Notre Dame], at Maulévrier?[73]

Fr. Séguin insisted that he come to Rome. Hence, on December 3 he wrote:

I will come, my friend, as I have telegraphed, because His Eminence insists—without doubt in view of our own interests. But if I am made the object of reproaches, especially if it be in anybody's presence, I will withdraw in silence and definitively give up the administration which had cost me so many contradictions and humiliations. I thought I deserved better of the Holy See for a devotedness that dates back forty years, for right from my ordination to the priesthood I struggled against Gallicanism through fourteen years of teaching theology, then served as an instrument of Providence for the foundation of the Good Shepherd, of Holy Cross, of Vigna Pia, and I see that now, last of all, I have to undergo a final trial that hurts me deeply, that of passing for someone who has disobeyed the pope.

Once more he reviewed briefly the trials of the last few, especially the last three, years. Then he concluded: "All of this is enough to discourage the most zealous of men, and I do not understand how they can refuse my resignation to the present day since there have been so many complaints against me."

On December 12 he left Le Mans. Fathers Drouelle and Champeau, summoned to discuss their grievances with him in the presence of the cardinal, made the journey from Marseilles to Rome with the superior general.

Fr. Moreau was amazed to discover all that had been done against him since the general chapter. He answered the grievances one by one verbally and in writing. He tried to resign three times, but Cardinal Barnabo and Pius IX refused to accept his resignation. In a circular letter dated January 16, 1864, he notified the congregation briefly of the reason for his visit to Rome. Then on January 31 he wrote:

> My last circular has already informed you why I came here. If I write you again on the eve of my return to France by way of Algeria, where I have promised to visit our schools, it is, first of all, to put certain anxious minds at rest concerning myself. Then, I wish to tell you how we stand in the eyes of the Holy See and to acquaint you with the results of my trip and, finally, to exhort you to turn my visit to profit by submitting to whatever measures may be demanded by circumstances.
>
> I need not assure you that I harbor no ill feeling against those who made it necessary for me to undertake this journey and thus to occasion new expense to the congregation. As a matter of fact, I was under obligation to make this visit as the result of a promise made more than three years ago to the worthy vicar of Christ, but I was to have come alone and for altogether different motives. My feelings are not what one would expect after all the opposition I have had to cope

with. The consolations I have experienced in the holy city are rewards sufficiently great to make me forget certain ways of acting which are naturally disagreeable and to make me see only the good which has been intended, notwithstanding a mistaken choice of means. How good is the God of Israel toward those who are of upright heart! Consequently, I would refrain from mentioning recent events, were it not that the demands of my office in the Congregation of Holy Cross and my duty of preventing a recurrence of the painful incidents which followed our last general chapter oblige me to discuss these matters with you.

It is well for you to know, then, in case you are not already acquainted with the fact, that for quite some time a mysterious campaign of opposition had been waged at Propaganda. Strange complaints indeed were lodged against my administration, and I was depicted in such an extraordinary light that I really had to read these documents or hear them read in order to believe that such things had actually been written. At the same time that they accused me of being domineering and harsh and of engaging in business transactions which would ruin our finances, these informants were careful to affect a show of respect and politeness for a poor old man who had to be humored because of his title of founder and the need of his signature for certain financial transactions, but whose stubbornness and eccentricity were beyond all hope of improvement.

It is true that no one either on my council or in the general chapter ever gave expression to such thoughts. But if one were to listen to the complaints, the general councilors were either simple children with no experience of men or affairs or else timid and spineless men who dared not contradict me. The general chapter delegates, for their part, it was said, had been cowed by the fear of offending me or deceived by subtle intrigue. Consequently, certain elections, particularly that of the procurator general to the Holy See, were null and void. Nor was this all. In order the better to dupe the good faith of the cardinal prefect of Propaganda, countless letters were sent to him, many of them anonymous, others signed by laity who pretended to be acting out of devotedness to the congregation and to be animated with veneration for its superior general. Among these names were some which appear in the minutes of our chapter. They evidenced such a spirit of contradiction that on seeing them the illustrious prince of the Church could not refrain from exclaiming in the presence of our general secretary: "Either these men are fools or criminals, or else they are staging some kind of devilish comedy for my benefit!"

Over and above all this, reverend fathers and dear brothers, a memorandum had been sent to Rome and to the bishop of Le Mans at the close of our chapter, although it had been prepared long before. With an evident view to bolstering up the defamatory correspondence which I have just mentioned by other calumnies against the mother house, this document completely ignored our decisions on certain administrative details. Furthermore, it was supplemented by certain conclusions which aimed at nothing short of the emancipation of the community from higher authority. The resulting picture of the general administration was so somber that someone wrote to me: "The whole congregation is falling to pieces." What made the situation still more critical was the fact that after having unsuccessfully offered my resignation to the general chapter, I had later sent it to Cardinal Barnabo and refused to reconsider it since it was my wish to take myself out of the way of those who believed me an obstacle to the welfare of the congregation.

Such was the state of affairs when I consented to reply to the requests which had been made to me and to come to clear myself of all these strange accusations. I shall not go into any details lest I offend anyone and also lest I lose precious time in acquainting you with this disloyal opposition in which most of you have had no part. Moreover, I am convinced that those of you who know of this whole affair will demand justice for these attacks against the mother house, the general officers, and the general chapter. As for my own personal justification and that of my nephew in connection with his visit to Notre Dame du Lac, I am satisfied to know the opinion of higher authorities, and I am no more worried than he by human judgments when they attack me alone. After all, you know what attitude you should take on this matter as well as on our financial situation and those responsible for it. . . .

Let us thank heaven for what has already been done here to thwart both the visible and the invisible enemies of our congregation. Let us accept with gratitude the means with which we are provided in order to atone for the past, save the present, and assure for ourselves a better future. May there not be a single one of you, reverend fathers and dear brothers, who will refuse to carry out the measures taken by the Sacred Congregation of Propaganda, the chapter, or the general council, whatever may be the cost to self-love. . . .

Unite, then, in one same spirit of obedience not only with the Holy See, which still deigns to protect us, but also with all your lawful superiors. . . .

I conjure you in the name of the sacred interests which have been entrusted to us and for which we must all answer; in the name of Jesus Christ and the ten thousand children whose education has been confided to us; in the name of his divine mother, Our Lady of Holy Cross, whose adopted children we are; in the name of Saint Joseph, our patron and our model; in the name of our eternal salvation and of all that we may have done or suffered out of fidelity to our vocation, let us forget past wrongs. Let us bear in mind the reply of our divine Lord to Saint Peter, who, after asking how many times he ought to pardon, received from his sacred lips the equivalent of these words: Always and without ever tiring. As for myself, I wish to remember only the devotedness of each one of you and the consolations which were unexpectedly procured for me by those who forced me to come to Rome.[74]

Despite these statements it was difficult, after so many intrigues, for the superior general to act as though nothing had happened. On February 15, after his return to Le Mans, he wrote to Br. Vincent, one of the first religious to go to Indiana and a member of the Notre Dame council: "I have just got back from Rome, my dear friend, and found your New Year greetings in my mail. I would not answer a word if I had not known you for so long a time because your letter is in such little accord with the signature which you placed on a memorandum which caused a cardinal to say: 'Those people are fools or criminals. . . .' I beg God to pardon all of you, to open your eyes, and to make you more obedient to the authorities constituted to govern you."

This defeat in Rome did not discourage Fr. Moreau's opponents. On the contrary, it made them all the more determined.

The vicar of France, Fr. Drouelle, and his assistant, Fr. Champeau, refused to take office until Propaganda determined the rights of provincials, and Fr. Drouelle left Rome for a visit to the languishing foundation in Dalmatia without even informing Fr. Moreau. When he returned to France in February, he complained that Fr. Moreau had regulated certain matters in his absence for which no one else was making provision. He began the canonical visit in France and sold property below value without even consulting the superior general.

At the same time Fr. Sorin and Bishop Luers were still working for the separation of the Indiana sisters. The Indiana vicar sent two reports and the bishop one to Propaganda. Then in May the bishop left for Rome.

In the preceding December Fr. Sorin had closed the brother's school in Cincinnati despite the local bishop's objections and without the knowledge of the mother house. In March without warning, he closed all six of the brothers' and sisters' schools in Philadelphia (he had begun to recall the brothers in the preceding December)—probably to prevent the possible establishment of a provincial house there: it would have been just the sort of "neutral" location that Fr. Rézé had requested in the general chapter. The reasons given, however, were that the brothers were exposed to being drafted into military service, which they could have avoided by payment of sixty dollars, and that the archbishop of Philadelphia wanted to make the sisters independent of the mother house! Fr. Moreau learned of the closing of these houses only indirectly.

In May Fr. Sorin wrote to Mother Mary of the Seven Dolors that if she did not come to take up residence at Notre Dame, the bishop of Fort Wayne would obtain total separation. Fr. Moreau protested futilely and waited.

A year had passed since the general chapter, and the only tangible result of its deliberations was a new edition of the rules. In accord with the decisions of the chapter, Fr. Moreau had attempted to revise the rules with the help of the general council.[75] Disagreement and bickering finally led to his redoing the rules himself in order to have them ready for the July deadline set by the chapter, as he explained in offering them to the religious:[76] "At last I have been able to finish the new edition of our rules conformably to the decrees of the general chapter in its session of 1863. . . . Obliged as I was to do this work myself because none of my assistants would consent to undertake it, although they agreed to examine it, I have kept in mind as far as possible all the observations submitted in writing or verbally in our chapters and in my council." But his outlook on this rule was quite different from his conception of the 1858 edition. He explained: "Notwithstanding all the attention I have given to this new collection of directives on regular discipline, I am far from presenting it to you as perfect. By its very nature such a work remains subject to whatever revisions experience or the expansion of the congregation may render necessary."

VI. THE TWO PROVINCES

The decisions of Propaganda on the 1863 general chapter reached Le Mans only at the end of September. They came in the wake of a provincial chapter that had made the founder's position all the more difficult, and they only made it more difficult still.

In early August 1864, Fr. Moreau wanted to discuss the approaching chapter of the French vicariate with Fr. Drouelle and asked him to call a preparatory session. The latter refused and threw all responsibility for the chapter on Fr. Moreau. The superior general tried unsuccessfully to elicit the vicar's cooperation. Finally the chapter met, invited Fr. Moreau to preside, and decided to move the residence of the vicar from Paris to Le Mans. Fr. Drouelle interpreted this as an insult to Bishop Fillion, who had presided over the general chapter which had decided the vicar should reside in Paris—since the bishop had not been consulted before this decision of the chapter—and from this moment Bishop Fillion seems to have moved more and more to the side of the opposition.

At the end of September the decisions of Propaganda arrived. Rome had decided to establish two provinces: a French province with the provincial residence in Paris and an American province with the provincial residence at Notre Dame du Lac. The letter of Cardinal Barnabo also stated:

On the question of the relations of the superior general with the other officials, Propaganda has decided that, since the administration finds itself on more solid footing because of the establishment of provinces, the superior general should leave administrative details to subordinates and limit himself to general supervision and the approbation of whatever measures may be submitted to him by the same officers. He should never interfere with their jurisdiction except in cases of grave negligence or real urgency. In such instances the general will keep the other officers informed of any measures he may have deemed conducive to the general welfare of the congregation.[77]

Fr. Moreau, in reporting this point to the congregation in a circular letter of November 22, could add an explanatory note to the paragraph just quoted: "This procedure has always been followed in dealing with our houses abroad and has been adopted in France since the last provincial chapter." Before that date the French Province had not been able to function normally, as we have already seen.

The cardinal also "thought it necessary to take an extraordinary but temporary measure in order to put a stop to the disagreements and end the factions which have arisen between the sisters and the priests and brothers in America." This move was to place "the sisters under the jurisdiction of the bishop of Fort Wayne until the Sacred Congregation shall have made known its definitive judgment with regard to them." Even more, the cardinal "put the fathers and brothers under the immediate supervision of the same bishop for the formation of this province."[78]

The cardinal's letter concluded: "The Sacred Congregation manifested a readiness to adopt measures of extreme rigor which would be most painful for Your Paternity unless it receives evidence that the above-mentioned directives are being carried out promptly, loyally, and in their entirety, and unless the institute take steps toward successfully attaining its goal by the observance of its constitutions and by a government functioning according to rule."[79]

In announcing these decisions to the congregation, the superior general commented on the one which effectively removed the American foundations from his control:

> Perhaps this decision will surprise the houses in Canada, New Orleans, and New York, which have remained aloof from the troubles in Indiana, as also those among you, my dear brothers, who, for fear of breaking with the mother house, have preferred to obey me rather than to abandon the places which certain parties wanted to make you leave without my consent. But now that the cardinal prefect has made known his decision, you will, I trust, be the first to give an example of obedience and to provide me with further proofs of your loyalty.[80]

The French provincial chapter met and elected Fr. Drouelle as provincial. Fr. Moreau wrote on January 10, 1865:

> I am availing myself of my very first spare moments since the close of the provincial chapter of France to thank you for your New Year's greetings and to revive your confidence for the future of the work entrusted to us, notwithstanding its manifold trials during the year 1864. I know full well that these troubles have caused you no little worry. . . .
>
> For my own part, reverend fathers and dear brothers, I am not the least surprised by all these trials. Thanks be to God, they have only increased my confidence in him who alone has founded and maintained this congregation. . . .
>
> Jesus Christ is faithful, and he will not permit you to be tempted beyond your strength. If we but know how to awaken him from his apparent sleep by our prayers, he will command the winds and the storm, and we shall have once more

the calm of bygone days. This peace of mind and heart has already made itself felt in the chapter over which I have just presided, and the members of the chapter found therein new light and encouragement.

Bear in mind and do not forget, reverend fathers and dear brothers, that just as divine Providence has willed its greatest works to begin in humility and abjection, it has also decreed that they should expand only at the price of difficulties and contradictions, trials, crosses, contempt, calumny, and detraction. . . .

The many different trials to which we have been subjected are indubitable marks of the divine will in regard to our congregation and of the presence of our Lord in our midst. . . .

Be glad then, reverend fathers and dear brothers, that you have been found worthy to suffer in body and soul and to share in the sufferings of this institute. Be glad and increase your confidence in proportion as I suffer personally more tribulations since these trials are a sure guarantee of the divine will toward us and the work whose instruments we are. . . .

I shall have no fears for the congregation, and even if all of you had abandoned me on hearing of our catastrophes, I should have begun all over again as soon as I could, so convinced am I that what I have undertaken is the will of God. If indeed you had then looked back, Jesus Christ would have chosen other workers to take your place.[81]

The American chapter of sisters met in March. That of the priests and brothers met in May. By Bishop Luers' decision chapter membership was organized not according to the decree of Propaganda and the constitutions but on the basis of numbers, which gave the Indiana houses an absolute majority in both chapters. The sisters' chapter introduced constitutional modifications; the priests' and brothers' legislated, among other things, one novitiate for the entire North American continent at Notre Dame despite language differences. The bishop obtained from Cardinal Barnabo the faculty of naming Fr. Sorin provincial of the priests and brothers and superior of the sisters. The sisters were even forbidden to correspond with their superiors in France. The delegates who were not from Indiana protested as did some of their bishops, and the general council sent a memorandum to Rome. Nothing happened.

Fr. Moreau, in accord with the instructions he had received from Rome the preceding autumn, had had nothing to do with the American chapters; in fact, he had been able to write Cardinal Barnabo on February 15, 1865: "I do not know when you will receive the chapter proceedings from America because I do not even know when the capitulants will meet, and, in conformity with the recommendation of Your Eminence, I am playing dead and will do so until further orders."

The only consolation that came from Rome was a letter of Cardinal Barnabo to Mother Mary of the Seven Dolors dated January 13, 1865, and promising early examination of the sisters' constitutions in view of papal approval. The founder, however, could not fail to find some consolation in the fact that despite all the struggles and scandals the congregation was larger than ever, that candidates continued to come, that a new Association of Saint Joseph already had about three thousand members without diminishing membership of the old association, that notable people were still delighted to be chosen members of the Academy of Holy Cross and invited to preside at its sessions, and that the missions preached by the priests, in which the founder still took part, were meeting with the same success.[82]

The new superior of Saint Bridget's in Rome now began to cause trouble. When the general council had shown itself unwilling to agree to his purchase of an adjoining property and had referred him to Cardinal Barnabo, the cardinal gave him encouragement, and he involved himself financially. The mother house then found itself with new debts, and after the superior received a rebuke from the superior general, Propaganda received new complaints against Fr. Moreau.

In France Fr. Drouelle was continually causing problems for the superior general. For example, at Maulévrier after scandalous conduct by a religious, Fr. Moreau had to dismiss the man. Fr. Drouelle refused to have anything to do with the house. Fr. Moreau had to replace the superior and reorganize the house. When the general council complained about the provincial's negligence, Fr. Drouelle decried the "dictatorship" of the superior general![83]

When the regular provincial chapter opened at Le Mans on August 11, 1865, Fr. Drouelle requested that some of his houses be suppressed. He informed the general council that he had no preferences and that the houses could be chosen by drawing their names out of a hat! The next day Fr. Moreau announced that the French provincial had sent his resignation to Cardinal Barnabo and that at Fr. Drouelle's own request the religious should no longer come to him for anything. Nevertheless, he then resumed his canonical visit of the French houses! The matter was taken to Bishop Fillion, who agreed that Fr. Drouelle should continue to act as provincial until Cardinal Barnabo had replied! Fr. Drouelle mailed another memorandum to the cardinal against Fr. Moreau. Even more, some of the religious were told not to correspond with the superior general without showing their letters to their local superiors.[84]

In Paris Fr. Champeau wanted to purchase a new building for his college since the lease on the building he was occupying would expire in 1867. The general council, after several meetings, decided instead to close the college. The bishop of Le Mans agreed. Fr. Champeau, however, asked to organize an independent corporation to take over the college. Fr. Moreau saw no difficulty but told him to sign no documents without previously notifying the general council. By January 1866 the corporation, in which Fathers Drouelle and Champeau were shareholders, was organized and owned valuable property, and Fr. Champeau refused to provide the general council with any information, stating that he had informed Cardinal Barnabo!

The superior general's position was now absolutely ineffective. The American Province had been placed outside his control by Rome, and the French provincial successfully nullified all control in France. The superior general was as ineffective as if he had been a prisoner, and that was being prepared. In late 1865 Fr. Moreau received a letter from Cardinal Barnabo inviting him to Rome "to be informed" of steps taken by Propaganda to insure "proper administration" of the congregation. According to Fr. Drouelle, he was to be kept there![85] The superior general, preaching a retreat at Grand-Lucé when he received this letter, wrote immediately to the pope:

> It is as one crushed under deepest affliction that I come to prostrate myself at the feet of Your Holiness to beseech you humbly to allow me to tell you that for some time the good faith of the Holy See has been deceived in regard to me and my council. God is my witness that if I were the only one to suffer, I would keep silence and drink the chalice to the very dregs without complaining to anyone. But there is question here of the existence of a foundation which Your Holiness has blessed and which the enemy of good has wanted to sift through the intrigue and ambition of certain of its members. Assuredly, after having spent my entire life in the service of the Church, I was not expecting from some of my fellow religious such a rich harvest of trials, and it is solely in order not to become an obstacle to the measures I am told have been taken by Propaganda and which I know nothing about that I place in the hands of Your Holiness all the authority I

received from you to govern the foundation of Holy Cross, while asking pardon for the faults by which I may have unwittingly saddened the Holy See.[86]

He informed Cardinal Barnabo that he had submitted his resignation and that he would readily receive any communication that should be sent but that because of the grave situation in France, he could not leave his council. On December 6, the cardinal wrote to Fr. Moreau that the earlier invitation was an order and that certain reports sent by the general council (perhaps the report on Fr. Drouelle's resignation) were "unreasonable." Fr. Moreau was apparently waiting to find out whether his resignation had been accepted or, if not, whom he could designate to govern the congregation in his absence. To leave everything in the hands of Fathers Drouelle and Champeau would have been to risk ruin. At least so he informed Bishop Fillion when he received Cardinal Barnabo's third letter on December 29, and the majority of the general council agreed with his stand.[87] As if to confirm his position, news of Fr. Champeau's corporation arrived as the new year began. The bishop wrote the cardinal that the founder was looking for excuses to avoid going to Rome and yet admitted that the congregation's creditors would be disturbed by his absence.[88]

These events served as the background to the last New Year's circular letter of Fr. Moreau's term as superior general:

If the year just past was full of trials for me, the coming year gives no indications of lessening either their number or their gravity. But the expressions of affection I have received and your devotedness to the Congregation of Holy Cross sweeten the bitterness of my sorrows, although they do not relieve my soul, which is crushed down by the spirit of division which the demon of discord has sown among us. In the midst of all these trials, our only course is to pray God to give us his peace and, in order that we may merit this peace,

314 PORTRAIT OF A FOUNDER

to ask him to renew us in the spirit of fidelity to our rules and our vows.

Hence, I beg you to walk more and more perfectly in the path of obedience, tightening the bonds of fraternal charity, and meditating frequently on your individual responsibility in the work of Holy Cross. As for myself, the sight of my declining years makes me tremble at the thought of the account I shall have to give; and while I thank you for your good wishes for my happiness, I cannot but implore the aid of your prayers and pardon for the faults by which I have caused you sorrow or disedification.[89]

On January 21, the procurator general arrived in Le Mans to plead with Fr. Moreau to leave for Rome, informing him that he would receive no further communication from the Holy See. On January 29 he left.

He wrote of his first visit to Propaganda in a letter of February 5: "I went to Propaganda for my first visit, reflecting on these words of the *Imitation*: 'Son, you must still be put to the test on earth and exercised in many things.'"[90] Nevertheless he was delighted by his reception in Rome. He wrote to the congregation on February 11: "I have again found here in this city the same friends and the same kindness as during my last visit." But he added: "Keep yourselves close to God by avoiding sin and by frequent reception of the sacraments, close to your superiors by obedience, and close to all your confreres by charity, for the demon of discord has done us untold harm."[91]

He once again offered his resignation. He was told it was not accepted. On May 27, the day after his final interview with Cardinal Barnabo, he wrote him the following letter:

In order that the sacred congregation may have no doubt about the dispositions which I manifested in the audience which Your Eminence did me the honor of granting me yesterday and in which you showed me such a fatherly kindness, I feel it my duty to declare before God that I am ready to offer my resignation either to His Holiness or to our general chapter and without any condition, provided that I will then be freed of all temporal responsibility, committing myself to take all the means that will be judged desirable to facilitate freedom of action for my successor whether in regard to the goods that were given me for the institute or in the matter of my leaving the mother house or fulfilling the tasks that may be confided to me, promising exemplary obedience to the superior general canonically elected.[92]

During his stay in Rome he had made a thorough canonical visit of Saint Bridget's and Vigna Pia. Nor had he neglected his correspondence with the religious. An interesting letter of March 27 to a brother who had not yet made his perpetual vows showed that the heartaches of the preceding months and the worries of his stay in Rome had not hardened or embittered him. He wrote in part:

I must tell you, my dear friend, how much delight your fine little letter gave me, and I must thank you especially for remembering me to Saint Joseph. It was a great consolation for me to learn of the edifying way in which the feast of this illustrious patron of our congregation was celebrated at Holy Cross. . . . I have too much affection for you, my dear Marie-Auguste, to forget you, even though we are separated by such a great distance, and I shall ask our Lord to be mindful of you as a spoiled child of his providence so that you may become worthy to consecrate yourself irrevocably to his work by indissoluble bonds. The sooner you do this, the greater consolation you will have at death, provided that you intend generously to die to yourself all the days of your life. Ask him to give this grace to me too.

The founder reached Le Mans on Sunday, June 10, as the community came away from vespers. After greeting and blessing them and announcing that his resignation had not been accepted, haggard and worn though he was, he immediately met with his council for three hours. He then resumed his normal chores.

Two days later he was surprised to receive a telegram from the procurator general: "Departure from Rome judged severely." Confused, he immediately wrote the cardinal, begging that his resignation be accepted. On June 19 he received from Bishop Fillion a letter from Cardinal Barnabo dated June 14, the feast of Saint Basil, announcing that his resignation had been accepted, though Fr. Drouelle's had not, and that Fr. Chappé, his assistant, would act as vicar general until the general chapter could convene to elect a successor. The cardinal ordered him to refrain from interfering either in the general affairs of the congregation or in the future election and urged him not to run the risk of ruining everything by refusing to submit. The founder's last circular letter as superior general announced the event and concluded:

> Surely, reverend fathers and dear brothers, I can only thank God for this news, and it is my fond hope that at the next chapter everything will take place in accordance with our rules and the prescriptions of the Holy See.
>
> In the meantime, let us pray, and count always on my devotedness to the congregation, as also on the affectionate interest with which I shall be to my last breath, reverend fathers and dear brothers,
>
> Yours in Jesus, Mary, and Joseph,
Moreau.

Fr. Séguin, the general secretary, recorded what happened at Holy Cross:

On June 21, after evening prayer, His Reverence entrusted Fr. Chappé, his first assistant, with the reading of his letter announcing to the institute the decisions taken by the Sacred Congregation and approved by His Holiness. After this communication, the very reverend father founder, practically the only one who was maintaining a perfect calm, rose and before the silent tears of his children, pronounced these words, recorded as faithfully as the profound emotion which that assembly experienced could permit:

"My reverend fathers and my dear brothers, the letter which you have just heard read has perhaps surprised you, at least most of you; but it should not worry you because everything has been provided for and arranged with wisdom. It is a precious grace for me, and it will also be a grace for you if you know how to profit from it. At times in the works of God there are names so compromised by the struggles inseparable from their foundation that it is useful for them to disappear so that passions may subside and opposition incited by the enemies of good may cease. That is why for nine years I have often offered my resignation either to general chapters or to Propaganda and last November to the sovereign pontiff himself. Besides, the responsibility that was weighing upon me frightened me at the thought of my eternity and of the account that I will soon have to render for my office. His Holiness, after having refused several times to free me of this responsibility, has finally deigned to grant my petition, and in naming Fr. Chappé to replace me, one of the two religious that I was permitted to suggest, he has given you a bond of union between those who sympathized with me in mind, heart, and action and those who did not understand my administration. The letter in which God sends me this good news was addressed to me on the feast of Saint Basil, and it is really for me the best of feast day gifts.

"I have long felt that something was lacking to my mission in this work, and I bless the providence that gives me today the means of accomplishing it. Until the present, by my position it was impossible for me both to command and to obey. However, from now on, I hope with the grace of God to give to all of you the example of submission and obedience. And now, before inviting Fr. Chappé to take my place here, I want only to ask your pardon for the bad example which I may have given you during my long term as superior and for the obstacles that I may have placed to the sanctification of each of you and to the prosperity of God's work."

When he finished these words, the very reverend father founder quite simply left the superior's place in order to take his place according to rank among the professed religious. The first general assistant then spoke. He protested in the name of all that "it was not for His Reverence to ask pardon of us but rather for us to throw ourselves at his feet and to beg his kind forgiveness for each one and for the entire congregation which he had founded at the cost of so much labor, to which he had consecrated, even sacrificed, his life, for which he had struggled for thirty years, suffered so many contradictions, and undergone so many trials without letting himself be overcome for a moment by ingratitude or by calumny or by the human judgments which God and the future will take care to reform." He added that "this entire sorrowing family would be happy at least to acquit a part of its debt of gratitude toward its father and its founder in surrounding his old age with care, respect, and love, and in profiting even to the end from his lights, his example, his experience, and his devotedness." Finally, at the request of the assistant, the father founder blessed for a final time as superior general the community and the congregation, and a moment later he had taken his place after the general officers. The sacrifice had been accomplished.[94]

CHAPTER 8

CONSUMMATION (1866–1873)

I. PEACE AND PERSECUTION: 1866–1867

Reactions to the founder's resignation were varied. Mother Mary of the Seven Dolors wrote to Fr. Moreau: "Very reverend father, my practice of revealing all my preoccupations to you and the kindness with which you listen to them encourage me to express to you my deep sorrow. . . . Be assured that I understand your suffering very well and that I feel it deeply."[1] Fr. Drouelle, when he informed the Marianites of Vendôme and noted their sadness, remarked: "It's really nothing at all. Practically all founders of orders were deposed like that."[2] A Le Mans newspaper asked whether the removal of Fr. Moreau as superior general would mean the sale of Holy Cross. When he answered that he had not been "removed" but had freely resigned as he had resigned as superior of the Good Shepherd monastery earlier, the paper replied: "If we have been mistaken on the interpretation we have placed on the change, the error is common to a great number of people in Le Mans."[3]

Mother Mary of the Seven Dolors wrote to a sister in America:

> What grave events have taken place! And what will their consequences be? That is God's secret. Let us pray very much, for if there was ever a difficult time, it is the one in which we are

now. . . . A veil of sadness envelops Holy Cross. Its founder and father, become a simple religious, is there in a room doing what they tell him to do and nothing more, taking his place everywhere after the councilors [the place which belonged to him as the oldest of the religious not holding an office], and asking the least permissions. They say he is lighthearted. Yes, I understand in what sense: in the sense in which God's friends are always happy. But he is a father, and as a father he must feel all the bitterness that there is in the cup which his children have prepared for him. He has not given me any indication of what he may be experiencing; I can see only the most perfect contentment and calm in his features and in his words. But his faithful children are weeping and praying for everyone. . . . Please keep these things to yourself, for discretion is more necessary than ever: everything is being misinterpreted, and the most innocent things can be used to go on calumniating our founder, who, however, is saying and doing and writing nothing more.[4]

Fr. Chappé wrote to Cardinal Barnabo: "Far from hindering my freedom of action, the father founder is facilitating it by a humility and an obedience which put all of us to shame."[5] In fact, in keeping with the teaching he had given the religious, he asked Fr. Chappé to become his spiritual director. Fr. Moreau wrote later: "I chose this priest as my director after my resignation, seeing in him only the priest and the superior. I went to him in all simplicity, enjoying the happiness of my resignation and of complete obedience."[6]

Fr. Drouelle showed himself as little disposed to cooperate with the new superior as with the old: he offered extensive advice on how to carry on the general administration and on the forthcoming chapter and prepared for the sale of Holy Cross, while at the same time declining Fr. Chappé's invitation to make the canonical visit of the Algerian houses and without the knowledge of the general administration proposing the sale of the Maulévrier property to the donor's heirs. This last step spurred the heirs to have the donation annulled. With the agreement of Bishop Fillion and Fr. Chappé, Fr. Moreau wrote the heir but in vain. The property was lost to Holy Cross, and the founder could succeed only in freeing the congregation from the obligation to reimburse the income received during the time since the donation had been made. Mortgages were transferred from this property to the mother house.

Propaganda had decided that the chapter of 1866 would have the same membership as that of 1863, but Fr. Moreau was not invited. Bishop Fillion informed him that he had lost his seat in the chapter by his resignation. This rule, however, did not seem to apply to other delegates. Even more, Fr. Champeau, who had not been in the chapter of 1863, was invited by the bishop. Fr. Moreau did not object, and several weeks before the chapter convened he retired to the Solitude of Saint Joseph so as to be absent when the delegates met.

Nevertheless, at his nephew's instigation, he prepared a lengthy report for the chapter on his administration. He wrote as vigorously as ever, concluding:

> [As the former superior general,] I have a final duty in regard to the congregation, the duty of vindicating my administration, all of whose acts were accomplished, first of all, with my council, and which have been falsely calumniated, although they were in conformity with our rules and constitutions. There is also the obligation of enlightening the good faith of the members of the chapter, whom efforts are being made to deceive in such a way, as I see it, as to ruin the foundation of Holy Cross under the pretext of saving it. Now in the presence of this twofold duty, silence cannot be excused. I do not think that any councilor or member of the chapter can keep silence in conscience, once he is made aware of the scheming

and the conspiracy which is boldly lying and spreading contempt for the authority regularly constituted for the government of the congregation. . . . In any case, it would be better to be stricken with dissolution by the Holy See than to die by inches through a compromise with injustice and ambition.[7]

The general council decided to present to the chapter an account of the debts it had assumed but without the founder's commentary. The chapter, which convened on August 23, decided that it was not "called upon to discuss and to judge the acts of him whom the congregation would always regard as its founder and father."[8] In fact, a motion was made that all the records of his administrative acts be burned! But it failed to carry. So unwilling was it to treat of the founder that the chapter did not even give Fr. Moreau the release from financial responsibility he had requested.

The delegates decided to petition Rome for permission to sell as much of the Le Mans properties as should be necessary to pay the debts. They also decided, at the insistence of the Canadian and Louisiana superiors, to ask the Holy See to establish Canada, Indiana, and Louisiana into three distinct provinces. They elected Bishop Dufal of Dhaka as superior general—a man who had for years been far from the scene of the struggles and who had not come for the chapter.

The founder now had more time for prayer. In gratitude for gifts sent to him by the sisters, he mailed them some verses he composed in his time of prayer and leisure. One of them began, "What am I doing on earth, so far from you, my savior?" And another, a lengthy "Visit to the Blessed Sacrament," concluded, "I hope in you and offer you my life, which I should like to end here in this place." To one sister he wrote, "God is giving me great peace and has freed me from all worry during the storm. I pray that he will in the end convert to himself the stubborn wills."[9]

In a letter to some American sisters he wrote: "Our Lord is giving me the grace of living in his peace in the midst of the storm which is threatening to swallow up our foundation, and he enables me to will nothing but his good pleasure. Whoever has Jesus has everything, and I urge you to repeat often the prayer found in the twenty-ninth chapter of the *Imitation* along with the thirtieth chapter."[10]

To Mother Mary of the Seven Dolors on the twenty-fifth anniversary of her reception of the habit, which occurred that August, he wrote:

> I understand all the sentiments of your heart on the anniversary day of your reception of the habit twenty-five years ago. It took place in such unusual circumstances and was followed by events which you were then far from suspecting. But grace must win out over nature, and on this occasion I would recommend that you recite from time to time the beautiful twenty-ninth chapter of the third book of *The Imitation of Christ*, sure that you will find it helpful. It is really consoling to recall that it was not in vain that you were given the name of daughter of our Lady of the Seven Dolors. As you behold the devil unleashed against the foundation we have undertaken, you must not have the slightest doubt but that it is snatching many souls from him. Hence, let us learn how to suffer and to surrender ourselves after the example of Jesus and Mary, and let us gather the bitter fruits of the cross in order to taste eternally the fruits of the tree of life with which God nourishes his elect in glory.[11]

The founder returned to Holy Cross some time after the chapter, and there he resided between the missions he preached. Already in August 1866 he could write to Mother Mary of the Seven Dolors of his "little but frequent retreat preaching." At the end of 1866 he had preached a three-week mission at Grand-Lucé.

During the Lent of 1867 he preached a twelve-day retreat at Flée and a fifteen-day mission at Coulombiers, where, he wrote, there were "miracles of conversion; poor sinners in great numbers are finally coming to the confessional, which they had abandoned fifteen, twenty, thirty, forty, and fifty years ago. I have had to ask the help of two neighboring pastors for the confessions."[12] Just before he left there, full of gratitude to God, for another mission at Saint-Christophe-du-Jambet, he wrote to his sister:

> I am tired, but I hope to come back to you still alive on Easter Monday. I really did not think I was capable of so much work. Yesterday I was able to speak in the morning to the women at 6:30, to the men at 8:15, to both at 10:30, in the afternoon to the women at 2:30, to the men at 4:00, to all of them together at 6:30, on each occasion for almost an hour, and with the church full every time. They tell me I look tired, but if I do not lose my voice, I will begin my next mission this evening.[13]

During that same mission he wrote to Br. Urban: "Miracles of grace are taking place here, and yesterday the church was too small three times on the same day. So far my health is holding out, and I am still able to fast."[14] He was then sixty-eight years old.

Later in 1867 he returned to Flée for another mission and gave still another at Château-du-Loir. As had always been his practice, he was training the people in community singing, writing and printing hymns for their use, and supplementing his preaching with carefully organized prayer services.

At Holy Cross where he resided between missions, opposition to him had not ceased. He was blamed for almost everything unpleasant that happened. His very presence proved provocative to some. He could no longer eat in the school dining room with the professors and students as he had formerly done but ate in the room reserved for the religious attached to the mother house.

Priests invited to preach the community retreat were warned against him.

Fr. Chappé, still governing the congregation until the new superior general should arrive, was said to be under the founder's influence or even his tool. At the same time Fr. Moreau was rumored to have denounced him to Rome. This alienated the vicar general, who at first had been so favorably disposed as to think of making Fr. Moreau prefect of religion at the college. The alienation even led to painful scenes.

It is difficult to reconstruct some of these scenes since conflicting reports on them have survived. On one occasion, after having been unjustly reprimanded in public, Fr. Moreau is supposed to have left the room inviting the other religious to follow, but according to another account Fr. Chappé left the room after offering the same invitation. On another occasion, after the painful exchange occasioned by a mention of the proposed sale of Saint Bridget's, Fr. Moreau is supposed to have said publicly in his characteristically blunt way, "The Saint Bridget's affair is becoming a comedy!" On still another occasion he presided at mental prayer and suggested reflections on the state of the congregation, offering as motives for hope "the protection of the holy hearts under whose patronage the congregation was founded . . .; humility, which makes us practice charity; and charity, which brings about the union of minds and hearts: God can show mercy for the sake of a small number of souls that have remained faithful to him."[15]

Fr. Moreau finally decided that he could no longer get the spiritual direction he needed and wanted from Fr. Chappé. He turned to the Trappist Fr. Paulinus.

Denunciations of the founder continued in Rome, and Cardinal Barnabo reprimanded the former superior general for having disobeyed his order to refrain from scheming, for having interfered in the chapter, and for having caused the loss of the Maulévrier property! Fr. Moreau replied with a long memorandum in his usual style: vigorous language with none of the niceties of diplomacy, a request for evidence, and a detailed presentation of the facts.

To Br. Urban, who had informed the founder of rumors that he had been scheming, Fr. Moreau explained on March 28, 1867, that he had done nothing beyond offering advice to religious who had asked for it. He added: "I have kept silence for seven months, and I will continue to keep it . . . as long as indiscreet tongues do not force me to justify myself. . . . In any case, I bless God for the calumnies of which my administration has been and is still the object. I pardon the forgetfulness and the ingratitude of some with all my heart. I mourn in secret over the scandalous violations of our rules and am happy not to have to behold divisions in the mother house [by being away so often]."[16]

In the same vein he wrote to his sister Josephine: "We must not be surprised that we are reported to have said things that we had not even thought of and that forgetfulness and ingratitude are often all that we receive for our interest and devotedness. The disciples must not be better treated than the master."[17]

He was deeply grateful to those who remained faithful to him. On January 2, 1867, he wrote to Br. Hilary:

I know your sentiments too well, my dear Hilary, to have doubted for a moment that you would remember me [at the coming of the new year], but it is a joy to have tangible proof that the charity which unites souls is not subject to the inconstancy of human friendship. That is why I thank you for your manifestations of affection and your good wishes.

Since Providence permitted the good faith of Propaganda to be deceived by intrigues, I bless it for the peace which my soul enjoys, but it pains me to see the provisional arrangement prolonged indefinitely, and I fear that Bishop Dufal will not be here before Easter.

That same day he wrote to Br. Narcisse: "As always, my dear friend, I am touched by your good religious greetings. . . . The year that has just ended has left me with peace of soul but deeply pained at the blows struck against our poor congregation."

It was at this time, near the beginning of 1867, that the founder had the great joy of seeing the constitutions of the Marianite sisters receive preliminary approval from Rome. The mother general received word of the approval on February 26, 1867, while she and another sister were on pilgrimage at Chartres with the founder to pray for this intention. On May 16, Fr. Moreau wrote to Mother Mary of the Seven Dolors, who had sent him a printed copy of the newly approved constitutions:

> Until the end of my life, I shall bless divine Providence for having provided me with the great consolation of seeing your congregation approved at Rome, along with the rules which I submitted to the Holy See, notwithstanding continual opposition, and for having enabled me to find in you, for the foundation of this congregation, a soul so generous. We have not yet sufficiently paid for this unexpected favor, and our debt of gratitude toward God can be paid only through numerous sacrifices, especially through the intercession of our Lady of the Seven Dolors, to whom you and all your daughters owe everything for this great act of the vicar of Jesus Christ. Consequently, rejoice in this decision in a spirit of gratitude and in the habitual disposition to do in everything, everywhere, and always the adorable will of God.[18]

Against this background of sorrow and joy and with peace in his heart, Fr. Moreau composed his "spiritual testament." He had gone to make a retreat at the Trappist monastery of Mortagne. He dated the document June 13, the vigil of the feast of Saint Basil:

> This is my spiritual testament, which I make on the second day of my retreat at the Grande Trappe of Mortagne in

the name of the Father and of the Son and of the Holy Spirit, whom I humbly beg not to allow it to contain anything which may be dictated by nature because in this, as in everything else, I wish to heed only the voice of grace.

I thank the Lord and hope to thank him eternally in the sojourn of his glory for having willed that I be born in the bosom of the Roman Church, to whose judgment I submit myself respectfully and with the docility of a son for his mother in everything I have written, published, and done until this day, as also whatever I shall say, do, write, or publish in the future.

I beg, and until my death I shall continue to beg, pardon of the three divine Persons for all the faults by which I have offended them and may offend them in the future in thought, desire, word, and omission. Humbly I beseech the Father, who created me, to restore in me his likeness defaced or disfigured by sin; the Son, who redeemed me, to apply to me in an ever increasing measure the fruit of his satisfactions to supply the insufficiency of my own expiation; and the Holy Spirit, who has so often sanctified me by the sacraments, to sanctify me ever more and more and to enkindle in me his gifts along with the theological and cardinal virtues.

With all my heart I pardon those who have harmed me in the exercise of my ministry by their calumnies, probably without evil intentions. I beg God to pardon those of our religious who have unknowingly paralyzed the development of the Congregation of Holy Cross by having recourse to means which are both out of harmony with the spirit of our constitutions and rules and opposed to religious obedience, simplicity, truth, and self-denial. If they could read in the depths of my heart, they would see there no bitterness but only indulgence and love for all the members of our family. My conscience tells me that I would gladly suffer much more if I could thus strengthen the congregation which has been so severely rocked. Heaven grant that at least it may in the future go back to our first constitutions and traditions and may not forget the saying of Saint Bernard: The greatest of persecutions which Christ endures comes from those who induce others to relaxation. Let this be said without personalities, and may the past serve as a lesson to all those who might still want to form parties or organize factions in order to satisfy their ambition.

I must in truth ask pardon of all those whom I may have unintentionally saddened, offended, or scandalized. I beseech all of them to forget any word or action of mine which may have seemed unworthy of my priestly character and the mission entrusted to me on earth, in the path of which I know I have placed many obstacles. Hence, I beg our Lord Jesus Christ to wipe out through the power of his blood, in those whom I may have disedified, the faults of which I may have been the occasion, and to make up by his mercy for my own deficiencies toward the souls whose salvation depended on my ministry.

As I think of my spiritual family, I cannot forget my family in the order of nature. . . . I congratulate you, beloved relatives, on having had faith strong enough to understand that I was not ordained a priest in order to make you rich, and for having been happy over the foundations organized under my direction although they brought you no advantage in this present life. May all of you live and die as good Christians and bequeath to your children the example left to you by your parents and mine.

I sincerely thank all those who were kind enough to assist me in the foundations of which I was the instrument. I recommend myself to their faithful prayers, promising not to forget them before God if, as I hope from his infinite mercy, he grants me to live and die in his love.

But it is to you that I address myself in conclusion, my dearest friends, priests, brothers, and sisters of Holy Cross, beloved sons and daughters in Jesus Christ who in the midst of my trials have never ceased to show for me the deepest interest, the most tender attachment, and the most generous devotion. Receive here the last expression of my gratitude, esteem, and affection. Although separated in body, let us remain united in spirit and in heart; and by constant fidelity to your rules, by your devotion to the Sacred Heart of Jesus and the Immaculate Heart of Mary, obtain the grace of entering into eternal union with God and his elect. It is there that we shall meet after the farewells of this earth if you are faithful to your vocation and acquire its spirit and its virtues daily in an ever increasing degree. To this end observe inviolably the three vows of your religious profession, meditate on your rules and my letters, and, lastly, pray for the poor priest who has been to you a father and has turned his dying looks and last thoughts to each of you to bless you all. Fiat, Fiat![19]

During this same retreat at Mortagne the founder prepared a letter of thanks to those who had sent him feast day greetings to be mailed after the arrival of the new superior general and with his permission. In this document he wrote:

My heart tells me that, while it harbors no bitterness against anyone, it beats with deep gratitude for anyone who shows an interest in me. You have done more, you who, when everyone was abandoning me, did not fear to manifest to me an even greater affection [by sending feast day greetings]. Be blessed and thanked for this once more. But do not show pity for me. Instead of sending me condolences, rejoice with me for having been at last liberated from a frightening responsibility. In the eyes of faith, that is a great grace and a sweet consolation for my old age.

His thoughts then went back to earlier years:

> Surrounded by a small number of fellow priests and worthy children of Saint Joseph, we all tasted the sweetness of a regular and fervent life in the midst of privations and the labors of a young community. Oh, who will bring back to us those early years which have flitted away all too quickly? Then we did not know the promptings of pride, the yearnings of ambition, the refinements of sensuality, or the spirit of criticism, jealousy, and division. But each one, to the best of his ability, set himself to practice humble obedience, the mortification of his senses, and the simplicity of religious poverty along with the silence demanded by rule and all-embracing charity. Thus, notwithstanding all the efforts of the devil to destroy it, God blessed our work, and financial resources arrived as we needed them because, instead of being worried about them, we were searching first of all for the kingdom of God.
>
> If we want to save our poor congregation, we must return without delay to the spirit which animated us during those first years. Doubtless the present is marked with heavy crosses and the future with grave worries. But the situation is not at all hopeless if we know how to profit by the means of salvation held out to us. Hence, let us rekindle our courage; let us take up our rules and our former practices and forget all the promptings of self-love in order to live only in obedience and fraternal union. Let us work seriously to ground ourselves in sincere humility, in a generous spirit of self-sacrifice, and in putting off the old in order to arrive at greater union with God and to implant more deeply in our souls that spiritual life which subjects to grace all the lower tendencies of nature. It is only on these conditions that we will be able to re-enkindle within us the fire of the Holy Spirit, which seems to be fading out, and to second the designs of Providence in the foundation of Our Lady of Holy Cross. . . . This is the only point

334 | MOREAU: PORTRAIT OF A FOUNDER

which worries me today. And if, before I die, I were privileged
to see the divine Spirit once more upon us, I would thank God
for the trials which he has sent me in his mercy. Then all our
tribulations would turn to his glory, our sanctification, and
the edification of others. I would also find there peace of soul,
for my conscience often bothers me at the thought that I may
perhaps have hindered your progress in the path of holiness
by not having been the right kind of leader. At least it seems
to me that I want to do my duty now as never before and that
with the help of your prayers and assistance from on high, I
will give you an example of obedience to him who is soon to
replace me in the government of our congregation.[20]

II. CHAPTER OF 1868

Bishop Fillion had delayed notifying Bishop Dufal of his election
until late in September, a month after the conclusion of the 1866
chapter. Fr. Moreau had written to the newly elected superior
general before the bishop of Le Mans did, apparently mentioning
nothing but his own resignation and the bishop's election. Bishop Dufal was unwilling to assume the office and tried to decline
it. Propaganda insisted. Matters were not finally settled until July
1867 when the Bengal missionary finally accepted.

While everyone was awaiting the arrival of the new superior
general, debts were mounting in France: the new administration
was much less efficient in checking the ventures of the French
provincial and in finding benefactors than the retired superior
general had been. There was a noticeable decline in religious
spirit, and a number of cases of flagrant disobedience. Many
of the temporarily professed religious were growing hesitant
about renewing their vows. Fr. Galmard, who had denounced Fr.
Moreau in the French provincial chapter of 1862, now addressed
a scathing denunciation of Fr. Drouelle to Rome.

All of this pained Fr. Moreau, who waited in silence for the arrival of his successor but also prepared for him a lengthy memorandum. This was not the only memorandum prepared for the new superior general. Letters were already informing him of the divisions within the congregation.

Bishop Dufal finally reached Le Mans on September 25, 1867, more than a year after the election. He gave Fr. Moreau the release from financial responsibility which the founder had fruitlessly requested ever since his resignation. He turned the former superior general's memorandum over to Fr. Drouelle and his associates for their reactions. The French provincial replied with a report entitled "Historical Outline Intended to Recall to the Very Reverend Father Founder Certain Facts Which He Seems to Have Completely Forgotten," in which he described mainly his own services to the congregation. The new superior general found himself unable to solve the financial problems of the congregation and unable to heal its divisions. After three months in France, he went to Rome with Fr. Drouelle. It was the beginning of 1868. Less than two months later, on February 24, he wrote to Fr. Chappé and the general council at Holy Cross that he had offered his resignation to Propaganda and requested permission to return to Bengal!

In sending the founder a copy of the circular in which he announced his resignation, he added a note:

> You will understand, very reverend father, why I have refrained from entering into any detail on the grave measure which I have taken; the congregation must already know enough about it. I wish only to make known to you one of the accusations brought against me, to which I allude in my circular and which profoundly humiliated and disgusted me. They have not hesitated, in letters from Paris and from Le Mans, to accuse me of preparing here in Rome the means of driving you and [your nephew Fr. Charles] from the house at

Holy Cross. I had already heard other more or less serious accusations leveled against my short administration and borne them in silence, but with this one it was impossible.[21]

Already in the preceding October Fr. Sorin had written inviting Fr. Moreau and his nephew to Indiana, and Fr. Drouelle was then insisting that a solution to the congregation's problems would be found if the general administration would "send the founder away from the mother house . . ., while assigning him a fitting pension, with permission to live wherever he wishes, completely free of all the obligations of the religious life," and if it would "dispense from their vows all those who might ask to leave."[22]

Having offered his resignation, the superior general was now unwilling to do anything. The French provincial, with him in Rome, was making all arrangements and barely getting from Bishop Dufal the minimal cooperation needed to make the steps he was taking effective. Meanwhile letters of complaint were still reaching Propaganda, some of them from Fr. Charles Moreau.

Propaganda agreed to an extraordinary general chapter to be held in Rome to which the superior general could summon all those whom he judged should be convoked "even in excess of the number fixed by the constitutions."[23] In fact, however, not even all those whom the constitutions named as members were summoned. The general officers and the provincials were summoned along with a number of religious chosen, it would seem, by Fr. Drouelle—twenty in all. Among their number was the founder, whom, however, Bishop Dufal refused to summon—he merely invited him—although Fr. Drouelle very much wanted him present. The plan was that he would be "judged irrevocably."[24] At this point Br. Leonard, a delegate, began collecting signatures once again to petition for the separation of the two societies; one other of the signers was, like him, a delegate.

At the beginning of June the delegates were on their way to Rome. Fr. Moreau, resting at Holy Cross after a series of missions at seven different localities, had chosen to ignore Bishop Dufal's invitation. One look at the list of delegates, and he had exclaimed: "This is a lightning flash in the dark for me. It reveals a final intrigue. I see nothing but ruin ahead! As far as I am concerned, I shall wrap myself in absolute silence unless an order comes from His Holiness, to whom I will then tell the whole truth."[25] He judged the chapter to be irregularly constituted since the constitutions had not been observed in the determination of its membership.

Plans had already been made by Fr. Drouelle for the election of Fr. Sorin as superior general and the sale of the Le Mans properties. When the founder heard rumors of the sale, he notified Cardinal Barnabo that the chapter could not decide on a sale without the consent of the civil society of Holy Cross and that he was still legally the owner of the properties. He also indicated what he thought of the sale. Finally, he sent a copy of the financial report he had prepared for the chapter of 1866.[20]

The capitulants were waiting in Rome for the arrival of the founder. In Le Mans he was receiving feast day greetings.[27] When Fr. Hupier, acting superior at Holy Cross during the delegates' absence, was notified that he should transfer all records and archives from Holy Cross to the Le Mans chancery, he drew up an inventory of what he found and turned everything over to Fr. Moreau! Though the delegates asked him to intervene, Bishop Fillion refused to urge Fr. Moreau to leave for Rome.

The founder prepared a circular letter, as he had done the year before, for all those who had sent him feast day greetings. He could not avoid mentioning the conflict which was brewing between the chapter, which he considered illegal and which was determined to sell Holy Cross, and himself, who was not prepared to agree. He wrote:

> God forbid . . . that I should ever weaken vocations which are already so terribly tried or give you an example of defection.

> There are already too many wayward minds and too many wandering souls for me to add to our misfortunes that of thus scandalizing you. On the contrary, if it were possible, I would wish to collect all the scattered stones and to strengthen the edifice which is falling into ruins by putting it back on its original foundation and thus contributing to the re-establishment among us of harmony, regular discipline, and sound financial administration.

He promised to accept whatever decision the Holy See should impose and added:

> This, however, does not mean that I wish to anticipate that decision, which all of us are anxiously awaiting, or, especially, to commit myself beyond my strength to a future which I cannot yet appraise. I say only that I already feel ready to offer myself, along with those in whom God might inspire the same courage, in order to save Our Lady of Holy Cross from the ruin which threatens it and to safeguard the interests of those who have been so kind as to honor me with their confidence. May God take pity on us all and save his foundation.[28]

The very day that he wrote this letter, June 18, a telegram came from Cardinal Barnabo ordering him to Rome. On June 23 another telegram arrived stating that the order had come from the pope. Fr. Moreau wrote to Pius IX immediately, stating that he was willing to do whatever the pope asked but not to share in the actions of the chapter. He explained his refusal. He feared that his absence from Holy Cross would provide the occasion for destroying all the records, which contained the only evidence that could exonerate all those persons, now calumniated, who had been associated with his administration. He feared that he would consequently become personally responsible for the debts of Holy Cross and that the creditors would be deeply disturbed by his absence. He added that he also feared that a trip to Rome in the heat of July might prove fatal to him. He sent his spiritual director, the Trappist Fr. Paulinus, his reasons for not going to Rome. The Trappist replied:

> As for the question which you raised in your good letter of July 14: whether you have offended God in not going to Rome, this is what I think. The convocation of the chapter seems to me to have been irregular. According to your letter, the threat of ecclesiastical censures seems to me, as you say, only the effect of a deception. Since you have made known your excuses and, now that they know them, they have not repeated their order, it seems clear to me that they have accepted your reasons. If despite these reasons the order should be repeated, that would be different. As things stand now, I think you can remain calm—at least until you are summoned again.[29]

Every effort was being made to get the founder to Rome, including a signed letter from the delegates publicizing in Le Mans his refusal to go. At the same time Fr. Moreau's friends wrote to Rome, and one of them even had an audience with Pius IX to intervene on his behalf.

Fr. Moreau seems to have felt somewhat uneasy about not going. On July 27 he wrote to Cardinal Pitra, who had proved a good friend on an earlier visit to Rome:

> Finding myself on the verge of occasioning great scandal involuntarily as a result of the threat of censures intimated to me in the name of His Holiness unless I leave for Rome immediately . . ., I have the honor to appeal once more to your charity, Your Eminence, and to beg you humbly to let me know: 1) if it is true that the sovereign pontiff has read, and not merely received, my explanatory letter dated June 23, of which I am enclosing a copy, and 2) why I am wanted in Rome although no one wants to tell me why, and if I cannot in conscience at least wait until the bad season is over.

In any case, Your Eminence, please assure His Holiness that I want to obey him no matter what the cost, even though his good faith has been duped, and that I am ready to die a victim of calumny and persecution rather than resist the clearly expressed will of the worthy representative of God upon earth. In the name of truth, be so kind as to assure the sovereign pontiff that I am ready to make all sacrifices he may deign to ask of me. They will be the best reward I can hope for in this world for all the works of which I have been the unworthy instrument.[30]

The delegates could wait no longer. Of the seventeen who were present at Saint Bridget's pressing business forced one of them, the superior of the college of Saint-Brieuc, to leave.[31] The sessions began on July 14. Fr. Drouelle saw most of his projects accepted. Fr. Sorin became superior general; the sale of the Le Mans properties was decided. Fr. Champeau served as secretary of the chapter and wrote not only the minutes but the circular which would notify the congregation of the chapter's activities and deliberations. Cardinal Barnabo spoke harsh words at the opening session, telling the delegates that the existence of the congregation hung upon the outcome of their deliberations. They had an audience with Pius IX at the end of their meeting—an audience in which the pope began sadly: "God is love. I would like to hope that your congregation . . . will henceforth live in harmony. But I am hesitant in this hope." Before they left Rome, they were informed that the services of the congregation were no longer needed at Vigna Pia.

The first capitulants to reach Le Mans arrived on July 30 just after Fr. Moreau had presided, at Fr. Hupier's request, over what was to prove the last graduation exercises of the Institution of Our Lady of Holy Cross. Fr. Sorin mailed a circular to the congregation from Paris on July 28, in which he warned against "hotheads in the congregation" and explained that because his presence was urgently needed in America, he was leaving Europe immediately. The next day the chapter's letter reached Le Mans. It had already been circulating in Paris and was known in the city of Le Mans before the community at Holy Cross, and in particular Fr. Moreau, saw it.

The letter was dated July 20. It bore on its paper cover the title: "Circular Letter of the General Chapter of the Congregation of Holy Cross Held in Rome by Order of His Holiness and Presided Over by His Eminence the Cardinal Prefect of the Sacred Congregation of Propaganda." On the inside of the cover was an indication that it had been printed on the presses of Propaganda. On its final page it bore the imprimatur of two high Roman officials. The founder had his nephew read it to him, stopping him only to have him reread certain passages. Then at the end he "looked sadly at the indication of the printer . . . and said: 'Is that true?'"[32]

The letter began: "Blessed be the God of mercies, who gives calm after the storm and who, after tears and sighs, fills hearts with joy! We come to calm your worries by words full of hope." A brief page outlined the sad state of the congregation before the chapter. Then the letter described how in Rome "the delegates bravely set to work" preparing for the chapter as they awaited their founder. A page was devoted to the history of the orders and appeals addressed to Fr. Moreau to get him to come to Rome. Since, to the great displeasure of Cardinal Barnabo and Pius IX, he refused to go, the chapter finally began. A brief paragraph described the work of the chapter, noting how the delegates invoked "our Lord and his holy mother . . . in all the sanctuaries of the holy city," how "union, calm, and peace . . . reigned among the delegates, almost all of whose votes were unanimous," and how they concluded from this "God is with us, unworthy though we are." Another paragraph suggested that the solution which they had found to the congregation's problems and which would be announced later would demand sacrifice but that the members of the congregation would be willing to make it, even though they were not responsible for their hardships. The letter continued:

> But here we must turn to the fulfillment of a very painful duty. To convince us to do it, we need the urging of the sharp voice of conscience and all the authority of advice received from on high. For there is question of raising our voice against our reverend father founder, repelling his attacks, refuting his allegations, and warning you against his provocations to schism. May God deign to direct our pen so that we may do it with all possible moderation without, however, neglecting anything which may be necessary to enlighten you.

There followed a lengthy presentation of Fr. Moreau's crimes: a statement that he had "in reality resumed all authority at the mother house" and was writing "publicly with the tone of an independent superior." This "poor misguided priest" was opposing the vicar of Jesus Christ, suggesting that the vows of the religious were invalid, and yet with "revolting temerity" declaring that he did not want to weaken vocations—what a "flagrant contradiction" between words and deeds! "This unfortunate father founder, whose guilt cannot make us forget his labors, zeal, virtues, and kindness for each one of us," might still profit from their prayers, for he was not yet eternally lost. Besides, might not his resistance be due "to a weakening of his mental faculties, to his advanced years, or to the first movements of an impetuous and proud nature which has never given in to anyone and which now finds itself constrained to bow beneath a sovereign will?" God might yet "put back into his mind and heart the religious principles and sentiments which were his glory and which he preached to us so often." A brief discussion of the way in which he had supposedly falsified the debts in order to absolve himself from responsibility followed. Finally came the statement that "if our dear reverend father, who had expressed the desire to be freed of his office of superior general so often, so publicly, and with such touching marks of sincerity, had only been content to live in peace among us without opposing the new administration in any way, he would have been surrounded with respect, because he was founder, and considered a patriarch in the midst of his numerous family. The different houses would have considered it their honor and their happiness to receive him, one after the other, at his visits, and everyone would have listened to his counsels as to the advice of a man sent by God."

After having finished this task—"and God is our witness how much it has cost us"—the letter expressed regret that the delegates could not reveal the chapter decrees until the approval of the Holy See had been given. But it assured the members of the congregation that a solution to their problems had been found, although like men caught in a shipwreck they would be "obliged to surrender to the storm a part of their belongings" in order to save their lives.

The delegates were interested in having quality rather than quantity in the congregation—a principle contrary to the one that had been followed until then. All who had asked for secularization had received it, and those who, without having asked for it, would show themselves unworthy of their holy vocation would be invited to "take their bad example elsewhere. From now on, we want to present to the eyes of the world a religious community like the most fervent that we find around us; we want to live in peace, with true brothers, with true servants of God, finally with all people who have no other thought, no other ambition than the glory of Jesus Christ and their own sanctification."

A final suggestion was that it would be well to meditate on "these important truths" during the annual retreat, which was about to begin. Then came a final reminder of the "extreme kindness of the most eminent Cardinal Barnabo" and a request for prayers. The letter bore the names of all the delegates who had gone to Rome, including the superior of Saint-Brieuc, although he had left the city before the chapter began. A postscript announced the election of Fr. Sorin.

That same day, August 1, Fr. Moreau received a canonical warning, ordering him to make known within four days, under the penalty of suspension, whether or not he would go to Rome. When Bishop Fillion assured Fr. Moreau that Pius IX had seen his letter, without waiting for a reply from Cardinal Pitra the founder informed the bishop he would leave for Rome as soon as he could "take certain steps" forced upon him by the "libelous letters just published against" him.[33] One of these steps was the preparation of the twenty-nine page mimeographed reply to his detractors. He wrote: "If, as we find in the circular of our general chapter, which has just been given to me, I were not afraid of becoming for you a source of scandal, I would maintain absolute silence on the treatment accorded me in the aforesaid letter."[34] He answered the circular's allegations with facts and citations of letters, minutes, and other documents. He concluded:

> This is sufficient, and more than sufficient, to enlighten your consciences in my regard and to prove to you that I am not in my second childhood today any more than I was insane in Rome a few years back. With all my heart I pardon those who have treated me so badly, and I am grateful for the calm and resignation in which God is pleased to keep my soul. I no longer look for any justice upon earth but only for divine mercy in a better life, counting myself fortunate to receive humiliations and contempt as my reward for the foundations of which I have been the unworthy instrument. I hope that it will be my lot until my dying day to drink uncomplainingly of the chalice of our Lord's passion. It seemed to me so bitter when it was first offered to me ten years ago during a terrible trial, and so it does today. But it becomes sweet when one drinks it to the very dregs.[35]

There was also a two-page reply to the insinuations of Fr. Sorin's circular letter.

III. FINAL VISIT TO ROME AND THE SALE OF HOLY CROSS

With Fr. Lemarié, a religious who had remained faithful to him, he left for Rome on the evening of August 10 and reached there on August 15. The next day he met with Cardinal Barnabo. On September 1 he sent an account of this visit to his nephew:[36]

> When I went to Propaganda . . ., I was received by His Eminence Cardinal Barnabo with an enthusiasm and kindness which astonished me, no less than it astonished my traveling companion and the superior of the French Seminary, who were present, as also Br. Vincent. Hardly had I entered the office of the cardinal prefect when he exclaimed: "At last there you are! Help us get out of this difficulty." Then abruptly changing both his tone and the topic of conversation, he complained of what I had said in a circular, namely, that the circular of the chapter at Saint Bridget's had been printed with his approval by Propaganda's presses. He added that he had not seen the manuscript and that he would issue a clarification on this point. Then, alluding to three letters whose authors had complained of the deplorable consequence of all the scheming and calumny, he exclaimed: "Poor Séguin! And Charles Moreau with his Whereas this and Whereas that! And that Mr. Bernard [who had interceded in Fr. Moreau's behalf]! When I replied that these gentlemen had reasons which they had not made known to me, that they were in fact very devoted to me, but that I could not be responsible for correspondence which they had not communicated to me, the cardinal added, "But you do not recognize the authority of the chapter!"

> "I believe that it was organized arbitrarily and composed of members designated by Fr. Drouelle and Bishop Dufal, all of whom were religious who opposed me when I was trying to insist on the constitutions approved by His Holiness, but the pope can make everything legitimate, and since he has done so, that is enough for me."
>
> Thereupon, having resumed his gracious and kindly tone, His Eminence did me the honor of accompanying me to the stairs leading to the office of Msgr. Simeoni, the secretary general [of Propaganda], to the great astonishment of the superior of the French Seminary, who told me the following day of his utter surprise at a reception like this.

On August 17 the founder wrote his nephew: "I took the liberty of criticizing the cardinal and the secretary general for the printing and publication of the two circulars [that of the chapter and that of Fr. Sorin]. Both of them assured me that they had not even read them and that since that time the printer had been strictly forbidden to accept or to print anything at all which did not come from Propaganda itself."[37]

Fr. Bardeau, the procurator general, later sent to Fr. Chappé a version of the founder's visit to Propaganda which showed a much less friendly cardinal. The account was a reconstruction based on questions the procurator had put to Cardinal Barnabo three weeks later. Doubtless each of the reporters, the founder and the procurator, saw and interpreted what had happened from a different vantage point. In any case, Fr. Moreau was told that he would have to make a retreat before seeing the pope—certainly a penance for his delay in coming to Rome, but as he saw it a "grace which I could not refuse."[38]

Before he saw the pope, he saw the Jesuit general and tried to persuade him to take over the Institution of Our Lady of Holy Cross as Bishop Fillion now wished, but without success. He wrote the following account of his audience on the very day he saw the pope, September 1.

On Monday at eleven o'clock, I threw myself at the feet of the pope. Instead of an irate judge, I found in him a father.

"There is Fr. Moreau," he exclaimed as he let me kiss his ring. "Get up and come here before me."

"Well, now, Fr. Moreau, you have not been sufficiently obedient. Ah, this has displeased me. And then, you have tried to administer too much since your resignation."

"Most holy father, will Your Holiness allow me to speak?"

"Yes, yes. Speak."

Then the pope put his head in his hands, his elbows resting on the arm of his chair as if the better to listen to me at his ease.

"Most holy father, Jesus Christ, of whom Your Holiness is in my eyes the image, is my witness, and, if need be, I would take an oath to this effect on the holy Gospels, that I never had for a single instant any idea of resisting your august will, but I was waiting to know it positively and to find out if my excuses had been accepted or not."

"What has displeased me is what has been printed against you."

"Since Your Holiness is so kind as to give me this proof of interest, I must tell you, and I take God for my witness, that this publication is nothing but one lie and calumny after another."

"I regret that. I did not know it before it was printed."

"What has afflicted me most, most holy father, is that they have been so bold as to write here that I had forgotten myself in the pulpit on the score of the respect due to the Holy See and to your sacred person and that I was not afraid of censures. Most holy father, I have consecrated my entire life to the defense of the doctrines of the Holy See and to the foundations which Providence has entrusted to me, especially to the foundation of Vigna Pia, and would I have forgotten myself in such a strange manner?"

"But they did not tell me that."

As I again mentioned the name of Vigna Pia, the pope kept silence and looked at me with compassionate eyes. Then I added that since my resignation I had not said or done anything that might look like an act of authority and that I had devoted myself to retreats and missions.

"So you have some Philotheas? A princess came here to plead your cause."

"Most holy father, she is not my Philothea, but a woman who is devoted to God's work and who is a relative of the bishop of Cahors [a mistake for Carcassonne], Bishop Bouillerie, who took the initiative for this.

"Your poor congregation is breaking up."

"Most holy father, this unfortunately is only too true, and had Propaganda been enlightened as Your Holiness was when you told me six years ago, 'You have three or four hotheads in your institute who are upsetting everything,' I would not see ruins piling up around me today. But no one wanted to pay any attention to me at Propaganda."

"At Propaganda?"

"Yes, most holy father, the good faith of the cardinal prefect has been duped up to this very day! If Your Holiness would at least permit those who have remained faithful to the former constitutions to come together and live in a house by themselves. . . ."

"I cannot do that, dear Fr. Moreau; this would mean schism in the congregation."

"Then, most holy father, everything is lost."

"They will end up turning over all the houses and their subjects to their respective bishops."

Then I was silent after adding, "We have been placed in the hands of Fr. Sorin, who is in America, and of Fr. Champeau, Fr. Drouelle, and Fr. Chappé, who are destroying Holy Cross."

"The Jesuits do not want it. Offer the sacrifice of what can be sold, if it is necessary, to pay the debts."

"With all my heart, if God so demands. And where shall I go to live, most holy father?"

"Wherever you wish. Remain in that part of Holy Cross which will not be sold."

As I knelt down again, the pope, to whom I had drawn close, blessed me and asked: "Are you staying in Rome?"

To this I replied that I would leave as soon as possible. Then he allowed me to kiss his ring affectionately and said: "Goodbye. God bless you."

In another account of the same audience, the founder pointed out that he had explained: "My presence will be necessary in France to settle matters, although I have chosen a layman as my representative."[39]

The French assistant to the superior general of the Jesuits told Fr. Moreau before he left Rome: "Do not abandon your congregation." On another occasion he said, alluding to the trials of the founder of the Redemptorists: "Remember Saint Liguori." The founder commented on this last remark: "But precisely what is lacking here is a saint." Cardinal Barnabo went even further. He said: "Are you afraid of being kept here? Well, they dragged Blessed Joseph Calasanz across Rome in a cart to the Holy Office, and then they beatified him." To this the founder answered: "I'm not interested in beatification at that price."[40]

Leaving Rome two days later, he reached Le Mans on Sunday, September 6, as the annual community retreat preached by Fr.

Champeau ended. Understandably, the confusion following his return was great. He came back from Rome consoled and not censured. He wrote on September 17 to the Marianites' superior in New Orleans: "My trip to Rome was a real consolation for me, and, whatever may have been said or written by different people, I was received with a kindness which I will never forget. I was in Rome for only a few days because the pope let me leave as soon as I wanted."[41] He had abundant information on the July chapter. He had been told by the pope that he might live where he chose.

When rumors began to circulate about what he had been told, he decided to cut them off by distributing the following statement to the local community:

> Since there is doubt as to what I said about the manner in which the letter of the general chapter was printed and how it has been judged in Rome, I do not fear to put my thoughts in writing so that, if anyone so wishes, they may be sent to Propaganda for verification. I said, and I repeat: 1) that this document was composed by Fr. Champeau, who read it to the meeting at which neither His Eminence nor the secretary general [Msgr. Simeoni] was present; 2) that Fr. Drouelle had a hand in it and that Br. Gregory copied at least part of it; 3) that His Eminence and Msgr. Simeoni assured me that they never saw the manuscript before it was turned over to the printers; 4) that the delegates paid the printing expenses; 5) that the two imprimaturs are not from Propaganda but from the vice-regent, or from that authority which "civilly" grants to all printers of Rome permission to print what is presented to them.
>
> I add that the Sacred Congregation of Propaganda has not yet even examined the acts of the chapter. Fr. Sorin's election is the only item approved so far.[42]

In fact, he prepared a circular to be sent to the members of the Association of Saint Joseph, which he was still directing, and the religious of the French Province, making these same points. He wrote to Msgr. Simeoni for permission to print and distribute it. Presumably, he considered the request merely a matter of courtesy and the permission certain because, when Msgr. Simeoni's answer came, the letter was already being distributed. After all, Cardinal Barnabo had, according to a letter of the procurator general to Fr. Chappé, told Fr. Moreau the chapter's letter had simply been a matter of self-defense, "the right of anyone who is accused."[43] The same right could hardly be refused him. Msgr. Simeoni, however, asked him not to send it.

Fr. Chappé had the procurator general go several times to Propaganda to find out what had happened during the founder's stay in Rome. Although Cardinal Barnabo was clearly displeased about what had followed on Fr. Moreau's return to Le Mans, he and Msgr. Simeoni refused even to issue a denial of anything he had said even when his circular letter became known in Rome, where it "more or less impressed" several cardinals.[44] In fact, Propaganda issued no further rebuke of any sort.

Matters now moved fast to a climax. The resources of the French Province were dwindling. The property at Flers had been sold and the college at Saint-Brieuc abandoned. The community at Holy Cross was living off the sale of furniture, cattle, and food supplies. Fr. Drouelle was hastening the sale of Holy Cross and the two Solitudes. In the meantime the movable property was being carried away.

Although Fr. Moreau spent much of November and December away from Holy Cross preaching, he was aware of what was being done. To him this procedure was a defrauding of the creditors. Therefore, on November 19 he and Br. Hilary, as members of the civil society of Holy Cross, filed a request with the civil tribunal of Le Mans for the dissolution of the civil society in order to provoke a court seizure and protect the rights of the creditors.[45]

Fr. Sorin had returned to France in October. When he learned on November 22 what Fr. Moreau had done, he ordered him to withdraw the request and sent the order to a Le Mans newspaper, which published it on November 23. On December 11 Bishop Fillion wrote to the founder: "A formal order has been given to you, and you have not obeyed. You have not even seen fit to make known the reasons which courtesy as well as obedience made it your duty to manifest. Hence, you are either in open revolt or are the victim of a delusion which I find it difficult to explain."[46]

On December 13 Fr. Moreau replied from Commerveille:

> Though busy with two instructions, services to be sung in the place of a sick pastor, and confessions to hear, I have the honor to reply to your letter of December 11. . . .
>
> You criticize me, my lord, for disobedience to my legitimate superiors and for my silence regarding the order I have received from them to suspend all steps to bring about the dissolution of our civil society. I have received no other orders, and hence Your Lordship cannot be referring to any others.
>
> Consequently, you ask me on what principles my conscience can be at ease. First of all, I have consulted men who were conscientious and devoted to us, and they have advised me of the steps to be taken. In addition, I have based my conduct on the following considerations.
>
> First of all, not even legitimate superiors can command in virtue of the vows of religion except in so far as their orders inflict no grave harm on truth, justice, and charity. Now, in the present circumstances, I cannot obey without violating these three virtues.

He commented in detail on "the present circumstances," the obligation of his vows, and the impossibility of any alternative procedure. He went on: "You close your letter, my lord, by asking me what I would have thought if, when I was superior, one of my religious would have disregarded my authority. Alas, my lord, I have had only too many occasions to show my stand on similar incidents." He then indicated many instances in which the very people who were now in control of the congregation had disobeyed him.[47]

On the day before he wrote this letter, he had written to Cardinal Barnabo: "I am letting things take their course, limiting myself in the ruin of Holy Cross to dissolving the civil society which I had founded in order to safeguard the interests of the sisters, my family, and certain other creditors whom the others are boasting that they will not pay off. If they take away everything belonging to me, at least I shall then be able to practice absolute poverty."[48]

Bishop Fillion manifested his reactions to the founder's letter to him in writing to Fr. Sorin on December 16: "If there should ever be question of canonizing Fr. Moreau, as his friends seem to think there will be, all his writings would have to be burned, since they give rise to terrible objections against him."[49]

That same day Fr. Sorin published in four Le Mans newspapers a letter on the financial situation of the congregation, which consisted in a "progressive scale of the debts of Holy Cross since its beginnings in 1835" as a summary of the founder's administration![50] There followed a very disagreeable exchange of letters in the papers between the superior general, who insisted that the letter had not been meant for publication, and the editors who had published it.

Denunciations continued at Rome, and when Cardinal Barnabo answered the founder's letter of December 12, he informed him that he was reported not only to be impeding a peaceful solution to the problems of Holy Cross but even to have taken steps to found a new institute independent of Rome. "If this were true, and I cannot believe that it is," wrote the cardinal, "I would not see how this project could be reconciled with your former fidelity and with the loyalty due to the sovereign pontiff."[51] Fr. Moreau replied in his characteristic way. He demanded concrete evidence for charges: "I defy anyone to quote a word, a line, or anyone at all in support of these diabolical inventions." He stated exactly what he was doing. He insisted that there was no other way to prevent injustice to the creditors.[52]

The publicity had reached such a point that Fr. Moreau felt that he could avoid being an occasion of scandal only by offering the newspapers the statement of why he had requested a dissolution of the civil society and by sending to the associates of Saint Joseph, many of whom had made considerable contributions to him for the work of Holy Cross, a letter explaining in detail what he was doing and why. As director of the Association, he had always informed the associates of the circumstances in which the work of Holy Cross found itself. Besides, it was the beginning of 1869, and he regularly wrote to them at this season. The document began:

> The year which has just ended, far from ending our trials, has brought them to the full by the deliberate ruin of the magnificent establishment where Providence fixed the mother house of our congregation. That is still my heaviest cross and most painful sacrifice. . . . If only so many trials had at least brought souls to God! But alas! Until now only the demon, who has sifted us, has gained from our defeat, and in offering you my good wishes for the new year, my dear associates, I feel the need of recommending myself to your prayers that I may not become unworthy of the happiness of those of whom Saint Paul said: "For those who love God all things work together for their good."[53]

That he had no ulterior motives in the painful step he had taken, he made clear to Br. Hilary, to whom he wrote on January 29: "I have no desire to seize again an authority which I willingly renounced, and I do not want to depart in my old age from that rule of conduct which I learned at the novitiate of the Sulpicians: not to ask for anything attractive, not to refuse anything humiliating."

Every attempt was made to have the founder withdraw his request for the dissolution of the civil society. To Canon Dubois, Bishop Fillion's vicar general, who tried to persuade him to do so, he answered "that no authority on earth could make him change his determination on this point." The canon explained: "Confronted with such a clear-cut and positive declaration, I left. . . . For the rest, he seemed to appreciate the motive for my step and expressed his regrets at being unable to share my viewpoint."[54] Fr. Moreau described these steps in his usual straightforward way in a letter to Fr. Séguin on January 27, 1869. He observed: "Apparently they are all afraid of the light. They tried to get Cardinal Barnabo to make me desist, but he was unwilling to send the requested prohibition probably because he feared to be just as compromised before the court as they are. Now they are trying to escape the blow that is about to fall." The founder even received a letter from a fictitious associate of Saint Joseph, Sophie Martin, suggesting a detailed examination of conscience and asking him how he could continue to celebrate Mass—a letter written in a style which he recognized as Fr. Drouelle's.

The increasing isolation into which his position was forcing him at Holy Cross even made it more and more difficult for him to find a priest who would hear his confession. When the dissolution was finally pronounced on March 9, the superior general wrote the founder:

> From now on I consider you a simple religious. It is your desire I believe, to live among your fellow religious absolutely like the rest of them. You will be happy to recall the edifying words which fell from your lips on the day on which you surrendered your powers of superior to the vicar general of the

congregation, your temporary successor: "Until the present," you said, "it was impossible for me both to command and to obey; but from now on, I hope with the grace of God to give you an example of obedience and submission." Nothing better could have been said; let us hope that soon it will be possible to add: nothing better could have been done. . . . To remove from the way of obedience any possible stumbling block, you will certainly be happy to have me annul, which I do by this present letter, every privilege of any nature whatever permitted or granted you orally or in writing, except that of occupying the first place after the superior general [the place due him as the oldest of the religious in the congregation in accord with the rules on rank and precedence found in the constitutions].[55]

Shortly before the dissolution was pronounced, the general administration of the congregation had succeeded in getting one of the creditors to have a legal hold issued on the property to prevent the sale from getting completely out of their hands.

An attempt was made to persuade the founder to leave Le Mans before the sale of Holy Cross began. But the pope had told him he could choose his place of residence, and even an appeal to Rome did not succeed in getting this permission revoked. Besides, the founder still had responsibilities to the Marianites—this too by a decision of Pius IX. He refused to leave. The auctioning began on April 21. On April 27 he wrote to Br. Hilary:

Everybody is leaving Holy Cross on Friday, and I am leaving Wednesday to preach a little ten-day mission in the vicinity of Saint-Calais.

And so divine justice passes over us, and those who wished to put me out are put out into the street themselves.

At my return I shall move in with my sisters, while awaiting the final outcome and shall follow my rule as well as I can.

On April 28 he transferred his few belongings to his sisters' house across the street—a house on the old Barré property. He was aided by his nephew, who had, as a schoolboy thirty-three years earlier, helped him move into the Barré house from Saint Vincent's Seminary as he began the work of Holy Cross. It was exactly twelve years to the day since he had received word of the papal approval of the constitutions of the congregation. In two trips they carried all the founder had: a few articles of clothing, a few books worth about six francs in all, his ordination certificates in their little white wooden frames, and a thousand little hymnals which he used on the missions he preached. He laid claim to the bed that had belonged to his confessor Canon Fillion and was granted it. But he wanted it only as a souvenir. He continued to sleep in the armchair he had used for years. The Marianites had given him the money to obtain it at the auction.

He settled down in a room from which for three months he could hear the auctioneer's voice and see a large notice of the auction on the wall of the former Institution of Our Lady of Holy Cross. The general administration notified him on April 27 that the congregation could not provide for his support. Fortunately, the Marianites had already offered to provide meals for him and his two sisters.

The offensive against the founder continued. When in February 1869 the new superior general had asked the religious to assure him in writing of their fidelity to him, some took occasion to write vigorous criticisms of the founder and even to send them to him, although some of the religious also wrote to him of their loyalty. Public statements against him continued, which Fr. Moreau now simply forwarded to Propaganda. Denunciations continued to reach Rome, but Rome no longer replied.

Bishop Fillion notified him that he was no longer director of the Association of Saint Joseph. In June Fr. Galmard wrote him that plans were afoot to found a new congregation with the incumbent superior general as founder, without debts and without a sordid background. In July the definitive separation of the Indiana sisters from the Marianites was decreed. In October the property of Holy Cross and the two Solitudes were sold, although final settlements with creditors continued until well into 1873, some of them receiving only 20% of what was due them. Some months later, early in 1870, all the other religious of the congregation left Le Mans.

Fr. Sorin had left France in May and, despite Propaganda's prescription that the superior general reside in France, thereafter returned from America only intermittently. In January 1870 he addressed to the religious a letter on the glorious future of the congregation, which he said had until then lived only by spurts. When at this point Fr. Moreau had qualms about obtaining permissions needed in the matter of poverty and wrote to Propaganda, the superior general suggested that Rome give him a "complete dispensation from all bonds and obligations toward the congregation."[56] Then the Franco-Prussian war broke out. The superior general invited all the French religious to America. The Paris school was abandoned as the occupying army moved in. Finally, the Prussians occupied Le Mans, and this interrupted the founder's preaching ministry.

In June 1869 Fr. Hupier had sent the founder feast day greetings. He had written: "The good God is trying you, but it is consoling to know that by trials we are made more like our Lord. Suffering passes, but its reward will be eternal. 'Blessed are those who mourn, for they shall be comforted.'"[57]

IV. FINAL JOYS AND ETERNAL REST

By early 1870 the battles were over, and only his interior peace remained. The founder replied on January 10 to New Year's greetings from a Marianite: "I thank you, my dear sister, for the good wishes which you expressed for me. I owe to the prayers of charitable souls like yourself the peace which I enjoy in the midst of my trials, and I am very grateful."

He wrote to the sisters in New Orleans on January 14:

> You are kind enough to write me your condolences for the trials of the year which had just ended. I thank you with all my heart, and I bless the hand which has struck me. It is a great honor which our Lord grants me, and also a true source of happiness, to drink his chalice. Thus, thanks to the prayers offered for me, I have not been troubled or discouraged. After the tempest and the storm come calm and tranquility, and I hope I shall be allowed to pass the rest of my earthly life here in peace. It is enough for me to have no qualms of conscience over all the groundless accusations made against me and to have received, along with an expression of the kindliness of the vicar of Jesus Christ, a double blessing. With all my heart I pardon those who have persecuted me, and I wish them well.[58]

Except for the five months of the Prussian occupation from November 1870 to April 1871, Fr. Moreau devoted himself to his work of auxiliary priest. Between November 1866 and January 1873 he visited fifty parishes, some of them several times and on occasion for missions lasting as long as three weeks. He also replaced sick or absent priests. Except when he was busy answering a request for help, he was always available. His preaching was as effective as ever. He wrote during one of these missions: "The harvest is going to be abundant here, and the church is too small. I have written to two pastors, since the pastor of the parish is sick, to come and help me with confessions. Yesterday, before a sizable crowd which filled the church for the third time at seven o'clock in the evening, I had to leave the pulpit to administer an emergency baptism since the child was in danger [of death]. I had the people sing hymns during the time and then came back to the instruction I had begun."[59]

Occasionally he received gratifying compliments like that of the pastor of a parish where he had preached a lenten series in 1840: "Not one of those who came back to the practice of their religious duties in 1840 has become negligent."[60]

There can be no doubt that the advice he gave to Fr. Séguin, now no longer a member of the congregation, in January 1869 was a description of himself: "I was happy to hear that you are less preoccupied with your preaching. You have certainly received from God more than enough to do a creditable job. What is hard is not so much the work and the delivery, which will become less demanding day after day if you put yourself wholly into it, but it is the spirit of prayer, of mortification, and of union with our Lord, without which no preacher will do anything more than beat the air."[61]

"This spirit of prayer, of mortification, and of union with our Lord" was so diffused throughout Fr. Moreau's life that, as one of his opponents said, "he preached immediately after an exhausting deliberation with as much calm, fullness, and blessing as if he had just come from prayer."[62]

Occasionally there were distasteful episodes as when a brother of the congregation burned all the hymnals the founder had distributed to the children during a mission. In most places, however, he was received in friendly fashion and even with sympathy or veneration.

He was most grateful to those, especially religious and former religious, who showed him some mark of affection. On June 14, 1870, he replied from Le Mans to Fr. Séguin's feast day greeting:

> I was very sure that your good heart would not forget the feast of St. Basil, and even if you had not written, I would not have thought otherwise. All the same, I was delighted to read this new expression of your unfailing attachment, and you

have given me too much proof of your affection for me not to remain grateful for the rest of my life. . . .

My health, about which you were kind enough to ask, has remained good throughout my four months of preaching, and it is getting better because of the rest I have been taking for three weeks now. . . .

None of the members of our poor congregation reside here anymore. . . .

Since my return from Rome, they have left me in peace, and I have the good favor of the pope thanks to that of Msgr. Simeoni, who has written me an affectionate letter. . . .

Fr. Drouelle goes on calumniating me, but I pardon him and am not at all troubled by it.

A year later, on June 13, 1871, he wrote to Br. Hilary that the religious need not fear the threat of dismissal for corresponding with their founder. He continued:

As for myself, I am happy in my solitude and in the midst of my retreats and missions, blessing God for having freed me from all responsibility in the administration of Holy Cross and for having inspired the pope to authorize me to live where I might wish.

May you enjoy the same peace, and in any case, my dear friend, we have to recall that life will soon be over and everyone will then be repaid according to his merits.[63]

A month later he wrote: "The only things I think of now are to continue my preaching and to prepare myself for death, which is still not here."[64]

For everyone he showed personal concern as the following letters indicate.

To the sisters in Louisiana: "Be assured, my very dear daughters, that I shall never forget you. . . . When our love is in

God and for God, we know nothing of the inconstancy of the friendship of the world since Christian charity always increases in proportion as we draw closer to the end of this present life."

To a young Marianite: "If in return for your New Year's wishes and out of gratitude for them I told you, my dear sister, that I hope you will get your diploma, my good wishes would certainly coincide with what you want yourself. But I prefer to wish for you very simply that the will of God be done. . . . Face your examinations in full confidence and all simplicity."

To an elderly sister: "After offering and sacrificing your health in the service of God, you can now edify others by your patience in sickness. This is another way of serving our Lord, and one which is both agreeable to him and still more meritorious than the first one. I am sure that you know how to profit by it."[65]

He thanked the Marianites for their gifts but insisted that they not send him more. On June 13, 1870, he wrote: "I regret that [the sisters] from New Orleans have incurred expense once again for my feast day, and I earnestly desire that they limit themselves from now on to praying for me so I may become less unworthy of the glorious name of my patron. . . . I have no need of a cassock, and as for trousers, I have been given enough of these in my lifetime."

On June 16, 1871, he wrote to the sisters in New Orleans: "I cannot conclude without thanking you again, my dear mother and my dear daughters, for the cassock which I am wearing at this moment, assuring you that I am in need of nothing except love for God."

His first biographer describes his daily life when he was not away preaching:

After his departure from Our Lady of Holy Cross, Basil used to celebrate Mass in the chapel of the Marianite sisters, where he returned in the afternoon for his visit to the Blessed Sacrament, his recitation of the breviary, and his daily way of the cross. In the evening he did spiritual reading for the sisters in the lives of the saints and said the rosary with them before night prayer.[66]

He dedicated to work all the time that remained to him from his preaching in the diocese. The preaching seemed rather to increase his strength than to sap it. . . . Although from 1869 on, his life was practically a continual retreat, he never let a year pass without going to the priests' retreat at the [diocesan] seminary. In order not to have to cover the long distance more than once a day under the July sun, he went in the morning to the house of Carmelites near the seminary, and there he received hospitality in the time between the retreat exercises. Since his sisters were worried about how he spent those days, he replied to the questions they asked by insisting he was so well taken care of that he needed nothing. All the same, every morning he took along a piece of bread and a piece of fruit, and it was only after his death that it was discovered that the devout retreatant had asked nothing more than that some water be placed in his room.[67]

In June 1871 the founder received feast day greetings from Fr. Sorin and Mother Mary of Saint Angela. The latter invited him to spend some time in Indiana, the former to spend his last days there. When he later came to France, Fr. Sorin renewed his invitation and asked to see Fr. Moreau. The founder explained: "I did not feel that I could reply because they were not retracting anything and because they doubtless wanted to use me as a shield to protect themselves against the charge of being responsible for the break [of the Indiana sisters from the Marianites]."[68] Besides, Propaganda had declared that the superior general should reside in France and the founder did not see how he himself could do anything that might seem to indicate approval of his residence in America.

On August 3 of that year he drew up the following document which showed that the sentiments expressed in his "spiritual testament" of 1867 had not changed:

> I declare before God, who will soon judge me, that I never took steps either to take back or to hinder the administration of the congregation; that I never even so much as thought of refusing to go to Rome at the request of the pope as soon as I had the assurance that His Holiness did not accept my excuses, even though I was convinced that the good faith of the holy father had been duped in my regard and also in regard to the membership of the Saint Bridget's chapter.
>
> I declare also that I never diverted to the foundation of Holy Cross anything given me for the house of the Good Shepherd.
>
> Neither have I ever enabled my family to profit by any public alms I received for the Good Shepherd, Our Lady of Holy Cross, or any other good work.
>
> I declare before the sovereign Lord who searches our consciences that, as I was satisfied with receiving only freewill offerings, I never sought out any legacy or donation in favor of the foundations which Providence entrusted to me, aside from the public subscriptions for the Good Shepherd. Thus, it is not difficult for me to offer up this sacrifice of everything of which I have been deprived.
>
> I beg all the creditors of Our Lady of Holy Cross to be convinced that, at the time of my resignation as superior general, I left the congregation with more than sufficient assets to pay off its debts and that I have never ceased in the meantime to defend their interests.
>
> With all my heart I pardon and humbly beseech the divine mercy, through the intercession of the Blessed Virgin and Saint Joseph, to pardon all those who have harmed my reputation or the goods which I held in trust, thanking God for

having found me worthy to suffer something on the occasion of works undertaken for his glory.[69]

The tireless old man worked to the very end. Despite his failing eyesight, which led him to request an indult to celebrate the votive Mass of the Blessed Virgin as he could not see clearly enough to read the book for Mass, he undertook a completely new edition of his *Meditations*, this one meant for the diocesan clergy and the laity.

On November 19, 1871, he wrote to the superior of the sisters in New Orleans: "I am still alive and I hope to be able to preach this coming Lent in a parish of our diocese despite my seventy-two years. However, old age warns me that I am getting close to my end, and I am impatient to see God and to be no longer capable of offending him. Ask him for this grace for me."

He wrote on June 13, 1872, to a Marianite:

> You have told me, my dear daughter, of the sacrifice that God has imposed on you in withdrawing from you the direction of the work which had cost you so much worry in order to confide another to your care. I bless our Lord for the generosity with which you have made your sacrifice. Nothing is better calculated to detach us little by little from this earth and to turn us toward a better world. These are inestimable graces to the eyes of faith, and the more you appreciate them, the more they will be your consolation. . . .
>
> I am growing quite old, but still I am not dying, and God has left me enough health to teach many others to know him and serve him better: I was even able to preach this entire past Lent as well as three weeks after.

On July 17 he wrote to Sister Mary of the Annunciation at Vendôme, explaining the tardiness of his reply to a letter from her:

It was not forgetfulness on my part, for your kind letter . . . frequently came back to my mind, and every time I almost felt remorse at not having answered you sooner. It is true I had a fairly voluminous correspondence to take care of and the work of the *Meditations*, which I am having printed. I want to let you know that it was not forgetfulness on my part: I would be ungrateful not to reply to so many manifestations of affection and interest, and that I do not want to be, or even seem to be, in your eyes.

My health is as good as ever, and the good God has chosen to give me enough to continue my retreats and missions in the diocese during three consecutive months.

Do not feel sorry for me because of the trials that he has sent me. They are a grace for which I bless him, and my mind is no more troubled by them than my heart is saddened.

If I regret the ruin of his work, I thank him for having saved at least the one of which you are a part, and for having developed by worthier hands the one which we were unable to keep, for the school at Holy Cross is doing well.

He heard echoes of what must have seemed to him the collapse of the remaining ruins of the congregation which had been his life's work. In 1871 he learned that Br. Leonard, who had been one of the first Brothers of Saint Joseph and for years a general councilor, but who had frequently attempted to separate the two societies, had been publicly stripped of the religious habit at the community retreat and sent as cook to one of the schools.[70] Fr. Moreau wrote to Fr. Séguin: "At the retreat poor Leonard was given a treatment which he did not deserve and which he should have reported to Msgr. Simeoni: he is professed, and he had the right to a canonical trial before being so humiliated and degraded. Even the hired help at the minor seminary of Précigné [where the retreat had been held] were talking about it."[71]

The founder learned that the general chapter was going to be held the following summer at Notre Dame despite the directive of Propaganda that the superior general and his council reside in France. To Fr. Hupier, who had informed him of his own assignment to Canada, he wrote on July 15:

> I did not know what had happened to you, when your letter informed me of your trip to America, something that surprised me all the more since you had always shown unwillingness to go abroad. In any case, you have obeyed, and your obedience has all the more merit because, according to our old constitutions, they did not have the right to give you such an order [since he did not have the foreign mission vow]. God will take account of it, and that is enough for you. He will reward you also for the charity which inspires you to keep praying for me, who always has such a great need of prayers, and for this I will remember you with as much affection as gratitude. Still, I regret that they made you move and sent you at your age into so murderous a climate. . . .
>
> And now the general chapter is going to be held at [Notre Dame], where Fr. Sorin is residing despite the decree of Propaganda obliging him to stay in France with his council and the French Josephite and Salvatorist novices. He wanted me to go too, but I am making use of the permission of the pope, who told me during my last trip that I could live where I chose. . . .
>
> I am continuing my retreats and missions in the diocese with the agreement of Bishop Fillion, who has just approved the third edition of my *Meditations*, which I have entirely redone.

It is not clear how many of the chapter's decisions he knew, but none of them could have been a consolation for him. It resolved on a thoroughgoing revision of the rules. It agreed on the abandonment of the Bengal mission, the Algerian houses, and the Cracow foundation. This chapter also marked the downfall of Fr. Drouelle, who was elected provincial of Canada and refused to go.[72]

The final great joy of the founder of Holy Cross was the celebration of his golden jubilee of priesthood. Because of the Franco-Prussian war it came a year late on August 12, 1872. He celebrated it with the Marianite sisters in Le Mans, the only other guests being his nephew, his two sisters, a niece, and two friends. One of the Marianites left this account:

> At seven o'clock, our venerated father offered the holy sacrifice in our chapel assisted by the chaplain of our community [Fr. Charles]. Before leaving the altar our father spoke, giving expression to his sentiments more or less in these terms:
>
> "If I heeded only my natural inclination, I would leave this altar in silence, but I would be afraid of disappointing your expectations and those of the devout persons who have joined their prayers to yours during this holy sacrifice, which renews within me so many memories and emotions. I would fear also to fail in my duty of gratitude toward God, who has filled me with so many graces since that memorable moment we are celebrating today in this anniversary. I will speak, then, to declare his great mercies to me and to correspond with your desires.
>
> "Yes, my very dear daughters, I can on this day cry out with David when, delivered from the hands of his enemies, he re-entered his capital, 'Glorify the Lord with me, and let us together celebrate the glory of his name!' And I can add with Mary, 'For the Lord has done great things for me.' Ah, how great is the dignity of the priest!"

After developing this thought somewhat, he turned to the "personal graces" he had received. He recalled his various ordinations, the foundations of which he had been the instrument, his great interior trial of 1855, his resignation in 1866, and the sufferings that followed. He concluded, the Marianite's account explains:

"Yes, my very dear daughters, I am happy to see your work grow and prosper, it is the consolation and the happiness of my old age, and I had good reason to invite you, when I began, to glorify the Lord and to celebrate the glory of his name."

During this beautiful talk, our venerated father, deeply moved, saw everyone's eyes flow with tears that expressed the sympathetic admiration of those present for all that the zeal of a priest can accomplish and his self-abnegation endure during [fifty] years.

At noon our beloved father presided at the community dinner; at the end one sister, in the name of the congregation, shared some verses inspired by filial affection and gratitude. This touched him, and he expressed his kind gratitude by a blessing for all his daughters. To complete the day, everything had been prepared for the giving of the habit to two young postulants from America. They were the last among us to have the good fortune to receive the holy habit from our father's hands. As we remember the consolations of this day, we will always include the homage of the grateful remembrance of His Holiness Pius IX, who filled up the spiritual joy of our venerable founder by giving him, as a jubilarian's reward, the graces of the apostolic benediction and a plenary indulgence through the cordiality of Cardinal Barnabo and Msgr. Simeoni.[73]

The next day, he wrote to Mother Mary of the Seven Dolors:

All day yesterday I was too happy. You did too much on the occasion of my fiftieth anniversary of priesthood for me to fail repeating my thanks to you and your companions dispersed over France and abroad.

Thirty-one years have passed since divine Providence brought you to this city and associated you with the work which God had confided to me. . . . You have spent yourself without reserve for the service of our houses, where several of you have already found the merit of a heavenly reward; and after the separation between your congregation and the one of which you had at first formed part, you never ceased to continue the work on which you had set out with devotedness that has been my principal consolation. For it I have blessed him who called you to work at fulfilling his merciful designs, and I bless him again, asking him that the work of his grace be achieved in each of you and through you the works of his charity. . . . The happy result of your efforts and of your confidence in God is a proof that you have been accomplishing his will, and at the same time it is a reward for your unlimited devotion to your holy vocation. May you be able to taste the first fruits of the crown promised to the "prudent virgins" in your approaching retreat, during which you will find yourselves in more intimate communication with your divine spouse! May you find there new strength to remain always watchful, with the lamp of good works in your hands, and to keep yourselves always ready to answer his call in fidelity to your constitutions, to your rule, and to your spiritual directory! Thus you will be able to sing, when you appear before the divine lamb, the song reserved to those souls who follow him in his heavenly ways, and you will continue to be the joy of my old age.[74]

As the year approached its end, the founder received a letter dated December 22 from a religious of the French Province who had made his vows in the early 1840s:

I feel the need of laying at your feet the tribute of my good dispositions toward you and the good wishes that I have formed for your happiness at the approach of the new year. The first sentiment that I wish to express to you, very reverend father, is regret, confusion for not having always shown in my relations with you all the respect and all the submission that I owed you. The bad example which some of our religious gave me is no excuse. Assuredly, I have always loved you as a son loves a good father, but I accuse myself of not having always been as reserved as I should have been with you in my words. I sincerely regret it, and I ask you pardon for all the suffering that I caused or occasioned you during the long and difficult years of your term as superior. My good wishes for you, very reverend father, are as ardent as they are sincere. I want the Lord to fill you with his sweetest consolations. I want those who have been ungrateful to become your friends once again. I want you to continue to be able to do on earth all the good which your strength will permit you to accomplish.[75]

Hardly a week after this letter was sent, Basil Moreau rendered his last service as an auxiliary priest. Mother Mary of the Seven Dolors sent the story to all the Marianites:

It was on January 1, 1873, that our excellent father found himself stopped in his labors. It was at the very moment that he was exercising his inexhaustible charity. The day before, with his usual cordiality and light-heartedness, he had received the good wishes of his family and of our community. Then he had gone to the village of Yvré-l'Evêque, near Le Mans, to visit the sick pastor, who had asked him to come and replace him for the services on New Year's Day and to preach in his place to his parishioners. Suddenly, during the night, our very reverend father was striken with sharp internal pains which did not permit him to say more than a few words to the parish and obliged him to return to Le Mans as soon as he had finished celebrating the holy sacrifice. The doctor began a treatment which was very difficult for our father, unaccustomed as he was to hospital care, who had been suffering in silence several months without having at all lessened his three days of fast and abstinence each week, without having added anything to his austere evening meal or to the water which had been his only drink for many long years.

On the fourth day, at the insistence of the doctor and our chaplain, the father founder consented to leave the armchair on which he had taken his rest for more than twenty-five years in order, he would say, to be able more easily to jot down the thoughts that came to him during the night. He also changed his room, which was not big and airy enough for his state of suffering, for a spacious room in which he agreed to have a fire lighted. From that moment our very good father resigned himself with perfect obedience to all the cares which were shown him, thinking of the divine infant savior in the crib "wrapped in swaddling clothes," as he said, in that Holy Christmas season, adding in a spirit of gratitude these words of the psalmist: "Lord, you have prepared a bed for your servant in his sickness."

As his illness got worse, the soul of the venerable sick man went up to God by more frequent invocations. During his last days he no longer ceased to pray. At whatever hour anyone approached him during the day or during his long sleepless nights, he could be heard reciting the invocations that his devout memory drew from the sacred books or from the liturgy. He turned most often to the holy Mother of God, from whom he must have received some help, some particular consolations, for at one moment he said: "They did well to consecrate me to the Blessed Virgin!" As we heard how patient his prayers were, as we saw how calm the movement of his lips was when his voice could not be heard, we could have doubted that the constitution of the venerated sick man really sensed that it was struggling with mortal sufferings. He was speaking only with God; he was asking for nothing to lessen his suffering; and nobody heard either a word or a sigh of complaint. And yet, with what gratitude he received everything that our sister nurse gave him! How readily he stretched out his hand to our father chaplain when he heard his voice in the most painful moments! But immediately he took up again that series of fervent outpourings which were only interrupted by rare intervals of sleep.

Our very reverend father, accustomed for so long a time and in so many ways to detachment from this life, nevertheless did not abandon the hope of being able to take up his apostolic occupations soon again. At the beginning of his illness, he had someone write to a pastor that his state of health would not permit him to come on January 19 for the mission that he had promised. But fearing that his absence would greatly embarrass the good priest, he had him informed some days later that he felt better and that he had a great desire to keep his engagement.

He expected from day to day to be able to assist at the holy sacrifice and even to celebrate it. When he saw that the time which he called his convalescence grew longer, he prepared to receive communion in his room. Despite his very great weakness, he wanted to get up as a humbler expression of his faith and devotion to the holy Eucharist. Since he could not kneel, he said one day before communion: "You see, my God, that my soul obeys my body at this solemn moment, and if I were not held back by suffering, I would not want to receive you seated in this chair, but rather with both knees on the ground and my head bowed deeply. At least, O my savior, I join the fervent desires of my heart to the adoration of the angels and the homage which the saints rendered your august majesty in similar circumstances. 'Jesus, whom I now see veiled, grant the object of my burning thirst: let me see your face unveiled and find eternal happiness in the vision of your glory.'" After he had communicated, he said Deo gratias (*Thanks be to God*); then he began the Te Deum (*ancient hymn of praise*).

Some days later, on the seventeenth, the feast of Saint Anthony his patron, when the persistent intensity of the illness had caused an alteration in the general state of the venerable sick man that made any illusion impossible, communion was given to him for the last time. On the evening of that same day, I asked our chaplain to let the entire community go in to our beloved father and to ask him for each and every one of us, my dear daughters, the favor of a last blessing. As soon as he had agreed to our desire, we went to kneel before his bed, and the chaplain said in our name: "My very dear father, here is the community of your spiritual daughters, who owe to you their religious life, who come to offer you their devout sympathy for your sufferings with the homage of their eternal gratitude for all the benefits of your devotedness and your example. They are kneeling to ask your blessing as founder and father, promising you the assistance of their prayers and an unwavering fidelity to the rule that you have given them."—"Yes, with all my heart," our father founder answered. "May God bless you by my hand. In the name of the Father and of the Son and of the Holy Spirit." He was asked to give his blessing to the entire congregation of the Marianites across the world. "Yes, to all," our good father said. "I will bless them again: blessing, absolution, all that I can give."

The venerated patient received the sacrament of anointing the next day and, in the evening, the apostolic blessing with a plenary indulgence. Sunday, January 19, was for us a day of very painful anxiety. I spent the night in the room of our dying father with our chaplain and three of our sisters. Toward morning his breathing became more difficult, and at half past nine his last moments began. It was not an agony, but a falling asleep, during which our father did not completely lose consciousness and seemed to be always aware of the voice that was recommending his soul to Jesus, to his holy Mother, to Saint Joseph, to the angels, and to all the saints, protectors of his journey to heaven, particularly to his baptismal patrons and the blessed whom he had most often invoked in his work as missionary and as founder: Saint Vincent de Paul, Saint Alphonsus Liguori, Saint Ignatius. At half past twelve the movement of his chest grew slower, and soon we could no longer see that he was breathing. At that moment the great and ascetic features of our father grew bright with a calm and serene beauty that those who stood around noticed. His soul seemed to shine out more vividly on the beautiful face that it still animated. Then our chaplain pronounced a final blessing on the dearly loved dying man whom our sobs could not hold back and gave him, as he breathed his last, the kiss of eternal peace.

The funeral of the venerable deceased was celebrated in the chapel of our mother house on Wednesday, the twenty-second, and until the departure for the cemetery, his body remained exposed with six of us keeping watch by turn day and night. It was then that we could see more clearly the real sentiments that the people had for the person of our father. Crowds of the faithful of every class were drawn to his coffin and tried to touch his hand with their religious articles. This manifestation continued during the liturgical prayer for the dead, many people trying to get to the open coffin through the crowds, which filled even our sanctuary beyond its capacity. It is true that our venerated father, dressed in his priestly vestments, drew people by the expression of peace and prayer which his last sleep had made clearer by softening the traces of his labor and austerity. During the two days that preceded the burial, it was impossible to notice any change in the air of the room where the coffin rested.

The pastor of the parish celebrated the mass of burial and gave the absolution. The dean of the [cathedral] chapter [of canons] carried the candle of honor. At the head of the funeral procession, the clergy was represented by several officials from the city and from the diocese and by the superiors of the religious congregations of Le Mans. After the family, the Marianite sisters, and the delegates of the monastery of the Good Shepherd and of other communities, there followed a large group of former students and friends, who had come out of the triple sentiment of veneration, gratitude, and sympathy for the man of great character and virtue in whom, as was written of the funeral procession . . . of Saint Basil, the holy archbishop of Cesarea, by Saint Gregory of Nyssa, his brother, "the poor came to honor their benefactor, the unfortunate their consoler, the young their master in the study of letters, and others him who had made himself all things to all people."[76]

How can we describe this man, whose personality we have seen expressed in his own words and deeds and the recorded reactions of others to him? Perhaps it can be done like this:

Basil Moreau, a straightforward man even to the point of being blunt.

Basil Moreau, a simple man, so simple as to be incapable of devious ways and incapable even of understanding or tolerating them.

Basil Moreau, an ardent man with an ardor that turned him into an enthusiastic and tireless worker for God, for the Church, for all people.

Basil Moreau, a warmly affectionate man full of love for Christ, and so a man of prayer; full of love for those who shared his labors, and so a kindly man unwilling to hold first place; full of love for "anyone who [was] perishing," and so an untiring apostle.

Basil Moreau, a man haunted by the ideal of union as a force that binds together into a great power for good all of those who would pool their labors, since "in union there is strength"; a man haunted by the ideal of union as a bond holding together the community of the religious of Holy Cross and enabling them to imitate the life of the earliest Church, fulfill the command of Christ, reflect the life of the family of Nazareth or even of God himself, and find the happiness of which the psalmist speaks: "How good it is and how pleasant when people dwell as one!"

Basil Moreau, a sign of contradiction and a "man of sorrows,"[77] who considered his choice of our Lady of Holy Cross as patroness of his work an inspiration, who thanked God for having found him "worthy to suffer something on the occasion of works undertaken for his glory,"[78] and who looked upon his trials as a "grace for which to bless" God,[79] never doubting through them all that "for those who love God, he makes all things work together unto good."[80]

AFTERWORD

This year brings to a close the 175th anniversary of Holy Cross in New Orleans, a moment that makes me humbly aware of the depth of commitment that our founder, Fr. Basil Moreau, had to the poor here. As a product of the missionary efforts that sent eight young Holy Cross religious to Louisiana, I see in Fr. Moreau a man of deep faith and unwavering trust in Divine Providence.

The author of this book, Fr. Thomas Barrosse, CSC, was also a native of New Orleans—the stories that he captures here offer valuable insight into our founder. As we reflect on how Fr. Moreau embraced the Cross in the ups and downs of the beginning of the congregation, some insightful lessons stand out as guideposts for us who follow his example today:

Simple beginnings: The small village of Basil's birth and those who were part of his earliest days were people of faith who held strong to who God was calling them to be despite the conditions of the time. Their example planted seeds in young Basil's heart that were nourished by the waters of baptism and grew over the years.

Family: Basil's parents nurtured in each of their children love of the Church, prayer in common, and respect for authority. These simple values played a key role in the expectations Basil held for himself, and went on to shape the development of the congregation.

Academic fervor: All who came to know Basil experienced his astuteness for learning, especially his ability to communicate to everyday people the messages of the Gospel that challenged them to reflect on their lives in the light of faith.

Integrity: Faced with numerous challenges, Basil was consistent in his efforts to search his soul with honesty and with the hope that at the end of time God would open to him the gates of heaven.

Forgiveness: As the challenges of building the congregation brought disagreements from every direction, Basil displayed a willingness to readily forgive and move on. This fortitude reveals a clear picture of a man with the openness to accept what cannot be changed and a determination to meet people anew.

Conscience: One of the extraordinary aspects of our founder's personality was his ability to seek advice, ponder, and then make firm decisions. His example calls us to enter the deep currents of transformation as we journey through life.

Missionary spirit: Fr. Moreau's vision and passion centered on the burning desire that *all people* should be invited to know, love, and serve the Lord. No place was too far to go to share the Good News. Despite untold suffering, the Congregation of Holy Cross continually goes out with the Gospel to encounter and serve new people.

Apostolic zeal: In today's terms, we might be tempted to speak of the founder as a workaholic. It is more accurate to describe him as a man who was truly on fire with the gifts he had been given. Until the end, Fr. Moreau was a man with a mission.

Soul work: Poverty, chastity, and obedience shaped Fr. Moreau's pursuit of holiness. Daily, this simple man of prayer and zeal left a blueprint for all who are willing to faithfully open our lives to the One who invites us to experience the Cross our only hope!

This book helps us explore the ways God led our founder on his journey of faith in the founding of the Congregation of Holy

Cross. Fr. Moreau's example challenges us to also examine the ways God is leading *us* in our day-to-day living. Like Fr. Basil Anthony Mary Moreau, may we strive to preserve peace in our hearts and thereby discover the Light of Life.

Sr. Ann Lacour, MSC
Congregational Leader
Marianites of Holy Cross
September 15, 2024
Feast of Our Lady of Sorrows

Notes

Foreword

1. Personal letter to Mother Mary of the Seven Dolors, September 9, 1853.

2. Conference to Holy Cross religious in Montréal, August 12, 1857.

3. CL 14, 1841 (I, p. 41).

4. Constitutions of Holy Cross, constitution 8, art. 118.

1. Background

1. The "department" is an administrative division of government intermediate between the national and the local ("commune") units.

2. Tony Catta, *Fr. Dujarié* (translated by E. L. Heston), Milwaukee, 1960 (hereafter referred to as "Catta, *Dujarié*"), p. 34.

3. Letters of Fr. Chappé to Bishop Bouvier, Dec. 3 and 24, 1847.

4. They had originally formed part of the 1682 declaration of the French clergy.

5. Philéas Vanier, *Recueil documentaire. Le très révérend père Moreau d'après ses écrits, ses correspondants et les documents de l'époque (1799–1835), pro manuscripto,* Montreal, 1945 (hereafter referred to as *"Rec. doc."*), p. 31; Etienne Catta and Tony Catta, *Basil Anthony Mary Moreau* (translated by E. L. Heston), Milwaukee, 1955 (2 vols., hereafter referred to as "Catta I" and "Catta II"), vol. 1, p. 35.

6. Catta, *Dujarié*, pp. 53f. and 105.

7. Catta I, p. 283.

8. April 13, 1823 (*Rec. doc.* pp. 34f.).

9. Charles Moreau, *Le très révérend père Basile-Antoine Moreau, piètre du Mans, et ses oeuvres,* Paris, 1900 (2 vols., hereafter referred to as "C. Moreau I" and "C. Moreau II"), vol. 1, p. 2.

10. *Rec. doc.* pp. 69f.

11. *Etrennes Spirituelles* 1846, pp. 37f.

12. April 13, 1823 (*Rec. doc.* p. 35).

13. *Rec. doc.* p. 59.

14. *Op. cit.* pp. 17–19.

15. Catta I, p. 30.

16. *Rec. doc.* pp. 18 and 20.

2. Preparation (1799–1823)

1. C. Moreau I, pp. 3f.

2. Conference of Aug. 3, 1920, pp. 3f.

3. C. Moreau I, pp. 4f.

4. *Op. cit.* pp. 5f.

5. Catta I, p. 19; *Rec. doc.* p. 19.

6. *Rec. doc.* p. 29.

7. *Op. cit.* p. 30.

8. *Op. cit.* pp. 27f.

9. *Op. cit.* p. 22.

10. *Op. cit.* p. 76.

11. Cf. *Rec. doc.* pp. 48, 50, 69.

12. *Op. cit.* pp. 30f.

13. *Op. cit.* pp. 45–48.

14. Aug. 14, 1822 (*Rec. doc.* p. 34).

15. *Op. cit.* p. 31.

16. *Op. cit.* p. 32.

17. Cf. *Rec. doc.* pp. 57 and 61.

18. Cf. *Rec. doc.* pp. 53f., 57, 65–68.

19. *Op. cit.* p. 68.
20. *Op. cit.* p. 50.
21. *Op. cit.* p. 61.
22. *Op. cit.* p. 63.
23. Cf. *Rec. doc.* pp. 49, 52, 62.
24. *Op. cit.* p. 56; cf. also p. 61.
25. *Op. cit.* p. 58.
26. C. Moreau I, p. 15.
27. *Rec. doc.* p. 33.
28. *Op. cit.* pp. 73–76.
29. *Op. cit.* pp. 78–80.
30. *Op. cit.* p. 73.
31. Cf. *Rec. doc.* p. 81.
32. *Op. cit.* p. 64.
33. *Op. cit.* pp. 82f.
34. *Op. cit.* p. 84.
35. *Op. cit.* p. 85.
36. *Ibid.*
37. *Op. cit.* pp. 35f.
38. *Rec. doc.* pp. 97 and 103.
39. *Op. cit.* p. 69. Since Sulpicians continue to belong to the diocese of their origin, the young priest would not have been lost to Le Mans.

3. Beginnings (1823–1835)

1. *Rec. doc.* p. 136. Note the somewhat anti-intellectual overtones; they left no trace on the Scripture professor's class notes.
2. *Op. cit.* p. 138.
3. *Op. cit.* p. 107.
4. Cf. Fr. Mollevaut's answers of Feb. 9 and July 1, 1826 (*op. cit.* pp. 113f. and 119).
5. *Op. cit.* p. 115.
6. *Ibid.*

7. Nov. 1, 1829 (*op. cit.* p. 134).

8. May 15; cf. also letter of Aug. 2 (*op. cit.* pp. 138 and 140).

9. *Op. cit.* p. 152.

10. *Op. cit.* p. 99; cf. also letter of Dec. 18, 1825 (p. 112).

11. March 11, 1824 (*op. cit.* p. 102); Dec. 8, 1824 (p. 105); July 9, 1825 (p. Ill); Dec. 18, 1825 (p. 112); Feb. 9, 1826 (p. 114); March 27, 1826 (p. 117); July 1, 1826 (p. 119); July 28, 1827 (p. 123); Jan. 11, 1835 (p. 154).

12. Cf. letters of May 11, 1824; Nov. 29, 1827; Aug. 2, 1831; Aug. 29, 1833; Jan. 26, 1834 (*op. cit.* pp. 104, 127, 140, 148, 150).

13. *Op. cit.* p. 121.

14. *Op. cit.* p. 128.

15. Cf. letters of March 20 and Nov. 12, 1828 (*op. cit.* pp. 128 and 130).

16. Letters of March 11 and Nov. 23 (*op. cit.* pp. 115 and 121).

17. Letters of Jan. 28, April 8, and Nov. 29, 1827; Feb. 20, July 5, and Dec. 21, 1828; May 20, 1829; June 6, 1835 (*op. cit.* pp. 123, 126f., 129, 131f., 155).

18. March 17, 1825; cf. letters of Jan. 5 and Dec. 3, 1833 (*op. cit.* pp. 107, 146, 149).

19. Montreal, 1923.

20. *Sermons* pp. 589f., an unfinished manuscript.

21. *Op. cit.* pp. 357f.

22. C. Moreau II, p. 464.

23. Conference of Aug. 3, 1920, p. 13.

24. Philéas Vanier, *Recueil documentaire. Le chanoine Dujarié (1767–1838), fondateur des Soeurs de la Providence de Ruillê-sur-Loir et des Frères de Saint-Joseph*, Montreal, 1948 (hereafter referred to as *"Rec. Dujarié"*), pp. 476f.; there were five, but one left after three days.

25. *Op. cit.* pp. 220–226.

26. *Op. cit.* p. 239.

27. *Op. cit.* p. 388. According to C. Moreau I, p. 87, there were 13 signatures, but according to the community's chronicles, 15 signed: *Rec. Dujarié* p. 493.

28. *Rec. Dujarié* pp. 407–411.

29. Letters of Aug. 18 and Nov. 14, 1834; April 18 and June 17 and 20, 1835 (*op. cit.* pp. 435–454, 458f., 467–471).

30. *Rec. doc.* pp. 186–192.

31. It contained the statutes of the Association, the indulgences accorded it by Rome, retreat readings from the Bible and the *Imitation of Christ*, and other devotions.

32. *Rec. doc.* p. 98.

33. July 1 and Nov. 23, 1826; April 8, 1827; Nov. 1, 1829; Jan. 1, 1830; Aug. 29 and Dec. 3, 1833 (*op. cit.* pp. 119, 121, 124, 134, 135, 148, 150).

34. Oct. 20, 1826; March 26, 1833 (*op. cit.* pp. 120 and 147).

35. Feb. 9, 1826; May 20, 1829; Jan. 10, 1831; March 6 and Dec. 3, 1833 (*op. cit.* pp. 113, 132, 138, 147, 150).

36. *Op. cit.* pp. 133f.

37. *Op. cit.* p. 126.

38. *Op. cit.* p. 139.

39. *Op. cit.* pp. 97f.

40. *Op. cit.* p. 101.

41. *Op. cit.* p. 110.

42. *Op. cit.* pp. 114f.

43. Cf. letter of March 26, 1830, cited above (*Rec. doc.* p. 136).

44. Oct. 10, 1823 (*op. cit.* p. 97).

45. Dec. 30, 1823 (*op. cit.* p. 100).

46. 1829, 1830, 1831 (*op. cit.* pp. 133, 137, 140).

47. Port du Salut, Soligny, Mortagne, and Thymadeuc in 1824, 1829, 1835, 1836, 1840, 1847, 1856, 1867.

48. *Rec. doc.* p. 41.

49. July 9, 1825 (*op. cit.* p. 111).

50. Catta I, p. 116.

51. Nov. 22, 1823; March 11, 1824; March 17 and Dec. 18, 1825; Feb. 9 and May 9, 1826; May 11, 1827 (*op. cit.* pp. 100, 101, 107, 112, 114, 118, 125).

52. *Op. cit.* p. 105.

53. Feb. 9, 1825 (*op. cit.* p. 113).

54. *Op. cit.* p. 124.

55. *Op. cit.* p. 155; cf. also letter of Oct. 10, 1829 (p. 134).

56. *Op. cit.* p. 153; cf. also letters of March 11, 1824; June 28, 1827; Dec. 21, 1828; Oct. 6, 1829; Jan. 5, 1833 (pp. 102f., 126, 130, 134, 146). From 1835 almost every other letter indicates how much Fr. Mollevaut admired Fr. Moreau and valued his friendship—see esp. letters of Jan. 31, 1837; Jan. 29, 1839; Jan. 12, 1842; Jan. 25, 1846 (*op. cit.* pp. 159, 164, 176, 184).

57. Cited in Catta I, p. 172.

58. Letter of July 24, 1826 (*Rec. doc.* pp. 37f.).

59. *Rec. doc.* p. 43.

60. *Op. cit.* p. 40. Carlism originated in Spain by those who wanted a separate line of the Bourbon family to take the throne. This movement was welcomed in France by those who wanted a restoration of the Bourbon line on the French throne.

61. *Op. cit.* p. 35.

62. *Op. cit.* pp. 70f.

63. Cited in Catta I, p. 178.

64. *Rec. doc.* p. 222.

65. *Op. cit.* pp. 222–224.

66. *Op. cit.* p. 232.

67. *Op. cit.* pp. 233f.

68. *Op. cit.* pp. 235–237.

69. Cf. St. Euphrasia's letter of Sept. 7, 1834, cited in Catta I, p. 259.

70. *Rec. doc.* pp. 248–250, cited in Catta I, pp. 215–218; cf. also his letter to Mother St. Euphrasia dated April 18, 1834 (*Rec. doc.* p. 252).

71. *Rec. doc.* pp. 259–262.

72. *Op. cit.* pp. 264–267.

73. *Op. cit.* pp. 269–274.

74. *Op. cit.* p. 269.

75. *Op. cit.* pp. 276–278.

76. Catta I, p. 239.

77. *Op. cit.* p. 248.

78. *Op. cit.* pp. 251f.

79. *Rec. doc.* p. 152.

80. Cited in Catta I, p. 259.

81. Cited in Catta I, p. 358.

4. Holy Cross (1835–1841)

1. Letter of Sept. 26, 1838 (*Rec. doc.* p. 163).

2. C. Moreau I, p. 146.

3. It grew from 48 pages in 1840 to 182 in 1848.

4. *Etrennes Spirituelles* 1844, p. 58.

5. *Circular Letters of the Very Reverend Basil Anthony Mary Moreau, Founder of the Religious of Holy Cross* (translated by E. L. Heston), Notre Dame, Indiana, 1943–1944 (2 vols., hereafter referred to as "C.L." followed by the number of the circular, usually its date, and in parentheses an indication of the volume "I" or "II" and the page), no. 5 (I, p. 11).

6. C.L. 1 (I, p. 2).

7. C.L. 5, Dec. 27, 1837 (I, p. 11).

8. C.L. 1 (I, p. 4).

9. C.L. 11, Jan. 8, 1841 (I, pp. 27f.).

10. *Rec. doc.* p. 155.

11. Fr. Dujarié had left no rules: cf. C.L. 26, Jan. 3, 1847 (I, p. 118).

12. Cf. Sister Mary Borromeo Brown, *The History of the Sisters of Providence of Saint-Mary-of-the-Woods,* New York, 1949, pp. 18–20; J. F. Alric, Histoire de la Congrégation des Soeurs de la Providence de Ruillé-sur-Loir, Paris, 1948, p. 42. On the origins of the rules

cf. *Rec. Dujarié*, pp. 302–304. Fr. Moreau may have had a part in composing them: cf. *Rec. Dujarié*, p. 318.

13. *Rec. Dujarié,* pp. 519–522.
14. Cf. C.L. 16, Feb. 4, 1842 (I, pp. 48f.)
15. C.L. 9 (I, p. 22)
16. Cited in Catta I, p. 423.
17. Cited in Catta I, pp. 423–425.
18. *Op. cit.* p. 426.
19. Aug. 3, 1840 (*Rec. doc.* p. 170).
20. Jan. 5, 1841 (*op. cit.* p. 171)
21. C.L. 14, Sept. 14, 1841 (I, pp. 38–45)

5. Growth (1842–1850)

1. Cf. C.L. 19 (I, pp. 73f.).
2. *Etrennes Spirituelles* 1845, pp. 131f.; for statistics on their number cf. C.L. 54 (I, p. 271).
3. *Op. cit.* 1846, pp. 55f.; 1847, pp. 106f.
4. *Op. cit.* 1845, pp. 135–145.
5. *Op. cit.* 1846, pp. 52f.
6. *Op. cit.* 1844, pp. 95f.
7. *Op. cit.* 1846, p. 52; cf. C.L. 36, April 15, 1849 (I, p. 166) on his fidelity to this moratorium; Fr. Mollevaut had warned him on July 3 and 15, 1843 (*Rec. doc.* pp. 179f.) not to expand too rapidly.
8. Cf. *Etrennes Spirituelles* 1846, p. 39.
9. *Annales* 1843, final entry.
10. *Op. cit.,* Feb. 22, 1844.
11. *Etrennes Spirituelles* 1841, pp. 66–69.
12. *Op. cit.* 1847, pp. 133–135; C.L. 64 (I, p. 305).
13. C.L. 45 (I, pp. 212f.)
14. General council minutes, Jan. 30, 1850.
15. P. 74.
16. 1843, p. 49; 1845, pp. 87f. and 126–130; 1847, pp. 74–93.
17. 1846, pp. 109–138; 1847, pp. 79f.

18. 1845, pp. 107–110; 1847, pp. 108–135 and 167–174.

19. C.L. 20 (I, p. 78).

20. C.L. 23 (I, pp. 88f.).

21. Pp. 79f.; cf. Catta I, pp. 614–618.

22. C.L. 35 (I, pp. 144–147).

23. C.L. 36, April 15, 1849 (I, pp. 164f.).

24. 1843, p. 46; 1845, pp. 87f.

25. Catta I, p. 427.

26. The 1846 rules provided in art. 24 that every novice eventually make at least annual vows of poverty and obedience; cf. also 1854 constitutions, art. 65.

27. 1838 constitutions, p. vi; 1846 directory, pp. 11–42 (the "directory" was a book containing the prayers and various practices—profession, responsibilities of chapters, etc.—in use in the Association of Holy Cross).

28. 1847 rules and constitutions, art. 66.

29. The particular superiors were all priests. It had been Abbé Dujarié's desire that the brothers have a priest superior. Given the situation in which the brothers and sisters then found themselves—limited education, greater instability, and at a decided disadvantage before civil law as well as before many of the bishops—this arrangement had much to recommend it for the time.

30. Cf. general council minutes, April 24, 1847.

31. Catta I, p. 539.

32. C.L. 25 (I, p. 104).

33. C.L. 26 (I, pp. 112f.).

34. Cf. C.L. 2, July 14, 1836 (I, p. 7); cf. also C.L. 20, Jan. 5, 1844 (I, p. 80) on his intention of bringing the aged and the sick back to Holy Cross to spend their last years or their time of trial in a closer community life.

35. Nov. 8, 1835 (I, p. 2), cited above.

36. C.L. 14, cited above at length.

37. Cf. C.L. 1 (I, p. 1), where he writes to the brothers: "I find consolation in the hope of discovering in each member of your community a sincere friend and a zealous co-worker in all the good which remains to be done."

38. C.L. 17 (I, p. 56).

39. C.L. 20 (I, pp. 79f.).

40. C.L. 26 (I, p. 113).

41. Cf. C.L. 20, Jan. 5, 1844 (I, p. 80).

42. 1845, pp. 111f.; 1846, p. 294.

43. 1845 directory, p. 43; 1846, p. 135.

44. C.L. 20, Jan. 5, 1844; 21, March 20, 1844; 28, Sept. 17, 1847 (I, pp. 83, 85, 125).

45. E.g., communications to Fr. Sorin dated Nov. 30, 1847, and Nov. 10, 1849.

46. "J.M.J." often occurs at the start of letters before this date, but this simply witnesses to a common practice of the time.

47. Devotion to the heart of Mary was linked to devotion to the heart of Jesus in the early nineteenth century. Abbé Moreau signed a letter of Aug. 14, 1822: "Yours in the hearts of Jesus and Mary" (*Rec. doc.* p. 34), and the 1835 Le Mans missal prescribed a commemoration of the Sacred Heart of Mary in every votive Mass of the Sacred Heart of Jesus. Fr. Moreau introduced the *heart* of Joseph into his thinking very early: cf. C.L. 8, June 26, 1839 (I, p. 19). But he seems to have hesitated over introducing it into the iconography and devotion of the Association until Fr. Mollevaut pointed out that images of the heart of Joseph existed: cf. letter of March 21, 1843, cited in C.L. 7, Jan. 10, 1843 (I, p. 69)—obviously, the circular, though dated Jan. 10, was finished after the reception of the March 21 letter which it quotes; that this letter is Fr. Mollevaut's seems clear from his later letter of July 3, 1843 (*Rec. doc.* p. 179).

48. Fr. Moreau had also published for the brothers a little office of St. Joseph in their manual (1841; cf. also directory of 1852). He offered them an office of the hearts of Jesus, Mary, and Joseph in

1846. But by 1855 the Little Office of the Blessed Virgin had practically completely replaced these (cf. 1855 directory).

49. C.L. 20, Jan. 5, 1844 (I, p. 80).

50. Explicitly in 1857 constitutions, art. 26.

51. C.L. 16-a (I, p. 48); cf. also C.L. 23, Jan. 4, 1845 (I, pp. 91f.) on
the conventual church as a symbol of the Association.

52. Constitution 9.

53. 1847 rules and constitutions, art. 21 and 62.

54. Session of Aug. 25.

55. Cf. 1845 "summary" submitted to Rome, signed by 12 priests
on Feb. 28 and by Fr. Moreau on June 20; cf. also the brothers'
acceptance of new rules based on those of 1845 at their major
chapter on Aug. 17, 1846: C.L. 25, Jan. 3, 1847 (I, p. 119).

56. Cf. minutes of Aug. 17.

57. 1838 constitutions, constitution 3.

58. C.L. 9 (I, p. 22).

59. *Rec. doc.* pp. 170f. and 177f.

60. Cf. C.L. 47, Dec. 8, 1851 (I, p. 259).

61. 1854 constitutions, art. 46.

62. *Rec. Dujarié* pp. 220–226.

63. Letters of June 28 and July 17, 1835; Sept. 26, 1838 (*Rec. doc.*
pp. 156f. and 163); cf. also Fr. Moreau's letter to Fr. d'Alzon April
10, 1856.

64. In addition to the texts already quoted, cf. letters of July 17,
1835, and Aug. 5, 1841 (*Rec. doc.* pp. 158 and 175).

65. Art. 299.

66. 1845 "summary"; C.L. 45, Jan. 1, 1851 (I, p. 221).

67. Art. 1.

68. C.L. 20, Jan. 5, 1844 (I, p. 79); cf. also C.L. 35, Jan. 5, 1849 (pp.
150 and 153) on continued favor from the nuncio and continued
attempts in Rome to get a decree of praise.

69. Cf. C.L. 42, April 12, 1850, and 43, May 13 (I, pp. 203 and 207f.).

70. C.L. 45 (I, pp. 210f. and 222).

71. Catta I, pp. 812–814; cf. also C.L. 45 (I, pp. 223f.).

72. Catta I, pp. 818f. The biographers explain: "This action of Pius IX was more than a mere pleasantry. It was his way of expressing distrust of the last remaining traces of Gallicanism, of which the special winged rabat of the French clergy was, rightly or wrongly, regarded as the symbol. The Roman collar, which became almost universal in France under the reign of Pius IX, symbolized devotion to the pope without any taint of nationalism."

73. Cf. C.L. 45 (I, p. 222); cf. also C.L. 46, May 2, 1851 (p. 225) on the delay.

74. He used the word of himself: letter of Oct. 21, 1841, cited in Catta I, p. 509.

75. Bishop de la Hailandière to Fr. Moreau, Aug. 13, 1840, and Feb. 25, 1842.

76. Fr. Moreau to Fr. Sorin Nov. 20, 1841, and April 8, 1842; Sorin to Moreau June 5, 1842; Moreau to de la Hailandière Sept. 14, 1842. To avoid similar misunderstandings elsewhere, Fr. Moreau wrote to Fr. Saint-Germain of Montreal that the Canadian foundation would be made on condition that it remain dependent on Holy Cross.

77. Minutes of Aug. 25; cf. complaints in C.L. 23, Jan. 4, 1845 (I, p. 88).

78. Fr. Moreau frequently tried to explain or defend the moves of Fr. Sorin and other foreign superiors: cf. general council minutes of Jan. 30, 1850, where he explains Fr. Barroux's unauthorized presence in France to beg for Notre Dame as necessitated by the Notre Dame fire of 1849; Fr. Moreau himself begged for the Indiana house on that occasion: C.L. 41, Feb. 1850 (I, pp. 195–200).

79. E.g., letters of Sept. 22, 1843; March 23, 1844; Jan. 20, 1845.

80. Cf. letter of March 17, 1845, cited in Catta I, p. 540.

81. Jan. 20, 1845, cited in Catta I, p. 535.

82. Cf. general council minutes of April 11 and 28 and May 11, 1846.

83. Cf. council minutes of Oct. 12 and Dec. 22, 1846; Jan. 12 and April 22, 1847.

84. Cited in Catta I, p. 561.

85. *Op. cit.* p. 563.

86. Council minutes of Jan. 4, 1848.

87. Session of Aug. 26.

88. Cf. C.L. 43, May 13, 1850 (I, pp. 206–208).

89. May 18, 1842.

90. Cf. letter of Oct. 18.

91. May 14, 1846.

92. Cf. letter of June 28.

93. Cf. C.L. 28, Sept. 17, 1847. (I, p. 123).

94. Catta I, pp. 785f. It will help to recall that Bishop Bouvier was well into his struggle with Dorn Guéranger, the abbot of Solesmes, in Rome at this time.

95. C.L. 29, Jan. 29, 1848 (I, p. 132); cf. also letters of Dec. 6 and 11.

96. Letter of Oct. 13, 1854, to Msgr. Barnabo, cited in Catta I, p. 831.

97. C.L. 17, Jan. 10, 1843 (I, p. 53).

98. *Rec. doc.* p. 183.

99. Algeria: Catta I, pp. 480, 483f., 488; Indiana: C.L. 17, Jan. 10, 1843 (I, pp. 56 and 64—penniless but happy); Canada: Catta I, pp. 582–584 and urgent letter of Fr. Moreau to Bishop Bourget July 13, 1849, on their suffering cold and hunger; New Orleans: Catta I, p. 935 (they begged leftovers from hotel kitchens); the Association in general: C.L. 20, Jan. 5, 1844 (I, pp. 76f.) on not being worried over food and clothing.

100. C.L. 135, Jan. 5, 1849 (I, p. 150).

101. C.L. 41, Feb. 1850 (I, pp. 199L).

102. Conference given on July 4, 1922, at Saint-Laurent, p. 3.

103. Catta II, p. 81.

104. Ordinance of Sept. 30, 1846, art. 10.

105. Art. 82–85.

106. *Rec. doc.* p. 167.

107. C.L. 11 (I, pp. 33f.).

108. C.L. 23 (I, pp. 89f). Quotation probably from St. Vincent de Paul.

109. C.L. 29 (I, p. 131); of. also 34, June 19, 1848 (I, pp. 141f.).

110. C.L. 31, Feb. 24, 1848 (I, p. 136).

111. *Rec. doc.* p. 180.

112. *Op. cit.* p. 178.

113. C. Moreau I, pp. 280f.

114. *Rec. doc.* p. 180.

115. C. Moreau I, p. 282.

116. She died in 1921 at the age of 91 in full possession of her faculties. Her recollections were written down by others during the last 16 years of her life.

117. *Rec. doc.* p. 183.

118. A French army had been organized and had marched on Rome to restore order and assure the return of Pius IX to the Eternal City, but their plans were frustrated by unexpected resistance which immobilized their forces before the gates of Rome for the entire month of June. Cholera was reported at Paris in the early summer of 1849 and before long had spread throughout almost the whole of France.

119. C.L. 37, June 14, 1839 (I, p. 168).

120. C.L. 39, Oct. 30, 1849 (I, p. 181); for further indication of his concern not to burden anyone in distributing the hours of adoration, cf. C.L. 45, Jan. 1, 1851 (I, p. 215).

121. Session of Aug. 30.

122. He entered Holy Cross in 1848 and made his profession in 1852; he was later a member of the general chapter.

123. Conference of Aug. 3, 1920, p. 14.

124. This brother had become a novice in 1853; he was later a member of the general chapter.

125. Conference of Aug. 3, 1920, p. 5.

126. Pp. 146f.

127. May 29, 1846.

128. Louis Veuillot, "Fragments inédits" présentés par François Veuillot in vol. 10 of the *Oeuvres complètes,* Paris, 1929, pp. 452f.

129. Louis Veuillot, *Correspondence,* tome 2, letter 190 (1931 edition), p. 184.

130. *Rec. doc.* p. 184.

131. C. Moreau I, p. 284.

132. *Rec. doc.* p. 185.

133. C. Moreau I, p. 285.

134. *Ibid.*

6. Culmination (1851–1860)

1. Cf. *Rec. doc.* pp. 305–326 for the ordinances for 1835–1847 and 1851.

2. C. Moreau I, p. 427.

3. C.L. 54, June 29, 1853 (I, p. 269) has 10,000.

4. Fr. Moreau to Fr. Drouelle March 25, 1852; cf. Catta I, p. 879.

5. C.L. 77, May 25, 1856 (I, pp. 356f.). This writing is now referred to as *Christian Education.*

6. Catta II, pp. 208f.

7. C.L. 70 (I, pp. 328f.).

8. C.L. 77 (I, pp. 357f.).

9. Cf., e.g., C.L. 54, June 29, 1853 (I, p. 278, art. 13); 90, Sept. 25, 1857 (II, p. 36): translation of the *Pedagogy*; 104, Jan. 2, 1859 (II, pp. 93f.).

10. C.L. 77, May 25, 1856 (I, p. 355).

11. Cf. Catta II, pp. 177–185. The initiative seems to have come from Bishop Bouvier's successor in Le Mans. Cf. Fr. Moreau's letter to Fr. d'Alzon April 10, 1856.

12. Seemingly suggested by the new bishop of Le Mans.

13. Catta II, pp. 273f., citing C. Moreau.

14. C.L. 92, Jan. 1, 1858 (II, p. 56).

15. C.L. 79, Jan. 1, 1857 (I, p. 383).

16. The diocesan newspaper of Le Mans published accounts of Fr. Moreau's activities in Rome.

17. Cited in Catta I, p. 832.

18. C.L. 46 (I, p. 225).

19. C.L. 47 (I, pp. 228–235).

20. Cf. also Fr. Moreau to Fr. Drouelle Dec. 4.

21. Catta I, pp. 860f.

22. Letter of Br. Leonard to Bishop Bouvier Feb. 13, 1853.

23. June 12, 1853.

24. Letter of Dec. 21, 1853.

25. June 30 (Catta I, p. 871).

26. Letter of Drouelle Feb. 14 (*ibid.*).

27. Letter of Champeau June 20 (*ibid.*).

28. Oct. 12.

29. Catta I, p. 875.

30. *Notes et souvenirs*, published by J. Chappée, Le Mans, 1925, pp. 16–20.

31. A. L. Sebaux, *Vie de Monseigneur Jean-Baptiste Bouvier*, Angoulême, 1886, pp. 95f.

32. Conference of Aug. 3, 1920, p. 12.

33. March 20, 1852.

34. Letter of March 29 (Catta I, p. 851).

35. Cf. C.L. 77, May 25, 1856 (I, pp. 345–347).

36. Sessions of Aug. 18 and 19.

37. C.L. 47, Dec. 8, 1851 (I, p. 259).

38. Session of Aug. 21.

39. Catta I, pp. 957f.

40. *Op. cit.* pp. 958f.

41. *Op. cit.* pp. 961f.

42. *Op. cit.* p. 967.

43. *Op. cit.* p. 973.

44. *Op. cit.* pp. 968f.

45. Catta II, p. 9.

46. Cf. Fr. Moreau's letter to the archbishop of New Orleans Aug. 27: "Before informing the Holy See of the sad affair of Notre Dame du Lac, I have felt it my duty to address to you the report which will serve as a basis for a canonical trial if poor Fr. Sorin does not come to his senses, and I inform Your Lordship that I am sure in advance of the severe judgment that His Holiness will pronounce. Please try to open the eyes of these blind men and to keep the matter from becoming public."

47. In the meantime Fr. Moreau had appealed to Fr. Rézé in Canada to go to Notre Dame to try to remedy a situation in which the canonical visitor seemed to be failing (cf. his letter to Rézé Sept. 29).

48. Catta II, p. 23.

49. *Op. cit.* p. 22.

50. March 21, 1854.

51. C.L. 65 (I, pp. 307–309).

52. This priest from Notre Dame seems to have held the title of provincial: cf. C.L. 77, March 25, 1856 (I, p. 360).

53. C.L. 71 (I, p. 332).

54. C.L. 74, Oct. 2, 1855 (I, p. 337); 76, Oct. 25 (p. 340); cf. also letter of Fr. Moreau to Fr. Granger Feb. 8, 1855.

55. Moreau to Drouelle April 24; to Granger May 30; to Sorin June 17 (this letter reviews the sad history of the New Orleans conflict and the confusion that followed).

56. Eventually Fr. Moreau asked Fr. Raymond, a Sulpician, to govern the New Orleans foundation until he could provide for it: cf. C.L. 77, May 25, 1856 (I, pp. 359f.).

57. Moreau to Granger Dec. 16, 1856, and Feb. 13, 1857; cf. Catta II, pp. 280–294.

58. To Granger Jan. 15, 1850, and to Bouvier March 2, 1850.

59. Letter of April 8, 1854, to his sister Josephine on the end of the trouble; letters to Drouelle April 24, 1855; to Granger May 30; to Sorin June 17.

60. In the spring of 1849, 20 children had died in 2 months (letter of Br. Vincent to Fr. Moreau May 18, 1849).

61. C.L. 54, June 29, 1853 (I, p. 272).

62. Between Aug. 27 and Sept. 28: C.L. 55, 56, 57, 59, 60—they contain some details on the New Orleans situation (I, pp. 280–291).

63. C.L. 60, Sept. 28, 1853 (I, p. 290).

64. C.L. 61, Oct. 12 (p. 292).

65. C.L. 65, June 15, 1854 (I, pp. 306f.).

66. C.L. 66, Sept. 19 (p. 318).

67. C.L. 67, Sept. 29 (p. 319).

68. C.L. 68, Oct. 13 (pp. 321f.).

69. C.L. 69, Nov. 4 (p. 324).

70. Cf. C.L. 58, Sept. 12, 1853 (I, p. 287); 64, Feb. 8, 1854 (p. 305).

71. C.L. 74, Oct. 2, 1855 (p. 337).

72. C.L. 76, Oct. 25 (pp. 340f).

73. C. Moreau II, p. 45.

74. The account is quoted from Catta II, pp. 107–112.

75. Cf. Catta II, p. 106.

76. C.L. 75, Oct. 15, 1855 (I, pp. 338f.).

77. Catta II, p. 110.

78. Conference of Aug. 3, 1920, p. 17.

79. Catta II, p. 114.

80. Cf. letters to Propaganda on the sisters March 29 and April 25, 1852, cited above.

81. Possibly he was referring to the opposition that anticlericals generally had for the title "congregation."

82. The statement that it was used for the union of the two societies means simply that it fulfilled the same task as "congregation"—i.e., to designate the entire Holy Cross community—and

not that it was particularly apt to signify the union of several societies in one larger organization. The founder used it for the Associations of the Good Shepherd and St. Joseph too, and they were not composed of several branches.

83. General chapter session of Aug. 26, 1855.

84. General chapter session of Aug. 25.

85. Session of Aug. 26.

86. After 1868 it met in 1872, 1880, and thereafter every 6 years.

87. General chapter session of Aug. 26, 1855.

88. Cf. general council minutes Feb. 20, 1856. Fr. Sorin's plan concerned only the religious in America, and Fr. Moreau added "except for Canada and New Orleans" in order to remove them from Fr. Sorin's jurisdiction. How well the founder understood the American form of government is not clear, but it is obvious that he left a very free hand to Fr. Sorin in Indiana, Fr. Rézé in Canada, and Fr. Drouelle in Rome, not to mention the superior in distant Bengal.

89. Session of July 16, 1868.

90. Cf. C.L. 77, May 25, 1856 (I, p. 359): the sisters should thank God for the modification in their status!

91. C.L. 77 (I, p. 342).

92. Cf. his numerous requests to Fr. Drouelle for Roman interpretations of the constitutions.

93. One of his first acts in Le Mans was to establish the Roman liturgy—something Bishop Bouvier had never done despite decisions taken years before.

94. Fr. Moreau also used this visit to go to Loreto to prepare for the founding of a refuge of Our Lady of Charity from the Good Shepherd monastery of Le Mans. It had been in the negotiation stage since late 1854: cf. Catta II, pp. 185–189; C.L. 77, May 25, 1856 (I, p. 347).

95. Catta II, p. 176.

96. Cf. C.L. 77, May 25, 1856 (I, pp. 358f).

97. Catta II, p. 230.

98. C.L. 79 (I, pp. 378f.).

99. Catta II, p. 233.

100. C.L. 86, July 3, 1857 (II, p. 1).

101. C.L. 86 (pp. 12–16); 102, Oct. 4, 1858 (p. 83).

102. C.L. 90, Sept. 25, 1857 (II, pp. 28–42); he could not go to New Orleans—C.L. 89, Aug. 11 (pp. 26f.)—or to Bengal; cf. also C.L. 90 (p. 35); 92, Jan. 1, 1858 (p. 45).

103. C.L. 92, Jan. 1, 1858; 93, Feb. 25; 94, April 13; 104, Jan. 2, 1859 (II, pp. 85–96, esp. pp. 86–88 on authority in the congregation); cf. also 96, June 16, 1858 (pp. 73–76).

104. C.L. 104, Jan. 2, 1859 (II, p. 88).

105. C.L. 80, Feb. 1 and March 1, 1857 (I, pp. 384–390) had been devoted entirely to this matter; warnings recur in C.L. 92, Jan. 1, 1858 (II, pp. 45f. and 57–59) and 104, Jan. 2, 1859 (p. 85).

106. C.L. 104, Jan. 2, 1859 (II, p. 85) refers to it as the "second" edition because the preceding edition of 1855 had departed so extensively from the original of 1848 as practically to constitute a new work; it was almost twice as long.

107. To appreciate this "method," it is important to note that the work was meant for the students as well as the religious and that many of the religious had an extremely limited education and found it most helpful to memorize answers to questions (cf. p. 5) and long sections of their rules as well.

108. An interesting point in these "rules" is the practice of having the students analyze or summarize the Sunday homily in the first study period after the Mass (p. 206).

109. Fr. Moreau does not give a complete presentation of his conception of the religious life anywhere else in his writings.

110. Pp. 105f., 110, 118f.

111. C.L. 94, April 13, 1858 (II, pp. 65–67).

112. Rule XIII, art. 2 and 4–6.

113. Rule XIV, art. 1–2.

114. Rule XVI, art. 1.

115. Rule XVII, art. 1–4.

116. Rule XXIII, art. 2.

117. Rule XVIII.

118. The text of the Marianite rules of 1858 was exactly the same as that of the Salvatorists and Josephites, at least for the passages quoted above. In the 1864 edition the rule on community spirit (rule XIII) replaced the paragraphs on those in business and the bees with the following: "The better to strengthen this union, the religious will strive to imitate the understanding and cooperation which exist among the members of the human body. St. Paul observes that they aid and serve each other: the eyes guide the feet; the hands protect the head; the stronger help the weaker; the pain and the pleasure of one are communicated to all the others; and in the distribution of nourishment each member retains only what suffices for itself and leaves the rest go to strengthen the others."

119. C. Moreau II, p. 318: its author was "one of them," i.e., Fr. Moreau's opponents—presumably, Fr. Champeau, who was the literary man among "them" and in Paris in 1858.

120. C.L. 86 (II, pp. 17f.).

121. C.L. 89, Aug. 11, 1857 (p. 25).

122. C.L. 90, Sept. 25 (p. 31).

123. Eugene Nadeau, *Mère Léonie*, Montreal, 1952, p. 45.

124. C.L. 90 (II, pp. 31f.).

125. Note, however, C.L. 90 (pp. 33f.) on the resistance Fr. Moreau met when he tried to effect the separation of material goods between the men's and women's communities.

126. C.L. 90 (p. 37).

127. C.L. 90 (p. 38).

128. For details on this man cf. Catta II, p. 216.

129. Pp. 4–6, 22f., 33.

130. Jan. 19, 1858.

131. C.L. 116, Oct. 31, 1859 (II, pp. 114–116), 118, Jan. 29, 1860 (pp. 118–122), 120, March 1 (pp. 124–126).

132. C.L. 116, Oct. 31, 1859 (II, pp. 114f.).

133. Catta II, p. 324.

134. C.L. 84 (I, pp. 400–402).

135. C.L. 94 (II, pp. 68f.).

136. Cf. C.L. 104, Jan. 2, 1859 (II, pp. 85f.); 105, Jan. 24 (p. 97).

137. C.L. 103, Oct. 20 (p. 84); cf. 100, Sept. 8, 1858 (p. 80); 101, Sept. 27 (p. 81); 102, Oct. 14 (p. 82).

138. Cf. letters of July 27 and 29, 1859.

139. C.L. 106 (II, pp. 98f.).

140. *Ibid.*

141. Cf. minutes of this session.

142. Letter of March 29, 1859.

143. Dated May 30, 1859, found after the council minutes of June 6 of that year.

144. C.L. 113, Sept. 5, 1859 (II, pp. 108–110).

145. Letter to Fr. Moreau Oct. 1, 1859, cited in Catta II, p. 361.

7. Resignation (1860–1866)

1. Cf. general chapter minutes of Aug. 11, 1860.

2. Document of Aug. 26.

3. Decrees 2 and 3 of the 1860 chapter; C.L. 131, Sept. 18 (II, p. 146).

4. Session of Aug. 24; decree 14, C.L. 131 (p. 147).

5. C.L. 133 (p. 157).

6. C.L. 136, Dec. 1, 1860 (p. 165).

7. C.L. 135, Nov. 12 (p. 163).

8. C.L. 136 (pp. 167–169).

9. General council minutes of Dec. 6, cited in Catta II, pp. 405f.

10. General council minutes of Jan. 31, 1861; Catta II, p. 420.

11. C. Moreau II, pp. 168–170; Catta II, pp. 411–420.

12. This projected American counterpart of the Association of St. Joseph never materialized: general chapter minutes of Aug. 16, 1863.

13. General chapter minutes Aug. 12, 1863.

14. C.L. 146, July 6, 1861 (II, p. 212); it was 235,130 francs, approximately 1.4 million dollars: Catta II, p. 437; cf. also C.L. 139, March 23 (p. 185); 140, April 9 (pp. 187f.); 141, May 3 (pp. 190f.); 151, Jan. 2, 1862 (p. 229).

15. Catta II, p. 422, giving references to the general council minutes.

16. *Op. cit.* pp. 437f.

17. C.L. 143 (II, pp. 198f.).

18. C.L. 131, Sept. 18, 1860 (II, pp. 147–151); 132, Oct. 8 (pp. 153–155); 134, Oct. 24 (pp. 159–161); 137, Jan. 3, 1861 (pp. 172–174).

19. C.L. 138, Feb. 6, 1861 (pp. 176–184); he proposed turning the brothers' novitiate, the Solitude of St. Joseph, into a place of pilgrimage.

20. C.L. 145, June 21 (pp. 202–211); cf. also C.L. 142, May 14 (pp. 193–197); there was also an interesting letter on love of relatives: C.L. 149, Sept. 23 (pp. 222–224).

21. General council minutes April 11.

22. General council minutes May 8 and June 6 and 27; C.L. 145, June 21, cited above; cf. also C.L. 163 and 164, Sept. 2 and 13 (II, pp. 262–264).

23. Letter of Aug. 18; C.L. 147, Aug. 27 (II, p. 217). The immediate occasion of the visit was a complaint to Rome from the bishop of Angers. He seems to have been influenced by the reaction of many people in his diocese against Fr. Moreau's acceptance of the Maulévrier property. He declined the task of making the visit, however, leaving it completely to the bishop of Le Mans (cf. letters of Fr. Moreau to Fr. Drouelle May 24 and July 2).

24. Aug. 27, 1861, cited in Catta II, pp. 444f.

25. C.L. 147, Aug. 27, 1861 (II, pp. 214–216); 149, Sept. 23 (p. 225); 150, Nov. 2 (p. 227): ". . . it is true that in general the dispositions and conduct of the members of the congregation have been a source of consolation in the misfortunes which have recently befallen us. Yet there are many who still leave much to be desired on this score, while they forget that in thus resisting the grace given them, they expose themselves to very grave dangers for their eternity." He asked whether, despite the American Civil War, Fr. Sorin might not be able to reimburse a loan he had made to him: C.L. 147 (II, p. 216). But the letters which the Indiana superior was receiving from Fr. Champeau against the founder at this time did not encourage him to offer help, and the help never came.

26. C.L. 148, Sept. 13, 1861 (II, pp. 220f.).

27. Letter of Dec. 12.

28. C.L. 153 (II, pp. 236–241; see esp. p. 238).

29. Cf. Catta II, pp. 484f., with references to his correspondence with Fr. Drouelle.

30. C.L. 153, March 26, 1862 (II, 236–238). The suffering and anxiety which lay behind the pleas voiced by Fr. Moreau in this circular appear in his personal letters too. On May 30 he wrote to Fr. Drouelle: "My heart is no longer capable of joy. . . . Rome no longer offers me any consolation, and I am thinking only of disappearing as soon as settlement of the financial affairs will enable my successor to undertake a regular administration." On June 21 he wrote to Fr. Sorin: "You do not seem even to suspect the anguish into which the financial embarrassment of which you are well aware has cast and is casting me day and night." Again, on July 2 to Fr. Drouelle: "How deep the chalice is, and how bitter the dregs!" However, he could add: "Despite it all, our work is making progress today, and even the interest of the clergy of Le Mans is being renewed."

31. C.L. 159 (II, pp. 250f.).

32. Catta II, p. 460.

33. C. Moreau II, p. 181: "all but two or three out of sixty" signed it.

34. Cited in Catta II, pp. 514f.

35. General council minutes May 30 and June 16; C.L. 159, June 15, 1861 (II, p. 252).

36. Cf. general chapter minutes Aug. 11, 1863.

37. Pp. 7f.

38. Cf. letter of Oct. 15 (Catta II, p. 517); he even suggested an extraordinary general chapter as a remedy.

39. Catta II, pp. 517f.

40. Oct. 15. While this correspondence was going on, Fr. Moreau was paying bills for which Fr. Drouelle was responsible. After having paid 13,000 francs (78,000 dollars) in the space of a few days, he wrote: "What anguish you have caused me!" (Oct. 23, cited in Catta II, p. 519). Fr. Moreau's concern over the progress of the American visit appears from the fact that between January and August 1862 he wrote 25 letters to the visitor.

41. Catta II, pp. 494f; he notified Fr. Sorin of the steps on Sept. 20.

42. Letter of Sept. 14.

43. Catta II, pp. 520–523.

44. Letter of Dec. 24, cited in Catta II, pp. 523f.

45. C.L. 165 (II, pp. 265f. and 273). He addressed them as "reverend fathers and dear brothers," practically abandoning from that date the expression he had regularly used until then: "My dear sons in Jesus Christ."

46. Catta II, pp. 535f.

47. *Ibid.*

48. *Ibid.*

49. Cf. letter to Fr. Drouelle March 24, 1863.

50. Letter to Drouelle May 4.

51. May 16 (Catta II, p. 549).

52. C. Moreau II, pp. 192f.

53. Minutes of Aug. 11.

54. An 1865 *Guide to the University of Notre Dame du Lac* published in Philadelphia contains the following description of Fr. Moreau's portrait in the Notre Dame administration building; it was written by Fr. Sorin: "The portrait at first is not striking; but, after becoming a little accustomed to it, you feel as if you were in the presence of a person who would read more of you by seeing you one moment, or hearing one sentence from your tongue, than an ordinary person would know of you after a long acquaintance. You feel a little nervous under the penetrating gaze of those eyes, and think you would prefer to hear a few words drop from those lips before subjecting yourself to so rigid a scrutiny. You feel that you are in the grasp of a strong but kind man; a man that never fails to know what he is about; one who digests to perfection all facts that come before him. However, those who have the honor of a personal acquaintance with the Abbé, lament that they are of necessity obliged to make content with so poor a likeness of their loved Father General."

55. Minutes of Aug. 17.

56. Minutes of Aug. 14.

57. Minutes of Aug. 18.

58. *Ibid.*

59. Minutes of Aug. 20.

60. Minutes of Aug. 19 and 20.

61. Minutes of Aug. 20.

62. Letter of Fr. Moreau to Fr. Séguin Nov. 26, 1863.

63. Minutes of Aug. 20.

64. C.L. 170 (II, p. 293).

65. C. Moreau II, p. 196.

66. Catta II, p. 575.

67. *Ibid.*

68. C.L. 172, Oct. 27, 1863 (II, pp. 298–301).

69. Letter to Fr. Moreau Sept. 12, cited in Catta II, p. 580.

70. Catta II, pp. 587f.

71. *Ibid.*

72. Catta II, pp. 595f.

73. Letter of Nov. 26.

74. C.L. 174 (II, pp. 307–313).

75. General council minutes Oct. 15, 17, and 22, 1863.

76. Cf. C.L. 176, June 27, 1864 (II, p. 330).

77. C.L. 177, Nov. 22, 1864 (II, p. 335).

78. C.L. 177 (p. 336).

79. P. 337.

80. P. 336.

81. C.L. 179 (II, pp. 347–351).

82. C.L. 181, May 12, 1865 (II, pp. 358 and 361); cf. also letter to Fr. Séguin Nov. 26, 1863.

83. Cf. general council minutes May 31 to July 6; C.L. 183, July 7, 1865 (II, pp. 366–369).

84. C.L. 184, Sept. 27, 1865 (II, p. 370).

85. Letter to Fr. Sorin Dec. 21, 1865; the bishop of Angers had suggested this.

86. Catta II, p. 660.

87. Cf. his letters to Cardinal Barnabo Nov. 28 and to Pius IX Dec. 30.

88. Letter of Jan. 3, in which he also discussed possible successors to the superior general.

89. C.L. 186 (11, p. 375).

90. C. Moreau II, p. 246.

91. C.L. 187 (II, p. 376). On Feb. 9 he had written Mother Mary of the Seven Dolors: "The work of the devil has been really terrible here, but I am not frightened, and the welcome accorded me has encouraged me greatly. . . . I am now dealing with Fathers Drouelle and Champeau, and I feel determined not to yield to them in anything" (Catta II, p. 674.)

92. C. Moreau II, p. 252.

93. C.L. 188, June 21, 1866 (II, p. 378).

94. C. Moreau II, pp. 253–255.

8. Consummation (1866–1873)

1. C. Moreau II, p. 256.
2. *Ibid.*
3. *Op. cit.* p. 257.
4. *Op. cit.* pp. 258f.
5. *Ibid.*
6. *Op. cit.* p. 264.
7. Letter to Fr. Chappé Aug. 23, 1866, cited in Catta II, pp. 709–711.
8. Session of Aug. 26, 1866.
9. C. Moreau II, pp. 270–272.
10. *Op. cit.* pp. 272f. cited in Catta II, pp. 724f.; these chapters of Book Three of the *Imitation of Christ* are entitled, "How God Is to Be Invoked and Blessed in Tribulations" and "That We Must Ask God's Help and Await Confidently the Return of Grace."
11. Letter of Aug. 4.
12. C. Moreau II, p. 276.
13. *Ibid.*
14. March 28, 1867.
15. Cf. Catta II, pp. 746f.
16. Letter of March 28, 1867, written during his mission at Coulombiers.
17. C. Moreau II, p. 276.
18. Cited in Catta II, p. 734.
19. *Op. cit.* pp. 1008f.
20. *Op. cit.* pp. 749f.
21. C. Moreau II, pp. 301f.
22. Catta II, p. 773.
23. Decree of May 12.

24. Catta II, pp. 803–806.

25. C. Moreau II, p. 309.

26. Letter of June 11, 1868.

27. In the absence of their superior, the members of Fr. Champeau's house in Paris sent a warm letter of sympathy and gratitude to the former superior general, applying to him the words of Scripture: "Blessed are those who suffer persecution for justice' sake."

28. Catta II, p. 814.

29. C. Moreau II, pp. 316f.

30. Catta II, pp. 840f.

31. Fr. Rézé of Canada had excused himself by letter. He was the only other religious convoked who was not present.

32. C. Moreau II, p. 347.

33. Letter of Aug. 3.

34. Catta II, p. 843.

35. *Op. cit.* pp. 846f.

36. *Op. cit.* pp. 852f. Aug. 16 was the day on which Fr. Charles Moreau was dispensed from his religious vows.

37. *Op. cit.* p. 854.

38. *Op. cit.* p. 855.

39. *Op. cit.* pp. 858f.

40. *Op. cit.* pp. 857 and 862; the latter of these two saints was imprisoned for 2 weeks in 1643, and 3 years later his congregation was suppressed; it was not reorganized until 8 years after his death.

41. C. Moreau II, p. 362.

42. Catta II, p. 872.

43. Letter of Aug. 26, cited in Catta II, p. 850.

44. Fr. Bardeau, the procurator general, to Fr. Chappé Oct. 22, 1868, cited in Catta II, p. 884.

45. Cf. his letter of Dec. 4: "I am taking this step because a new administration is selling everything, is unwilling to reimburse

any of the sums [due creditors], and has accumulated more than 130,000 francs of debts since my resignation. If I succeed in having a court administrator appointed, at least this waste will come to an end, and we shall perhaps be able to safeguard the interests of those of our creditors who hold only promissory notes." Cf. also his letter of Dec. 6: "I owe it to those persons who have honored me with their confidence, with or without mortgages, to take their cause in hand. . . . Should it be necessary, I would keep for myself nothing of what may belong to me personally. Before all else, in so far as may depend on me, I do not want to cause any loss to anyone who loaned me money while I was superior. This is why I petitioned for the dissolution of the civil society . . . and asked for the appointment of a court administrator who can settle everything immediately and impartially" (Catta II, pp. 901 and 908f.).

46. Catta II, p. 909.
47. *Op. cit.* pp. 910–912.
48. *Op. cit.* p. 914.
49. *Op. cit.* p. 912.
50. *Op. cit.* pp. 917–920.
51. Dec. 31, 1868.
52. Jan. 7, 1869.
53. C. Moreau II, pp. 386f.
54. Catta II, p. 930.
55. C. Moreau II, p. 394.
56. Catta II, pp. 969f.
57. *Op. cit.* p. 959.
58. *Op. cit.* p. 969.
59. C. Moreau II, p. 423.
60. *Op. cit.* p. 460.
61. Letter of Jan. 27, 1869.
62. C. Moreau II, p. 338.
63. *Op. cit.* p. 466.

64. To Br. Hilary July 19, 1871.

65. Catta II, pp. 975f.

66. Often he commented on the reading and offered his own personal remarks, which were jotted down on occasion by some of the sisters.

67. C. Moreau II, p. 462.

68. Catta II, p. 981.

69. *Op. cit.* p. 1010.

70. Br. Leonard commented on this treatment: "I often contradicted Very Reverend Fr. Moreau and opposed his government, but he never gave me any indication that he even remembered it" (C. Moreau II, p. 436).

71. Jan. 2, 1872.

72. A statement to the creditors of Holy Cross published by the general administration in a Le Mans newspaper after the 1872 chapter (Nov. 9) provoked a final public rebuttal by the founder.

73. C. Moreau II, pp. 455–458.

74. *Op. cit.* pp. 458f.

75. *Op. cit.* pp. 486f.

76. *Op. cit.* pp. 470–474.

77. Remark of Bishop Charbonnel of Toronto (Catta II, pp. 848).

78. Conclusion of his declaration of Aug. 3, 1871.

79. Letter of July 17, 1872, to Sister Mary of the Annunciation.

80. A text frequently quoted by the founder in his trials.

Index

Fr. Thomas Barrosse, CSC (1926–1994), was ordained a priest in 1950. He taught at the University of Notre Dame in Indiana and Holy Cross College in Washington, DC. In 1974, he was elected superior general of the Congregation of Holy Cross. In this position, he visited all the houses of the congregation, meeting personally with every religious to reassure them of the mission and future of Holy Cross.

Fr. Barrosse promoted devotion to Fr. Basil Moreau, the founder of Holy Cross, and compiled his letters. He also worked for the 1982 beatification of Br. André Bessette, CSC, who was later canonized as the first saint from the congregation. Fr. Barrosse played a large role in the 1986 revision of the Holy Cross Constitutions, which is the version that remains in effect today.

After leaving office, Fr. Barrosse went to Bangladesh where he taught in the major seminary until he died on June 14, 1994.

Br. Joel Giallanza, CSC, is a member of the Moreau Province of the Congregation of Holy Cross and offers spiritual direction and retreat ministry.

Br. Paul Bednarczyk, CSC, is the superior general of the Congregation of Holy Cross. He is the first brother to serve as superior general in the Congregation's history.

Sr. Ann Lacour, MSC, is the congregational leader of the Marianites of Holy Cross.

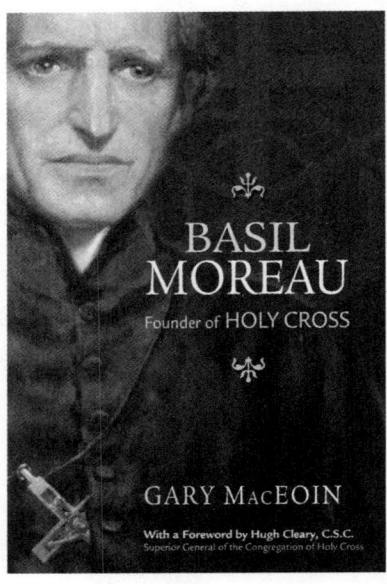

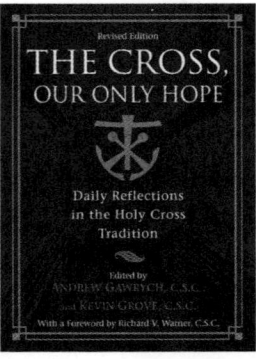